OUT OF
THE
DARK

For Beth, Michael and Bobby

'Remembrance'

Across the lonely fields of history lie
The shattered bones of countless thousands,
who fought and died for freedom.
And yet, some restless souls still wander our land,
In search of remembrance from their own.

–Ken Kinsella

The Great War Memorial commemorating
thirty-nine officers and men who fell in the
Great War is situated in the village of Kilgobbin,
County Dublin.

OUT OF THE DARK

1914–1918

South Dubliners Who Fell in the Great War

KEN KINSELLA

MERRION

First published in 2014 by Merrion
an imprint of Irish Academic Press
8 Chapel Lane
Sallins
Co. Kildare
Ireland

British Library Cataloguing in Publication Data
An entry can be found on request

978-1-908928-59-7 (paper)
978-1-908928-60-3 (cloth)
978-1-908928-61-0 (PDF)

Library of Congress Cataloging in Publication Data
An entry can be found on request

Designed and typeset by Sin É Design
Printed in Ireland by SPRINT-print Ltd

Contents

Foreword

I regard it as a privilege to have been invited to write the Foreword to this book and I do so with great pleasure.

I assumed the appointment of President of The Royal British Legion in the Irish Republic towards the end of the 1980s and I set myself the objective of doing all I could to 'bring back the memory' of those Irish who were casualties of the Great War as well as those who survived and returned to Ireland but were forgotten and 'swept under the carpet'.

Since the end of the 1980s, following the IRA ceasefire and the Good Friday Agreement, attitudes began to change and gradually Irish people began to talk about relatives who had served and those who had not come home. A significant number of books were written telling the story of men and women who went to that war. Also, local initiatives in counties of Ireland produced books of Roles of Honour listing the names and details of the casualties of that county.

This is one of the books which adds significantly to our knowledge of those who went to the war, and sometimes why, and of their families. The book is an account of various families living in South County Dublin who were known to, or known by, the author. It tends therefore to be more personal than simply a list of names and therefore makes fascinating and at times powerful reading.

The book gives an interesting background to the Great War and the story of Irish involvement in it and I would like to congratulate the author on the large amount of research involved and on the most interesting way in which he has introduced readers to the areas of South County Dublin from which they came, as well as recounting the frequently poignant stories of their gallant service.

Major-General David Nial Creagh, The O'Morchoe CB,CBE, KLJ
June 2013

Preface

In this book of remembrance, as in the hearts of people for whom they fought and fell, their memory is honoured forever

The desire to contribute to the remembrance of forgotten Irishmen sprang from a passionate interest in the stories of those who fought and died in the First World War. The military life of my great-uncle, whose name is commemorated on the war memorial situated in the picturesque village of Kilgobbin, was a well-kept family secret until I was in my forties.

Later, my involvement with the restoration of this memorial further heightened my level of interest in their stories. It is not possible for anyone living today to appreciate the horrors faced by soldiers in this war. However, Father Willie Doyle's description of Ginchy, Guillemont and Leuze Wood in August 1916, helps just a little bit:

> The first part of our journey lay through a narrow trench, the floor of which consisted of deep thick mud, and the bodies of dead men trodden under foot. It was horrible beyond description, but there was no help for it, and on the half-rotten corpses of our own brave men we marched in silence, everyone busy with his own thoughts ... Half an hour of this brought us out on the open into the middle of the battlefield of some days previous. The wounded, at least I hope so, had all been removed, but the dead lay there stiff and stark with open staring eyes, just as they had fallen. Good God, such a sight! I had tried to prepare myself for this, but all I had read or pictured gave me little idea of the reality. Some lay as if they were sleeping quietly, others

had died in agony or had had the life crushed out of them by mortal fear, while the whole ground, every foot, was littered with heads or limbs, or pieces of torn human bodies. In the bottom of one hole lay a British and a German soldier, locked in a deadly embrace, neither had any weapon but they had fought on to the bitter end. Another couple seemed to have realised that the horrible struggle was none of their making, and that they were both children of the same God; they had died hand-in-hand. A third face caught my eye, a tall, strikingly handsome young German, not more, I should say, than eighteen. He lay there calm and peaceful, with a smile of happiness on his face, as if he had had a glimpse of Heaven before he died. Ah, if only his poor mother could have seen her boy it would have soothed the pain of her broken heart.[1]

It was unacceptable that so many Irishmen lay forgotten in foreign fields and were written out of Irish history. Young men of different religious denominations, middle class and working class, poor and wealthy, the cream of Irish manhood, were slaughtered in their thousands and forgotten by successive Irish governments until the late twentieth century. The teaching of history in Irish National Schools omitted the heroic contribution of Irish men and women in the First World War. Their names and the history of the war became part of the collective amnesia that gripped the new state and lasted for decades. The hurt felt by relatives of soldiers, who were ridiculed and sometimes accused of being traitors, was understandable in the years that followed the war, and is no less relevant today.

My research project extended over a period of thirteen years and meeting like-minded friends who encouraged and assisted me, made the long journey easier and more enjoyable. Whatever the motivation, the book represents my small contribution to forgotten Irish heroes who were born or lived in South County Dublin, close to my place of birth.

Acknowledgements

I wish to thank my wife, Liz, for coping with the disruption to our lives and her patience and assistance over a period of thirteen years. Her help in proof reading and editing the manuscript was greatly appreciated. My children, Hilary and Ken were always encouraging throughout the period of research. This is an opportunity to pay tribute to my cousin and friend, the late Drew Kinsella, whose grandfather and great-uncle fell in the war. His enthusiasm for remembrance and commemoration of our local Great War heroes was inspiring.

A special word of thanks to Philip Lecane, author of, *Torpedoed: The RSM Leinster Disaster*, for his work in reading the manuscript and offering advice on style and structure. Michael Lee is another great friend, who offered information, assistance, advice and much encouragement. I thank him for the many enjoyable hours spent in discussions at his home in Dun Laoghaire.

Thanks to Sean Connolly, Honorary Secretary of the Royal Dublin Fusiliers Association for reading the manuscript and offering valuable advice. My thanks to military historians, Liam and Conor Dodd, for their constant assistance and encouragement. I wish to thank Mal Murray of the Gallipoli Association, who was always available to provide assistance in the difficult areas of research. A special thanks to Dr T.K. Whitaker, architect of the modern Irish economy, who contributed a splendid article dealing with the economic difficulties encountered by the first government of the Twenty-Six County Irish State.

My grateful thanks to the management and staff of the National Archives at Kew in London for their generous assistance and permission to publish information from its archive. I wish to thank D.P. Cleary MBE, Irish Guards Regimental Headquarters, London, for providing attestation papers for fallen soldiers of his regiment. My thanks to the management and staff and of The National Library of Ireland; The Irish

National Archives and The National Museum, Collins Barracks, all situated in Dublin. My sincere gratitude is offered to Margaret Doyle and Caroline Mullen, archivists at Clongowes Wood College and Blackrock College, who were most generous with their time in assisting me with information on former pupils of their colleges. Thanks to Mary Furlong and her staff at the Representative Church Body Library in Rathgar, for their assistance in researching Church of Ireland families. Thank you to the late Jean Kelly for permission, and Lar Joye for allowing me access, on a closed day, to inspect Mrs Dorothea Healy's scrap book relating to her son John, in the National Museum's exhibition, 'Soldiers and Chiefs'.

My sincere thanks to the following relatives of war dead who kindly allowed me permission to use extracts of their books and articles: Louise C. Callaghan's poem, 'Brother', from her book of poems, *Remember the Birds*, relating to her uncles, Major Joseph C. Callaghan MC, Captain Stanislaus C. Callaghan and Second Lieutenant Eugene C. Callaghan; Morgan Dockrell from his book *SIATLOF*, relating to the part played in the Great War by his great-uncles, Major George Shannon Dockrell and Major Maurice Henry Dockrell MD; Enda Cullen, from 'A Journey of Remembrance' published in *Three Rock Panorama*, relating to his great-uncle, Private Stephen Joseph Hayden; Alex Findlater, from his book, *The Story of a Dublin Merchant Family 1774– 2001*, where it relates to his great-uncles, Captain Alexander Findlater, Lance Sergeant Charles Findlater and Lance Corporal Herbert Findlater; Rob Goodbody from the book *The Goodbodys: Millers, Merchants and Manufacturers* by Michael Goodbody, relating to their relative, Lieutenant Owen Frederick Goodbody; Noel Kidney from his essay, 'The Picture on the Mantelpiece' relating to his great-uncle, Lieutenant Henry Burke Close; Charles Lillis, from the book, *I Just Happened to be There* by Mary Lillis Jensen, relating to her uncle, Lieutenant Martin Lillis; Clive C. Martin, by kind permission of; *Mary Martin's Diary*, relating to her son, Captain C.A. Martin; Honor O Brolchain from her books, *All in the Blood* and *16 Lives & the Biography of Joseph Plunkett* relating to extracts on the family of Sub-Lieutenant Gerald Anthony Plunkett, Joseph Mary Plunkett and Captain Kenneth O'Morchoe; Consuelo O'Connor (nee Cruess Callaghan) from her book, *Consuelo Remembers*, relating to her uncles, Major Joseph C. Callaghan MC, Captain Stanislaus C. Callaghan and Second Lieutenant Eugene C. Callaghan; Joan McPartland (nee Verschoyle), from the family book, *Gens Van Der Scuylen, 600 years of Verschuijl and Verschoyle Family*, by Virginia Mason, Verschoyle Mason Publications, relating to Captain William Verschoyle and Second

Lieutenant Francis Verschoyle; Anne Pedley, The Royal Welsh Fusiliers Association, for information from her unpublished work, *The Gunners Hell, Zillebeke Lake,* July 1917, relating to Second Lieutenant John Henry Leland; Elizabeth Dowse, from her book, *A Jackdaw's Gleanings*, relating to her father and uncles, Richard Victor Dowse, Major-General John C. A. Dowse, Lieutenant Henry H. Dowse and Lance Corporal Charles Edward Dowse; Hugh Sweeney and George Sweeney, from their unpublished work, *A Tale of Two Brothers*, the story of their uncles, George and Michael, who went their different ways – one enlisted in the British Army and the other joined the IRA; John Weafer from his article in the journal of the *Dun Laoghaire Borough Historical Society* relating to his great-uncle, Private John Joseph Weafer.

I am most grateful to relatives of war dead who offered me military and family information and permission to photograph letters, medals and other memorabilia: Ian and Ann Ainslie; Jasper C. Brett; John Byrne; Fintan Byrne; Alex Beavan; Graeme Donald; Brendan Doyle; Alex Findlater (Edinburgh); Carmel Forrestal; Patrick Glynn; Paul Glynn; Delores Gobett; Rob Goodbody; Nuala Howell; John F. Joyce; John Kelly; Patrick and Catherine Kelly; Ronan Lee; Owen Lemass; Patsy Mooney; Tara Owens; Michael Richardson; Scott Rossitor; Leslie Shaw; Mary Sheppard; Brian Tierney; Father Philip Tierney OSB; Rosemary Tierney; Andrea Tingleff, Patrick Vaughan and Mary White.

Other important family contributions came from: David Collen; Claude Cronhelm, Canada; Jo-Anne Crossing; Angela Doyle; Gregory Geoghegan; Brendan Jackson; Margaret Kinsella; Anne Kinsella, Chris and John Kinsella; Gethin McBean; Colm McQuinn; Nancy Malone; Maureen Martin; Oliver Murphy; Father John Slater; Turtle Bunbury; Joe Walsh and Bill Webster.

My thanks also to all those who offered information, assistance and encouragement: Jim Craddock; Ger Doyle; Jamie Deasy; Alan Geraghty; Margie Geraghty; Noelle Hughes; Joseph Ledwidge; Alan Murphy; Joseph Murphy; Pat O'Daly; James and Mary Rigney; Tony Roe; Noel Ryan; Reverend Niall J. Slone; Frank Spain.

Websites and forums were important to my research and I am most grateful to Alan Greveson's 'World War One Forum' for its support. Alan's extraordinary knowledge of the Great War and willingness to assist throughout the period of research was of immense benefit. I am also grateful to Chris Baker and the 'Pals' of the Great War Forum website, together with thanks to his website, 'The Long, Long Trail – The British Army in the Great War'. Ancestry.com was most useful for contacting relatives of Great War dead. Included in my thanks is the wonderful website, Irish War Memorials, created and managed by Dr Michael Pegum, which was of immense value in locating soldiers commemorated on Great War Memorials in Ireland.

Newspapers, magazines and journals were an important source of information. I would like to thank Alan Geraghty and his editorial team at the *Three Rock Panorama Magazine* who gave me enormous assistance in making contact with relatives of Great War dead.

I am indebted to all of the aforementioned relatives, friends, institutions and publishers for their valuable assistance and constant encouragement to keep going despite the many barriers and disappointments met along the way. Please accept my humble apologies if I have unwittingly omitted any person's name.

Alessandro Portelli, an Italian-born oral historian and scholar of American literature and culture, said of history: 'All sources, oral and written, are equally inaccurate.' The author wishes to assure readers that he has taken great care to check all military and family information contained in the book, but cannot be responsible for the accuracy, reliability or currency of the information, written or oral, provided by institutions, publications, relatives and local historians.

Abbreviations, Terms, Name Changes

AA Guns	Anti-aircraft guns
AIF	Australian Imperial Force
ASU	Active Service Unit
Capt	Captain
Cpl	Corporal
CWGC	Commonwealth War Graves Commission
CO	Commanding Officer
BEF	British Expeditionary Force
DSO	Distinguished Service Order
HE Shell	A high explosive shell used during the Great War which exploded its fragments in all directions and could be fired by high-angle weapons such as howitzers.
IRA	Irish Republican Army
IRFU	Irish Rugby Football Union
K1	Kitchener's first volunteer army or the first 100,000 men to enlist, took just two weeks to achieve in August 1914
K2	Kitchener's second volunteer army. Kitchener asked for another 100,000 men to enlist on 28 August 1914
K3	Kitchener's third army. This division was established in September 1914. It was March 1915 before makeshift drab uniforms arrived and July before rifles were issued.
L/Cpl	Lance Corporal
L/Sgt	Lance Sergeant

Lt	Lieutenant
Lt-Col	Lieutenant-Colonel
MC	Military Cross
Maj	Major
MM	Military Medal
OTC	Officers Training Corps
Pte	Private
TNT	Explosives
WWI	World War One
WWII	World War Two

Name Changes

Chanak is now Cannanakale.

Queenstown is now Cobh.

Kingstown is now Dun Laoghaire.

Sackville Street is now O'Connell Street, Dublin.

Kings County is now Offaly.

Ypres is now known as Ieper.

Mesopotamia is present-day Iraq.

Wytschaete is now known as Wijtschate.

Queens County is now Laois.

Terms

Coloured lines:

A plan of attack outlining the four coloured objective Lines; Black, Red, Blue and Brown.

Heavies:

Heavy artillery, i.e. a 60-pounder battery.

Lachrymal:

A tear-producing gas; its effects are not as fatal as asphyxiating gas, but could put men out of action for hours.

A second is lachrymal shells, which make it difficult for men to serve the guns.

A third type of lachrymal shell could linger for several hours and was most useful when an army needed to prevent the enemy from bringing up reinforcements.

Chlorine gas:

Could destroy the respiratory organs of its victims and led to a lingering death by asphyxiation.

The following towns, villages and institutions are all situated in
Dublin City or County

Ballinteer, Ballybrack, Ballycorus, Barnacullia, Blackrock, Booterstown, Brennan-stown, Cabinteely, Carrickmines, Churchtown, Clonskeagh, Cornelscourt, Dalkey, Dean's Grange, Donnybrook, Dundrum, Dun Leary, Foxrock, Golden Ball, Glasthule, Glencullen, Harold's Cross, Howth, Kilgobbin, Kilmacud, Kill-of-the-Grange, Kilternan, Kingstown (now Dun Laoghaire), Leopardstown, Milltown, Monkstown, Mount Jerome Cemetery, Mount Merrion Avenue, Rathfarnham, Rathgar, Rathmichael, Rathmines, Ringsend, St Stephen's Green, Sandyford, Sandycove, The Scalp, Shankill, Stepaside, Stillorgan, Terenure and Windy Arbour. Trinity College (also known as Dublin University) is in Dublin city, unless otherwise stated.

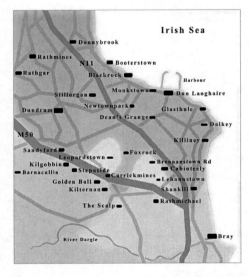

Map of towns and villages in South County Dublin by Billy Moore.

List of Photographs

Maps

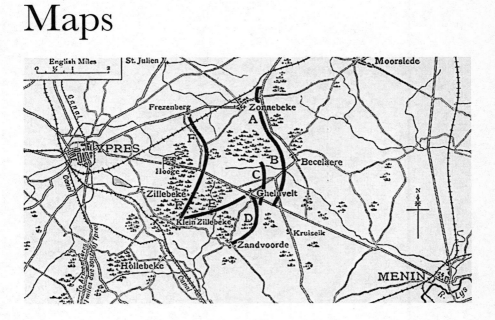

1. First Battle of Ypres, Flanders, from 19 October 1914 to 22 November 1914. Shows British positions in October 1914. Courtesy of Chris Baker, The Long, Long Trail.

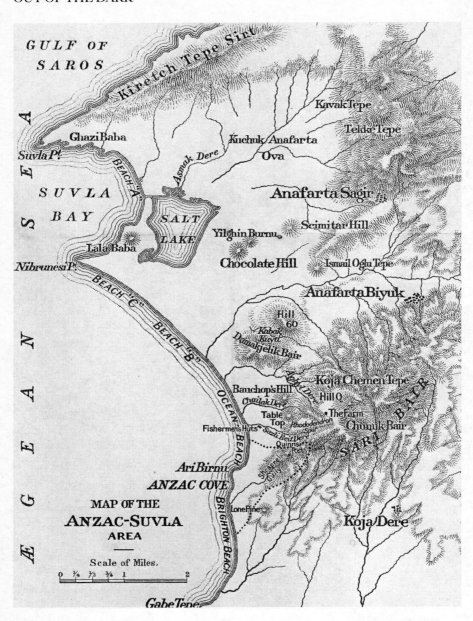

2. The Gallipoli Campaign – April to September 1915. Courtesy of Paul Read.

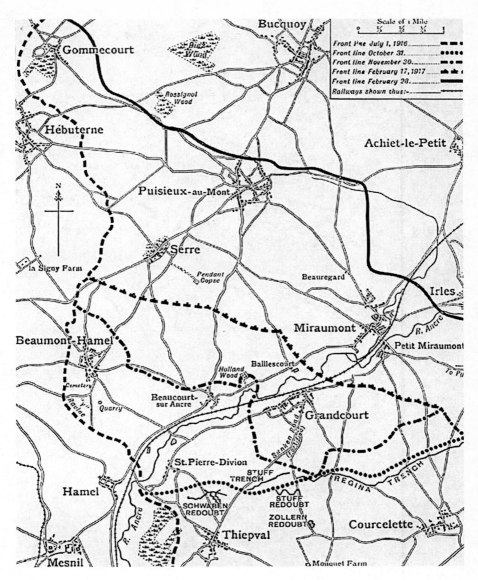

3. Battle of Ancre: showing British advances from July 1916 – February 1917.
The Long, Long Trail.

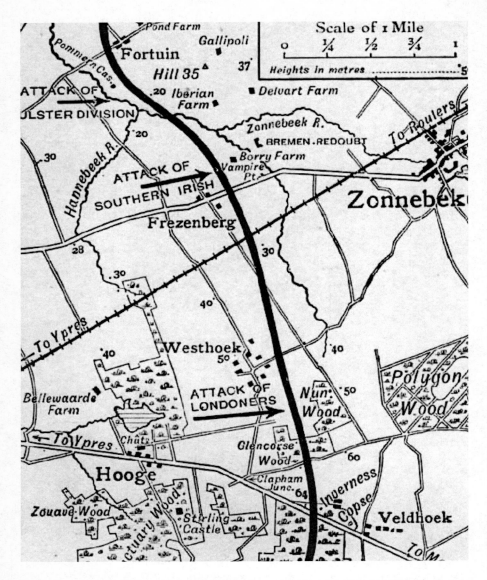

4. Battle area east of Ypres showing line before attack on 16 August 1917. The Long, Long Trail.

Introduction

The horror and devastation of the First World War, frequently described as the Great War, was on a scale never witnessed before. Nearly 36 million from all countries involved in the war were casualties.

How and why this global war began is not the subject of analysis in the book, however, for the sake of clarity it should be stated that it opened with the Austro-Hungarian invasion of Serbia on 28 July 1914. On 1 August Germany declared war on Russia and two days later it declared war on France and invaded Belgium. The next day, 4 August 1914, Britain declared war on Germany. The Great War ended on Armistice Day, 11 November 1918.

The book is aimed at expanding the limited military and family information available in the public domain on soldiers and their families from South County Dublin. It is also an attempt to keep before the public eye the story of heroism and heartbreak of Irishmen who fought and died together in appalling circumstances on the western and eastern fronts. War Diary reports from Irish and British Regiments, together with letters and anecdotal information reveal extraordinary tales of courage in the face of impossible odds. The reader will also get an insight into the compelling human story of the war which affected so many lives, not only on the frontline but also those at home. While the Roll of Honour for officers and men is the main theme of the book, the author has also attempted to analyse the complexities of the economic and political difficulties in South County Dublin throughout the war years and in its aftermath.

The plight of Irishmen, who returned home following the war, and the years of shameful neglect up to the end of the 1980s, is featured also. There is an enormous change in the attitude of the state and among people who held the view that Irishmen and women who enlisted in the British and Allied services should have stayed at home to fight the British.

The main body of the book is divided into seven districts, each beginning with a brief history of the people, events and institutions relating to the Great War. Each chapter concludes with the Roll of Honour for selected officers, men and a small number of nurses. This will include a military and family profile of those who fell, together with siblings and other family relations who served and survived the conflict. In the Roll of Honour for each district the profiles of soldiers are presented in military rank and in alphabetical order. However, brothers who perished are kept together, irrespective of rank.

Readers will observe that there is more detailed information on officers when compared with other ranks. Men from families with wealth and power were more likely to be remembered. Original documents of officers were available for inspection at the National Archives in London contrasting sharply with the poor availability of service records for other ranks. A German bombing raid on the London War Office repository in September 1940 destroyed about 60 per cent of service records for other ranks, the exception being attestation papers for soldiers attached to the Irish Guards Regiment, which were not affected.

The other anomaly in the information available for a soldier's last days in action was the paucity of information in battalion war diaries on other ranks in comparison with officers, whose names were frequently referred to in war diaries, while the names of other ranks were rarely mentioned.

The success of any historical research depends largely on the willingness of others to share resources. One of the biggest problems associated with a project of this kind is the difficulty of making contact with relatives of Great War dead, especially those who served in other ranks. Relatives known to me were extraordinary in their willingness to share information. The difficulty encountered in making contact with relatives was partly due to the emigration of approximately 1.2 million Irish people in the years between 1891 and 1922, a trend that was to continue until the late 1960s. It is also true that many returning soldiers and relatives of war dead remained silent to avoid ridicule and unpleasantness in their communities by not speaking about the heartbreaking loss of loved ones. This situation often resulted in a failure to pass on anecdotal information, letters, photographs, medals and other memorabilia that were hidden away to be lost or sold by the generations that followed.

Readers may feel that letters written to parents by senior officers, following the death of a son, were repetitive and a little trite, but what was the alternative? In their great sorrow and distress, parents derived some consolation from a letter that expressed the sad loss of a brave and gallant son, who was much loved and respected by his comrades.

While this was a man's war, all too often women have been overlooked. Irishwomen served as nurses and worked in munitions factories in Ireland and England. Far away from the action a network of women's committees was formed to support men at the front. One such committee was the Dundrum County Dublin Prisoners of War Committee, responsible for food distribution to Irish soldiers who were prisoners of war in Germany. A young lady, Monica Roberts, who lived at Kelston, Stillorgan Road, set up a society called 'Band of Helpers to the Soldiers'. The primary aim of this society was to supply comforts to soldiers at the front. The Monica Roberts Collection is in the Royal Dublin Fusiliers Association's archive with Dublin City Library and Archive, where it is available for public consultation in the Reading Room.

The Roll of Honour also includes information on a small number of Voluntary Aid Detachments (VAD), young women who worked as temporary nurses in hospitals and clearing stations, often near to the front line. They were frequently described as 'Lilies of the Fields'.

This was a terrible time in Irish history and it behoves the present generation to have an open mind about all Irishmen who fought against the Germans in the Great War as well as those who stayed at home to fight the British in the 1916 Easter Rising and the War of Independence that followed.

Chapter One

ENLISTMENTS

South County Dublin in the early twentieth century was an unequal mix of working-class Roman Catholics and Protestants and a powerful minority of wealthy middle-class people. We may never know how many Irishmen of birth or blood fought and how many died in the Great War. The official figures vary between 200,000 and 300,000 enlistments and 35,000 to 49,400 fallen, but there is a body of opinion that believes the numbers were much greater.

Tens of thousands of first and second generation Irishmen joined the armed forces of adopted countries, many of whom were not allowed for when the numbers of enlisted and dead were being calculated. The figures do not take into account all of the Irishmen in the Royal Navy and in non-military services, like the Merchant Marine, who served and suffered in the Great War. We do know that about 28,000 Irishmen were serving in the British armed forces at the outbreak of war with a further 30,000 reservists, who were immediately called up.

One of the many examples of recruitment of Irishmen living abroad was given in the *Freeman's Journal* on 1 January 1915. It published details of a report in the *Dumfries & Galloway Standard*, 'Over 350 Roman Catholics of the St Andrews pro-Cathedral congregation joined various regiments. It may be assumed that a large proportion of the above are Irish or of Irish descent.'[1] The leading article in the *Kilkenny Journal*, in September 1918, suggested: 'Irishmen to the number of 300,000 have fought in the armed forces representing Ireland and Great Britain in the Great War, and they were summoned to the fray in the name and for the sake of Ireland – far more than 300,000 men of Irish birth or blood – probably nearly 1,000,000 are enrolled in the American and Colonial armies.'[2]

Irish participation in regiments, from Ireland, Britain, Canada and USA, included:

Ireland:
Connaught Rangers
Royal Irish Regiment
Leinster Regiment
Royal Irish Fusiliers
Royal Dublin Fusiliers
Royal Irish Rifles
Royal Inniskilling Fusiliers
Royal Munster Fusiliers
South Irish Horse
North Irish Horse

Britain:
4th Royal Irish Dragoon Guards
6th (Inniskilling) Dragoons
8th King's Royal Irish Hussars
London Irish Rifles
5th Royal Irish Lancers
Irish Guards
1/8 (Irish) Kings Liverpool Regiment
Tyneside Irish Brigade

Canada:
Irish Fusiliers of Canada
The Irish Regiment of Canada 199th (Duchess of Connaught's) (Own Irish Rangers) Battalion
208th (Canadian Irish) Battalion
121st (Western Irish) Battalion

South Africa:
1st South African Irish Regiment

USA:
69th Infantry Regiment

Irishmen also enlisted in the Royal Navy, Royal Merchant Navy, Royal Flying Corps, Royal Engineers, Royal Army Medical Corps and other British, American, Canadian, South African, Australian, and New Zealand Regiments. Many soldiers of Irish blood and descent were also listed in the Royal Newfoundland Regiment.

WHY DID IRISH MEN AND WOMEN JOIN IN THE WAR AGAINST THE GERMANS?
There were several reasons why Irishmen joined the fight against Germany at the outset of the Great War; not least was the centuries-old tradition of Irishmen serving in the British armed forces. There were 159,000 Irishmen in the British service in 1815 and in 1830 over 42 per cent of all non-officers in the entire British Army were Irish born.[3]

Irishmen have been an important part of the English (British) army for hundreds of years. The Royal Dublin Fusiliers Regiment was created from 102nd and 103rd Regiments of Foot, but can trace its origins back to 1661. The Connaught Rangers Regiment was formed in September 1793 as the 88th Regiment of Foot, and it played a major role in the French defeat at Salamanca in 1812. The 86th Regiment (Leinster) of Foot, between 1806 and 1812, spent more than twenty-three years overseas, fighting in Egypt, India, Ile de Bourbon, Ceylon, and as marines aboard men-of-war. The regiment was recruited from Leinster and other parts of Ireland and it won fame as the 'Irish Giants' and 'Bourbon Heroes'.[4] 'More than 30,000 Irishmen fought for Britain in the Boer War, 1899-1902, and a few hundred fought on the opposite side, for the Boers.'[5] In one of the greatest tributes ever made to a regiment of the British Army Field Marshal Sir Evelyn Wood VC said in reference to the extraordinary bravery of the Royal Munster Fusiliers, following the landings at 'V' Beach, Gallipoli, on 25 April 1915:

> It is perhaps only soldiers who can fully appreciate the enduring courage of the Munster Fusiliers who, after losing half their numbers by drowning, and by fire and shrapnel and bullets, with their brigadier-general, his brigade major, and most of their regimental officers down,

could re-form into remnants of companies, and after a night without food, follow a staff officer, Lt-Col Doughty-Wylie, from the beach up to the Old Castle, and assault successfully Hill No 141. These men are indeed worthy descendants of their predecessors who carried the walls of Delhi in 1857.[6]

While tradition was a factor, the scourge of poverty and unemployment in Ireland in the late nineteenth century and early twentieth century was responsible for much of the emigration and enlistment in the armed forces of Britain and adopted countries. Emigration had tormented the Irish nation from the years of the Great Famine and by 1900 it had become an enforced pattern of life for many families. Thousands of boys and girls left school early; often as young as ten years. Adolescents whose parents were poor, and as a consequence did not have the privilege of a full education, were frequently forced into emigration. Prior to the outbreak of war Dublin had the most poverty stricken, poorly-housed population in Europe. Complete independence from Britain was a noble aspiration, but for thousands of Irish people who were starving, emigration and a new life in a foreign land was the only option.

It has been said, with justification, that the failure of successive British governments to provide employment and a standard of living in Ireland equal to that of its people living in mainland Britain was at least partly responsible for the hunger and deprivation that forced Irish people into emigration. In 1911 Dublin's working class had the worst housing conditions of any city in the United Kingdom, with more than 20,000 families living in one-room dwellings.

When joining the armed forces of Britain or other English-speaking countries, Irishmen could look forward to a regular pay packet, three meals daily, medical services and pension benefits. In 1914 a soldier in the British forces could expect to get one shilling and six pence per week, but this could increase when he acquired a skill. An infantry man began in 1915 with the basic pay, but this increased to two shillings and nine pence per day in 1916, when qualified as a machine gunner. An aeromechanic was paid four shillings per day in 1917 and this could rise to five shillings with promotion to corporal. Irishmen who enlisted in the Australian and Canadian forces could expect five or six shillings per day. British troops referred to Australians as 'the [redacted] five bobbers'. One shilling and six pence per week may not seem much, but in 1914 it provided a regular income for working-class families in Dublin city and county, where the rates of pay were lower than those in Britain.

THE PALS' FACTOR

The pals' factor, which operated in villages and townlands all over the country, is sometimes overlooked. In the period 1900 to 1918 many Irishmen joined the British armed forces because their pals did. A young unemployed man of meagre means with that spirit of adventure common to most Irish people often followed a pal into the same regiment.

Those who enlisted from the Golden Ball and Stepaside, tiny villages in South County Dublin, joined the Irish Guards. Edward Farrell and his pal, Denis Doyle, both unemployed farm labourers, enlisted on the same day, and when Denis was killed in 1914, his younger brother, John, also joined the Guards. In the case of two nearby villages, Foxrock and Carrickmines, young men joined the Connaught Rangers; pals who wanted to be together in the same regiment. Dominick Reynolds, of Foxrock, enlisted on the 3 May 1915 with neighbour and pal Daniel Byrne – their friend, Richard Murphy, had already enlisted. 'According to the *Evening Herald*, forty-six members of the successful Young Ireland Fife and Drum Band in Newtown Park, Blackrock, enlisted in the forces. Many of these men joined the Royal Dublin Fusiliers.'[7]

On a larger scale more than two hundred rugby footballers enlisted at Lansdowne Road and formed the Dublin 'Pals', 'D' Company of the 7th Battalion, Royal Dublin Fusiliers. They were, by and large, middle-class men from universities and Dublin sports clubs, but not all professional men. Many of them refused to accept a commission out of loyalty to their pals, and were known, with affection, as the 'The Toffs Among the Toughs', the 'Old Toughs' being a nickname for the Regiment. The defeat of the unions in the 1913 Lockout left many skilled and unskilled workers who had joined a union with no prospect of employment until the recruitment for the war began. A full company of Dublin Dockers enlisted and were known as the 'Larkinites' after their Trade Union leader James Larkin. Soccer players, pals from the Dublin clubs Bohemians and Shelbourne volunteered also. Whatever the reason for Irishmen joining the British and Allied forces, they were innocent of the charge that they were traitors.

Middle-class Protestant Irishmen volunteered as part of a family tradition of service in the British armed forces. Some of those in the three southern provinces may have been influenced by the prospect of Home Rule, but it is more likely that they were Unionists and saw it as their duty to defend Britain and its Empire. In the words of Alex Findlater: '...for most Irish Protestants, the reaction was visceral and instinctive'.[8] Working-class Protestants were fewer in number, but would have enlisted for the same reasons. The situation for educated Roman Catholic men from the professional classes was the same. Hundreds of ex-pupils from Roman Catholic schools followed the example of great men, like Tom Kettle MP, Willie Redmond MP, Father Willie Doyle SJ and others who joined the war effort to fight an enemy seen as common to Britain and both traditions in Ireland.

NATIONALIST LEADERS

Nationalist MPs, John and Willie Redmond, Stephen Gwynn and Tom Kettle, had actively campaigned against participation by Irish soldiers in the Boer War, however, the Great War was a different matter. John Edward Redmond MP, the Nationalist leader, and his brother, William, who were born at Ballytrent, Co Wexford, were the sons of William Archer Redmond MP and Mary Redmond (née Hoey). John Redmond saw it as an opportunity for Irishmen, of both traditions, to fight side by side in support of Britain and its Allies, believing that the country would be rewarded by Britain with self government. Redmond pushed for a distinctly Irish Brigade in the same way that other countries within the Empire were contributing their own military units. However, Irish-born Lord Horatio Kitchener became a major stumbling block to Redmond's plan.

Kitchener did not like Home Rule and disliked even more the idea of a private Irish army. There was great excitement in Catholic Ireland when on the 18 September 1914 Royal Assent to Home Rule was given to Ireland. Now Redmond urged his Irish National Volunteers to join the war on the British side, and his pleadings with all Irishmen to support Britain were responsible for widespread recruitment. In a public speech intended for northern Unionists and in support of Irish participation on the side of the Allies, he stated:

> As our soldiers are going to fight, to shed their blood, and to die at each other's side in the army, against the same enemy, and for the same high purpose, their union in the field may lead to a union in their home, and ... their blood may be the seal that will bring all Ireland together in one nation and in liberties equal and common to all.[9]

In another speech delivered in London in 1915, appealing to Unionists, Redmond said: 'Let Irishmen come together in the trenches and spill their blood together and I say there is no power on earth that when they come home can induce them to turn as enemies one upon another.'[10]

Having won the enactment of Home Rule, Redmond was a little naive in his expectation that Unionists and Nationalists fighting as allies would bring about reconciliation in a war that was not expected to last more than a few months.

He saw his prize slipping away. The Ulster Volunteers would have to enlist and his first proposal was that Irishmen would take over the defence of Ireland; this would free British troops for Flanders. He had little option but to match Carson's stakes in a great poker game. He did not join the War Cabinet. He had almost become the first Prime Minister of an Ireland with its own Parliament. Redmond was soon overtaken by history and there was no payback for the sacrifices made by those who enlisted at his request. The Wexford MP was out-manoeuvred by Carson and his Tory supporters.[11]

Lieutenant Thomas Michael Kettle MP, barrister, writer, poet, economist and soldier, was one of the greatest Irishmen of the twentieth century. He was born in Artane, Co Dublin, the son of Andrew Kettle, one of the founders of the Land League. Tom Kettle married Mary Sheehy, a fellow graduate of the Royal University, on 8 September 1909. She was a suffragette and, like Kettle, a member of a well-known Nationalist family. Her father, David Sheehy, was a Nationalist MP. Mary's brother, Francis Sheehy Skeffington, a pacifist, was murdered by a British officer during the 1916 Easter Rising. The couple's daughter, Elizabeth, was born in 1913.

In an orgy of rape in the villages and towns of Belgium, the Germans burnt and destroyed everything in sight, killing thousands of innocent citizens, many of them women and children. The burning to the ground of the Roman Catholic University library in Louvain also infuriated Irish people. On 25 August 1914, German troops deliberately set fire to the library by pouring petrol on the building, destroying nearly 300,000 priceless books and medieval manuscripts.

Tom Kettle was in Belgium at the outbreak of war, where he was running guns for the volunteers. In reference to this German act of terrorism, his wife Mary Sheehy Kettle wrote in her memoir, '...and in this capacity was a witness of the agony of Belgium. He returned to Ireland burning with indignation against Prussia. He referred to Germany as "the outlaw of Europe". He said: "When they burned Louvain, the Barbarians lit a fire which is not easily put out".[12]

His burning ambition and dream was that Ulster Protestants would be reconciled with the rest of Ireland. He wrote to his wife: 'One duty does indeed lie before me, that of devoting myself to the working out of reconciliation between Ulster and Ireland. I feel God speaking to our hearts in that sense out of this terrible war.'[13]

In his Political Testament he makes a dying plea for the realisation of his dream:

> In the name, and by the seal, of the blood given in the last two years I ask for Colonial Home Rule for Ireland, a thing essential in itself, and essential as a prologue to the reconstruction of the Empire. Ulster will agree. And I ask for the immediate withdrawal of martial law in Ireland, and an amnesty for all Sinn Fein prisoners. If this war has taught us anything, it is that great things can be done only in a great way.[14]

He prophesied that the Easter rebels of 1916 would be remembered as heroes while Irishmen serving in the European war would be deemed traitors: 'These men will go down in history as heroes and martyrs; and I will go down – if I go down at all as a bloody British officer.'[15]

Although he had little sympathy with the rebellion, Easter week had been for him a harrowing and terrible experience and allied to the awful conditions in the trenches his health began to deteriorate. Not surprisingly, he refused to accept a safe job behind the lines choosing instead to stay with his comrades in the Dublin Fusiliers. Lieutenant Thomas Michael Kettle MP was killed in action on 9 September 1916 while leading a company of his men at Ginchy during the Battle of the Somme. His wife wrote: 'Perhaps the greatest proof of his magnetic personality lies in the fact that all classes, the Unionist and Nationalist, the soldier, the Sinn Feiner, and, as the *Freeman* wrote, "those wearing the convict garb" of England, united in mourning his death and paying tribute to his memory.'[16] His batman, an 18-year-old Belfast lad called Robert Bingham, wrote to his widow, Mary Kettle:

> I am writing to you in respect of my late officer which I had been servant to him since he has been out in France … he was a brave officer and he was like a father to me as I am myself an orphan boy … I was

awfully sorry when God called such a brave man away. He told me just before his death that I was going home and he was staying where he was. With that he gave me his watch and I will be willing to forward the watch to you, when you write to me as I am not certain of the address.[17]

It is not known if Robert Bingham returned the watch to Mary Kettle or if she allowed the young Belfast orphan to keep it as a memento.

William Hoey Kearney Redmond MP, a nationalist and brother of John Redmond MP, took the view that it was a fight for all small oppressed nations and that Irishmen should not stand apart from the struggle. Although well over the military age he made his decision to wear a British uniform. In an extract from long letter to his close friend, Patrick Linnane, he wrote about his reasons for joining the army: '...if the Germans come here – they will be our masters and we at their mercy. What that mercy is likely to be, judge by the mercy shown to Belgium.'[18]

William Redmond was a land reform agitator, a determined advocate of Irish Home Rule, and was imprisoned three times. At the age of 56, he succeeded in obtaining special permission to join his battalion, returning to his beloved 'A' Company of the 6th Battalion, Royal Irish Regiment. The Irish troops of the 16th (Irish) and 36th (Ulster) Divisions advanced shoulder-to-shoulder in the great attack on the Messines Ridge towards the small village of Wytschaete next to Messines. Men of both traditions marching side by side into battle fulfilled the dream of his brother John, but did not result in the unity of minds and hearts that he thought might result from such a historic occasion. On 7 June 1917 Major William Redmond MP for East Clare was mortally wounded while leading the Royal Irish Brigade to victory at the Battle of Messines Ridge, at Ypres in Belgium.

Francis Ledwidge of Slane was one of the country's finest poets and an office bearer in the Irish National Volunteers at local level. Ledwidge came from a working-class family and at one stage in his young life he was working as a road mender; ironically when he was killed, aged 29, at Boesinghe, in Flanders Fields on 31st July 1917, he was back where he began, repairing roads.

When asked why he enlisted, he said: 'I joined the British army because she stood between Ireland and an enemy common to our civilisation and I would not have her say that she defended us while we did nothing at home but pass resolutions.'[19]

Stephen Gwynn MP, a Protestant Nationalist, strongly supported John Redmond's encouragement of Irish Nationalists and the Irish National Volunteers to join the Allied and British war effort. Redmond and Gwynn expected that wholehearted participation by Irishmen would ensure implementation of the suspended Home Rule Act. Gwynn was born in St Columba's College, Rathfarnham, where his father John, a biblical scholar and Church of Ireland clergyman, was warden. He had strong connections with the Gaelic revival movement. Stephen Gwynn was over fifty when he donned the British Army uniform in January 1915, initially with the 7th Leinster Regiment, and later in 1915 he was promoted to Captain and served on the Western Front with the 6th Connaught Rangers. Many months after the attack on Wijtschate, on the 21 September 1918, the *Galway Observer* recorded the following:

> In a letter to the mayor of Derry (Mr R.N. Johnston) on Irish achievements in the war, Capt Gwynn recalls that he saw Derrymen at a place where 'there was no thought of anything but our common credit' on the ridge in front of Messines, where the 16th (Irish) and 36th (Ulster) Divisions lay side by side. 'Once it happened', he says, 'that our right flank was moved up a little and I was the officer sent up to take over the section of the line from the Ulster troops who were holding it. They were the Inniskillings, and the commanding officer, Colonel McRory, showed me round the line. All the trenches had names that were very familiar to me, but at last we came to a very strong point at the head of a mineshaft, where there was a great accumulation of sandbags'. Colonel McRory said to me rather sadly: 'We call this place Derry Walls, but I suppose that when your fellows come in here they will be changing all the names'. I said to him: 'we won't change a name of them, and we will hold Derry Walls for you'. We did hold Derry Walls for four months and gave it back to the Ulster people and it was from there they went over the top on that day, when the two divisions, side by side, captured Messines and Wytschaete.[20]

FAMILIES DIVIDED

It was not uncommon for families to have had divided loyalties; one member of a family fighting for the British and Allied armies and another on the Republican side against the British. Sub-Lieutenant Gerald Plunkett was killed in action in Gallipoli in 1915, and his half-nephew, Joseph Mary Plunkett, was executed for his part in the 1916 Easter Rising.

At the time that Herbert Lemass (19) and Edwin Lemass (21) were in the trenches on the Western Front, their second cousin, Séan Lemass (17) was fighting the British in the General Post Office. Séan Lemass was later to become Taoiseach in the new Irish State.

Lieutenant Gerald A. Neilan, with the 10th Royal Dublin Fusiliers, was killed by a rebel sniper at Usher's Island on Easter Monday 1916, and his younger brother, Anthony Neilan, was sent to Knutsford Detention Barracks in England, on 1 May 1916, arising out of his participation in the 1916 Easter Rising.

Sergeant William Malone, 2nd Battalion, Royal Dublin Fusiliers was killed in action on 24 May 1915, at St Julian, France. His brother, Lieutenant Michael Malone, was killed when the British Army bombed No 25, Northumberland Road, Dublin, in the Battle of Mount Street Bridge during the 1916 Easter Rising.[21]

On the same day that Private John Weafer of Glasthule received his fatal wounds in the Battle of Hulluch, his Enniscorthy kinsman, Captain Tom Weafer, Irish Volunteers, was fatally wounded building a barricade at the junction of O'Connell Street and Lower Abbey Street, Dublin. He died in the *Irish Times* paper store in Lower Abbey Street, now Madigan's Pub.[22]

Bridget and Hugh Sweeney, the owners of a fruit shop on Harold's Cross Road, Dublin, were active Republicans. One son, George, as a result of a family dispute, left home and joined the Royal Munster Fusiliers and was killed in 1917. Meanwhile, his younger brother, Michael, aged 15, fought under Cathal Brugha in the South Dublin Union and also lost his life.[23]

William and Edward Dodd, brothers of Newtownpark, Blackrock, enlisted in the British Army at the outbreak of war. Sergeant William Dodd was killed on the first day of the Battle of the Somme, 1 July 1916, and his brother Edward left the British Army and joined the IRA.[24]

RECRUITING

It is accepted that Catholic Ireland suffered under British Rule. Religious persecution, Penal Laws and the unnecessary starvation of hundreds of thousands of Irish people in the Great Famine were just some of the British failings. And yet, despite the long wait for an Irish Parliament and the suspension of the Home Rule Act in 1914, Irishmen flocked behind Redmond and Kettle to join the British Army. The anti-recruiting lobby in Ireland before the outbreak of war did not prevent about 170,000 men staying with Redmond, becoming the National Volunteers, while 11,000 of the more extreme Nationalists broke away, retaining the name The Irish Volunteers.

The Rapturous reception given to the 6th & 7th Royal Dublin Fusiliers as they marched through the streets of Dublin on their way to Gallipoli was captured by the *Irish Times* on 1 May 1915:

> Led by the band of the 12th Lancers and the pipers of the Trinity College Officers Training Corps, they marched off from the Royal Barracks. Along the Liffey quays, crowds on the pavements, spectators in the windows cheered and waved. Outside the Four Courts, a large group of barristers, solicitors, officials and judges shouted goodbye to their friends. Little boys strutted alongside the marching column, chanting their street songs:
>
> > 'Left, right; left, right, here's the way to go;
> > Marching with fixed bayonets, the terror of every foe,
> > A credit to the nation, a thousand buccaneers,
> > A terror to creation, are the Dublin Fusiliers.'
>
> Not for them the direct route along the Liffey quays to the ships. Diverting along Essex Bridge, they marched through the commercial centre of Dame Street, then College Green, passing the Bank of Ireland and Trinity College where many of the battalion had been students and one a professor. Spectators became dense as the marching column crossed O'Connell Bridge and right wheeled onto the quays skirting the statue of O'Connell the liberator. Emotion rose when well-dressed ladies from the fashionable Georgian and Regency squares of south

Dublin mingled with their poorer sisters in shawls from the Liberties and lesser squares of north Dublin. Together they joined their husbands and sweethearts in the ranks to keep step with them the last few hundred yards.[25]

This was in marked contrast to the reception given to the paltry few, who survived Gallipoli, France and Flanders, when they sneaked home through the back door in 1918–19.

THE 1916 EASTER RISING

The 1916 Easter Rising did not have majority backing from the Irish people at its outset and Dubliners, in particular, were furious at the devastation of their city and the killing of so many civilians. It is recorded that during the five days of fighting, more than 300 civilians were killed, 2,200 wounded and nearly 1,800 suspected activists were eventually deported. In the immediate aftermath of the surrender, many Dubliners in the city were 'baying for blood' as the rebels were rounded up, however, the harsh response of the British Government following the Easter Rising brought about a dramatic change in the mood of the people.

P.S. O'Hegarty, republican, revolutionary, writer and civil servant, wrote: 'The European war had shown Ireland to be less Irish and more anglicised than ever she had been in her history, had shown Ireland to be more than three-fourths assimilated to England.'[26] However, when General John Maxwell was appointed by the Army Council as British Commander-in-Chief in Ireland on 27 April 1916, his actions would change the course of Irish history. Public revulsion at the execution of fifteen leaders of the 'Rising', and the arrest and murder of the pacifist, Francis Sheehy Skeffington, by the British officer Capt Bowen Colthurst, on the grounds that he was a criminal further incensed Irish people and assisted the growing alienation from the British administration in Ireland. O'Hegarty also wrote: 'When Sir John Maxwell shot to pieces the Government of the Irish Republic, he put an end to the English domination of Ireland. If the English government had laughed at it, tried the promoters before a magistrate and ridiculed the whole thing, with no general arrests and no long vindictive sentences, they could have done what they liked with Ireland.'[27]

Following the Easter Rising, life became more difficult for Irishmen serving in the British forces, especially those attached to British Regiments. While tens of thousands of Irish soldiers were risking their lives on the Western Front, the British administration, who felt betrayed by the 1916 Easter Rising, no longer trusted them. General Maxwell reported that he found it '…very difficult to differentiate between Sinn Feiner and Redmondite. It is merely a question of degree'. Captain Stephen Gwynn said of the soldiers of 16th (Irish) Division, 'I shall never forget the men's indignation. They felt they had been stabbed in the back.'[28] But the greatest betrayal of Irish servicemen in the British armed forces took place in their own country.

In the years following the 1916 Easter Rising, Irish history would gradually change. The pride and adulation emanating from those large crowds cheering their fellow countrymen as they went to war, would soon dissipate, to be replaced at the end of the war by loathing for almost everything British. The slowing down of recruitment to the British forces began following the disastrous Gallipoli campaign in 1915. An advertisement in the *Evening Herald* on 30 October 1915 read 'Irishmen, you cannot permit your regiments to be kept up to strength by other than Ireland's sons! It would be a deep disgrace to Ireland, if all her regiments were not Irish, to a man.'[29]

The *Irish Times* published an article from the military correspondent of the *London Times*, under the heading of 'An Indelible Stain', which provides an insight into the official British attitude to the slow-down of recruitment in Ireland at this time:

> The time has come for a drastic reform of the Services Act and, if this action is not taken quickly and thoroughly, Germans will beat us in the organisation of her man power. All that is necessary to say about Ireland is that compulsion is necessary on military grounds, if the Irish Divisions are to be maintained, and that, if we are not to expect the additional 150.000 men that Ireland could give us, and then we must make good the deficit elsewhere. We shall all very much regret the disappearance from our armies of the Irish element, but it is bound to happen unless a change is quickly made. The good humour, dash and soldierly qualities of the Irish are prized in the army. They are the finest missile troops that we possess when they are led and officered by Irishmen who understand them, and it will be an indelible mark

upon this gifted race if a German war against the liberties of Europe and integrity of all small nations find Ireland absent from the roll call at the end.[30]

It must be stated that the slowdown in recruitment was not confined to Ireland – there were problems in other parts of Britain also, especially among those who worked on the land. Conscription spurred the British anti-war movement into new life. 'By 1916, 200,000 Britons signed a petition calling for a negotiated peace in response to the rise of conscription by the British government, with more than 20,000 military men of military age refusing to enter the British armed forces before the war ended.'[31] The British government's answer to replacing the appalling wastage on the Western Front and earlier in the Balkans was to introduce conscription, which came into force on 2 March 1916. John Redmond MP strongly resisted introducing conscription in Ireland and in the end it was not enforced anywhere on the island. The anti-conscription campaign received huge support from Sinn Féin and the Roman Catholic Church and paved the way for armed resistance.

On 10 October 1918 the war came closer to south Dublin when the Kingstown to Hollyhead mail boat, RMS *Leinster*, was torpedoed and sunk with the loss of over 500 lives.

THE END OF THE WAR

'The Send-off'
Shall they return to beatings of great bells
In wild trainloads?
A few, a few, too few for drums and yells,
May creep back, silent, to still village wells
Up half-known roads.[32]

–Wilfred Owen

Following four terrible years of war the guns fell silent on 11 November 1918. The *Evening Herald* reported on the scenes in Dublin city following the announcement that the war was over: 'Aeroplanes swooped and swirled through the clear air over

Dublin. Crowds in the streets cheered the loops and stunts of the aviators. Young ladies and old sported small flags and wore the British and Allied colours. In some parts of the city groups of schoolboys and girls were to be met carrying flags and singing.'[33] And the *Irish Times* wrote that:

> Rejoicings were on an extensive scale. The news had quite an exhilarating effect, however, on all classes, and it soon became evident that work and business had been disorganised for the day, a spirit of holiday making being quickly evoked. In the afternoon and until after nightfall the scenes in the principal streets recalled a public festival day of the pre-war period.[34]

For those Irish soldiers still on the front line, the end of war did not come one minute too soon. Captain Terence Bernard Poulter, Royal Dublin Fusiliers, survived the war and years later remembered the relief felt by the men on 11 November 1918: 'This was joyous news approaching eleven o'clock in our sector. You could hear a pin drop and when eleven o'clock came there were wild cheers. The war was over as far as we were concerned.'[35] The feeling of elation at the ending of the war was not received with the same enthusiasm by many nationalists and republicans. Geraldine Plunkett, sister of Joseph Plunkett, executed for his part in the 1916 Easter Rising, wrote: 'The war ended in November with Germany defeated. The men in jail thought that this was the end of our hopes, but we, outside, did not feel quite like that. Public opinion was much more informed and support for us had been growing. Armistice night in Dublin was a very ignorant demonstration by the English.'[36]

THE WAR WAS OVER, BUT FOR MANY, THE NIGHTMARE CONTINUED

The war was over for millions of Europeans, and it was certainly over for tens of thousands of Irishmen who lost their lives following four years of the bloodiest war imaginable. But for the wretches who returned home with missing limbs, tortured by shellshock or suffering with pain from lingering wounds the nightmare continued. Many men were so damaged by shell shock that they spent the remainder of their miserable lives in mental hospitals or institutions like Leopardstown Park Hospital in South Dublin. And then there were thousands of ex-servicemen, who by all outward appearances were leading normal lives, but were so disturbed by the horror experienced in the war that they were unable regain their self confidence. These were the men who could not reconstruct relationships with their loved ones and thus became withdrawn from family and friends. Many survivors became victims of depression and alcoholism, and some even committed suicide. Men were so badly damaged, physically and mentally, that they may have wished a shell or sniper had finished them off. Great War heroes, who finished up as human wreckage living in their homeland, mostly unwanted, except in nursing homes and hospitals, where devoted doctors and nurses did their best to comfort them in their pain and anxiety.

In the months and years that followed the war, survivors who came home having witnessed tens of thousands of comrades being killed or maimed on the battlefields of Europe, most of them believing that they were fighting for Ireland, were confronted by a people whose attitude had changed dramatically in four years. British bungling of the 1916 Easter Rising, its betrayal of John Redmond and his Irish Parliamentary Party, and the party's subsequent annihilation by Sinn Féin in the 1918 elections all contributed to this change. Instead of the expected welcome home, Irish soldiers who fought in the war were frequently branded as traitors and some were subjects of assassination attempts. Many soldiers and their families found it difficult and uncomfortable having to live in this hostile atmosphere, and frequently found themselves in conflict with Sinn Féiners. At the conclusion of an interview for this book in 2006, an elderly lady (now deceased) showed genuine concern that the published information about her uncle in this book would result in upsetting IRA activists in Dublin. While this was unrealistic in today's Ireland, she was remembering the fear experienced by her grandparents when her uncle joined the British Army. Another example of anti-British feeling in the country following the war involved a statue of the Sacred Heart donated by a town in Northern France to Kingstown as a token of gratitude for the sacrifice made by many young Irishmen from the district who gave their lives in the defence of freedom. The statue was refused by the Christian Brothers and the local parish church also declined the offer. However, the sisters at the Dominican Convent in Kingstown accepted the statue. The Oratory was built at the Dominican Convent, Kingstown, in 1919 to celebrate the end of the Great War and as a place to display the statue of the Sacred Heart. In 1919 Sister Concepta Lynch started to decorate the Oratory in the Celtic style. The work is completely hand painted and the intricate and complex design rivals that of the 'Book of Kells'. Sister Lynch continued her work until her death in 1939.[37]

Poor housing, high unemployment and some discrimination in state jobs led to the formation of various old comrades associations to relieve the plight of veterans. In 1919 the unemployment ratio of ex- servicemen was 46 per cent in Ireland compared to just 10 per cent in Britain.[38]

Many of those who stayed at home received help from the Royal Dublin Fusiliers Old Comrades Association which was formed in the late 1920s: 'Thousands of veterans found that they were "surplus to requirements" and, either unable to find work, or no longer accepted by their community, they emigrated in the hope of a better life abroad.'[39]

The likely feelings of Great War survivors were summed-up by Captain Stephen Gwynn, of the 6th Connaughts:

> And when the time came to rejoice over the war's ending, was there anything more tragic than the position of men who had gone out by the thousands for the sake of Ireland to confront the greatest military power ever known in history, who had fought the war and won the war, and who now looked at each other with doubtful eyes?[40]

HEARTFELT APPRECIATION FROM A FAMOUS FRENCH SOLDIER

Irishmen who fought and died in the Great War and comrades that survived were not completely forgotten in the aftermath of the war. Marshal Ferdinand Foch commanded France's Ninth Army during the Battle of the Marne, which was the first major engagement of the war. He also commanded an army group in the battle of the Somme in the summer of 1916. Later, his generalship at Ypres saved the Channel Ports for the Allies. Marshal Foch was eventually given unified command of all the Allied troops in France. He halted the German advance during the second Battle of the Marne. On 18 July1918, Foch mounted the counter-attack that turned the tide of the war. The following is an extract of his moving tribute to Irish soldiers delivered in Paris on Friday 9 November 1928, which, in its own right, will stand as a monument to all Irish soldiers who fought in the Great War:

> The heroic dead of Ireland have every right to the homage of the living
> for they proved in some of the heaviest fighting of the world war that
> the unconquerable spirit of the Irish race – the spirit that has placed

them among the world's greatest soldiers – still lives and is stronger than ever it was. I had occasions to put to the test the valour of the Irishmen serving in France, and, whether they were Irishmen from the North or the South, or from one party or another, they did not fail me. Some of the hardest fighting in the terrible days that followed the last offensive of the Germans fell to the Irishmen, and some of their splendid regiments had to endure ordeals that might justly have taxed to breaking-point the capacity of the finest troops in the world. Some of the flower of Irish chivalry rests in the cemeteries that have been reserved in France, and French people will always have these reminders of the debt that France owes to Irish valour. We shall always see that the graves of these heroes from across the sea are lovingly tended, and we the French people shall try to ensure that the generations that come after us shall never forget the heroic dead of Ireland.[41]

THE EARLY YEARS OF THE NEW STATE

The first Irish Free State administration, in 1922, faced enormous economic difficulties, compounded by the bitterness that existed between politicians who were former comrades, but took opposing sides in the Civil War. To put the economic difficulties into perspective, Dr T.K. Whitaker, architect of the Modern Irish Economy, writes of this period as follows:

The 26 County Irish state which achieved independence in 1922 was a frail entity, faced with a destructive civil war. It was predominantly agricultural and relatively poor, with average incomes less than one-half those in Britain. The population of 3.25 million included a workforce of 1.25 million. Only one person was employed in industry for every eleven said to be 'engaged' in agriculture. 'Engaged' is a euphemism – for most it merely meant being unpaid relatives on farms too small to afford them an independent livelihood. These so called 'relatives assisting' formed a reservoir of poverty-stricken underemployed who filled the emigrant ships for decades. The main ruling parties of the period to the mid-fifties were joint inheritors of the Sinn Fein (self-sufficiency) idealism of a founding father, Arthur Griffith, himself a disciple of Friedrich List, the apostle of protection for infant industry. However, the prior attention of the earlier, 1922/32, administration had to be given to quelling a civil war, repairing the infrastructural damage consequent on many years of disturbed conditions, and establishing the financial viability of the new state.[42]

Despite these difficulties, W.T. Cosgrave, leader of the Free State Government, gave serious thought to the process of a Great War Memorial and it was through his efforts in 1919 that a trust fund was created together with a number of plans and designs. His proposal was accepted on 16 December 1931. As President of the Irish Free State Executive Council, Cosgrave, said at the time: 'This is a big question of remembrance and honour to the dead and it must always be a matter of interest to the head of the government to see that a project so dear to a big section of the citizens should be a success.'[43] In 1927, William Cosgrave's government contributed £50,000 towards a site along the South Bank of the River Liffey at Islandbridge, and Sir Edwin Lutyens, the great English architect and memorialist, was appointed to design the Garden of Remembrance. Due to the outbreak of the Second World War the official opening was postponed on completion of the project in 1939. In the years following its completion, the annual armistice day ceremonies drew large crowds and the Garden of Remembrance became an important place for Dubliners to visit and remember their loved ones. Then came the years of shame when the Great War dead were forgotten and the Garden of Remembrance became dilapidated and was allowed to operate as an open site for caravans and animals of the Irish Traveller community.

LATE TWENTIETH CENTURY BRINGS A NEW DAWNING AND A CHANGE IN ATTITUDES

Remembrance became part of the peace process. With an end to conflict in the north and a growing interest in family history a welcome change of attitude began to take place in the late 1980s and 1990s. The Garden of Remembrance, which had been badly neglected for many years, underwent extensive restoration by the Office of Public Works and was opened officially on 10 September 1988. Today, the Garden is one of the most beautiful Great War Memorials to be seen anywhere in the world. The Trustees responsible for its restoration said: 'It is with a spirit of confidence that we commit this noble memorial of Irish valour to the care and custody of the Government of Ireland.'[44]

Other positive moves towards official recognition of those Irish men and women who died in the Great War were beginning take place around this time. The Royal Dublin Fusiliers Association was founded in 1996. The aim of the association was to promote a better understanding of the Irish involvement in the Great War. The former Taoiseach, Bertie Ahern, at a State Reception given in 2001 to honour the work of the association, said: 'In the past, official attitudes to commemorating the fallen of World War I tended to be censorious.'

The former Fine Gael TD for Donegal, Mr Paddy Harte, supported by northern unionists of like mind, was the driving force behind the north-south project to construct a round tower at the Island of Ireland Peace Park at Messines Ridge in Flanders to honour the Irishmen from north and south who fought and died side by side on the Western Front. He wrote:

This often meant the sharing of blood soaked trenches; attending to each other's wounded, and gladly accepting the comfort of a clergyman from the other side of the religious divide. It had always been my intention to visit the war graves but somehow there was never the time nor the opportunity. Then in 1996, Rosaleen suggested that perhaps we should go before I left public office – I was still a Dail Deputy at the time. Rosaleen and I spent three very emotional and fulfilling days in early September visiting some of the cemeteries and monuments. I felt very emotional when I came face to face with the evidence of the slaughter of young men and women in a war that should never have happened. I also felt ashamed that we who share the peace and comforts of a new Europe seldom thought of them. I suggested that people should stop to think what kind of Ireland would have emerged if the First or Second World War had been lost. The young people who had sacrificed their lives for our freedom did not die so that Protestants and Roman Catholics should behave the way they were behaving.[45]

The plan to construct an Irish round tower at the Island of Ireland Peace Park at Messines Ridge won the goodwill of both governments together with influential people on both sides of the border. Importantly, it had support from the Unionist community. The round tower structure is 34 metres tall and was partially built with stone from a former British Army Barracks in Co Tipperary. Harte spoke with Sir Patrick Mayhew MP, Secretary of State for Northern Ireland, who expressed his admiration for his speech at the Peronne War Museum in the Somme, France, and immediately pledged financial support. When Paddy Harte ran into difficulties about the arrangements to put in place a system to have the Peace Park properly maintained, he found An Taoiseach, Bertie Ahern, most receptive. First and second Ministers of the Northern Ireland Executive, David Trimble and Seamus Mallon also gave their full support to the project. Another important factor in gaining Protestant Irish support was the positive part played by the clergy representing most Protestant denominations in all of Ireland. When all the problems were overcome and everything was in place, there remained one last task, which required finance and goodwill from all sides. Paddy Harte used his considerable influence to find a solution and the finance to send the Irish Army Number One Band to Belgium to attend the official opening. He wrote of this wonderful moment in Irish history: 'It was a historic occasion and a very moving moment when they paraded with a British Army Band from Northern Ireland to remember men who had been forgotten for eighty years.'[46] A bronze plaque near to the entrance of the Island of Ireland Peace Park is inscribed with a peace pledge:

> From the crest of this ridge which was the scene of terrific carnage in the First World War, where we have built a peace park and Round Tower to commemorate the thousands of young men from all parts of Ireland who fought a common enemy, defended democracy and the rights of all nations, whose graves are in shockingly uncountable numbers and those who have no graves, we condemn war and the futility of war. We repudiate and denounce violence, aggression, intimidation, threats and unfriendly behaviour. As Protestants and Roman Catholics, we apologise for the terrible deeds we have done to each other and ask forgiveness. From this sacred shrine of remembrance, where soldiers of all nationalities, creeds and political allegiances were united in death, we appeal to all people in Ireland to help build a peaceful and tolerant society. Let us remember the solidarity and trust that developed

between Protestant and Roman Catholic soldiers when they served together in these trenches.

On 11 November 1998 the President of Ireland, Mary McAleese, joined Her Majesty Queen Elizabeth II of England and His Royal Highness King Albert and Queen Paola of the Belgians, to perform the official opening of the Island of Ireland Peace Park. The attendance also included ambassadors, governors, generals and leading dignitaries from all three countries. Twelve hundred people from all over Ireland travelled by sea and air to be present.

This was followed on 24 March 2010 by a historic event when Mrs Mary McAleese, accompanied by her husband, Dr Martin McAleese, travelled to Green Hill Cemetery in Turkey to unveil a plaque commemorating nearly 4,000 Irishmen who fought and died in the Gallipoli campaign. When asked by the *Irish Times* how she hoped Ireland might mark the centenary of 1914–1918, the President responded as follows: 'By restoring to memory a generation who, of their time and in their circumstances, made sacrifices that they believed to be important … [restoring] in such a way that those memories no longer divide us in the way that they have done historically but allow us a shared commemoration.'[47]

Chapter Two

Barnacullia, Kilgobbin and Stepaside

HISTORY AND ROLL OF HONOUR

The villages and townland of Barnacullia, Kilgobbin and Stepaside are in close proximity and in 1914 they would have formed a single community. Barnacullia was renowned for its granite quarries that provided employment for stonecutters. Some stonecutters also farmed small plots of land. A limited number of labouring and domestic jobs were available on farms and in big houses. There appears to have been two publicans in Barnacullia, Patrick Cannon and J.J. Doyle. The population of this townland in 1911 was 291, occupying 45 houses.[1]

The name Kilgobbin may have come from St Gobban. The ancient monastic site, on which the ruined church stands in a prominent position, is surrounded by the old cemetery on the highest point of elevated ground offering good views of the countryside. Not far from the ruined church stands Kilgobbin Castle. It was necessary for those living on the borders of the Pale to build castles to protect the land from attacks or incursions by the native Irish. Kilgobbin Castle dates back to the Norman period. The church was built in 1707 by Archbishop King and went out of use in 1826. 'The 1911 census recorded a population in Kilgobbin of 224 occupying 47 houses.'[2]

The Great War Memorial is situated on the south-west of the site of the ruined church and old cemetery. Apart from the National Monument at Islandbridge, the memorial at Kilgobbin is one of the few monuments in Dublin city and county erected by a local community to commemorate our Great War dead. The author established that minutes of the Rathdown Rural District Council meeting for 7 June 1924 had survived and it revealed that Mrs Belinda Barrington Jellett of Clonard House, Sandyford, was granted permission to erect a Celtic cross at the old cemetery in memory of the officers and men from the district who fell in the Great War. Stonemasons from Barnacullia designed and crafted this beautiful Celtic cross using local granite.

The Rathdown Rural District Council took over the old cemetery and church at Kilgobbin from the Church of Ireland in 1878. Today it is in the care of the Cultural, Community Development and Amenities Department of Dun Laoghaire / Rathdown County Council. In the late 1990s it became clear that the limestone plaque, which had been subjected to severe weathering, would eventually result in the names of the original twenty-nine soldiers becoming illegible. When the author approached the chief executive of the Council's Environmental Department with a plan to restore the memorial, he unhesitatingly provided the finance to complete the work. The original plaque contained the names of twenty-nine officers and men, but during restoration a second plaque was added, bringing the total to thirty-nine casualties commemorated. Very few people in South Dublin were aware of the memorial's existence because it was hidden away on the southern slopes of the old cemetery, surrounded by scrub, briars and small trees. An old photograph of the memorial may be seen on the first page of Michael Pegum's *Irish War Memorials* website. The construction of a new housing development in the adjoining field exposed the monument to the public for the first time in many years, and it was fortuitous that the landscaped area in the estate was situated alongside the cemetery. The granite walls and steps, constructed by the developer, have facilitated easy access to the memorial for people of all ages. John McCann from the Cemeteries Department, Dun Laoghaire / Rathdown County Council arranged the landscaping and cleaning-up of the area around the memorial in time for the rededication ceremony, which took place at the memorial on 27 September 2008. More than a hundred people, including many relatives of the commemorated men attended the very moving ceremony. The Reverend Canon David Moynan, rector of the Church of Ireland, Kilternan, assisted by Reverend Terry Lilburn, and Reverend Father Eamann Cahill, parish priest of St Mary's Roman Catholic Church, Sandyford, conducted a short religious ceremony.

The Dun Laoghaire/Rathdown County Council was represented by Councillor Lettie McCarthy, who also assisted in the ceremony. A haunting lament was played by an Irish Army piper as the names of officers and men memorialised were read out. Representatives from the following Great War organisations were also in attendance: Combined Regiments Association, London; Connaught Rangers Association; Irish Guards Association; Irish United Nations Veterans Association (IUNVA); Leinster Regiment Association; Organisation of Irish National Ex-Servicemen and Women (ONET); Royal British Legion; Royal Dublin Fusiliers Association and Royal Munster Fusiliers Association.

The population of Stepaside fell in the years following the Great Famine and in the census of 1901 there were only eighty-seven people occupying twenty houses.[3] Prior to the outbreak of war in 1914, the village had a police barracks, dispensary, grocery shop owned by Mrs Ellen Smyth, the pound for stray horses and a forge run by Ned Deering, who was related to the Roe stonecutting family.[4]

TRIPLE TRAGEDY FOR THE KILGOBBIN FAMILY

MANLY, Eric Cecil John
Lieutenant, 'B' Battery, 82nd Brigade, Royal Field Artillery. Secondary Regiment, Royal Garrison Artillery (Special Reserve).

Lieutenant Manly was the first artillery officer from the 18th Division to be killed in action before the terrible artillery duel that took place prior to the opening of the Third Ypres on 31 July. His end came, aged 21, at Zillebeke Lake near Ypres, on 18 July 1917, when a shell exploded in a gun-pit, which also killed two of his men and wounded three others. A letter from his Colonel stated: 'He was one of our senior subalterns, always keen and cheerful, and his loss will be very much felt. I much regret he did not live longer to continue his career in the army, in which his outlook was very promising. He was a general favourite with us all, and had a delightful personality.' A letter from his Major stated:

He died a good death, fighting his guns, just as he would have willed it. The infantry were to raid the German trenches, and we amongst other batteries, were to fire on the trenches adjoining those to be raided. Unfortunately, our position was apparently known to them, and they put several big shells into us. The unlucky one amongst these fell in one of the gun-pits in Eric's section. He was in it at the time superintending the shooting. Two gunners were struck down alongside Eric. The other three were badly hit, but managed to get out into the next gun-pit. To us it is a frightful blow. We all loved him and his cheery ways and we will miss him dreadfully. His men will miss him too; he has always been a good friend to them. And I know that those of his section who are left appreciate to the full the fact that he died amongst them, sharing their dangers. For my own part, I was always glad to have him alongside me. It was worth a lot to have such a stout-hearted companion, as well as such a cheery one, when in warm corners.[5]

Lieutenant Manly's grave is at II. D. 9. Dickebusch New Military Cemetery Extension, Ypres, Belgium and is he commemorated on the Roll of Honour at the Church of Ireland, Kilternan; Great War Memorial, Kilgobbin; Great War Memorial, Bilton Grange (Preparatory) School, Rugby and on a plaque in his parents' plot at Kilgobbin Cemetery. He was awarded the 1915 Star, British War and Victory medals.

Eric Manly left school in 1913 and received a commission in the Special Reserve of Officers, Royal Garrison Artillery, and was promoted lieutenant in February 1915. The following July he went to France with an Ammunition Column and later in the year was attached to the 82nd Brigade, Royal Field Artillery. He saw much fighting, including the Somme offensive in 1916.

Eric Manly was born in Kilgobbin on 14 July 1896 and attended Bilton Grange (Preparatory) School, Rugby. Lieutenant Christian Carvar was not only a fellow artillery officer, but also had been in school with him at Bilton Grange. He mentioned Eric in a letter to his parents: 'Lieutenant Eric Manly of B/82 Battery – that cheerful Irishman who loved horses more than guns, was blown to pieces while directing night firing on the 18 July.'[6] Eric was the elder son of Arthur Manly and Violet Maud McIllree Manly, who lived at Clonlea, Murphystown until 1896, when they moved the short distance to Greenfields, Kilgobbin. They had four children: Aileen, Eric,

Laurence and Joan. Their mother, Violet, died in 1916. Some years later, Arthur married his second wife, Margaret Elizabeth Oswald, a Scottish friend of his two daughters, and they lived at Oldtown House in Kilgobbin. His daughter, Joan, was killed in a traffic accident on the Ballyogan Road in 1940, while on her way to play tennis at Carrickmines Tennis Club.

When Arthur died in August 1941, Margaret went to live with her sister-in-law, Aileen Freeman, in Springfield, Rathfarnham, Co Dublin. She died at Rathdrum Nursing Home, Dartry, Dublin on the 3 December 1956. Aileen married Lt Charles Henry Freeman, 2nd Battalion, Royal Irish Regiment. Charles Freeman was one of the cadets involved in the defence of Trinity College during the 1916 Rising. He died in 1950 and Aileen passed away in 1981.

Eric's brother, Lieutenant Colonel Laurence Arthur Manly MC, 2nd Battalion, Lancashire Fusiliers, was wounded in the Great War, but survived and served again in the Second World War. Laurence married his wife, Jane, in 1925 and they had two children. He was killed aged 43, in North Africa on 25 November 1942 while commanding the 2nd Battalion, Lancashire Fusiliers. Lieutenant Colonel Manly was awarded the Military Cross for gallantry in the field.

His grave is at the Oued Zarga War Cemetery, Tunisia.

From little towns in a far land, we came
To save our honour, and a world aflame;
By little towns in a far land, we sleep
And trust those things we won, to you to keep.[7]

–Rudyard Kipling

KILGOBBIN FRIENDS GASSED IN FRANCE

Patrick O'Driscoll and Philip Connor, two Kilgobbin men from the 8th Battalion Royal Dublin Fusiliers were posted to France the same day and were both killed on 29 April 1916. On this day in Dublin, Nurse Elizabeth O'Farrell was sent with a Red Cross flag to inform General Lowe that Padraig Pearse wished to negotiate surrender terms.

O'DRISCOLL, Patrick Daniel

Lance Corporal, Service No 13756, 8th Battalion, Royal Dublin Fusiliers, 48th Brigade in the 16th (Irish) Division.

The 8th Dublins were among other Irish Regiments preparing for a German gas attack and bombardment in the Hulluch region on 27 April 1916. Blankets soaked in Vermorel, an anti-gas agent, were to cover entrances of all dug-outs. Vermorel sprayers, used to dissipate gas, were checked and ready for use and personal respirators made ready. Compared to those that were to come later, the sack gas-helmet then available was of inferior quality and would only reduce, and not prevent the possibility of asphyxiation.[8] At 3.30am on 29 April 1916 at Hulluch,

> the gas attack signal was given again. Two clouds of gas, one from the Hulluch front, met and settled over the Dublins trench with no wind to move it. Scarcely a man could survive this attack. The casualties from gas poisoning were more severe than on the 27th owing to the gas clouds meeting and remaining stationery and concentrated over the trenches. Dublin casualties during the two days amounted to several officers killed, wounded or gassed; 81other ranks killed; 53 wounded; 122 gassed and 102 missing.[9]

Lance Corporal O'Driscoll, aged 37, was one of the many Dublin Fusiliers to die from the effects of gas poisoning and shell-fire during the attack at Hulluch, France, on 29 April 1916.

He is commemorated on the Loos Memorial, Pas de Calais, France, and the Great War Memorial, Kilgobbin. Lance Corporal O'Driscoll was awarded the 1914–15 Star, British War and Victory medals. Unfortunately for his family the War Office was unable to make contact with his next-of-kin, resulting in the Dublin Medal Office requesting permission to dispose of his medals on 5 January 1922.

Patrick was the son of Cornelius O'Driscoll from Valencia Island, Co Kerry and Bridget O'Driscoll (née Murphy) from Saggart in Co Dublin. Bridget passed away in 1881 aged 45, and Cornelius died in 1885, aged 65. His family said that Cornelius was the first teacher in St Mary's National School, Sandyford. There were eleven children in the family: Margaret Maria, Ellen, John Ambrose, Bridget Maria, Edmond Francis, Cornelius, Timothy William, Denis Joseph, Johanna Maria, Ambrose Thomas, and

Patrick Daniel. Patrick was born at Kilgobbin on 4 November 1878 and baptised at St Marys Roman Catholic Church, Sandyford.

CONNOR, Philip

Private, Service No 16351, 8th Battalion Royal Dublin Fusiliers, 'A' Company, 48th Brigade in the 16th (Irish) Division.

Private Philip Connor was with fellow Kilgobbin man L/Cpl O'Driscoll and died, aged 42, from the effects of gas poisoning and shell-fire during the attack at Hulluch on 29 April 1916. Further information of his last days in action is contained in the profile of L/Cpl Patrick Daniel O'Driscoll, earlier in this chapter. He has no known grave and is commemorated on the Loos Memorial, Pas de Calais, France, and the Great War Memorial, Kilgobbin. Private Connor was awarded the 1914/15 Star, British War and Victory medals. He was born in Sandyford, the son of John and Mary Connor, Stepaside, and it is recorded that he had at least one sibling, Peter, born in 1877. In the census of 1901, John and Mary Connor were living at house No 20 in Kilternan.

BARNACULLIA MEN GASSED IN FRANCE

Gas! GAS! Quick boys! – an ecstasy of fumbling
Fitting the clumsy helmets just in time,
But someone still was yelling out and stumbling
And flound'ring like a man in fire or lime. –
Dim through the misty panes and thick green light,
As under a green sea, I saw him drowning.[10]

–Wilfred Owen

DOYLE, Joseph

Private, Service No 7528, 2nd Battalion Royal Dublin Fusiliers, 10th Brigade in the 4th Division.

He was declared missing on 24 May 1915 at Mouse Trap Farm, Flanders, Belgium, and his date of death is recorded as 25 May 1915. His wife, Mary, wrote to the War Office on 20August 1915 enquiring about her husband because, 'I have not heard from him in a long time.'[11] This evidence suggests that she did not get confirmation of his death until after the War Office received her letter, nearly three months later.

He was aged 35. His comrade, Private Laurence Mooney, also from Barnacullia, fell with him on this day. At about 2.45am on the morning of Monday 24 May 1915 the Commanding Officer of the Dublin Fusiliers, Lt-Col Arthur Loveband was standing outside the door of his dugout with Capt Tom Linky when they saw a red light fired from the German lines to the north-west of the farm. This was immediately followed by three more red lights directly over Mouse Trap farm. Further red lights were seen over the German lines south-east of where Loveband and Linky were standing. Within seconds of the final red light going up, a dull roar was heard. Loveband shouted to his men: 'get your respirators boys, here comes the gas'. A German advance captured nearby trenches. The Dublins came under artillery fire and machine-gun fire from the adjacent captured trenches. Eventually the Germans broke into the Dublin trenches. Fierce fighting followed, during which Lt-Col Arthur Loveband was killed. The wind changed and took the gas back to the German lines. There was fierce fighting throughout the day and the site at Mouse Trap farm was taken and retaken. Losses were heavy on both sides. The Dublins held on until the afternoon when only their headquarters and transport sections remained. The last message from Capt Basil McClear was: 'Very many of our men are surrounded. We must have reinforcements.' McClear was killed leading a grenade assault on the occupied Dublin trenches facing the farm. His brother officer, 2nd Lt Kempston, got another note through to battalion headquarters: 'For God's sake send us some help. We are nearly done.' At 12.45pm the only surviving officer of the 2nd Dublins, Capt Tom Linky, sent a note to headquarters of the 10th Infantry Brigade: 'Reinforce or all is lost.' At 9.30pm one officer and twenty men marched out and reported to brigade headquarters. At the end of the battle, seventeen officers and 175 men from the 2nd Battalion Royal Dublin Fusiliers were killed. Many others were wounded, gassed or taken prisoner. The battalion had lost over 50 per cent of its strength.'[12] Among those killed were Joseph Doyle and Laurence Mooney, neighbours from Barnacullia.

Private Joseph Doyle's grave is at II. D. 5. Roeselare Communal Cemetery, Belgium, and he is commemorated on the Great War Memorial, Kilgobbin. He was awarded the 1915 Star, British War and Victory medals. Joseph Doyle (stonecutter) enlisted on 8 August 1901, completed a course in Siege Ballooning on 8 March 1904 and was discharged to the army reserve. He was called up at the outbreak of war in 1914 and posted to France on 31 August 1914.

Joseph was born at Ryan's Hill, Barnacullia on 28 February 1880, the son of

Thomas Doyle (stonecutter) and Elizabeth Doyle. There were four children in the family; Joseph, Thomas, John and Elizabeth. Joseph married Mary Doyle at the Church of the Assumption, Sandyford, on 16 May 1910 and they had two children; Elizabeth and Annie. Mary, who was born at the Big House in Barnacullia, had two children, Christopher and Joseph Doyle, from a previous marriage.

Joseph Doyle's grandchildren; Nancy Doyle, Noel and Michael Malone live in the Barnacullia and Sandyford area. Another grandson, Brendan Doyle, who lives in Dundrum, has researched his grandfather's part in the Great War. Brendan's five sisters – Elizabeth, Helen, Noleen, Teresa and Monica – also live in the district.

GRADY, Edward

Sapper, Service No 12047, 5th Field Company Royal Engineers in the 2nd Division.

In 1914 the 2nd Division, under Major-General Charles Munroe, was sent to support the French and Belgians. The division took part in the long retreat from Mons, and suffered heavy casualties in the first Battle of Ypres. Sapper Edward Grady was wounded in action on 22 October 1914, while fighting east of Boesinghe in the First Battle of Ypres on the 21 and 22 October and he died on 2 November 1914 in one of the General Hospitals in Boulogne.

His grave is at III. A. 34. Boulogne Eastern Cemetery, Pas de Calais, France and he is commemorated on the Great War Memorial, Kilgobbin. He was awarded the 1914 Star, British War and Victory medals, which were sent to his mother in October 1921.

Edward Grady enlisted in Dublin on 24 December 1903. He was based at Aldershot, having completed nine years service, and decided to commit to a further period of service in Section 'C' of the Army Reserve. 'The 5th Field Company, Royal Engineers was based at Aldershot at the outbreak of war. It was one of the first formations to proceed to France with the BEF in August 1914 and remained on the Western Front throughout the war. In 1914 it was in action in the Battle of Mons and its subsequent retreat; Battle of the Marne; Battle of the Aisne and the first Battle of Ypres.'[13]

Edward (stonecutter) was the son of the late John Grady (stonecutter) and Catherine Grady (née Doyle), Barnacullia. There were four children in Catherine's first marriage: Edward, Joseph, John and Ellen. His mother remarried and lived with her second husband at 2, O'Neill Buildings, Dublin. Edward, like most children in Barnacullia and Stepaside, would have attended St Mary's National School in Sandyford. He trained as a stonecutter, before joining the British Army. Edward's attestation papers revealed that at the time of enlisting he had eight nieces and nephews, the children of his sister, Ellen Byrne, together with three aunts and one uncle, all of whom resided in Barnacullia. He was 5ft 8ins, fresh-faced with grey eyes and sandy hair. His effects included a leather purse, two emblems, tobacco pouch and pipe. Prior to departing for France, he was billeted at 88, Hut Rosyth, Dunfermline, Fife in Scotland.

His brother, Private John Grady, Royal Engineers, served and survived the war. When John was demobilised he married a Yorkshire girl, but was killed in car accident in his adopted country.

MOONEY, Laurence

Private, Service No 9383, 2nd Battalion Royal Dublin Fusiliers, 10th Brigade in the 4th Division.

On 15 November 1916, at the end of the Battle of the Somme, his battalion transferred to the 48th Brigade, 16th (Irish) Division.

Private Mooney was reported missing in action, presumed to have been killed on 24 May 1915 at Mouse Trap Farm, Flanders, Belgium. The circumstances in which Laurence was killed in action are given under the profile of Private Joseph Doyle, earlier in this chapter.

On 14 August 1915 the *Evening Herald* carried his photograph with a message stating that his family was seeking information following a report that he was missing.[14] He is commemorated on the British War Memorial, Menin Gate, Ieper, Belgium and the Great War Memorial, Kilgobbin. Private Mooney was awarded the 1915 Star, British War and Victory medals.

He was the son of Patrick Mooney and Rose Mooney (née Ellis), of Stepaside Hill, Barnacullia. There were six children in the family: Patrick, Laurence, Mary, Catherine, Anne and Rose. The family also fostered two children: Anthony Farrell, who married and lived in London, and Teresa, always known as Teresa Mooney. 'Laurence's sister, Rose, remembered that he was turned away when he first attended the Recruiting Office, but undaunted, returned the next day when he was accepted by a different officer on duty. Her abiding memory of him was of the day he left home and walked down Stepaside Hill for the last time to go to war.'[15]

Laurence was born in Kingstown and educated at St Mary's National School in Sandyford.

His father, Patrick 'Colours' Mooney was a colour sergeant in the Royal Dublin Fusiliers, and fought in the Boer War. Following his army service he worked as a grave-digger in Kilgobbin Cemetery and was in charge of the 'Pound' at Stepaside. He is interred with his wife, Rose, in Curtlestown Cemetery. A member of his family said that career soldiers, attached to the British Army, lived in provisional housing provided for retired rank and file and some of these houses were situated in an area near Stepaside, known locally as, Mooneystown.[16]

O'NEILL, Patrick

Private, Service No 2040, 1st Battalion The Welsh Regiment, 84th Brigade in the 28th Division.

He was killed in action, aged 39, on 8 May 1915, on the first day of the Battle of Frezenberg. 'A strong attack on British trenches, left and centre of 83rd Brigade, was broken by concentrated shell-fire leaving the right of 84th Brigade exposed. Germans prised a way in and up to the 84th Brigade.'[17]

He enlisted at Bridgend, Wales. His battalion was in Chakrata, India when war was declared in August 1914. As soon as a territorial unit arrived to replace them the 1st Welsh returned to England. The battalion landed at Le Havre in France on 18 January 1915 and was in action in the Second Battle of Ypres and the Battle of Loos. Private O'Neill has no known grave and is commemorated on the British War Memorial, Menin Gate, Ieper, Belgium, and the Great War Memorial, Kilgobbin. He was awarded the 1915 Star, British War and Victory medals.

Patrick was born in 1876, the son of John O'Neill (stonecutter) and Catherine O'Neill (née Murphy) of Stepaside. There were seven children in the family: Patrick and twin brother, Gabriel (presumed to have died at birth), Catherine, Mary, James, John and Anne. Patrick was a stonecutter and prior to 1914 he emigrated to England with his brother John in search of work. They lived at 8, Guilford Street, Egremont, Cheshire, but John returned home to Ireland prior to the outbreak of war. As the war ended the world was hit with an influenza pandemic in 1918/1919. It spread throughout the globe causing an estimated fifty million deaths, of whom nearly three-hundred thousand were from the United Kingdom, including Ireland. This pandemic also had an impact on the O'Neill family. The late Mrs Jane Morgan, who lived in Barnacullia was a niece of Private Patrick O'Neill, said: 'During the epidemic my grandmother, Catherine O'Neill lived in Stepaside and worked tirelessly with her next-door neighbour, Nan Roe, to comfort the sick and dying until she also succumbed to the illness and died.'[18]

DOUBLE TRAGEDY FOR THE ROBINSON FAMILY

Patrick Robinson (bootmaker), married Bridget Shakespeare and they had five children: Anna, Catherine, Elizabeth. Two other children, Mary and John, died in infancy. When Bridget died, Patrick married Jane Rochford, as his second wife, and they had twelve children. Their names were Bridget, Patrick Joseph, James Thomas, Margaret Mary, Emelie, Jane Mary, Peter, Joseph, Mary, Thomas, William Patrick and John. The Robinsons lived in Kilgobbin and later at Cornelscourt, Foxrock. Four of their sons enlisted in the British Army and fought in the Great War. James and John were killed in action during 1914 and 1917 respectively. A third brother, Joseph, survived, but he suffered from bad health most of his life as a result of war wounds. The name of the fourth son who served and survived is unknown.

Shoemaking was a tradition in the Robinson family for generations and family lore says that Patrick made the first pair of boots for Arthur Richard Wellesley, 2nd Duke of Wellington. The Wellesley's were from the Anglo-Irish Ascendancy. Patrick Robinson had a shop on Florence Road, Bray, Co Wicklow and owned a detached, red-bricked house, Arno, in the area.[19]

His daughter, Jane, was a nursemaid employed by the Elvery family and lived close to the Robinson's shop in Bray. The Elverys were the proprietors of the Elephant House shop in Sackville Street, Dublin (now Supermac's). Jane was a beautiful woman, and ideal subject for the budding young artist, Beatrice Elvery, later to become Lady Glenavy. Beatrice invited Jane to pose for a nude painting, but she declined the offer, saying that not even her husband had seen her in the nude.[20] Beatrice Elvery was referring to Jane Robinson when she wrote: 'The nursemaid's favourite walk was by Carrickmines Railway Station where she was having a flirtation with the porter.'[21]

ROBINSON, James Thomas

Private, Service No. 1236, 1st Battalion Irish Guards, 4th Guards Brigade in the 2nd Division.

Private Robinson was declared missing, presumed to have been killed in action, aged 39, during the First Battle of Ypres in the area of Zillebeke Wood, three kms south-east of Ypres in Belgium, on 6 November 1914. His comrade, Private Edward Farrell, from nearby Golden Ball, was killed in the same place on this day. 'At 1pm on 6 November 1914, at Zillebeke Wood, following a quiet morning, the enemy began shelling again; directing most of their fire at the support trenches, and at the same time bombarding the front trenches with field guns and machine guns. This lasted until 2pm when the German attack developed against the French, on the right. They at once retired leaving the right flank of 2nd Company open, and then the enemy came down onto the right flank – after firing for some time it became clear that No 2 Company was untenable and they withdrew. The Company "in good order and fighting" fell back by platoons to its support trenches, but this left No1 Company practically in the air, and at the end of the day the greater part of them were missing.'[22]

James Robinson enlisted in London on 13 February 1902 and served a period of twelve years before being discharged. He signed up for a further period of four years on 19 May 1914. On 29 September 1915 the *Evening Herald* carried his photograph with a message stating that his family was seeking information following a report that he was missing.[23] Most Irish Guards massacred in the First Battle of Ypres, including Private Robinson, have no known graves and are numbered among the many thousands commemorated on the British War Memorial at Menin Gate, Ieper in Belgium. He was awarded the 1914/15 Star, British War and Victory medals.

James Robinson was born in 1875 at Kilgobbin. He married Catherine McKenna at St Michael's Roman Catholic Church, Kingstown, on 17 January 1911 and they had three children, Patrick Joseph, James William and Edward, and at the time of James's death, his family was living at 6, Peterson's Lane, Dublin. He was described as being 6ft in height with blue eyes and black hair.

ROBINSON, John
Private, Service No 10368, 1st Battalion Royal Irish Fusiliers, 10th Infantry Brigade in the 4th Division.

Private John Robinson was killed in action, aged 27, East of Fampoux, during the Battle of Arras on 11 April 1917. 'On 11 April the battalion left Brown Line for a position of assembly, north-west of Fampoux and as part of the 10th Infantry Brigade in conjunction with the 11th and 12th Infantry Brigades assaulted the German positions east of Fampoux. The assaulting troops were in position by 11.30am and the concentration was observed by two hostile aeroplanes flying very low. Two Allied planes were shot down shortly before this incident.'[24]

Robinson spent nine years in India with the 1st Royal Irish Fusiliers before going to France with his regiment. During his time in France he was wounded and invalided home, where he recuperated and returned to the action at the front. His grave is at 11. H. 22. Browns Copse Cemetery, Roeux, France and he is commemorated on the Great War Memorial, Kilgobbin. Private Robinson was awarded the 1914/15 Star, British War and Victory medals, but having failed to make contact with his next-of-kin, the Dublin Medal Office requested permission to dispose of his war medals on 11 January 1922.

John Robinson was born in 1890 at Kilgobbin and resided in Foxrock. He was very close to his sister Jane and when home on leave he walked the short distance from Kingstown to Dean's Grange, where he stayed with her at her home. Johnny, as he was known to Jane, would invariably arrive in the early hours of the morning and waken Jane by throwing a stone to her upstairs bedroom window. She would come down and prepare a meal and bed for him. This situation lasted all through the war and when he was leaving her for what would be the last time, he said goodbye and told her that this would be the last time she would see him alive. Jane replied in a positive tone, saying 'do not be silly of course I will see you again.' A couple of days after his death in April 1917, at a time when Jane was heavily pregnant, a policeman knocked on the door at 6am with the news that Johnny was dead. Her husband asked the policeman to keep his voice low, because he was afraid that it would upset his wife and cause shock, which could induce premature labour, but Jane called down to him, 'It is alright Dan, I know Johnny is dead.' Later that evening she told her husband that she heard the stone at the window during the night, as usual, but when she opened the window to call down, there was no one there; she knew instinctively that Johnny had been killed.[25]

WHITE, Anchoretta Louise,
Voluntary Aid Detachment (VAD), British Red Cross Society.

Cora White (as was she was known to her family) lived on the north side of city, but came to live at Jamestown, Kilternan before the outbreak of war. She trained in Mercer's Hospital, Dublin, and then went to Leeds for further training before being posted to Rouen, France, where it is likely that she met a fellow VAD, Violet Barrett, of Carrickmines. Voluntary Aid Detachments trained for a very short period before being sent to hospitals, specialising in caring for wounded soldiers, situated in Ireland, Britain, and elsewhere in Europe. Cora White married Arthur William Rutherfoord in 1919 and they resided at Elmfield House, Ballyogan Road, Kilgobbin, the former home of the Moss family. The Rutherfoord home was adjacent to the Manly home at Greenfields. Patricia and Tom Farrell have a wonderful piece of Great War memorabilia at their home, Knockrose, The Scalp, given to them by Jane Glanville, a relative of Cora Rutherfoord. It is a collapsible canvas bed with Cora's initials, ALW, printed on it. Mrs Glanville also has an autograph book containing signatures of the many soldiers nursed by Cora White. When she died in 1973, Cora Rutherfoord was interred with her husband, Arthur, in the churchyard at Kilternan Church of Ireland, Kilternan.

Chapter Three

Golden Ball and Kilternan

HISTORY AND ROLL OF HONOUR

The tiny village of Golden Ball, which nestles under the Three Rock Mountain, is an extension of Kilternan and may date back to 1768.[1] It seems likely that the village got its name from the two large gold-speckled granite balls perched on the piers of the impressive gateway at the entrance to Kilternan Abbey, an eighteenth-century Georgian house. The original granite balls on the gate piers, which were missing for many years, were found in the late 1990s and securely attached on the piers by a small team of dedicated local men. On the mountainside to the north-west of Kilternan Abbey there is a fine dolmen or portal tomb, where the capstone is estimated to weigh eighty tons.[2] Among the other notable monuments that have survived is the Giant's Grave on the slope of the Two Rock Mountain. Kilternan Abbey was originally known as Kilternan House until changed by the Strong family. Count George Noble Plunkett MP, barrister, Irish Nationalist politician and curator of the National Museum, purchased the last seven years of its lease in 1900. He was created a Papal Count by Pope Leo XIII in 1884 for helping the Blue Nuns and presenting them with a villa as their house in Rome.[3] Count Plunkett was the father of Joseph Mary Plunkett, the Irish Nationalist, poet and journalist, who was executed along with fourteen other leaders of the 1916 Easter Rising. Joseph Plunkett was educated at Belvedere College, and from the age of fifteen he was a boarder at Stoneyhurst College in Lancashire. He suffered poor health throughout his life. The 1901 census revealed that Joseph was at home in Kilternan Abbey with his siblings,

Geraldine, George and Josephine (known as Moya). His parents were not at home on this evening, but three housekeepers, Ellen Fitzhenry, Liz Burke and Mary Murphy, were present. Kilternan Abbey was destroyed by fire in 1912 and only the basement walls and part of the gardens remain today.

Count Plunkett was a cousin of the Protestant Unionist, Sir Horace Plunkett of Foxrock. They came, respectively, from the Killeen (Fingall) and Dunsany branches of the Plunketts, and 'were descendants of brothers, who were uncles of Saint Oliver Plunkett (1625–1681), but many degrees apart'.[4]

A RELATIONSHIP THAT CROSSED RELIGIOUS AND POLITICAL DIVIDES

The Reverend Arthur O'Morchoe, rector at Kilternan Church of Ireland from 1894 until his death in 1921, lived in close proximity to Count Plunkett in Golden Ball, and despite their opposing views on religion and politics, they were friends and their children enjoyed meeting socially. Joseph Plunkett's sister, Geraldine, wrote:

> The nearest house to ours on the Dublin side in Kilternan was the Grebe House, the Church of Ireland rectory. Pa (Count Plunkett) and the rector, Reverend Arthur O'Morchoe, were friends (they were both book people) so we got to know the O'Morchoe boys from the time we moved there. They were the same age as ourselves and we roamed all over the countryside, playing complicated games with them. They were good people and we liked and respected them. These friendships lasted into adulthood, although being from different religions and traditions; we went into different schools, universities and armies. The O'Morchoes joined the British army at the same time that we were becoming deeply involved in nationalism.[5]

Joseph married his fiancée, Grace Gifford, at midnight shortly before his execution.

She also wrote that:

> Grace Gifford told me that there were six soldiers with fixed bayonets in the little chapel with them, and there were soldiers with them again

when she saw him later that night in his cell for just ten minutes. She had not believed that Joe would be shot; the officer in charge told her several times that he thought Joe would not be shot, that he was dying. I did not know until long afterwards that the officer was Niall O'Morchoe; he and Joe had played together as children in Kilternan. If Joe had shown any signs of life after the rifle shots O'Morchoe would have had to finish him off with a revolver. He refused to give the order to fire and was dishonourably discharged and ruined as a result.[6]

A later version of this incident was given by Eilís Dillon, daughter of Geraldine Plunkett, who in her contribution to the book, *Victorian Dublin*, under the title, 'A Victorian Household', wrote as follows:

A sad story and an astonishing coincidence are fixed in my mind concerning Kilternan. The nearest big house on the Dublin side was the Protestant rectory. The rector and my grandfather were friends and the children played and grew up together in warm friendship also. As time went on the Plunkett family became involved in the Irish Republican Brotherhood and the plans for the rising in 1916. The rector's sons, their old friends, naturally joined the British army at the outbreak of the 1914 war. In the fullness of time, my oldest uncle, Joseph, was court-martialed and condemned to death, and of all people, his old boyhood friend, Kenneth O' Morchoe, was instructed to command the firing party which would execute him. He refused, was himself court-martialed and cashiered from the army and died not long afterwards, or so I have been told. But I have not checked the end of this painful story.[7]

Both versions of what happened on that tragic evening for the Plunkett family were only partly correct. Three of Reverend O'Morchoe's four sons, Arthur, Kenneth and Niall, joined the British Army and served throughout the Great War. It was Captain Kenneth O'Morchoe, who was on duty that night and had refused to shoot a friend of his childhood. Kenneth was not court-martialed and dismissed from the army, nor did he die some time afterwards. In the weeks that followed the Easter Rising he was transferred, or may have requested a transfer, to the Leinster Regiment. It is recorded in the War Diaries of the Leinster Regiment that 'he joined the 2nd Leinsters on the Western Front at Red Lodge in Belgium, on 17 June 1916. He proceeded to take charge of 'A' Company during the same month and was wounded on 18August 1916 at Carnoy near a place called Irish Alley.'[8] Later, he transferred to the 1st Battalion, Royal Dublin Fusiliers. He was a member of the Army Rifle Association and was a leading shooter on his battalion team that won the Queen Victoria and Henry Whitehead Cups in 1921. When the Royal Dublin Fusiliers disbanded in 1922, O'Morchoe continued his military career with the Gordon Highlanders from 16 September 1922 until he retired in 1947–48, with the rank of Lieutenant Colonel. He remained unmarried, and when he died on 22 December 1962, at aged 68, he was interred in the family plot in the churchyard at Kilternan Church of Ireland. All three O'Morchoe brothers survived the war.[9]

Kilternan, probably meaning the 'Church of Tiernan' was described in 1914, as a 'post-town at the junction of four parishes; Tully, Kilternan, Kilgobbin and Rathmichael'.[10] The old church lies ruined at the picturesque Bishop's Lane, off the Glencullen Road at the foot of the Dublin Mountains, and was the site of a monastery long before the Norman invasion. The spelling of the place name, Kilternan or Kiltiernan has varied over the years going back to the seventeenth century. 'The ancient parish of Kilternan consisted of the following townlands; Ballybetagh, Boranaralty, Brockey, Glebe, Glencullen, Glencullen Mountain, Kilternan, Kilternan Domain, Kingston and Newtown. The population of the parish in 1841, just before the Great Famine, was 1019, but by 1871 it had reduced to 696.'[11] Glencullen, a beautiful mountain village, had a national school and Carnegie library, which opened in 1914.

The poet George Darley (1795–1846) spent his childhood at Springfield near The Scalp. Writing in years after a long absence from Ireland, Darley asserted that 'a single fern in the Three Rock Mountains was worth a whole English forest'.[12] The Mining Company owned a smelting works in Ballycorus, where in 1836 forty people were employed, but a few years later employment had reduced by half. It gradually became uneconomical to produce Irish ores and in the late 1800s it was used for processing ore from the Isle of Man. It closed down around the time that the Great War broke out in 1914. 'There was a tower near the mine used for making shot, and furnaces for smelting and rolling lead into pipes.'[13] A good number of stonecutters and labourers were employed in the quarries around Glencullen and Barnacullia. Farm labouring, gardening and domestic work in the big houses remained the most important source of employment for working-class people in this part of south Dublin. Farms in the late nineteenth and early twentieth century were in the ownership of: M. Byrne, W. Byrne, Peter Dolan, Thomas Fisher, H.J. Fox, William Hicks, P. McCann, Philip Reilly and James Sutton.

A paper-mill started by Captain Anderson passed through a number of owners, including, Healey, Walter McMahon and Thomas Brown, before it closed down in 1867. The stream, which operated the paper mill, flowed under the road, past Kilternan Lodge and supplied another mill which produced cotton.[14] The family of L/Cpl Arnold Moss, killed in Gallipoli in 1915, were the owners of the mill until 1875 when the Kilternan Lodge and mill passed on to a new owner and it closed down in 1902. The mill house and the dried-out mill ponds still survive today.[15] The Moss family built a row of cottages for their workers, known today as Moss's Cottages, situated close to the location of the old mills. The forge in Kilternan, owned by Charles Walsh, was situated on the Glencullen Road, close to the home of Pte Denis Higgins, who was killed in the war. Willis's post office, grocery and hardware, acquired in the 1890s by Edward Willis, was the focal point in the village. Most children in this district attended the local national school in Ballycorus, a short distance from Kilternan.

The Scalp, a geological feature formed by the melting waters of a glacier, is a spectacular rural landscape situated close to Kilternan at the border of Co Dublin and Co Wicklow. 'Knockrose, which was built in the mid 1700s, adjacent to Springfield, was a mixed farm of some thirty-eight acres, and has been in the ownership of the Stevenson family for many generations. In late 1914, with the Great War in full swing, the first casualties were shipped back to Ireland from the various battlefields, and Knockrose was to play its part in the rehabilitation of wounded soldiers. In the late Victorian era a large wooden bungalow known as The Chalet was erected to the east of the farm buildings overlooking the sea. It became the clubhouse of The Vagabond Club, a cycling club with many members drawn from the medical and judiciary professions. The Vagabonds went on to form Ireland's first motor club, the Irish Automobile Club (IAC) in 1901. In late 1914, when the injured soldiers were brought back to Dublin and left in hospitals, the former Vagabonds, many of them doctors, recognised the peaceful atmosphere in The Scalp and sought permission from the War Office to open a home for wounded soldiers at Knockrose. It was to this place that more than 3,500 soldiers were brought for recuperation in the private cars of the members of the IAC (for which the club was awarded the Royal Warrant, hence RIAC).

In 1916 the Red Cross took over the Chalet and set up a Field Hospital for the victims of gas attacks. It was the ideal place for sufferers of gas poisoning due to its pure air and beautiful country surroundings. The field in front of the building was covered with tents so the injured could get as much fresh air as possible. The chalet was used as the hospital in which dressings were applied and examinations carried out. Some of the victims succumbed to their injuries and to this day, guests in the chalet have reported sightings of ghosts in military uniforms around it.[16] Almost one hundred years later with its beautiful gardens situated 500 feet above sea level, Knockrose is still caring for those troubled by poor health. Many visitors get a sense of the peace that exists there and find it hard to leave. Some also report of seeing Vikings, monks and soldiers as they wander around the garden; perhaps they do not want to leave either! Lieutenant William Drury, whose family home was situated close to Knockrose, was the third soldier from this small area to be killed in the war.

DRURY, William Symes
Lieutenant, 8th Battalion Royal Dublin Fusiliers, 48th Brigade in the 16th (Irish) Division.

Lieutenant Drury was killed, aged 38, while on active service in France, as the result of a bomb accident, which took place during an officers' exercise on 29 January 1916. His tragic end came at the 47th Divisional Bombing School in Labeuvriere, France. Proceedings of Court Enquiry were held in the field on Sunday 30 January 1916 to ascertain the cause of death. The officer in charge at the time of the exercise stated that he gave the order for trainee officers to duck down behind the parapet. When the explosion had taken place the officers stood up but Lt Drury was still on the ground. A small particle of shrapnel had pierced his back and went through his heart. The Court, having reviewed the scene of the accident and heard all the evidence of opinion, decided that the accident was caused by the premature burst of a Mill's hand-grenade, due to a faulty fuse. The report concluded as follows: 'There seems to have been an absence of close personnel supervision referred to as necessary in the commandant's statement.' Subsequent to the accident, Lieutenant-General Harry Wilson, Commanding, 4th Corps, stated in his report: 'I do not consider that this practice of throwing for "shrapnel effect" should be carried out as it is too dangerous. I have issued an order to this effect.'[17]

His grave is at 1. K. 25. Nœux-les-Mines Communal Cemetery, Pas de Calais, France and he is commemorated on the Roll of Honour at the Kilternan Church of Ireland; Great War Memorial, formerly at St Matthias Church, Dublin, and now at Christ Church, Leeson Park, Dublin, and the Great War Memorial, Kilgobbin. He was awarded the1914–15 Star, British War and Victory medals.

The battalion was formed in September 1914 as part of K2 army and moved to Ballyvonare, near Buttevant, Co Cork, and then in June 1915, it moved to Ballyhooley, near Fermoy, Co Cork. It was then transferred to Blackdown Barracks, Aldershot, before landing at Le Harve on 29 December 1915.[18]

William Drury was the son of Thomas Chalmers Drury BL, and Susan Anna Drury (née Symes) of The Lodge, Kilternan and Richmond House, Rathgar. Thomas died at Elpis Nursing Home on 10 April 1925 and Susan passed away at Greenan, Rathgar in 1936. There were fourteen children born to the couple, of whom nine survived infancy. Their names were Thomas William Ernest, William Symes, Henry Galbraith, Richard Gray, John, Thomas Chalmers, Katherine Anna, Gladys and Dorothy.

William, born in 1874 at Rathmines, was employed in the Secretary's Department at the Guinness Brewing Company in Dublin. Prior to the outbreak of war he was in lodgings at 80, Lower Lesson Street, Dublin. It is recorded in his original documents that he owned a car for a period of two years and drilled daily with the Irish Rugby Football Union Volunteer Corps at Lansdowne Road. Lieutenant Drury bequeathed his estate, in different proportions, to his siblings and godson, Francis McDermot Byrn. He also left money to the following club and institutions; £50 to the Orthopaedic Hospital of Ireland, Upper Merrion Street, Dublin; £25 to the Women's Shelter, James Street, Dublin, and £10 to the Powerscourt Boys Club, Lad Lane, Dublin.[19]

'Flanders Fields'
Oh, Flanders fields your secret keep,
Of where they died and now they sleep.
No stone or cross to bid farewell,
In your land of peace, that once was hell.

–Ken Kinsella

There were sixteen labourers' cottages in Golden Ball at the beginning of the twentieth century; eight were terraced and the other eight semi-detached. According to the 1911 census very few men in this tiny village were of an age eligible to join the British Army. Nevertheless, at least seven, including three pairs of brothers from the cottages, joined the British forces. Four of the seven died in uniform and all three survivors were badly affected by their war experience. Five men enlisted in the Irish Guards, of whom three were killed in the first week of November 1914 at Zillebeke Wood, and the fourth, who enlisted following the death of his brother, died in hospital in 1915. Three O'Morchoe brothers, who lived in Glebe House, close to the village, enlisted and survived the war. Sub-Lieutenant Gerald Plunkett, half nephew of Joseph Mary Plunkett, who was an occasional visitor to his relatives at Kilternan Abbey, was killed in Gallipoli. The Zillebeke Wood casualties are commemorated on the British War Memorial at Menin Gate, Ieper in Belgium. The site of the Meenenpoorte, known as the Menin Gate, was considered to be a fitting location to place a memorial to 54,389 missing British and Commonwealth soldiers. The traffic, which goes through the enormous archway, is stopped each evening just before 8pm in preparation for the Last Post. This moving ceremony has been conducted by officers of the Ieper Fire Service on each evening of the year since1929. The only exception occurred during the years of the Second World War when the Germans occupied Ypres for a second time. The three survivors from Golden Ball cottages were Corporal Hugh Strong, Royal Dublin Fusiliers; his brother, Able Seaman John Strong, Royal Navy and Private John Byrne, Irish Guards.

BYRNE, Edward

Private, Service No. 3049, 1st Battalion Irish Guards, 4th Guards Brigade in the 2nd Division.

He was killed in action on 2 November, 1914, aged 27, at Zillebeke Wood, near Ypres, Belgium. 'His battalion was reduced to three companies, since in No 3 Company all officers were casualties and only 26 men of it answered their names at roll-call. The battalion was heavily shelled all that day. They tried to put a little wire on their front during the night; they collected what dead they could; they received several wounded men of the day's fight as they crawled into our lines; they heard one such man calling in the dark, and they heard the enemy turn a machine-gun on him and silence him. One shell dropped in one of the support trenches killing two men.'[20]

Private Byrne is commemorated on the British War Memorial, Menin Gate, Ieper, Belgium; Great War Memorial, Kilgobbin and his parents' headstone at Glencullen Cemetery. He was awarded the 1914 Star, British War and Victory medals.

He enlisted in Dublin on 23 May 1908 and his battalion landed in Le Havre, France, on 13 August 1914. Many soldiers, when they first enlisted, found it very difficult to adapt to army discipline combined with home sickness, and some turned to alcohol for comfort. In his early days in the army he had some difficulties with discipline, but settled down to become an excellent soldier.[21] The *Evening Herald* carried his photograph in December 1915 accompanied by a message: 'His parents would be grateful for any news of him.'[22]

He was the son of Matthew Byrne and Bridget Byrne (née Fleming), 69 Golden Ball Cottages, Kilternan. There were nine children in the Byrne family: Stephen, John, Edward, Charlotte, Bridget, Mary, Anne, Ellen and Julia. Edward's father, like most men in that area, worked as an agricultural labourer. His mother, Bridget, worked in Willis's Post Office in Kilternan and may have been the first postwoman in Ireland, and she was assisted by her daughter, Mary.[23]

Edward was born on 2 February 1887 and attended Ballycorus National School. He was employed as a temporary farm labourer, most likely to have been during harvest time only. His brother, Pte John Byrne, Irish Guards, 1st Battalion, survived the war. John (known to his family as 'Johno') lost a leg in the war and returned to England where he spent the remainder of his life. Their sister, Mary, married Private Patrick Connolly, Royal Army Medical Corps, of Kilgobbin, who also served in the Great War. Patrick survived, but was wounded in action and hospitalised on a number of occasions during the conflict. When demobilised in 1919 he continued to suffer badly from the effects of shell shock and gas poisoning. He died in 1933 and is buried with his wife, Mary, in Glencullen Cemetery.[24]

Early-morning raids by the Black and Tans during 1920 were quite common in Golden Ball, as they were in other parts of Ireland. These early-morning sorties were in the form of a front door broken down at the least hesitation to open; family members thrown out of bed; the house ransacked; interrogation of the head of household and violence where family members showed any resistance. The Byrne and Farrell families were close neighbours and suffered the same humiliation at the hands of the Black and Tans. Family history says that Bridget Byrne and Mary Farrell discussed how best to handle the frequent raids on their homes. They came to the conclusion that the photograph of their fallen sons, in British Army uniforms, which hung proudly in their living rooms, should be brought to the attention of the Auxiliary officer in charge. This tactic usually had the desired effect of minimising interrogation and violence. Women were very fearful that during a raid on their homes a male member of the family would lose patience with the 'Tans' and react violently, which would also most certainly have resulted in a shooting. The Black and Tans frequently searched local houses for hidden guns and interrogated the head of household seeking information on the movement of local IRA activists. The action taken by two loving and astute mothers did prevent their homes from being targeted as frequently as their neighbours, but inevitably, this led to some speculation and rumours that the Farrell and Byrne families might be informing on local IRA men. However, in the years following the War of Independence it was accepted by the local community that the rumours were untrue.[25]

DOYLE, Denis

Private, Service No. 4003, 1st Battalion Irish Guards, 4th Guards Brigade in the Second Division.

He was killed in action, aged 23 on 1 November 1914. On the day that he died his battalion was fighting hard at Zillebeke Wood, outside Ypres, to prevent the Germans from breaking through the town, which would have given them access to Calais and the ports. The front trenches were drenched by field-guns, at close range, with spurts of heavy stuff at intervals; the rear by heavy artillery, while machine-gun fire filled the intervals. One of the trenches of a platoon in No 3 Company, under Lt Maitland, was completely blown in, and only a few men escaped. It was hopeless to send reinforcements; the machine-gun fire would have wiped them out moving and the Guards artillery was not strong enough to silence any one sector of the enemy's fire.[26] He is commemorated on the British War Museum, Menin Gate, Ieper, Belgium and the Great War Memorial, Kilgobbin. Doyle was awarded the 1914 Star, British War and Victory medals, which were sent to his parents in 1920. He enlisted in Dublin on 5 January 1912, with neighbour Edward Farrell. His late sister, Elizabeth O'Rourke, said that she remembered the sadness in her home when the news came through that Denis was killed in action.

Denis was the son of Michael Doyle, farm labourer and Margaret Doyle of 164, Golden Ball Cottages, Kilternan. There were seven children in the family: Denis,

John, Michael, Bernard, Margaret, William and Elizabeth. Denis attended Ballycorus National School and was employed as a casual farm labourer.

DOYLE, John

Private, Service No 9311, Reserve Battalion, Irish Guards, 1st Guards Brigade, Guards Division.

When Denis Doyle was killed his younger brother, John, enlisted in Dublin on 22 July 1915, despite suffering from bad health. It was not uncommon for a young man, grieving and angry following the death of a brother, to react by joining the army. He never made it to the front and died, aged 23, from scarlet fever at Beddington Isolation Hospital, London, on the 7 September 1915, 48 days after enlisting. John did not serve long enough to qualify for campaign medals, and the Silver War Badge was not instituted until 12 September 1916. His grave is at A. 447. Caterham and Warlingham Burial Ground, Surrey, England, and he is commemorated on the Great War Memorial in Kilgobbin. He attended Ballycorus National School, was unmarried and worked as a farm labourer when work was available.

FARRELL, Edward

Private, Service No. 3999, 1st Battalion Irish Guards, 4th Guards Brigade in the 2nd Division.

Private Farrell was killed, aged 23, on 6 November 1914, at Zillebeke Wood in the first Battle of Ypres. Details of Farrell's last days in action may be seen in the profile of his comrade, Pte James Robinson, in Chapter Two. In one week the battalion's casualties amounted to 6 officers killed, 7 wounded and 3 missing. Other ranks were 64 dead, 339 wounded and 194 missing.[27]

Edward Farrell enlisted in Dublin on 5 January 1912, with his friend and neighbour, Denis Doyle and their battalion landed in Le Havre, France on 13 August 1914. He was awarded the 1914 Star, British War and Victory medals. His grave is unknown and he is commemorated on the British War Memorial, Menin Gate, Ieper, Belgium, and the Great War Memorial, Kilgobbin. Edward was born in Golden Ball, on 3 May 1891, the second eldest son of Patrick Farrell and Mary Farrell (née

Grennan) of 67, Golden Ball Cottages, Kilternan. Ten children were born to the couple of whom six survived infancy: Elizabeth, Patrick, Mary, Edward, Richard and Francis. Edward attended Ballycorus National Primary School, where the majority of children from Kilternan, Golden Ball and Ballycorus, got their early education. He worked as a farm labourer when employment was available, usually at harvest time. The late Kate Sinnott, who was born in Golden Ball in 1916, said: 'I was acquainted with the Farrell family before they emigrated to England in 1936, and I remember my parents saying that Edward was a popular young man in the village and inherited his father's skill as a boxer.'[28] Some weeks before the Farrell family received the telegram from the War Office informing them of Edward's death, his mother had a dream in which she saw Edward being killed.

His brother, Frank, enlisted in the Royal Air Force at the outset of the Second World War and had passed the examinations to train as a fighter pilot, but was hit by a lorry that went out of control on icy roads. He died in hospital a few days later.

HIGGINS, Denis

Private, Service No 11226, 1st Battalion Royal Dublin Fusiliers, 86th Brigade in the 29th Division. Having survived the massacre during the landings at 'V' Beach, on 25 April, Pte Higgins was killed in action five days later, aged 21, at Krithia, Gallipoli, on 30 April 1915. On the morning of the 30 April Colonel H.G. Casson, was appointed to command the brigade. About 1.10pm a strong skirmishing line was observed to be advancing from the direction of Achi Baba. The Royal Munster Fusiliers and the Royal Dublin Fusiliers, under Major Hutchinson, were temporarily amalgamated into one unit, owing to its losses. On this night, by the order of the Major-General Commanding the 29th Division, Brigade Headquarters were withdrawn from the vicinity of the firing line.[29]

As Pte Higgins and his comrades tried bravely to get ashore on the 25th, General Sir Ian Hamilton, Commander of the Allied Mediterranean Expeditionary Force, watched the landings from the deck of HMS *Queen Elizabeth* with Admiral Sir Roger J.B. Keyes. He wrote:

> Here we watched as best we could over the fight being put up by the Turks against our forlorn hope on the *River Clyde*. Very soon it became clear that we were being held. Through our glasses we could quite

clearly the sea being whipped up all along the beach and about the *River Clyde* by a pelting storm of rifle bullets. We could see also how a number of our dare-devils were up to their necks in this tormented water trying to struggle on to land from the barges linking *River Clyde* to the shore. There was a line of men lying flat down under cover of a little sandbank in the centre of the beach. They were so held under by fire they dared not, evidently, stir. Watching these gallant souls from the safety of a battleship gave me a hateful feeling: Roger Keyes said to me he simply could not bear it. Often a commander may have to watch tragedies from a post of safety. That is all right. I have had my share of the hair's breadth business and now it becomes the turn of the youngsters. But, from the battleship, you are outside the frame of the picture.[30]

Major-General Hunter-Weston, Commanding the 29th Division, often referred to as the 'Butcher of Helles', said of the 1st Battalion Royal Dublin Fusiliers, following the landing at 'V' Beach: 'Well done the Dubs! Your deeds will live in history for time immortal.'[31] Due to his disregard for the welfare of the men under his command, the 'Dubs' may have considered this compliment to be a little hollow.

Private Higgins's grave is at 9. 'V' Beach, Special Memorial Cemetery, Turkey, and he is commemorated on the Great War Memorial, Kilgobbin. He was awarded the 1914 Star, British War and Victory medals. The Officer Commanding the Medal Office in Hamilton, Scotland, requested disposal of his medals on 5 January 1922. The assumption is that the War Office received no reply to its standard letter seeking confirmation of his next-of-kin. The letter was addressed to his mother, who by then was deceased, but it would have been delivered to his home at the small family farm in Kilternan, where his brother and sister were living. The onus was on them to respond and claim his medals. The sum of £6:3:8 in his favour remained unclaimed on 26 June 1917, more than two years after his death.[32]

The 29th Division returned to Britain, from Madras in India, and landed at Plymouth on 21 December 1914. It moved to billets in Torquay, but in January 1915 it went on to Nuneaton. The battalion came under orders on 16 March 1915, and sailed from Avonmouth for Gallipoli, going via Alexandria and Mudros, where it halted on 9 April, before landing at Cape Helles on 25 April 1915.[33] 'While in Torquay the

1st Battalion Royal Dublin Fusiliers commanding officer, Lieutenant-Colonel Rooth, handed over the regimental colours to the town mayor for safe-keeping. When they returned to Torquay on St Stephen's day 1918 the town handed back the regimental colours to a Guard from the 1st Dublin Fusiliers. Out of a battalion 1,100 strong that had arrived in Torquay four years previously, only forty were now left, the regiment having been decimated by the landing at Suvla Bay and the next three years of war.[34]

Denis was born in Dublin city and at age seven he was living with his parent, Elizabeth Dolan, widow of Bryan Dolan, a small farmer from Glencullen Road, Kilternan. There were three children in the Dolan family, Mary, Peter and Ellen, together with two orphaned children, Denis Higgins and Fred Keegan. The 1911 census revealed that Elizabeth's son, Peter Dolan (farmer), aged 26, and his sister, Ellen Dolan, aged 21, both single, were living in the family home at Kilternan.

Chapter Four

Dundrum, Rathmines, Rathgar, Sandyford and Windy Arbour

'Asleep'
Under his helmet, up against his pack,
After so many days of work and waking,
Sleep took him by the brow and laid him back.
There, in the happy no-time of his sleeping,
Death took him by the heart. There heaved a quaking
Of the aborted life within him leaping,
Then chest and sleepy arms once more fell slack.
And soon the slow, stray blood came creeping
From the intruding lead, like ants on track.[1]

–Wilfred Owen

HISTORY AND ROLL OF HONOUR

In the early twentieth century 'the neighbourhood of Dundrum abounded in richly diversified scenery, commanding views of Dublin Bay and Mountains and was studded with numerous seats and elegant villas. It was recommended for the purity of its air, and summer is much resorted to by invalids.' Windy Arbour, situated between Dundrum and Miltown, was visually dominated by the sheer height of the granite walls that surrounded Dundrum Lunatic Asylum (now the Central Mental Hospital). Among the Magistrates appointed to attend Petty Sessions, on alternate Mondays, were Richard H. Davoren; George N. Plunkett; William H.F. Vershcoyle; Dr Isacc Usher, all of whom lost sons in the Great War and the parallel war of Irish Independence.[2]

Dundrum was a town with an approximate population of 535, and offered more opportunities for employment than the nearby villages of Sandyford and Kilternan. The Manor Mill Laundry was the largest employer of female labour in the region. Its hooter sounded a number of times during each the day between 7am and 5pm. The Lunatic Asylum in Windy Arbour also offered some employment. Other sources of employment came from the many retail shops, public houses, together with gardening and domestic work. The Mill Pond situated in the heart of Dundrum Town Centre was first mentioned in 1821, when a map of Dublin city and county showed two buildings straddling the River Slang.[3] Eva (Evie) Sydney Hone, a Cubist painter and stained-glass artist, was born at Roebuck Grove, Dundrum in 1894. She received international recognition following her design of a window at Eton College Chapel. Evie Hone produced about 155 glass panels, together with many oil and watercolour paintings. Her early work, *The Annunciation* (stained glass) was commissioned for St Nahi's Church of Ireland in Dundrum.

Sandyford was a small village situated between Dundrum and Kilternan. In 1914, it had a Roman Catholic Church, National School, Post Office and Carnegie Library. The Post Office was first opened in the 1880s by Thomas Burton and later managed by his daughter, Miss Alice Burton. The local hostelry, Sandyford House, was owned by Denis Flavin, and the first librarian, in 1907, was Bess McNally of Stepaside. On the southern end of the village, at Murphystown, Richard 'Boss' Croker, purchased the property, Glencairn, from Mrs Mary Murphy, widow of James Murphy, a High Court Judge who died in 1901. Croker earned his fortune in America and trained racehorses at Glencairn, including 'Orby', winner of the English Derby in 1907. Today, Glencairn is better known as the former residence of the British Ambassador, Christopher Ewart-Biggs, who was killed in a fatal ambush, which took place near his residence in 1976.

During the early part of the twentieth century, Countess Markievicz, artist and republican, was the first Irish woman to be elected to the British Parliament. She retained a cottage in a laneway off the Blackglen Road, about one-and-a-half miles from the village and close to the home of Christopher Mulligan, who fell in the Great War. The countess, who was a member of the Gore-Booth family of Sligo, married a man of Russian–Polish origin. The employment situation in Sandyford was similar to Kilgobbin and Kilternan, where they relied heavily on domestic work, farming, gardening and quarrying.

Rathmines and Rathgar was an extensive Suburban District in the parish of St Peter, Uppercross and Rathdown baronies in Dublin County and in 1911 it had a population of 37,840 inhabiting 7,050 houses.[4]

TWO DUNDRUM BROTHERS FALL IN WAR

Robert W. Jameson, FSI, JP of Clonskeagh Castle, Clonskeagh, and Katherine Anne Luscombe of Milltown Castle, were married in September 1879. The couple resided at Campfield House, Dundrum, and had six sons: Arthur George, Cecil, James, Francis, Thomas and Harold Gordon. Two of their boys, Arthur and Harold, fell in the Great War.

JAMESON, Arthur George
Lieutenant Commander, Commander HM Submarine, *D2*, Royal Navy.

Lieutenant Commander Jameson, aged 31, was swept overboard and lost on the HM Submarine *D2*, on 23 November 1914. The following day the *D2* failed to return when under Commander Lt C. Head; it is believed that she was sunk by a German Torpedo. The body of Lt-Com Jameson was not recovered.

Arthur joined the Royal Navy in 1898 aged 15, and was appointed Naval Cadet in May 1900 and midshipman on 30 May 1901. He served on board HMS *Thescus* and *Repulse* on the Mediterranean Station before being promoted to Sub-Lieutenant on 30 July 1903. He went through the necessary courses and examinations to qualify for the rank of Lieutenant, taking four 'firsts' in July 1905. Jameson then served at home on the destroyer, HMS *Waveney*, and on the North American Station on HMS *Ariadne*, flagship of Sir Day Hort Bosanquet GCVO, KCB. He was promoted Lieutenant on 30 July 1905, in the same year he joined *Forth* to specialise in submarine duties and afterwards was appointed to the command of *A8*, on which he served until May 1908. In January 1911 he was appointed to HMS *Neptune*, Sir Francis Bridgeman's Flagship in the Home Fleet. He was selected for the War Staff Course in 1912 and having completed the course the following year, he was appointed to the HMS *Antrim* for

War Staff Duties, where he served under Rear-Admiral Madden and Rear Admiral Pakenham. Two months later he joined HMS *Forth* having spent some time in command of the 'B' class and was made Captain of the 'C' in 1908–1910. In 1911 he was lieutenant on the HMS *Neptune*, and was one of the first officers to qualify in April 1912. On passing out at the end of that year he served on HMS *Antrim* for War Staff Duties in the 3rd Cruiser Squadron. He was promoted to lieutenant-commander on the 3 July 1914 and in March 1914 he returned to the submarine service, being appointed to the command of *D2* in the 8th Flotilla. Lieutenant-Commander Jameson took part in the Battle of the Bight, off Heligoland, on 28 August 1914.[5]

He is commemorated on the Portsmouth Naval Memorial; War Memorial in the school chapel at Monkton Combe School, Bath, and the War Memorial, Christ Church of Ireland, Dundrum. Lieutenant-Commander Jameson was mentioned in the despatches of Commander Keyes, CM, MVO, on 17 October 1914 and was awarded the 1914 Star, British War and Victory medals, which were claimed by his widow.

Arthur was born on 30 September 1883 and educated at Monkton Combe School, Bath. In August 1908 he married Isabel Laura Katherine Pitman of, Clarence Villa, Rolle Road, Exmouth, at St Mary's Church in the parish of North Huish, Devon. They had one child, Isabel Valerie, born in December 1913 at Portsmouth.

JAMESON, Harold Gordon
Second Lieutenant, 65th Field Company Royal Engineers, in the 10th (Irish) Division.

Second Lieutenant Jameson was on a ridge at the Karakol Dagh, Gallipoli, having followed a call to his company to help in a holding operation. He was killed in this action, aged 26, on 16 August 1915.

> It was about 2am on 16 August when Capt Scovell, considering that the entrenchments were completed, ordered the company to return to bivouac, which they did. The company had only been there a quarter of an hour when they were ordered to return to the firing line and returned to the ridge about 3am, where they found the Turks had broken line and the Royal Engineers were pushed into a gap. Captain Scovell and Second Lieutenant Jameson fell in the first couple of minutes of this

skirmish. Fierce fighting took place and the Royal Engineers held the gap until about 7pm when infantry took up position. It lost 2 officers, 4 men killed and 1 officer and 28 men wounded.[6]

Jameson's commanding officer, who was himself wounded on 14 or 15 August, wrote to his parents: 'He was a general favourite amongst officers and men. We had a hard time at the Dardanelles, but your son's never failing courage and cheerfulness under these adverse circumstances were of the greatest help to us all. His death is a great loss to the 65th Company, and to the Royal Engineers of the 10th Division.'[7]

Second Lieutenant Jameson is commemorated on the Helles Memorial, Turkey; War Memorial, Christ Church of Ireland, Dundrum; Hall of Honour, Trinity College and the War Memorial in the school chapel at Monkton Combe School, Bath. He was awarded the 1914–15 Star, British War and Victory medals. Jameson was gazetted 2nd lieutenant on 1 October 1914 and following his training at Chatham and the Curragh he left for the Dardanelles with the 10th Division, landing at Suvla Bay on 7 August 1915.[8]

He was born in 1889 and educated at Monkton Combe School, Bath, where he entered the junior school in the Lent term of 1901 and the senior school in the summer of 1903, completing his education in the summer term of 1907. He is mentioned in the school magazine, where it is stated that 'he won a form prize and as a rower (Cox) steered with his head as well as hands, and generally kept a good course'. Harold is also mentioned for winning a history prize.[9] He entered Trinity College and passed through the Engineering School, receiving his BA in 1911 and BAI in 1912. Following college he was appointed to the Sudan Irrigation Service, but volunteered to join the colours during a visit home to Dundrum in 1914.[10] His cousin, Frieda Catherine Thompson was the sole executor and beneficiary of his estate.[11]

FOUR BEVERIDGE BROTHERS SERVE IN WAR

John Francis Barry Beveridge BL, Town Clerk of Dublin, in his second marriage to Jane Blackhall (née Healy) had eight children: Annie, Charles Vincent, Gerald O'Hagan, Edmund (died at age 13) Mary, Georgina, James O'Shaughnessy, and Arthur Joseph (twins). They resided at 33, Belgrave Square, Rathgar East. John Beveridge died just three months after the birth of the twins, aged 48, and the family moved to a smaller house in Rathmines. Jane Blackhall, in her first marriage, had one child, Jonas. John's first marriage to Elizabeth Teeling in 1870 produced five children: Elizabeth (Lizette), Katherine, William John, Jane and John Francis. Their mother, Elizabeth, died in childbirth during 1877.

BEVERIDGE, James O'Shaughnessy
Captain, 137th Field Ambulance Royal Army Medical Corps.

In 1916 James and his identical twin brother, Arthur, were transferred to Aldershot in England and underwent three months officer training, which included horse riding lessons. James was put in charge of the 137th Field Ambulance and in the late summer of 1916 he was sent to the front with his unit. In the meantime, Arthur was posted nearby and they managed to meet about once a week.[12] Captain James Beveridge was killed in action, aged 24, on 22 November 1917 at Cambrai, France. When the telegram came, two of his sisters intercepted it and walked around Belgrave Square for a couple of hours debating how to break the news to their mother, before returning home. A report in the *Belvederian* in early in 1917 noted that James was unwell, being cared for in Rouen, but had recovered enough to return to the front with the Field Ambulance.[13] On the day that he was killed he continued attending to the wounded until stricken down by many wounds. In this state he was found by the Catholic chaplain, who administered the last rites of the church. He was deeply loved by his men. One of them, speaking to his mother shortly after his death, said, 'You may rest assured that Capt Beveridge was not left lying out for long after he was wounded, as his men would follow him anywhere, they loved him so much.'[14] When the news broke at home there was profound grief not only within the immediate family, but throughout his extended family and friends. Following his death his commanding officer wrote of him as 'an exceptionally brilliant officer.'[15]

His grave is at I.C. 11 at Lebucquiere Communal Cemetery, a village situated eight kms east of Bapaume, France. He was awarded the British War and Victory medals, which were sent to his mother in October 1921.

James Beveridge was born in Rathgar on 21 March 1893, attended Belvedere College and entered University College Dublin, Medical School in 1910. He did his clinical training at St Vincent's Hospital where he won the Junior Class prize in 1913. James joined the Royal College of Surgeons OTC in February 1914 and received his commission in the Royal Army Medical Corps Special Reserve. This provided a small, but much-needed source of income in his final year. In 1915 he graduated with honours. James and his twin brother, Arthur, enjoyed their social life, belonging to a group of young men and women who called themselves 'The horsy fellows'. They were also co-founders of the UCD Swimming Club.[16] James's twin brother, Major-General Arthur Joseph Beveridge CB, OBE, MC, 137th Field Ambulance, Royal Army Medical Corps served and survived the First and Second World Wars. Arthur Beveridge matched his twin brother stride for stride, academically. They were together at Belvedere College, University College Dublin Medical School, St Vincent's Hospital, Royal College of Surgeons and both graduated with honours at the same time. Arthur received his commission in the Royal Army Medical Corps Special Reserve at the same time as James and they were both attached to the 137th Field Ambulance. 'When James fell the chaplain did not have far to go to break the news to Arthur, who had had a premonition that something dreadful was about to happen. He was so grief-stricken that he could not carry on at the front, and was given three months compassionate leave. When he returned to Dublin he spent six weeks shut up alone in his room, speaking to no-one.'[17] At the end of his leave he returned to war and performed with great distinction, being awarded the Military Cross: 'For conspicuous gallantry and devotion to duty. His dressing station was heavily shelled during an engagement, but owing to his determination, courage and initiative, a large number of wounded were attended to and evacuated from the danger zone.'[18] When the Great War ended Dr Beveridge continued to serve with many different medical units in various parts of the world until he retired on 21 March 1958. He received the General Service Medal and clasp for his service in Iraq during 1919–20 and was also awarded the OBE. Major-General Beveridge was awarded the Norwegian Military Cross, Norway's highest ranking military decoration, and he was 'Mentioned in Despatches' on two occasions. He married Sheila Mary Macnamara and they had seven children. Sheila died in Dublin in 1952, aged 47, and Arthur passed away aged 66 in 1959, while in Venice, Italy.[19] Sheila was the daughter of Lieutenant-Colonel William John Macnamara of Corofin, Co Clare, an army physician. He served in the Army Medical Service from 1880 to 1898, transferring to the Royal Army Medical Corps when it was formed in June 1898. His foreign service also included Madras from 1881 to 1886, West Africa 1890 to 1891 and South Africa in the Anglo-Boer War from 1901 to 1903. Among other things he was responsible for the concentration camps (a British, not a German invention) in which the wives and children of the Boer Commandos were confined in very bad conditions, as part of a military strategy to 'starve them out' by denying them the help of wives and children who kept the farms going by commanding black labourers. He was appalled by the conditions he found in the camps, and gradually dismantled the system over a period of two years. This valuable experience led to Lt-Col Macnamara being recalled to service during the Great War, serving as Assistant Director of Medical Services for Ireland from 1914 to 1922. He signed the death certificate of Thomas McDonagh in Kilmainham Jail in 1916 and signed a petition (along with other medical staff) asking for the death sentences on 1916 leaders, McDonagh, Clarke and Connolly to be commuted on grounds of ill-health.[20]

Irish doctors made an extraordinary contribution in the Great War. According to Dublin surgeon Dr Joe Duignan, about one third of the medical doctors in the Royal Army Medical Corps were Irish born and 176 medical students from the Royal College of Surgeons in Ireland enlisted at the outbreak of the Great War.[21]

The Beveridge family's contribution is just one example of the courage and expertise displayed by Irish doctors in both World Wars. Dr Brian Beveridge, son of Major-General Arthur Beveridge, pointed out that 'during WWI there were many horrendous injuries from shrapnel and machine gunning, causing severe wounds, contaminated by soil, animal faeces (from horses)'. This led to high incidence of tetanus and gas gangrene, which were almost invariably fatal. As the war progressed more soldiers were protected by tetanus immunisation (rather than tetanus serum). One way to save the lives of soldiers with such injuries to limbs was to amputate the affected limb (and thus protect the victim from the toxic effects of these clostridial bacteria), so amputation became frequent, in the absence of any alternative.

By the start of Second World War things were better organised. Much had been learned towards the end of First World War about rapid evacuation of the wounded, soldiers were immunised before going to the front and the advent of the antibacterial sulphonamides meant that there was more success in treating wound infections, and also outbreaks of diarrhoea, etc. Basic hygiene in the arrangements of camp latrines also helped considerably, so the scale of losses was much smaller. One feature was a revision of policy about amputation, which it was felt had been over-used in the

First World War. During the Second World War permission to amputate had to be sought from the Commanding Officer of each Royal Army Medical Corps unit.[22] To illustrate the difference between the wars, Dr Brian Beveridge related a story of his father's chance meeting with surviving soldiers from both wars:

> The first was of a WW1 situation when he found himself in a barn near Cambrai with about 250 soldiers in need of immediate surgery, and only himself and one orderly to deal with them. Almost the only measure available was to amputate for severe contaminated limb wounds, so some amputations took place. Many years later, in 1949, we were on holiday in Rosslare, and went into a pharmacy to have a film developed. When writing down details, the one-armed pharmacist asked my father's name. When my father replied, he looked up, stared intensely for a moment and then said 'ah!', and clutched his left shoulder. He had recognised my father from the barn in France. There followed a long conversation, reminiscing about the Battle of Cambrai and other events in the war.
>
> The WW2 story was from the ill-fated landings in Norway during 1940, when my father commanded the Army Medical Services in the Namsos area of Norway. A surgeon to one of the units asked him for permission to amputate the leg of a soldier with severe shrapnel damage – he opined that the soldier's future might be better served with an artificial limb. My father, after seeing the soldier and some discussion decided that he could survive evacuation to Scotland, where amputation could proceed if thought necessary, and the soldier was evacuated. Some years later, in the mid-50s, my father, who had left the army in 1953, was working as an Assistant Medical Officer of Health in North Lincolnshire, when he examined a youth with special needs, who was accompanied by his parents. He noticed that the boy's father limped slightly, and wore a special boot. At the end of the consultation the father turned to him and asked: 'Dr Beveridge, are you by any chance related to a Colonel Beveridge who was in Norway during the war?' My father replied that he was, indeed, the same Colonel. The father replied 'It was you who stopped them taking off

my leg!' The father then recounted his story of a series of operations in Scotland at the end of which he was left with a short leg, for which he wore a surgical boot. Invalided out of the army, he had returned to his Lincolnshire home, where he eventually got a job as a tractor driver on a large farm, and was still in secure employment.[23]

Another brother, Warrant officer Gerald O'Hagan Beveridge, South Irish Horse, served from 1914 to 1919 and was awarded the Meritorious Service Medal. He married Eileen O'Connor, who served in the war as a Voluntary Aid Detachment (VAD). When Gerald retired from the army he worked as manager of the Bank of Ireland in Fairview, Dublin. The couple had no children.[24]

Captain William John Beveridge, enlisted in the Australian Army Medical Corps, in early 1918 and served both in Egypt and the Western Front. He was a half-brother of the above-mentioned soldiers, being the son of John Francis Beveridge from his first marriage with Elizabeth Teeling. William Beveridge was educated at Clongowes Wood College and studied medicine at the National University in Dublin. Willie (as he was always known) graduated LRCPSI, LM, at the Rotunda Hospital, Dublin in 1896. He married Beatrice Maude Latham in June 1907 and they had two children, Muriel Jane and Beatrice Amy.[25] While serving on the Western Front Dr Beveridge was present in a place where a plane was shot down, and the pilot badly injured. He gave first aid to the pilot, but having no paper with him, tore a piece of cloth from the wing of the plane, and jotted down a summary of the pilot's injuries, and what he had done for him, before sending him on to the Casualty Clearing Station. Eventually the piece of cloth was sent back to him, and he kept it as a war souvenir. After his death in 1943 his widow kept it, but when she died some years later, her daughter decided to present it to the Australian War Museum in Canberra, where it has remained and is occasionally exhibited.[26]

LEASK, James Cunliffe MC
Captain, 5th Battalion Northumberland Fusiliers, 149th Brigade in the 50th Northumbrian Division.

Previously, Service No. 3689, 5th Battalion Royal Highlanders. Captain Leask was killed in action, aged 43, on 30 March 1918. 'He stayed at his post whilst everyone was evacuated and was severely wounded by a shell and was seen at the bottom of a shell hole with both legs blown off, then a little later, another shell struck in the same place. Prior to embarking on this mission he was promoted to Acting Major, however, this was not upheld following his death.'[27] His wife Mary wrote to the War Office on 22 January 1919, requesting information regarding her husband, who was reported missing and presumed to have been killed. She wrote: 'It is now ten months since my husband was reported missing and I have not received official confirmation that he is dead'. The War Office responded on 29 January 1919 with the usual explanation when an officer was reported missing, declaring that the Army Council was not in a position to issue a formal Certificate of Death. However, the letter also stated that due to the length of time that had elapsed since the officer was reported wounded and missing and the fact that his name had not appeared as a prisoner of war on any list received from the German Government, the Army Council was constrained from concluding that Capt Leask was dead. The Army Council went on to explain that its letter may be used instead of an official Certificate of Death and is usually accepted.[28]

He has no known grave and is commemorated on the Pozieres Memorial, situated about nine kms north-east of Albert, France; War Memorial at the Presbyterian Church, Adelaide Road, Dublin and Christ Church (Presbyterian), Highfield Road, Rathgar. Captain Leask was awarded the Military Cross. His citation stated: 'for conspicuous gallantry and devotion to duty in leading a counter attack through a village. After severe fighting, he successfully cleared the village and enabled a force to be extricated, thus greatly assisting the withdrawal that was in progress. He behaved with gallantry and skill.'[29] His wife, Mary, refused an invitation to attend the investiture at Edinburgh Castle for his Military Cross. She always believed that Cunliffe had been abandoned by his senior officers and never forgave them.[30] He was awarded the 1915 Star; British War, Victory medals and the Territorial Force

War medal. Mrs Leask applied for her late husband's medals on 4 November 1921, when she was living at 20, Harley Terrace, Gosforth, Newcastle-on-Tyne. Cunliffe (he was known by his second name) served as a volunteer in the Royal Highlanders Volunteer Corps from 1908 to 1912. In July 1912 the Colonel Commanding the Northumberland Infantry Brigade signed a certificate stating that in his opinion, 'Mr J.C. Leask can be recommended as in every way eligible and suitable for a commission.' He was commissioned 2nd Lieutenant on 12 July 1912. Leask was a training officer with 5th Battalion Northumbrian Fusiliers and was posted to active duty in France, despite his age. His battalion was at Walker, Newcastle in August 1914 as part of the Northumberland Brigade in the Northumbrian Division and in April 1915, it landed in France.[31]

Cunliffe, an insurance executive, was born in Dublin in 1876 and married a Dublin girl, Mary Anderson, on 1 June 1901. They lived with their two children at 11, Churchtown Lower, Miltown. The family emigrated to England some time before the onset of war and resided at 54, Harley Terrace Gosforth, Newcastle-on-Tyne, where Cunliffe was the manager of the Yorkshire Penny Bank in Newcastle. He was a talented illustrator and illustrated the *Official History of the Royal Scots Regiment*, which is now in the library at Edinburgh Castle. His daughter later sold the original drawings at Sotherbys in London, where they were bought by the regiment for its museum. During the war he always carried his pencil and paint box. He made many sketches, which is believed were lost or sold. Cunliffe was also an enthusiastic stamp collector and his large spare collection is now in the possession of his grandson Ian Ainslie.[32]

They had two children, Clara Gladys (known as Gladys) and Ronald (Ronnie). Ronnie's life changed when his father was killed. He had planned to become a naval architect and was an indentured apprentice, but following Cunliffe's death it was no longer possible for his mother to pay for his studies. Ronnie served as a flight sergeant in bomber command during the Second World War and flew thirty-eight missions, for which he received the Distinguished Flying Medal, awarded for acts of valour, courage or devotion to duty whilst flying in active Service.[33]

Gladys inherited her father's talent for drawing and painting and before she was married was employed by Armstrong Whitworths, in Newcastle, as a tracer. She married James Ainslie and they had two sons, James Cunliffe and Ian. Gladys painted pictures throughout her life and was very successful in art exhibitions around

Berwick where they lived. Her husband James served on a Corvette minesweeper in the Royal Navy during the Second World War. James died in 1966 and Gladys passed away in 1983.[34]

James Cunliffe Leask, was the son of the late Robert Heddle Leask and Anna Louisa Leask (née Molloy) of 52, Harold's Cross Road, Terenure. Robert was both an architect and engineer and came to Dublin from Scotland in the 1860s. There were seven children in the family; Elizabeth Harriet, Anna Katherine, Ethel, Henry Norman, James Cunliffe, Robert and Harold Graeme.

Cunliffe's brother, Henry Norman (known as Norman to his family), served in the Royal Navy during the Great War and survived the conflict. His family understands that he made a model of every ship in the fleet around the time of the Great War. He died in 1942, aged 70.[35]

ALL FIVE POULTER BROTHERS SERVE IN WAR

Henry Chapman Poulter and Alice Sarah Poulter (née Barnard) lived at Woodfield, Roebuck, Dundrum. They had seven children: Henry Chapman, Edgar Alan, Terence Bernard, Wilfred Forman, Cecil Edward, Alice Dora and Marjorie Constance. Henry and Wilfred were killed in the Great War and Cecil was killed in action during the Second World War. The other brothers, Edgar and Terence, survived. Henry Poulter senior was manager of the Yorkshire Insurance Company. His wife, Alice, died in 1962, aged 96, when living at 14 Adelaide Street, Dun Laoghaire.

Lieutenant Edgar Alan Poulter, 7th Battalion 'D' Company (the 'Pals') Royal Dublin Fusiliers, survived the war. He enlisted at Lansdowne Road and remembered years later that, 'we all turned up, and incidentally, paid half-crown for the privilege of joining up'.[36] Arrival in Gallipoli was an eye-opener for these young men, who had been enjoying happy, eventful and sheltered lives in Ireland. Edgar also said:

> I saw the odd fellow coming back with his leg blown off or wounded
> with stick bombs or land mines … we all began to feel a little funny in
> the pit of the stomach. At 7pm that evening we were ordered to occupy
> Chocolate Hill. From the time we landed until we reached Chocolate
> Hill we had had nothing to drink. We landed without filling our water
> bottles and I don't know whose mistake that was, and didn't remedy
> the situation until later that night. We couldn't use the Artesian wells,

because the Turks had thrown bodies in the wells and polluted the water.[37]

Edgar Poulter also remembered what happened when he suggested to his Brigade Major that he should use mules to take rations up to his men in the trenches:

> Would you have any objections, sir, if I brought the rations up to the men in the trenches? The major replied: 'Good God man do you know what you are talking about, you might get the mules killed.' Edgar argued that nine or ten men were killed or wounded every night coming down with rations. The Brigade Major explained that there were plenty of men but not mules. Edgar's persistence resulted in the superior officer agreeing to a week's trial, with a warning; 'God help you if you lose the mule.'[38]

Edgar married Doddie Baird and he died in 1975. Doddie died in 1986 and they are buried in Mount Jerome Cemetery, Dublin. His brother, Captain Terence Bernard Poulter, Royal Dublin Fusiliers, also survived the war.

A fifth brother, Private Cecil Edward Poulter, Natal Mounted Rifles, South African Forces, which formed a fifth part of General Montgomery's 'Eighth Army', was killed in action, aged 38, at the Battle of Tobruk on 22 June 1942. Cecil was underage all through the Great War, but enlisted in the British Army and fought in the Second World War. He was buried in Halfaya Sollum War Cemetery, situated on the main coast road from Mersa Matruh through to Libya and is commemorated on the War Memorial at St Andrew's College, Booterstown.

POULTER, Henry Chapman
Captain, 8th Battalion Royal Dublin Fusiliers. Previously, 7th Battalion, 'D' Company, (the 'Pals') Royal Dublin Fusiliers.

He died of wounds, aged 23, in No 11 Field Ambulance at Fontaine-lès-Croisille, on 29 November 1917. On 9 December 1917, his father wrote to the Secretary of the War Office, stating:

> I received a telegram in your name on the 4th inst., stating that my

son was wounded and no further particulars have come to hand so far from the War Office. But, on the morning of the 7th inst., his mother received two letters, of which I enclose copies, and if you will do me the kindness of sparing a few moments to peruse them you will easily appreciate the severe shock she received. She naturally expected them to contain news from the boy's friends of how he had met his wounds and of the progress he was making, because it is generally understood that the War Office invariably classify casualties under three headings; 'wounded', 'seriously wounded' and 'dangerously wounded', and therefore all our friends who heard that he was 'wounded' were assuming that it was good news. It seems clear to me there must have been a mistake in classifying this case and I think there should be no excuse for this under the elaborate War Office system. I write, not in anger, but in sorrow, to draw your personal attention to the matter for the sake of other poor relatives with whom your officials correspond. We got first intimation that this same boy was wounded in August last through letters in the post and when I tell you we have three sons (commissioned) still serving you will better understand our anxiety.[39]

Captain Poulter's grave is at H.5. St Ledger British Cemetery, twelve kms south of Arras, France, and he is commemorated on the War Memorial at St Andrew's College, Booterstown. He was awarded the 1914–15 Star, British War and Victory medals. Henry enlisted in 7th Battalion, Royal Dublin Fusiliers at Horsham, Essex on 18 September 1914 and was posted to Gallipoli on 7 August 1915. His Medical Sheet reveals that he contracted pyrexia on 27 September 1915 and diarrhoea two weeks later, while serving in Gallipoli. Following the evacuation of troops from Gallipoli, he was admitted to hospital at Port Said on 10 November 1915 suffering with enteric and four days later he was sent back to England and was in the General Hospital in Portsmouth.

We know from Lt Harry Laird's writings that he was in Naas Barracks in 1916, before returning to the front. He was discharged to a commission on 7 February 1916 and returned to France with the 8th Dublins. His effects included a cheque book and pass book.[40]

Lieutenant Harry Laird was another Dub who fought in Gallipoli with the 'Pals'

'D' Company, but was taken prisoner and lived to tell his story. He was wounded in Gallipoli and returned home to Ireland to recuperate. When he recovered he was stationed at Naas Barracks, Co Kildare, and mentioned that he met Harry Poulter, a comrade from 'D' Company. Laird returned to the front along with Poulter and they were at Strong Point 13, near Kemmel. On 21 February 1917 they pushed off and occupied billets at Locre, where they shared a comfortable hut, later taking over a farmhouse for their mess. They were in the company of two Australian officers, Thompson and Hughes, and Laird mentions that he joined Poulter for a game of Bridge, opposing the two Australians. But this relative comfort was short lived as they returned to Locre on 6 May to prepare for an offensive.

Laird said about his regiment: 'I had always thought that the German army was a model of smartness and neatness, but whether the shine had been taken out of them by 1918, or I was fortunate in the specimens I met, I never saw any of them up to the standard of the Royal Dublin Fusiliers.'[41] Henry Poulter was born in Westham, Essex in 1894 and educated at St Andrews College, Booterstown. He was single, 5ft 9ins in height with brown hair, and worked as an insurance clerk before enlisting.

POULTER, Wilfred Forman
Second Lieutenant, 24th Squadron Royal Flying Corps.

He was shot down in flight action at Villers-Outréaux, on 5 March 1918 and succumbed to his wounds the next day aged 19. At the time of being shot down he was flying a SE5a B145. His squadron was based at Matigny a short distance from Béthencourt. According to Greg VanWyngarden, Poulter was most likely shot down by Adolf Schreder of Jasta 17. Schreder claimed an SE5 south-east of Vendhuille at 3pm on 5 March. The German officer was himself killed in action twelve days later on 17 March. Poulter's parents received a letter from the War Office on 24 May 1918 stating: 'With reference to your letter of 6 March 1918, I am directed to inform you that in an official list of dead received from Germany through the Geneva Red Cross Society, the following report appeared concerning 2nd Lt W.F. Poulter; "Died on 6 March in hospital; buried in civilian cemetery at Villers Outreaux. Reported by intelligence officer."'[42]

His grave is at 11. D. 14. Honnechy British Cemetery and is commemorated on the War Memorial at St Andrew's College, Booterstown. At some later time his body was exhumed in the civilian cemetery at Villers Outreaux and re-interred at Honnechy. He was awarded the British War and Victory medals.

Wilfred served two years in the Dublin Cadet Corps stationed at Portobello Barracks, before enlisting in the Royal Flying Corps at South Farnborough on 2 May 1917. He began as an engineer's apprentice and was discharged on 1 August 1917, having been appointed to a temporary commission, and was attached to the 24th Squadron, formed at Hounslow, London, on 21 September 1915. There were twenty-nine items in his effects, including; pilots' log book, correspondence, fountain pen, diary, large photo, letters and photos.[43] Wilfred was born in Co Dublin in 1898, educated at St Andrews College, Booterstown and was single.

VERSCHOYLE BROTHERS KILLED IN ACTION

William Henry Foster Verschoyle (solicitor) and Frances Harriet Hamilton Verschoyle (née Jackson), Woodley, Dundrum, lost two sons in the war. It is said that Frances, who was born in France, never recovered from her tragic loss and died in 1924 aged 65. There were four children in the family: George John Foster, William Arthur, Francis Stuart and Kathleen. During the War of Independence, William Verschoyle received threatening letters, and on one occasion was even shot, but managed to chase his assailant across the fields before capturing his gun. When Frances died, William married Winifred Mary Letts, his second wife, in 1926. Winifred Letts was known for her novels, plays and poetry. William Verschoyle died in 1943 and was interred with his first wife in Rathcoole Cemetery, Co Dublin.[44]

Captain Reverend George John Foster Verschoyle MA, Chaplain 4th class, served from 1916–1919 and survived the war. He was curate at St George's, Dublin, during the years 1919–1925, followed by three years at Christ Church, Taney, Dundrum. In later years, he was rector of Killennel and Ardamine, Killenagh, and he died in 1954. Reverend Verschoyle married Frideswide Frances Hornidge in 1925 and they had two children, Peter and Patricia. He enjoyed landscape painting in oils, which led to a family art exhibition in 1929 at the Mills Hall, Merrion Row, Dublin. His wife Frideswide, sister Kathleen and other family members took part in the exhibition.[45]

VERSCHOYLE, William Arthur
Captain, 1st Battalion Royal Irish Fusiliers, 10th Brigade in the 4th Division.

He was killed in action, aged 27, while leading his company in an assault on German trenches during the Battle of Arras on 11 April 1917. His Brigadier wrote of him that he was 'never more cheerful than when in action'. Private John Robinson of the same regiment, from Kilgobbin, was killed with Capt Verschoyle on this day. 'His battalion was east of Fampoux on 11 April 1917, but left Brown to take up a position of assembly, north-west of Fampoux and as part of the 10th Infantry Brigade. The assaulting troops were in position by 11.30am, but the concentration was observed by two hostile aeroplanes flying very low, two allied planes having been shot down shortly before. On the left, "C" Company did not succeed in advancing quite so far having suffered severely. It was here that Capt Verschoyle was killed, whilst gallantly leading a bombing party in an endeavour to put an enemy machine gun out of action, which was holding up troops on his battalion's left, all the officers of the two leading companies having become casualties.'[46] Two men in his battalion, Privates, O'Brien & Baker, wrote:

> Arti was first of all hit in the shoulder by a bullet. Barker dressed his wound and advised him to go back; this of course he refused to do. (He was a very gallant fellow and on all occasions and nothing would stop him short of death). On reaching the German front line he collected some of our bombers and proceeded to bomb up a communication trench towards the German second line. When he got about half way up this trench he was hit by a bullet in the head, which killed him instantaneously. Unfortunately a heavy counter attack drove our men back and they were unable to recover his body. This is all the information it is possible to gather.[47]

A report on William Verschoyle from Marlborough College stated that:

When he passed out at Sandhurst Military College he joined the Royal Irish Fusiliers and was posted to India in 1912. He was still in India at the outbreak of war and when his regiment sailed for France he was left at Bombay suffering with malaria, which he had tried to conceal throughout the six days' journey from Quetta. When fit, he joined his old battalion in May 1915, just after his brother Frank, had been killed in Flanders. He was wounded, went through a heavy gas attack, in which his company was blown up in their trenches, and later succumbed to trench fever. William was sent home to Ireland and was offered a staff appointment, but refused it, preferring to return to his regiment at the front. During an offensive, in April 1917, he was hit in the shoulder but after his wound had been dressed, he collected some bombers and worked up a communication trench towards the German second line, where he met his death. This record is just what those who knew him best at school would have expected of him. Though he suffered at first at Marlborough from all the trials of a sensitive nature, his friends will remember him for a desperate sincerity that was almost disconcerting, a real affection for anyone he thought he could trust, and a latent cheerfulness that stood him in good stead throughout his soldiers' career.[48]

He is commemorated at Bay 9, Arras Memorial, Pas de Calais, France; the War Memorial and Verschoyle Memorial, Christ Church of Ireland, Taney, Dundrum; Aravon School Memorial, Bray, Co Wicklow; Marlborough College Roll of Honour and on the walls of the College's Memorial Hall and the Royal Irish Fusilier's Panel in the chapel at Sandhurst Royal Military Academy. He was awarded the 1914–15 Star, British War and Victory medals, which were sent to his father in 1922. His battalion was at Shorncliffe in August 1914, and moved to Harrow on 18 August 1914, before landing at Boulogne on 23 August 1914.

VERSCHOYLE, Francis Stuart
Second Lieutenant, 2nd Siege Company, Royal Anglesey Royal Engineers.
He was killed in action, aged 19, near Ypres, Flanders, on 25 April 1915. The previous month, on 25 March at Dickebusch, 2nd Lt F. S. Verschoyle shared command of the

first and second sections of the Royal Engineers with 2nd Lt B.G. Holland. Following his death one of his men, Cpl Greenhalgh, wrote to his parents:

> On the 19th April we left for the trenches, your son being Lieutenant in charge of a mining party. Things went well with us until the Saturday of the 24th when at 4am the enemy commenced heavy shelling which lasted for five hours, and completely destroyed our mine and part of the trench. The shelling having ceased, your son ordered the roll of the men to be called and found there was only himself and two men left, of which I am one, the remainder having been cut off. I then asked him if he intended leaving the trench, but this was impossible, as there was no way out. We decided to remain until the following night, but unfortunately, for us they again started shelling our trench for seven hours. At the end of that time we were ordered to stand to. Your son called another man and myself to the lower part of the trench to man our rifles, as the Germans were advancing. This was at 1.05pm on Sunday 25 April. We were firing together with Capt Jollie of the East Surrey Regiment. After half-hour fighting, I was distressed to see your son and Capt Jollie shot. Thinking it was only a wound, I immediately bandaged his head, but, to my profound sorrow, he died. An officer of the East Surreys spoke in high praise of the coolness of your son, and said his name would be held in high esteem by the East Surreys. There being no other officer left, I was compelled to report myself to our Commanding Officer. I informed him of your son's death, and the major and officers and men were deeply grieved, as they felt they had lost a good leader and kind friend.[49]

A second letter to Mrs Verschoyle from Cpl J. Whelan stated that:

> He died fighting with only four men in a trench with him. Lt Verschoyle himself killed ten Germans in holding the trench so he died a noble and peaceful death. He never spoke a word; his wound was in the head. On the night of the 25th he was to come out of the trenches and one hour before he was to leave he met his death. The evening he was going

to the trenches he gave me his fountain pen to mind for him in the presence of our Quarter Master Sergeant, so I made a remark in an innocent way; 'what will happen if you do not come back? He said, 'keep it as a present from me', so of course Mrs Verschoyle if you would like it I will let you have it willingly, but if you do not want it, I assure you I will treasure it as a keepsake of the officer I loved to serve, not me alone but everyone in the company.[50]

His grave is at G.7, Ypres Town Cemetery, Belgium and he is commemorated on the War Memorial and Verschoyle Memorial, Christ Church of Ireland, Dundrum; Great War Memorial at Castlepark School, Dalkey; Hall of Honour, Trinity College and the Roll of Honour and walls of the College's Memorial Hall at Marlborough College, Wiltshire. He was awarded the 1914–15 Star, British War and Victory medals. 'The company was formed at the headquarters in Beaumaris, Anglesey, North, Wales and trained in drill, musketry and fieldworks in the period 1 September to 17 November 1914. It departed Le Havre for St Omer on Christmas Day, 25 December 1914.'[51]

Francis was born on 9 April 1896, educated at Castlepark School, Dalkey and Marlborough College, Wiltshire, leaving the latter in the summer term of 1914 to enter Trinity College. He was unmarried.

COLLEN, William Stewart
Lieutenant, 6th Battalion Royal Inniskilling Fusiliers, 31st Brigade in the 10th (Irish) Division.

Lieutenant Collen was killed in action on 7 August 1915, having disembarked at 5am on 'C' Beach, under shrapnel fire. His battalion advanced over a ridge to Lala Baba leaving packs and baggage. At 7am it received orders from GOC 3rd Infantry Brigade to proceed to north of lake and attack enemy position on Mastan Tepe. As it crossed over Sand spit, west of Salt Lake the battalion was heavily shelled. It received support on left from the 5th Royal Irish Fusiliers, during the advance on north side of Salt Lake. At 3pm the battalion was heavily shelled by shrapnel and sniped on reaching north corner of Salt Lake. The battalion suffered many casualties here, including the loss of its commanding officer. At 6.30pm, the open ditch at the foot of hill was heavily entrenched and fortified by enemy. At the end of the day, 2nd Lt Collen and 5 other ranks were killed, 7 officers, 66 other ranks wounded and 21 men were missing. This appeared to be the end of the action on this awful day for the 6th Inniskillings and the 10th (Irish) Division, commanded by Galwayman, Lieutenant General Sir Bryan Mahon.[52]

Lieutenant Collen is commemorated on the Special Memorial, Green Hill Cemetery, Turkey; Great War Memorial at Leys School, Cambridge, England; Great War Memorial, Wesley College, Ballinteer; Great War Memorial and Collen Memorial at Christ Church, Taney, Dundrum and the Roll of Honour, Miltown Golf Club. He was awarded the 1915 Star, British War and Victory medals, which were issued to his parents on 24 February 1922.

William Collen was appointed to a temporary commission on the 19 September 1914 and his battalion sailed for Mitylene at 6pm on 30 July 1915 arriving in Port Iero at 5.30am on the following day. When notified of his son's death, his father wrote to the War Office: 'Is there any chance of my son's remains being identified and sent home?' The War Office reply gave him little comfort, informing him that his son was buried in Gallipoli and there were no further details. There was a further letter to the War Office from his brother, John, who requested permission to try and get back any effects belonging to his brother, but no reply to this letter was recorded in Lt Collen's original documents.[53]

William Collen was born on 13 August 1889, the son of Joseph Collen (building contractor) and Hannah Moira Collen, Homestead, Dundrum. When his parents died in 1935 and 1941 respectively they were interred in the new cemetery at Kilgobbin. There were six children in the family: Mary Elizabeth Heron, Hannah Sophia, William Stewart, Margaret Robinson Beckett, John Black and Joseph Harcourt. William attended Wesley College for a period of one year before transferring to Leys School in Cambridge for a further year. 'Here, he played rugby with the school's 2nd XV.'[54] When he finished school he worked in the family business, the well-known construction company Collen Brothers managed by two branches of the family from Armagh and Dublin. He was well known in golfing circles around Dublin and competed in the Irish Close Golf Championship in 1913. William played to a four handicap and was a member of Carrickmines and Miltown Golf Clubs. It is said that 'he played a careful, methodical game and was a good match player'.[55]

DAVOREN, Ambrose Joseph Stainislaus
Lieutenant,Commanding Z Battery, Trench Mortar Battery Royal Field Artillery in the 25th Division.

He was killed in action, aged 27, at sector G15C, near Poperinge, Belgium, on 18 July 1917. On that day, near Poperinge, Belgium, 'the brigade sustained a severe military and personal loss in the death of Capt P.M. Chaworth-Musters MC and Lt A. Davoren, Commanding Z Battery of 25th Division, who were killed by a shell'. Following his death, Mrs Davoren received a letter from her son's chaplain, Father W.J. Smyth:

You will, no doubt, have received official news of your son's death. It is a sad loss to us all, officers, men, and myself not least. I went across to the Trench Mortar lines this morning and spoke in the same way about him. 'Such a splendid officer.' 'He was always so thoughtful for others.' 'We could afford to lose him least of all.' Since I was attached to the Artillery of the 25th Division four months ago I have always found him most kind and most ready to help me to get the few Catholics in the Trench Mortar Battery together for Mass. Two Sundays ago he was present at my Mass in an open field. He really enjoyed a chat with me about Clongowes and his old rector and masters, most of whom I knew very well. It always surprised me that one of his great ability and disposition took so readily to and seemed so much at home in the very rough and tumble life we had out here. Of course, his heart was in his work, and it was a pleasure to see him arranging his gun positions in the trenches, fixing up telephones and setting so quietly and so thoroughly about all the little details of his duty, as though he had never done anything else and never intended to do anything else in his life. He told me himself that the strangeness of things out here wore off for him in about a week after he came out. That admission meant a very great deal, I assure you, and reveals more than anything the quiet determination that was the stamp upon his character. This afternoon I have arranged to bury him in a cemetery away from the line, so he will lie in a blessed grave and the prayers of the church will be said over him as they would have at home in Ireland.[56]

A second letter received by Mrs Davoren from a fellow officer, Lt A.J. Cunningham, who had been a church minister in Scotland before the outbreak of war and was killed in action on 24 March 1918.

I write to express to you my deep sympathy with you and yours in the loss of your son and my own dear friend. It is hard for me to realise that even yet that he has gone, though I brought his body back from the line and saw him buried. He rests in a quiet military cemetery well behind the range of the guns, and we have had a cross made to mark the grave. Captain Nowell Usticke has checked the articles of your son's kit and is writing you an account of how they have been disposed. For friendship sake, I ask your permission to keep a little book of Shakespeare which he and I used many a time to read together. He was the best friend that I made in France, and there was none among us who did not admire his gentleness and humour, his ability and learning, his broad generous outlook and firm character. He was loved with equal warmth and sincerity by all his men, whether in his particular battery or not. I trust that God will send you comfort equal to the sacrifice he called you to make for he surely does not make love and worthy objects of love only to use them as a means to afflict us. You may rest assured that your dear son suffered no pain in his death, and he never feared his death while he lived. Captain Smyth, the padre who buried him, was a Roman Catholic, so that his burial was according to the rites of his faith.[57]

His grave is at II. B. 42, Poperinge New Military Cemetery, Belgium and he is commemorated on the War Memorial, St Mary's Roman Catholic Church, Haddington Road, Dublin, and the Great War Memorial, Clongowes Wood College, Co Kildare. He was awarded the British War and Victory medals. The War Office wrote to his father on 28 June 1917 seeking confirmation of his next-of-kin and referring to him as 'Second Lieutenant Davoren'. His mother replied immediately: 'As a consequence of the death of my husband, the late Richard Davoren, I am now the nearest living relative of my son, Lieutenant Ambrose Joseph Stainislaus Davoren. I may add that my son was gazetted 1st Lieutenant in August 1917 with precedence from June 1916.' A response from the War Office confirmed that her son was promoted to full lieutenant at the time stated by Mrs Davoren.[58]

Ambrose, born on 13 November 1889, was educated at Clongowes Wood College, Co Kildare; University College Dublin and King's Inns, Dublin. With a brilliant future ahead of him, Ambrose Davoren decided to join the Royal Field Artillery in 1915 and went to France in 1916. He was the son of Richard and Catherine (Ina) Davoren (née Nugent), of Friarsland, Roebuck, Dundrum, where the family resided during the years 1887 to 1914. Today, this elegant Mansion is named Glenard and is used as a University residence. Nine children were born to Catherine and Richard, of whom seven survived infancy; Catherine, Margaret, Mary, Esmey, Ambrose, Frances and Carmen. Ambrose bequeathed his estate to his married sister, Margaret McGonigal.[59] His father, a well-known Dundrum solicitor, was born in Co Clare and practised from his offices at Dame Street, Dublin. He died in 1917 and his wife, Catherine, passed away in November 1932, while staying at Coote Hall, Booterstown. In the period before her final illness, she resided at 68, Waterloo Road, Dublin.

The following is an extract from a master at Clongowes Wood College, who wrote of an incident involving Ambrose:

'I should like to add the following little incident which took place in the dormitory when Ambrose was in the Third Line. I was standing at the end of the dormitory when Ambrose came up to me and said:

> "Sir, there is a new boy just arrived, who says he has not brought any soap with him. May I give him some?" This little act of kindly consideration for others was to my mind, the key to his character. It was not confined to the boys but extended to his Masters and Prefects. To his mother and sisters and also to his nephew, who is at present with us, we tender the very sincere sympathy of his Masters and Prefects. We feel that his *Alma Mater* has lost a very devoted son. May his soul ever rest in peace!'[60]

The union of Clongowes past men was founded in 1897 and the first President was Chief Barron Palles. He had often discussed legal topics, as an equal, with a neighbour in Dundrum, a young Clongownian, Ambrose Davoren. A brilliant young law student at University College Dublin and at King's Inns, Davoren was not called to the Bar as he preferred to fight in the battlefield rather than in the courts.[61]

Following his departure from Clongowes Wood College he followed the Arts course in Classics and secured his BA with first place and first-class honours. He would have benefited by a Postgraduate Scholarship but for being a solicitor's apprentice in his father's office. Some years later he gained his LL B with first-class honours and was elected auditor of the Solicitors' Apprentices' Debating Society, reading a very brilliant paper on *The Rights of Minorities*. This society awarded him its gold medal for oratory. Ambrose was auditor of the Classical Society in University College Dublin from 1911 to 1915 and a member of the Council of the *National Student* to which he contributed several articles. He had completed his course for the Bar before he was actually 'called'. One might easily imagine that with such a splendid academic record he would not have had much time for the lighter side of University life. But such was not the case as he was one of the founders of the College Tennis Club. In fact, he took a large share in the college life and had made his mark as a very happy after-dinner speaker at college banquets. He was a committee member of the UCD Classical Society.[62]

USHER, Isaac William

Lieutenant, 2nd Battalion Royal Irish Regiment, 22nd Brigade in the 7th Division.

He was killed in action at Memetz Wood on 4 July 1916 aged 20. Lieutenant Usher was leading his platoon in a strong attack against a well-fortified German position and refused to leave his men when he was wounded in the foray. An informant, Lieutenant W. Todd of Royal Irish Rifles, stated: 'I saw him wounded in one leg by machine gun fire and then later he was shot again and was lying dead. It was 4 July 1916 at Memetz Wood.' A second informant, Dubliner, Private Byrne, Royal Irish Regiment wrote the following report from his hospital bed in Glasgow: 'It was the 4th July at 6am, at Memetz Wood; he was shot through the heart and killed instantly. The ground was lost and retaken five days afterwards.'[63]

His grave is at III. L. 6. Dantzig Alley British Cemetery, Mametz, Somme, France and he is commemorated at the War Memorial, Christ Church of Ireland, Dundrum, and the Hall of Honour, Trinity College. He was awarded the 1914–1915 Star, British War and Victory medals. 'Isaac Usher was nominated for the Royal Military Academy at Sandhurst in December 1914 and gazetted to the Royal Irish Regiment in June 1915, obtaining promotion to full lieutenant before leaving for France in November 1915.'[64]

He was the son of Dr Isaac William Usher, JP and Rose Cecilia A. Usher (née Meyler) of Laurel Lodge, Dundrum, who were married in the local Church of Ireland at Taney on 6 July 1895. There were three children in the family: Isaac William, Rosie Priscilla and Bloomfield Meyler. Isaac was born on 8 March 1897, educated at Strangeway's School, St Stephen's Green, and entered Trinity College in 1914, where he was a member of its OTC.

Rose Usher died on 2 August 1909 and her husband, Isaac, was killed tragically on 24 February 1917. 'He was hit by a car, driven by a local man, Batty Hyland, which was reversing near Dundrum Railway Station. Dr Usher was a bad time-keeper and was knocked down while rushing for a train. Mr Hyland was the chauffeur for Sir Joseph Redmond. The Usher family was successful in its court action for damages against Sir Joseph Redmond arising out of the death of Dr Usher.'[65]

Dr Usher was still dealing with the administration of his late son's estate when the accident occurred. He was the local dispensary doctor, serving mainly working-class Roman Catholics, and was a popular and highly respected man in the community. Among other local activities, Dr Usher was Vice Chairman of the fund-raising committee for Dundrum's Carnegie Library, which opened in 1914 and Vice Chairman Rathdown Rural District Council. In November 1917 some of his many friends responded to this great loss by erecting a monument in his memory. The monument is situated near the place where he was killed, adjacent to the present Dundrum Luas Railway Station. In the early years the fountain, which formed part of the monument, was filled with water and used by humans and animals alike. When the horse-drawn traffic disappeared, the trough was converted into a seat.

DE ROSSITER, Walter Wrixon

Lieutenant, 42nd Canadian Battalion, Royal High-landers, Canadian Infantry (Quebec Regiment), 7th Brigade in the 3rd Canadian Division, (formerly Service No 418907 in rank of Sergeant).

It was reported that in his battalion's war diary that he died from wounds on 12 October 1917 at Magnicourt-en-Comte, details not stated. A further report on 10 November 1917 confirmed that he died, aged 50, from a self-inflicted bullet wound to his head. He had been with the battalion since its organisation, having enlisted in Canada as a private on the 20 May 1915, but was promoted to sergeant almost immediately. He went to France with the battalion on 9 October 1915, and received his commission as a lieutenant on the 12 November 1915, becoming Transport Officer within a short period of time. During his whole connection with the battalion he gave most efficient and devoted service. He was 'Mentioned in Despatches' on 9 April 1917 and on numerous occasions showed courage and coolness under fire. Prior to enlisting in the Highlanders he had seen long service with the Royal North West Mounted Police, and also served in the South African Campaign as Squadron Sergeant Major with the 2nd Battalion 1st Canadian Mounted Rifles, and 'his loss was greatly felt by both officers and men of the battalion'.[66]

Corporal Will Bird was on sentry duty on the night of the tragedy and wrote:

> We moved away to Agincourt where there was to be an inspection by General Henry Horne … We were to act as sentries … The arrangement was such that it was the hour before daylight when I did my last round. Everything was in darkness and not a vehicle was passing. But as I went along, a shot rang out in the house I was passing. It was so unexpected that I stood for a moment, wondering what a guard was to do. Then I went to the door and tried it. It was not locked and a light shown from an inner room. I stood undecided, expecting a voice or voices. None came so I looked in the room. An officer was lying on the floor in his

pyjamas, a revolver beside him. No one else was there. One look was enough to see that he was dead. Then I saw a written note lying on the table beside a lighted lamp. The pen was there as if it had just been used. I scanned the note, went out and down the street to where I knew a senior officer was billeted. He was rather gruff at being aroused, until I told him my errand. Then he dressed very hurriedly and went back with me. He read the note and told me not to tell any person what I had seen. He would look after everything. I was to carry on with my round. There were rumours the next day, but I never mentioned a thing to anyone.[67]

His grave is at VI. H. 11. Aubigny Communal Cemetery Extension, Somme, France and is commemorated on the War Memorial, Christ Church of Ireland, Taney, Dundrum and his wife's headstone in the graveyard at St Nahi's Church of Ireland, Dundrum. He received the Queens Medal with five clasps following his service in the South African War and was awarded the 1914–15 Star, British War and Victory medals for his service in the Great War. He was also mentioned in Sir Douglas Haig's despatch following his bravery in the field during the first day of the Battle of Vimy Ridge on 9 April 1917, when his regiment covered itself in glory.

Walter de Rossiter joined the North West Mounted Police (NWMP) in December of 1888 and served the scarlet tunic for the next 12 years. In 1896, he was selected to join a troop of the North West Mounted Police to attend the Commonwealth events in London, leading up to the Diamond Jubilee of Queen Victoria, culminating in a gala finale on the 22nd of June 1897. He returned to Canada on the SS *Labridor* on the 16th of February of the same year. Walter de Rossiter enlisted in 4th Regiment, Canadian Mounted Rifles in Regina on 21 December 1899 and fought in the South African War (1899 to 1902). He resigned from the NWMP on 30 November 1900. When war broke out in Europe, Walter just couldn't resist the temptation for further glory.[68]

He enlisted in the 42nd Battalion Royal Highlanders in Montreal and served with the rank of sergeant. His attestation paper reveals that he falsified his age, stating that he was 'born in Ceylon in 1875' making him eight years younger. He also stated that he was 'not married' and gave his sister, 'Hattie Montgomery', as his next-of-kin; he had no sister with that name. The upper age limit for joining the Canadian Army was 45 years and at age 48 he would have been over the age limit in 1915.

On June 10 1915 the Highlanders embarked for overseas service in England. They arrived at Plymouth, England, on 19 June for training, and on 7 October 1915, the battalion began its journey to France, arriving at Boulogne the next day. Sergeant de Rossiter was promoted to temporary lieutenant on 12 November 1915 following a recommendation from Major-General Mercer, Commanding the 1st Canadian Division. The battalion quickly began its service in the front line, experiencing the many harrowing realities of trench warfare. The 42nd saw its first major action at Mount Sorrel a few miles to the east of Ypres from 2 June to 13 June 1916. The 42nd played a critical role, along with other British & Canadian units, in saving Ypres from massive German attacks, but at heavy cost of life.[69]

He was in a hospital at Warley for a period of eight days on 14 September 1916 suffering with arthritis in the left wrist and cellulitis on the right arm. On the 4 November 1916 he was granted ten days' leave and a further ten days' leave was granted on 3 July 1917, just three months before his death. The two periods of leave in nine months indicate that not all was well with Lt de Rossiter in the months before his death.[70]

He was born at Rosemount, Dundrum, on 24 January 1867, the son of Thomas Wrixon Rossiter and Annie Elizabeth Rossiter (née Cox) of Meadowlands, Dundrum. Thomas Wrixon Rossiter's first marriage to Catherine Hurley ended in tragedy when Catherine was hit by a runaway horse in 1859, at age 28. Thomas served as Inspector of Police in Galle, Ceylon, from 1852 until 1862. The couple had three children, all born in Ceylon: Catherine Elizabeth, Margaret Ann and Mary Ellen. In 1864, Thomas married Annie Cox, as his second wife, and they had four children: Charles Patrick Frances, Walter Wrixon, Eric Hamilton and Grace Emily. 'Thomas sold his coffee estate on sixteen acres of land in 1870, and returned to Dundrum.'[71] Walter's brother, Charles, arrived in Quebec with another Rossiter relative from Liverpool, on 18 September, 1882, and Walter followed four years later at age 19, arriving in Canada in 1886. They settled in the district of Assiniboia, Wapella, in the prairie province of Saskatchewan. Walter added the prefix 'de' to his surname in the period between his arrival in Canada and the time of the 1891 census. Today, many members of the wider Rossiter family use the prefix 'de', although no one used it in the time preceding Walter.[72]

When Walter returned to Canada after the Boer War he was eligible for a 'Volunteer Bounty Land Grant' entitling him to 320 acres, and there is a record of his receiving this land. However, he probably sold it, as on 18 October 1902 he returned to Ireland and married Catherine Frances Wright at Christ Church of Ireland, Taney in Dundrum. He started a family, perhaps working in his wife's family's dairy business in Churchtown. The marriage produced five children between 1903 and 1910. The children's names were Edward Wrixon, Annie, Walter, Frances and Constance. The family lived in the sprawling Frankfort Castle and one can only guess what it would have been like for Walter, now in his mid-thirties and just back from the war in South Africa, finding himself in the land of his birth that he had left at the age of 19. He was married with five children, and probably living in his mother-in-law's house. It may very well have been a stifling existence for a man used to a life of adventure on the prairies of Saskatchewan. He must have felt very much out of place, and it is not hard to imagine him developing an almost fanatical longing for his old life as a frontier lawman.[73]

Whatever the reason, Walter decided to go back to Canada in 1910, where he joined the Police Force in the notorious Wild West town of Moose Jaw, Saskatchewan and served until the spring of 1915 when he enlisted in the Canadian National Army at the outset of the Great War.[74]

At the time of Walter's death in 1917, he had been living apart from his wife and family for a period of seven years and his affairs, including his bank account, were in the charge of Hattie Montgomery, also recorded as his next-of-kin, with an address at c/o Mrs Beggs, 5, Kempville, Ontario, Canada. He was a colourful character and this brought him not only adventure and hardship but eventually led to his untimely demise at age 50.[75] 'Walter de Rossiter's three nephews, from his brother, Charles's marriage, also fought in the Great War. Eric Thomas, Charles Archibald and Terence Patrick were attached to the 88th Battalion, Victoria Fusiliers and survived the war. One of his nephews, Eric, visited him prior to Passchendaele, but was unceremoniously brushed off. When the news of Walter's death became known, Eric and his brother Archie came to Ireland to deliver the news to his wife Catherine, while they were on leave after Passchendaele.[76]

HALF-NEPHEW OF JOSEPH PLUNKETT KILLED IN WAR
PLUNKETT, Gerald Anthony
Sub-Lieutenant, Collingwood Battalion, Royal Naval Volunteer Reserve, in the 63rd Royal Naval Division.

Sub-Lieutenant Plunkett was the officer commanding the Collingwood Battalion, 'A' Company, 2nd Platoon, when he was killed in action, aged 27, during the 3rd Battle for Krithia, in Gallipoli, on 4 June 1915. 'He arranged for the men in his platoon to hear mass and receive their last confession in the glare of the sun before facing mortal battle against the Turks.'[77] At last 4 June arrived. It was the day of the great push, from which so much was expected and which proved such a bitter disappointment. The bombardment commenced at 8.30am and with only two short intervals continued until noon, when a general advance was made all along the line. On the right, the French stormed the Haricot Redoubt, whilst the Royal Naval and 42nd Divisions gained their objectives, but on the left both the 29th Division and Cox's Indian Brigade were unable to go forward any appreciable distance. Unfortunately the French, in face of repeated strong counter-attacks, had to evacuate their new positions, and the Collingwood Battalion, which was on their immediate left, was hence caught by enfilade fire and almost annihilated. The first wounded were cheery and full of the great success they had gained, but as time went on, and fresh batches arrived, the spirit of optimism gave place to one of shattered hopes, and they had no knowledge of victory to help them bear the pain of their wounds, the intolerable flies and the sickly smell of blood in those dirty stuffy aid posts, most of which were no more than an unoccupied portion of trench. The dressing-stations and trenches leading to the aid posts were full of wounded, and it was more than twenty-four hours before they were all evacuated to the beach.[78] One of his men wrote to his brother Oliver with the following account of his death:

> The captain ordered us to be ready in advance, starting at 12 noon on 4 June. We shelled the Turks for three-quarters of an hour, and then jumped over the top of our trench. We were in support of the Anson Battalion, who were in the firing line without losing a man. Our platoon commander (your brother) had given us great confidence before the charge by laughing and joking with us. He seemed as if he was going to compete in some sports instead of a life and death

charge. He told us there would be no Turks left by the time we got to their trenches. He was the first man over the trench, and he was a little ahead of us all the time until he got hit. We had got up to the Turkish first trench, and he was emptying his revolvers into them, when all of a sudden, he clapped his hands to his head and fell. I could nearly swear that he fell stone dead. He did all in his power to please us lads, and we would have done anything for him and gone anywhere with him. I can only say that everyone who knew him regrets his early end.[79]

Sub-Lieutenant Plunkett is commemorated on the Helles Memorial, Turkey and was awarded the 1914–15 Star, British War and Victory medals. There are contradictory views about the plight of the Collingwoods in Gallipoli. Contrary to reports that the battalion was 'almost annihilated', The Royal Marine Light Infantry website in an article titled, The Collingwood Myth, states that:

It is supposed by many, that the Collingwood Battalion was all but destroyed at Gallipoli on 4 June 1915. However; the 'Collingwoods' immortality within the Royal Naval Division history is mainly due to the fact they were a newly raised 2nd or replacement Collingwood battalion and that they lasted only ten days at Cape Helles before disbandment. From their total of approximately 1000 men, they suffered only 185 men killed in action on 4 June 1915, with 15 to 20 dying from wounds later, together with about 400 men wounded. This left about 400 men in the battalion, a number very similar to the strength of other Royal Naval Division Battalions in May (before the first reinforcements arrived).[80]

Readers will make up their own minds about the outcome of a battle, where only 400 out of 1000 men survived unscathed.

Gerald Plunkett was a member of the OTC at Trinity College and on 20 October 1914 he was gazetted temporary sub-lieutenant in the Royal Naval Volunteer Reserve. According to family history Gerald had a one slightly shorter leg, obtained in a skating accident and this caused him some difficulty initially when he decided to join the forces. He was the youngest son of Patrick Joseph Plunkett JP, builder, land owner and alderman, and Helena Plunkett (née O'Sullivan), of 14, Palmerston Road, Dublin. Patrick Joseph was son of the late Walter Plunkett of Bayna House, Co Meath, a member of the ancient house of Fingal. He was from the Killeen line of Plunketts and he came to Dublin when the Great Famine destroyed the family farm, which bordered Killeen Castle, Co Meath. Patrick married Elizabeth Noble who owned a leather shop in Aungier Street, Dublin, and on the strength of its proceeds he leased land at Rathmines and built on Belgrave, Palmerston, Cowper, Windsor, Ormond and Killeen Roads. He did all his repair work by direct labour, supervising it himself and, at ninety, was persuaded with difficulty to come down from the roof of one of his houses.[81] There was one surviving child from this marriage, George Noble, later to become Count Plunkett, who lived for a time with his family at Kilternan Abbey, Golden Ball. When Elizabeth died Patrick married her first cousin, Helena O'Sullivan, a widow, and they had five children, of whom four survived infancy: Germaine, Oliver, Gerald and Helena. She had been a governess in France and her children all spoke good French. 'Helena was a beautiful needlewoman and kept the house at 14, Palmerston Road, with elegant taste and efficiency.'[82] 'By the time that Patrick Plunkett died in 1918 he had lived through the imprisonment of his son, Count Plunkett, the Countess and two grandsons in 1916; the election to the Westminster Parliament of Count Plunkett in 1917 and his imprisonment again; the execution of his grandson, Joseph Plunkett for his part in the 1916 Rising and the death of his son, Gerald, at Gallipoli.'[83] Two other grandchildren fell in the Second World War.

Gerald was born in Dublin on 11 August 1887, entered the Junior School at Belvedere College in 1900, and left in 1905, having received excellent results in each year of Intermediate examinations. He went to the USA and Canada with his brother, Oliver, before entering New College, Oxford. At some time in his education he also attended Wimbledon College, London, founded by the Jesuits. He entered the Inner Temples, London and King's Inns, Dublin, was called to the Irish Bar in 1910 and served in the North-East Circuit Court.[84] His resignation from the Rathmines Board of Commissioners was announced at a meeting on 2 June 1915, as he was being posted to Gallipoli. The young barrister was a keen yachtsman, played golf at Rathfarnham Golf Club and was a member of the Bar Golfing Society. He was also very musical, and possessed a fine baritone voice. His niece, Shivaun Gannon, said of her great-uncles: 'Oliver and Gerald were very athletic and both took part in the

Henley Regatta each year.' She pointed out that Gerald 'was killed at Gallipoli, leading his men on to the beaches in that futile Dardanelles campaign. He had been more than a beloved brother to Oliver, they were close friends, sharing so much of their lives together including their student days at Oxford.' To his sisters, Germaine and Enie, he was the 'baby brother. My mother's (Germaine) eyes would fill with tears, whenever she spoke of him, through the years.'[85]

Gerald and his half-nephew, Joseph Plunkett, were born the same year, shared a cradle and later in their young lives were to die bravely for different causes. 'The two families followed different traditions' Geraldine Plunkett Dillon said, 'Helena liked English schools and sent her sons to Oxford and Count Plunkett and his children were firmly Irish Nationalists.'[86]

His brother, Oliver, was attached to the Army Horse Transport Service and was wounded twice, but survived the war. When Gerald went to war Oliver became a member of the Rathmines Board of Commissioners, but resigned before joining the Army. He married an Englishwoman, Cordelia (Dedee) Wheeler, and had a distinguished career as a lawyer in the British Colonial Service. Oliver was appointed a judge in Palestine and Egypt and was one of the judges in the 'Assassination of Haim Arlosoroff' trial, and became Governor-General of Saint Lucia. When Oliver retired, he returned to England with his wife, and they were to endure the loss of two sons during the Second World War. Flying Officer Oliver Peter Plunkett, Royal Air Force was killed in August 1941 and his brother, Lieutenant George W. Plunkett, light Anti-Aircraft Royal Artillery was killed in 1943. Their niece, Shivaun Gannon, concluded that the couple had five sons and in 2003, Paddy, the one survivor, was in his nineties and living in England.[87]

SCALLAN, Richard Talbot

Second Lieutenant, attached 90th Prisoner of War Company Labour Corps, Secondary Unit, 'B' Reserve Brigade, Royal Garrison Artillery, Royal Horse Artillery.

Second Lieutenant Scallan died, aged 27, when he was hit by a train on 31 May 1918. At a Court of Enquiry on 10 June 1918 it was stated that he was killed accidentally by a train, at a time after 2.30am on the railway line between the towns of St Sulpice-de-Faleyrens and Libourne in the Bordeaux region of France. The officer suffered multiple injuries when a train struck him in the back. He was given permission by Captain R.M. William to go to Libourne on the 5.45pm train and return by the train leaving there at 11.11pm. At approximately 2.30am, a French lady in attendance at the railway crossing reported that a British soldier asked her for the direction to St Sulpice-de-Faleyrens. In a letter to his father, the War Office wrote that the enquiry elicited that a ticket had been taken by an officer for the 11.11pm St Sulpice train to Libourne, but not given up at that station. His body was discovered by a French railway employee, Eugene Boyer and an American soldier, Cpl James Vannatter, who stayed with the body until it was removed.[88]

His grave is at 1.Talence Communal Cemetery Extension, Gironde, France and he is commemorated on the War Memorial, Belvedere College Dublin; Great War Memorial, Kilgobbin, and the Solicitors Memorial, Four Courts, Dublin. He was awarded the British War and Victory medals.

Having gained valuable experience as a member of the Dublin University OTC he was accepted for admission to an Officer Cadet Artillery Brigade at St John's Wood, London, on 14 July 1916. On 27 February 1917 he embarked at Folkestone, arriving in Bologna on the same day. Having spent some months in the front line he arrived back at Base Depot on 7 October 1917, following a period in hospital suffering from scabies. His Medical Case Sheet states that he returned to hospital eleven days later, on 18 October, with impetigo on his right arm and back. Following a further period of three weeks in hospital his condition had cleared up except for a small patch on the back of his neck and one finger. He was discharged and returned to duty, but his general condition was described as, 'somewhat debilitated, pale, and anaemic and it appears that his appetite is poor'. On 28 March 1918, he was transferred to the Labour Corps, attached to 90th Prisoner of War Company, stationed at St Sulpice-de-Faleyrens.[89]

Richard Scallan (Dick, as his family knew him) was the son of Francis Joseph Scallan (solicitor) and Marian Scallan (née Elliott), Ludford Park House, Ballinteer. His death was followed, a few days later, by another tragic death in the family, when his father died suddenly. There were seven children in the family: Mary, Ethel, Richard, Francis, Catherine, Eva and Nora. Richard was educated at Belvedere College (1901–1910) and entered the National University of Ireland. On the completion of his education he joined his father's firm of solicitors, J.L. Scallan, 25 Suffolk Street, Dublin, and was admitted to the Roll of Solicitors on 22 July 1915. In the years before the outbreak of war he practised as a solicitor with his father and brother, Francis. Richard was a member of Carrickmines Golf Club and won the coveted Carysfort Challenge Cup in 1915, before going to war.[90]

At some time following his father's death, the firm merged and became known as Scallan O'Brien Solicitors, and in more recent times it merged with the well-known firm of Arthur Cox Solicitors. Richard Scallan's nephew, Frank Plunkett Dillon, was a partner with Arthur Cox until his retirement. The late, Mrs Nonie Robinson, of Dun Laoghaire, gave the author a photograph of her uncle in uniform, which was carefully preserved in a beautiful leather wallet with his father's name and business address inscribed. The family home, Ludford Park House, was bought by Wesley College in 1963 and is now the residence of the College's principal.

TIERNEY, Herbert Stanislaus Joseph

Second Lieutenant, 8th Battalion Cheshire Regiment, 40th Brigade in the 13th (Western) Division. Secondary Regiment, 7th Battalion 'D' Company (the 'Pals') Royal Dublin Fusiliers.

He was reported missing during the attack on the Dujaila Redoubt in Mesopotamia (Iraq) on 9 April 1916 and it was confirmed later that he was killed in action aged 27.

> On 8 April at 7.30pm his battalion left bivouac and moved to take up allotted position in division for assault on the Turkish position at Sannaiyat, but the assault failed on the next day, 9 April. Failure to take up position was chiefly due to lack of a sufficient number of junior

officers to control the platoons. The battalion was much scattered by this operation, but began to get together after dark. In the aftermath of the battle, 5 officers were missing, including 2nd Lt Tierney, 1 wounded, 7 other ranks killed and 64 missing.[91]

He wrote his last letter, in pencil, to his mother on 7 April 1916, two days before he was reported missing. His letters were addressed to his 'Dear Mother' and signed 'Your fond son, Bertie':

> We started a deuce of a battle two days ago and we are still advancing, fighting heavily all the time. I have come through safe and I hope to say the same in a few days when the show is over. We are now in a position about three miles from where we started, but the first line is going forward well. You will read all about it in the papers long since. PS, Have just had a parcel from you on the battlefield. More welcome than anything could be.[92]

His body was not recovered and he is commemorated on the Basra Memorial, Iraq and the War Memorial at Belvedere College, Dublin. He was awarded the 1914–1915 Star, British War and Victory medals, forwarded to his father in June 1921. His father, Christopher Tierney, wrote to the Secretary for War on 4 November 1916:

> Am I to take it that your fear of that there being no hope of 2nd Lt H.S. Tierney being alive is based on the result of exhaustive enquiry, and therefore final – or merely surmise? I cannot understand if he was killed, why his body was not found or why the identification disc he wore did not turn up in some way. Please say is it in the bounds of possibility he may be a prisoner of war in the hands of the Turks?[93]

On 19 September 1916 Mr Tierney received a handwritten response from the Commander of the 8th Cheshires, Major J.W. Ley: 'I think that it will be a kindness if I tell you that I am afraid that you will not see your son again.' Despite this conclusive information the family still hoped that he might have been taken prisoner of war. A further letter from Mr Tierney to the War Office on 3 April 1917 requested a response to a statement in the House of Commons by Mr Hope MP to the effect that 470 officers and men were taken prisoners of war. The reply from the War Office stated that 2nd Lt Tierney was not on any prisoner-of-war list. It was not until the 19 July 1918 that the War Office sent a leaflet to Mr Tierney showing the steps taken to trace missing officers and men. On 22 July 1918, Mr Tierney confirmed that he had received no news from his son from the date of his being reported 'missing'. Finally, the agony for the family ended when a letter was received from the War Office on 21 August 1918: 'In view of the lapse of time since 2nd Lieutenant H.S. Tierney was reported missing, his death has been accepted for official purposes as having occurred on or since the 9 April 1916.'[94]

The matter of his effects was also a concern for his parents, who wrote that it was a matter of extreme surprise that the returns of his belongings should be so long delayed. Mr Tierney received a letter in 1916 notifying him that a package was awaiting in Bombay and would be shipped on the first available steamer. However, he wrote to the War Office on 12 July 1917 stating: 'I have to inform you that the effects referred to as having been forwarded in November last, consisted of a small wooden box sent for safe keeping to Cox & Company, Alexandria by the late Herbert S. Tierney before leaving Basra in February 1916 for active service, contained some heavy things he did not require at the time.'[95] Herbert Tierney applied for a commission in the army at the outbreak of war, but before receiving a reply from the War Office he enlisted in the ranks with 'D' Company (the 'Pals') of the 7th Royal Dublin Fusiliers. He was posted on 15 September and discharged to a commission on 21 November 1914. At a later stage he received his commission as 2nd lieutenant in the 8th Battalion, Cheshire Regiment. He was wounded while serving in Gallipoli and evacuated to hospital in Alexandria, Egypt, before joining his battalion in Mesopotamia (now Iraq).[96]

The Cheshire 8th Battalion was formed at Chester on 12 August 1914 as part of the KI 'New Army'. In February 1915 it moved from Chiseldon to Pirbright and in June embarked for Egypt and then to Gallipoli. It moved in January 1916 to Egypt and the following month it arrived in Mesopotamia where it remained.

He was the son of Christopher Tierney, bank manager at the Hibernian Bank, Lower Sackville Street, Dublin, and Frances Tierney (née Healy) of 14, Rostrevour Terrace, Rathgar. There were three children in the family: Herbert Stanislaus Joseph, Gerald Joseph and Marie. When Christopher passed away in 1924, Frances lived at 26, Wellington Road, Dublin, and she died in August 1952 aged 91. Herbert (known to his family as Bertie) was born in 1888. He entered Belvedere College in 1903 and later enrolled as a student in the Royal University of Ireland, where he graduated with a BA. In 1910 he was admitted to King's Inns and called to the Bar serving for four years on the Munster Circuit. *The Belvederian* of 1917 said of him, 'his many excellent qualities, his charm of manner and manly bearing made him conspicuous wherever he was. He was universally loved, and is now deeply regretted by a host of friends.'[97]

Most of the letters written by Herbert to his mother have survived and the following is a selection of edited extracts, which give an insight into the human aspects of a young man at war:

> HMT *Ivernia,* 3 July 1915:
> Here I am on a most lovely day sitting in a deal chair, got up in drill uniform, nice and cool, looking down into the loveliest sea that ever was. We are now a few hours from Malta where we hope to arrive about 4 or 5 this evening. This ship was out last voyage with the Naval Brigade and I find that Gerald Plunkett was aboard. It is a peculiar thing as the last time I saw him we were discussing which was the quickest way to the front. He got there first, but had bad luck poor chap!

(**Note:** A profile of Sub-Lieutenant Gerald Plunkett may be seen in this chapter.)

> Gallipoli 15 July 1915:
> I got a grand sheaf of letters on Sunday last. We have not got into the firing line yet but hope to do soon as this is a fairly rotten place. It is as hot as blazes. I took my knife out of my rucksack a few minutes ago and I could not hold the blessed thing it was so hot, but it's all in the game. We are in no danger but it is fairly rough. We are in bivouac, which means that we are under the skies, no tents or anything to give shade except what one can make by rigging up a blanket and a few sticks.

Lemnos, 3 August 1915:

I like the way you grouse about the rain. I can't conceive anything more heavenly than a wet summer at home, everything green and fresh instead of the d-d sun and dust and drab colours of this place. We move tomorrow to the place where our big show is going to be. I am not sorry, resting here is not the sort of rest that one enjoys much. Give my love to Eleanor and of course to Paddy and Mrs Lynch when they come out again. Nance will be on a hospital ship if she comes out here. There are dozens of them all lit up at night with green lights and a red cross. One feels that a slight wound would not be such a very unfortunate thing. All sorts of nice girls looking after one. One of our men was on one for a few days sick, he gave most glowing accounts.

(**Note:** Patrick Lynch KC, of the Irish Parliamentary Party was a family friend of Herbert's mother. Following the vacancy caused by the death of Major William Redmond MP, Lynch was unsuccessful in his bid to take the seat in the East-Clare by-election in 1917, won by Eamon de Valera.)

Gallipoli, 13 August 1915:

The big show is going on strong but just where we are there is an advance just now. I am in a wonderful dug-out now, perched upon the top of a hill, forming the side of a steep gully, with the enemy's trenches about 80 yards away – but they can't touch me. I keep extraordinary well, though this climate knocks some of the men about rather badly. The main difficulty is to keep clean. Water is much too precious to wash with, and a change of clothes is an undreamed of luxury. Now I must send my best love to you and Dad and all those people who have asked for me, I have not much chance of writing to them.

19th General Hospital, Alexandria, 16 November 1916:

I am feeling much better now, more like the man I was, more in *status quo ante bellum*. I was never very ill, but just as I was getting well from jaundice, I suddenly got a temperature of 102–5. I am going to get some kit together here before I leave. Socks you might send me a pair now and again. I hope dear old Dad is keeping fit and Gerald.[98]

MOSS, Arnold Wilson
Lance Corporal, Service No 14188, 7th Battalion 'D' Company (The 'Pals'), Royal Dublin Fusiliers, 30th Brigade in the 10th (Irish) Division.

Arnold Moss took part in the taking of Chocolate Hill on 7 August 1915, and as a result of his gallantry in the field was promoted to Lance Corporal on the 14th, two days before he fell. He was with his comrade, Sgt Edward Millar of Monkstown, on 9 August 1915, when he joined the party led by Capt Tobin.

Following a bayonet charge at Kiretch Tepe Sirt on 16 August 1915, he was reported wounded, missing and was assumed to have been killed in action on that date. He was aged 18. The fighting on Sunday and Monday 15 and 16 August was among the fiercest of the whole Gallipoli Campaign. His Colonel wrote: 'I knew him as one of the bravest of the brave.' And an officer present on that day wrote of the action:

Our Company was instructed to bring up a supply of ammunition to some troops on our left who were being hard pressed. Two parties were detached and Arnold and I were in the party of 40 led by Capt Tobin. When close to our objective the fire became so intense that we were ordered to lie down as low as we could and to open the boxes of ammunition and distribute the bandoliers. Arnold, Lea and I were lying on our backs, side by side, endeavouring to open the boxes when we got orders to fall back some distance, where there was a certain amount of cover. As soon as Lea lifted his head off the ground he was hit in the back of the head; Arnold immediately went to his assistance. There was quite a crowd at the spot, and Capt Tobin was in the act of rallying us, when I saw Arnold coming along supporting Lea, and I was surprised to see them, as I thought it would be impossible for Arnold to escape being hit. I understand that he was subsequently recommended for the Distinguished Conduct Medal for helping comrades under fire.[99]

Henry Hanna wrote: 'The sights I saw going along that place I shall never forget. Some of our fellows throwing back bombs which the Turks threw over and which had not exploded. Wounded and dead lying everywhere. The sun streaming down and not a drop of water to be had. Neither had we bombs to reply to the Turks and drive them out. The battalion was taken from Kizlar Dagh and marched back to their dug-outs on Karakol Dagh, a sad and downhearted crowd, with many faces absent. It was a sad roll-call for the regiment.'[100] The casualties during the night stood at 11 officers and 54 men killed or wounded, and 13 missing.

Lance Corporal Moss is commemorated on the Helles Memorial, Turkey; Great War Memorial, Sandford Church, Ranelagh; Aravon School War Memorial, Bray, Co Wicklow; Boys Scout Memorial, St Patrick's Cathedral, Dublin; Hall of Honour, Trinity College, and his parents' grave in the churchyard at Kilternan Church of Ireland. He was awarded the 1915 Star, British War and Victory medals, which were forwarded to his father in March 1920. He was recommended for the Distinguished Conduct Medal (DCM) when he assisted wounded comrades under fire at Chocolate Hill on 9 August 1915; however, there is no confirmation on his Medal Index Card that it was granted.

Arnold Moss enlisted in Dublin on 16 September 1914, and was posted to the Dardanelles in July 1915. He was the son of Henry William Moss (company director and freeman of Dublin City) and Susan Moss, daughter of John Webster, Stillorgan. The couple lived at Greenmount 4, Milltown Road, Rathmines, Dublin, and previously at Elmfield House, Ballyogan Road, Kilgobbin. Henry Moss was a well known landscape painter and exhibited in the Royal Hibernian Academy until 1934. He was, for many years, President of the Dublin Sketching Club. When the couple died in 1944 and 1946 respectively, their bodies were interred in the family plot in the churchyard at Kilternan Church of Ireland. Henry was a director-merchant of Greenmount, Milltown and his family was the former owner of the cotton mill in Kilternan. There were four children in the family: Henry Webster, Aileen Mary, Geoffrey Lawton and Arnold Wilson. Arnold's grandfather, Henry (1826–1883), purchased Elmfield House in 1856 and enlarged it during the 1860s. The house was demolished and rebuilt in 1914 by the new owners, William and Cora Rutherfoord.

Arnold Moss was born in Kilgobbin, on 15 April 1896 and educated at Strangeway's School, St Stephen's Green, before entering Trinity College, where he matriculated in 1914. His brother, Lieutenant Geoffrey Lawton Moss, MC of the Leinster Regiment, survived the war and was awarded the Military Cross on 28 August 1916 for gallantry and bravery in the field. He also served in the Second World War and was promoted to captain on 2 September 1939. In 1951 he illustrated a book, *The Elements of Fly Fishing for Trout and Grayling*, written by his brother, Henry Webster Moss.

FLEMING, Owen

Private, Service No 5699, 2nd Battalion Leinster Regiment, (Royal Canadians) 17th Brigade in the 24th Division.

The Leinsters were taking a beating at Prémesques, in the Battle of Armentières, which officially ran from 13 October to 2 November 1914, where Pte Fleming was reported missing, presumed to have been killed in action, aged 33, on 20 October 1914. This is one of a series of actions that tend to get overlooked in favour of the larger more dramatic first Battle of Ypres. Prémesques was the first occasion that the Leinster Regiment was heavily involved in the fighting of the Great War and the first time that it suffered a large number of casualties. Early on the morning of Sunday 18 October orders were received for 17th Brigade to attack the line Prémesques / Pérenchies with 2nd Leinsters being responsible for taking the small village of Prémesques. (There was a belief that dramatic events in the regiment's history always occurred on a Sunday.) The initial attack was made at 7.30am without reconnaissance or bombardment, by all four companies. German resistance was immediate and effective particularly in front of the 3rd Rifle Brigade whose advance was held up. The regimental history records the nuisance that snipers made of themselves, particularly targeting officers who at this stage of the war were still likely to be leading their men from the front with drawn swords. By 10am 'D' Company had entered the village of Prémesques. On the left, on account of the opposition and despite being reinforced by a battalion of the Royal Fusiliers, the Rifle Brigade did not attain its objective. This left the Leinsters in an exposed position with the Battery de Sénarmont, an outwork of the defences of Lille, still in German hands on their left flank. As the day drew to a close the battalion dug in on the positions reached. The following day the battalion remained in its entrenched positions under occasional shell fire and suffering a further twelve casualties. Once again the low-key tone of the war diary is worth quoting in full to set the scene for the events of the 20 October: 'At 8am enemy makes a strong attack in force, commencing with heavy artillery fire and the brigade fell back on the line Porteegal Farm – Rue de Bois. Casualties during the day were

30 other ranks killed; 70 wounded and 214 missing.' Similar losses were occurring throughout the British Expeditionary Force, literally bleeding the old professional army of its junior and middle ranking officers, NCOs and experienced men. These irreplaceable losses would cost the country dearly in the coming years. Thus ended an eventful few days for the battalion during which it was engaged in its first major action on the European continent. If it was in any mood for introspection it could take the satisfaction from giving a good account of itself against a numerically and materially stronger force albeit at a heavy cost. During the period 18–20 October, the 2nd Leinsters were reported to have suffered 434 casualties of whom 5 officers and 150 other ranks were killed.[101]

He is commemorated on the Ploegsteert Memorial, Comines-Warneton, Hainaut, Belgium. The Ploegsteert Memorial stands in Berks Cemetery Extension. The sounding of the Last Post takes place at the memorial at 7pm on the first Friday of every month. He was awarded the 1914 Star, British War and Victory medals. His photograph was carried by the *Evening Herald* on Monday 17 January 1916 with a notice to the effect that he was missing since an engagement on 18 October 1914. Private Fleming enlisted in Dublin in 1914. The 2nd Battalion was in Cork and moved through Cambridge and Newmarket in England, arriving at St Nazaire, France on 12 September 1914 as part of the 17th Brigade, 6th Division (later 24th Division), too late for the Battle of Mons and the subsequent retreat to the Marne. The 2nd Leinsters were present at the Battle of the Aisne although not heavily engaged and seemed to have suffered few casualties.

Owen Fleming was born in 1880 at Windy Arbour, Dundrum. His niece, Mrs Maureen Martin (nee Fleming) wrote:

> Nobody in the family knew he existed, yet alone was killed in the war. One of my sisters does remember a shield (Memorial Plaque) in the house with a military crest on it, but I was very young at the time and I don't know what happened to it, or what it was about. My uncle, James, emigrated to America and my father, Patrick, stayed in Windy Arbour, but nobody knows what happened to Christopher … maybe he also went to war. I am glad we read your article in *Panorama* as we would not have known of Owen's existence and he can now be remembered in our prayers.[102]

He was the son of James and Anne Fleming, 24, Rosemount, Dundrum. There were six children in the Fleming family: Anne, Owen, Mary, James, Christopher and Patrick. At the time of the 1911 census, his parents had passed away and Owen Fleming, aged 30, was recorded living with his sister and brother in law, Mary and William Mulhall and their children, William, James, John and Patrick, at 35, Windy Arbour, Dundrum. His brothers, James, Christopher and Patrick, his sister, Anne Gore and nephew Christopher Gore were also visiting the house on that evening.

KING, William

Private, Service No 40776, 1st Battalion Northampton Regiment, 2nd Brigade in the 1st Division.

Private King was killed in action, aged 25, on 24 September 1918. On the day that he fell, his battalion attacked at 5am and was on the left with the 2nd Royal Sussex on the right. Four tanks were to have gone in front of the battalion, but two got knocked out before starting; one lost its direction and did not appear. One seemed to get lost in Pontruet. They were therefore quite useless. Then 'B' Company on the left was held up; the 46th Division attacking Pontruet from the north failing to take the village, which was strongly held. The south-east corner remained in Boche hands and 'B' Company was enfiladed by machine-gun fire. 'D' Company got right onto its final objective, but as its left flank was exposed by 'B' Company failing to get forward, they had to withdraw to Sampson Trench, joining with the Royal Sussex. The casualties were fairly heavy, with 2 officers killed, 12 wounded, 195 other ranks wounded and 40 killed.[103]

He is commemorated on the Vis-en-Artois Memorial, in the village of Vis-en-Artois, near Arras, France The absence of the 1914–1915 Star medal from his campaign medal entitlement indicates that Pte King did not enlist until late 1915 or 1916. He was awarded the British War and Victory medals.

William was the son of Patrick (farm servant) and Mary King of 4, Innismore Terrace, Terenure. There were eight children in the family of whom seven survived infancy: Patrick, William, Thomas, Leon, Mary Jane, Kathleen and Andrew.

His brother, Pte Thomas King, who served in four regiments, finishing the war with the Royal Irish Rifles, survived the war. He was wounded during his service and discharged on 11 April 1919. Thomas was awarded the British War and Victory medals. He was born in Dublin in 1894 and married Elizabeth Curley in 1919. They had two children and lived in Churchtown. Thomas died in 1954, aged 60.

THE TRAGIC STORY OF AMBROSE LANGAN

LANGAN, Ambrose

Private, Service No 4486, 25th Battalion Australian Imperial Force, Australian Infantry, in the 2nd Division.

Ambrose Langan enlisted at Enoggera, Australia on 29 November 1915 and embarked for Egypt in May 1916 arriving in Marseilles later in the month. His battalion participated in its first major battle at Pozières between 25 July and 7 August 1916, during which it suffered 785 casualties. It was here at Pozières Ridge that Pte Langan was missing, presumed killed, aged 43, on 5 August 1916. 'At Pozières Ridge on 5 August 1916, the battalion was in difficulty with the enemy shelling with all calibre of shells. Many attempts were made to get to the RE stores, but due to enemy shelling it was practically impossible to get supplies forward. At 4am the enemy lodged a counter-attack but it was easily repulsed with heavy losses by the Australian machine gun and rifle fire. The men were working very hard consolidating their position heedless of heavy enemy fire, which at this time was terrific. The battalion held its position until 6pm when it was relieved. Casualties were 24 other ranks killed; 9 officers and 126 wounded; 1 officer and 178 other ranks missing.'[104]

He is commemorated on the Villers-Bretonneux Memorial, Somme, France and the Bundamba War Memorial, near Ipswich in Queensland, Australia. Private Langan was awarded the British War and Victory medals.

Private Edward Lynch, a comrade of Ambrose Langan serving in the Australian Imperial Force, kept a diary of his time in the trenches on the Western Front and wrote about his experiences. In one passage Edward describes how his friend Paddy wandered in search of his brother Jimmy:

> A chap comes past and tells me, 'Paddy's gone. A shell got him. Took half his face off as clean as a whistle.' 'Didn't you hear him scream?" No, I didn't hear him scream. We don't any longer notice screams. We're used to them. Paddy had gone to find his brother Jim, for whom he's spent the past three nights searching – crawling around in no-mans-land turning dead men over in a vain search for the brother who fell on that first day. Three nights exposed to rifle and machine-gun fire. In memory we still can hear that low, pleading call, 'Jim, Jimmy, Jimmo',

amid the rattle of enemy guns and rifles at him. Then silence as we wonder if they got him. Silence for ten minutes or so and again there would come from some other direction the pleading call. The call of brother, for brother laid low days before. Still we can see the agony in his face as he wandered the trench all day seeking news of Jim. Half a dozen men assured him that they saw Jim fall with a blue dot in his forehead, but he wasn't convinced. He must find Jim. He has found him![105]

The maiden name of Edward Lynch's mother was O'Shaughnessy and it is reasonable to assume that his parents were of Irish descent. Any person inspecting the graves and memorials of fallen soldiers in Belgium, France and Gallipoli is struck by the number of Irish surnames on headstones in cemeteries where soldiers of the Australian and New Zealand Armies sleep.

Prior to enlisting Ambrose worked for the Queensland Railways at Bundamba Station, a suburb of Ipswich, Queensland. His friend and colleague, Mr P. Delaney, who also worked at Bundamba Station, wrote to the Officer in Charge, Base Records, Defence Department, Melbourne, on four occasions during the first half of 1917, requesting information on his former workmate. In a letter from Delaney, dated 23 January 1917, he wrote: 'Further to your letter of the 15th inst., you are unable to supply anymore information regarding Pte A. Langan than I already know. Can you not obtain definite information from the authorities as to the fate of the man – advise me what myself and my co-executors should do to fix-up his affairs?' The response received on 2 January 1917, explained that until some substantial evidence was obtained regarding his date of death nothing further could be done. A letter was also sent to the Defence Department on 22 August 1917 from O'Shea & O'Shea Solicitors, 43, Queen Street, Brisbane, advising the authorities that they held the original Will of Ambrose Langan and requested a certificate of death. This information was not available to the solicitors or executors for some considerable time until the authorities were certain that Ambrose had been killed in action on the date stated.[106] In one of those extraordinary coincidences, Robert McFarlane, named as one of Ambrose's executors, had a son, also Robert, who was killed on the same day in the same place as Pte Langan.[107]

Ambrose Langan married Annie Byrne, the daughter of John Byrne and Elizabeth

Byrne (née McDonnell) of Castledermot, Co Kildare. The couple had two daughters: Elizabeth, born in Dublin in 1898 and Bridget, born in Glasgow during 1899, just before her parents returned to Dublin. It is recorded in the 1901 census that Ambrose and Annie were farming at Holylands, Whitehall, Rathfarnham. Their farm may have been situated on the site, where in later years the Nutgrove Shopping Centre was built. Then tragedy struck the family when Annie became ill and died in the Meath Hospital, Dublin, on 18 April 1905, leaving Ambrose with two children. She was aged 32.

When he emigrated to Australia on 8 August 1911, his daughters were taken to Castledermot, Co Kildare, where they were reared by three maiden aunts; they never saw their father again. The family is not aware of the circumstances that led Ambrose to emigrate a few years after his wife's death. His great-granddaughter, Gerada Mullane, noted that 'he was described as a railway worker' on the ship's manifest. His daughter, Elizabeth, married John Byrne, had two children and was widowed at an early age. The second daughter, Bridget, married Patrick Keatley and remained in the McDonnell property at Main Street, Castledermot. His daughter, Bridget, was recorded as his next-of-kin.[108] Why did Ambrose enlist at the age of 41? Perhaps, in the back of his mind there was the thought that while serving in France, he would get the opportunity of travelling home to Ireland to see his daughters.

Ambrose Langan, born in 1871, was the son of Ambrose and Brigid Langan (née Purcell) of 26, Farranboley, Windy Arbour, Dundrum. There were nine children in the family: Lana, James, Mary, Anne, Ambrose, Teresa, Catherine Mary, Edward John and Teresa Agnes. Two children, Lana and Teresa, died at a young age. Brigid, widowed at the time of the 1901 census, was the owner of a public house and thirteen acres of land in Windy Arbour. She died in 1911, age 70, and her mother, Jane Purcell, who was living with the family in 1901, died in 1902, aged 93. Following their deaths, most members of Langan family were interred at St Nahi's graveyard in Dundrum.

Private George Langan, 1st Battalion. Royal Dublin Fusiliers, a first cousin of Pte Ambrose Langan was killed in action, aged 32, in Gallipoli on 8 August 1915. He was the son of George Langan, who died in 1883, and Ellen Langan (née Rogers). There were five children in the family: James, Bridget, George, Elizabeth and Emma.

MAHON, George

Private, Service No 15762, 1st Battalion Royal Dublin Fusiliers, 86th Brigade in the 29th Division.

Having survived the slaughter during the landings at 'V' Beach on 25 April, Private Mahon died from wounds, aged 26, received at Marquette, Somme, on 21 May 1918. On the day that he was wounded at Grand Hazard and Battery Headquarters, his battalion was involved with training/baths and the camp was shelled at intervals by long range high velocity guns. This camp was condemned as unsafe for troops and the battalion moved to another location. Private Mahon died from his wounds, with three comrades who were also wounded in the shelling.[109]

His grave is at D. 22. Cinq Rues British Cemetery, Hazebrouck, Nord, France and he is commemorated on the Great War Memorial at Christ Church of Ireland, Dundrum and the Great War Memorial, Kilgobbin. He was awarded the 1914 Star, British War and Victory medals.

The information on his medal index card indicates that he enlisted during 1914 or earlier and may have been in India until 1914. Information on the movement of the 1st Dublin Battalion is contained in the profile of Pte Denis Higgins in chapter three. He was evacuated with his battalion from Gallipoli on 1 January 1916, arriving in Egypt seven days later and sailed from Port Said to Marseilles for service in France on 13 March 1916.

George Mahon, the only son of John and Annie (Nannie) Mahon, of 37, Ballawly Cottages, Dundrum was born at Rosemount, Dundrum on 21 July 1892. There were four children in the family: George, Annie, Martha and Mabel. George was described as a gardener in the 1911 census.

SANDYFORD FATHER AND SON KILLED IN THE TWO GREAT WARS

MASON, George

Corporal, Service No 3615, 6th Battalion, 'B' Company, Royal Irish Regiment, 47th Brigade in the 16th (Irish) Division.

He was one of two men killed, aged 26, in action on 10 August 1916. On the day that he was killed at Loos, 'the enemy displayed considerable activity with heavy trench mortar and aerial torpedoes. The Royal Irish Regiment replied vigorously with trench mortars and artillery. Casualties for the day were 2 other ranks killed and 5 wounded.'[110]

His grave is at 111. P.1. St Patrick's Cemetery, Loos, Pas de Calais, France and he is commemorated on the Great War Memorial at Kilgobbin. He was awarded the 1915 Star, British War and Victory medals, which were issued to his wife on 21 March 1923. George was drill instructor to the National Volunteers in the Sandyford district and enlisted in Dublin on 31 May 1915. He was posted to France in December of the same year. His effects, forwarded to his wife in December 1916, included a letter, cap badge, knife, pipe, wrist watch and strap, prayer book and photograph. His wife, Elizabeth, wrote to the Registry Office for 12 District in December 1916 stating: 'I received my late husband's belongings this morning. Everything that you mentioned, except the watch and strap, has come. I hope you will forward it to me.'[111]

He married Elizabeth Magee and they lived at 57, The Cottages, Sandyford Village with their four children, Elizabeth, Christina, Laurence, James Patrick, and Charles. Their son, Gunner James Patrick Mason, Service No 872568, The Royal Artillery, 125 Anti-Tank Regiment, fought in the Second World War and died aged 23, on 25 August 1943. His grave is at 5. K. 8. Chungkai War Cemetery, located at the Bridge over the River Kwai in Thailand and his gravestone carries the inscription 'Go ndeanfaidh Dia Trocaire ar a Anam (May God have mercy on his Soul).' On the 15 November 2005 Gunner James Mason was the subject of a RTÉ Documentary, titled, 'Who was Gunner Mason? He became a Japanese Prisoner of War during the Second World War, and worked on the railway made famous by the film, Bridge Over the River Kwai.'[112]

George Mason was the son of Laurence and Ellen Mason of 7, Murphystown, Kilgobbin, Sandyford. They had eight children of whom six survived infancy: George, Joseph, Patrick, (twins) William, Michael and Alice. His brother-in-law, Henry Magee, served in India with the British Army. George's great-grandchildren; Fintan Byrne, Oliver Byrne, Geraldine Dowling and Miriam Ivory, all live in South Dublin.

MULLIGAN, Christopher
Private, Service No 9936, 2nd Battalion Royal Irish Rifles, 74th Brigade in the 25th Division.

Private Mulligan was killed in action, aged 34, on 10 June 1917, the day before his battalion withdrew to bivouacs. The Battle of Messines (7–14 June 1917) was a momentous event in Irish history, because for the first time the 16th (Irish) and

36th (Ulster) Divisions fought alongside each other. Despite the Home Rule crisis and the Easter Rising, Irishmen of both traditions put aside their differences and marched together into battle. General Plumer, in a well planned attack, assisted his troops to see what lay ahead of them by making available a scaled model of the Ridge. Plumer detonated 9,500 tons of explosives under German defences in 19 mines. At Messines Ridge on 7 June, two officers and 23 men were killed or died of wounds and 5 officers and 216 men wounded. Nothing of note happened on the 8th and work on consolidation was continued. The German artillery activity increased, especially during the latter part of the day, but concentrated effort was made in the 2nd Rifles sector. By the time they withdrew to bivouacs on 11 June there had been additional casualties.[113]

His grave is at I. A. 9. Messines Ridge British Cemetery, south of Ieper town, Belgium and he is commemorated on the Great War Memorial, Kilgobbin. He was awarded the British War and Victory medals.

Tommy Kenny, a retired Irish Army Trooper, and one of only two soldiers to survive the Niemba massacre on 8th November 1960 is a great-nephew of Pte Christopher Mulligan. He told the author that two great-uncles were killed in the war; however it has not been possible to identify the second brother or confirm Tommy's story. Christopher was born in Sandyford, the son of Edward Mulligan (farmer) and Esther Mulligan (née Williams), of Blackglen, Sandyford. Edward and Esther were married in St Mary's Roman Catholic Church, Sandyford on 12 June 1864. There were at least fifteen children born to the couple, of whom ten survived birth, but it was possible to find records of only seven children. Their names were Thomas, Maria, Christopher, John, Cornelius, Bernard and Esther. Their father, Edward, passed away in the years between 1901 and 1911.

RICHARDSON, Michael Paul

Private, Service No 14784, 7th Battalion, 'D' Company, (the 'Pals') Royal Dublin Fusiliers, 30th Brigade in the 10th (Irish) Division.

Private Michael Richardson was the only soldier killed near Chocolate Hill, Gallipoli, on 4 September 1915, just four days after his 20th birthday. Ronan Lee, a relative, stated that Sergeant Anderson, of the Military Police, wrote to Pte Richardson's parents: 'Michael was sitting at the foot of a tree writing a letter when a shrapnel shell exploded over him. He suffered no pain and we buried him near to where he fell.' Family history says that the blood-stained letter was sent to his parents.[114] Private Richardson was the last soldier, of those profiled in this book, to die in Gallipoli before Sir Ian Hamilton, Commander of the Gallipoli Forces was recalled to London on 16 October 1915, effectively ending his military career. He was replaced by General Sir Charles Monro, who immediately recommended evacuation.

His grave is at I. A. 5. Green Hill Cemetery, Turkey and he was awarded the 1914–1915 Star, British War and Victory medals. He was one of many men, associated with rugby football, who joined the ranks of the Royal Dublin Fusiliers, 'D' Company, (the 'Pals') at Lansdowne Road in 1914. Further information on his progress from enlistment to death can be seen earlier in this chapter in the profile of his cousin, L/Cpl Arnold Moss.

Michael was the youngest son of John Paul Richardson (building contractor) and Ellen Richardson (née Courtney) of, Pembroke Lodge, which was on the site of the present-day Dundrum Credit Union.

He was born in Dundrum on 31 August 1895, and educated at St Mary's College, Rathmines, where he played rugby for his school. The Richardsons were a prominent family in Dundrum, where they owned many houses and shops built by John Paul. There were eleven children in the family: William, John, Mary, James, Arthur, Eileen, Florence, Michael, Charlotte, Irene and Ethel.

John Paul's grandfather, William Richardson (1796–1870) built Pembroke Cottages, situated opposite the Roman Catholic Church in Dundrum, whilst William's brother John Trimble Richardson, a farmer and builder, was responsible for building the present Kilternan Church of Ireland, which was consecrated on 10 December 1826. The marriage of Michael's great-grandfather, William Richardson to Mary Plunkett, a Roman Catholic, cut him and his descendants off from the rest of the family; however, today the relationship between the families is much closer. Michael Richardson was a third cousin of Arnold Moss, a fellow 'Pal' of 'D' Company, the families being related through Arnold's grandmother, Mary Moss (née Richardson).[115]

SAUNDERS, Thomas Ernest

Private, Service No 10/1329, 'B' Company, Wellington Infantry Regiment, New Zealand Expeditionary Force.

He was on service in Egypt in January 1915 before being sent to Turkey where he was killed in action, aged 26, in Gallipoli on 29 April 1915. At the tail end of the Battle of the Landing, 23 members of the Wellington Infantry Battalion were killed in action on 29 April. His battalion seized Russell's Top, on 27 April, and was still holding on when Pte Saunders was killed.[116]

He is commemorated on the Lone Pine Memorial, Gallipoli, Turkey; New Zealand Army Roll of Honour, and the Great War Memorial, Christ Church of Ireland, Taney, Dundrum. He was awarded the 1914–15 Star, British War and Victory medals. Thomas was a member of the Ulster Volunteers for a period of eighteen months before emigrating to New Zealand, where he lived at 164, Whittaker Street, Gisborne. He was employed as an accountant before enlisting in the New Zealand Army on 21 October 1914. Details on his attestation papers suggest that his mother may not have been informed of his death until 10 June 1916. He was born on 17 March 1889, the son of John Saunders (deceased) and Frances Anne Saunders of 1, Sydenham Place, Dundrum, who was widowed aged 32. There were three children in the family: Thomas Ernest, Evelyn and Gladys. In a short form of will he bequeathed all that he possessed to his mother, including his military pay left at the General Post Office in Gisborne, New Zealand.[117]

SWEENEY, George Columbus

Private, Service No 23837, 2nd Battalion Royal Munster Fusiliers, 3rd Brigade in the 1st Division. Secondary Regiment, Service No 7052 Lancers of the Line.

He was killed in action, aged 19, on 10 November 1917 during the Passchendaele campaign. On the 6 November 1917 the battalion numbered 20 officers and 630 other ranks when it arrived at Irish Farm in the Ypres salient. The ground was a quagmire full of water-logged shell-holes following four months of battle. The Munsters were to be one of two battalions leading the 1st Division's attack at 6am on 10th November. Weighed down with equipment they waded waist deep through mud and water, initially taking all objectives within forty-five minutes. Some hours later the battalion was reduced to 7 officers and 240 other ranks, over 400 officers and men having become casualties.[118]

He is commemorated on the Tyne Cot Memorial, situated nine kms north-east of Ieper town, Belgium. Private George Sweeney was named among twenty soldiers remembered by the staff and students at Kingstown School, Swindon, on Friday 9 November 2012. His name was proposed by a relative, who was member of staff at the college. He was awarded the British War and Victory medals. The 2nd Dublins landed at Le Havre on 14 August 1914; however, Pte Sweeney did not enlist until 1916.

He was the son of the late Hugh Sweeney and Bridget Byrne. Hugh hailed from Co Derry and worked with the grocery chain Leverett & Frye in Sackville Street and Bridget came from a farming background in Co Wexford. The couple opened a greengrocers shop at 5, Harold's Cross Road and had six children: George Columbus, May, Michael, Patrick, Hugh and Margaret Esther. Declan and Hugh Sweeney are the nephews of George Sweeney, and the following are extracts of their unpublished work, *A Tale of Two Brothers*.

The tragic story of Bridget Sweeney and her sons, George and Michael, has not been put in the public domain. Even the immediate family was torn between celebrating one or the other's life and death. George died on the winning side and was quietly forgotten, whilst Michael died on the losing side and was, together with his mother, relegated to whispered remembrances within the family.

> Hugh and Bridget came from strong Nationalist and Roman Catholic backgrounds and they instilled the same values in their children. Hugh died suddenly when he was only thirty-eight and Bridget had a hard struggle to run a shop and bring up a family on her own. Her two eldest sons, George and Michael, were constantly bickering, because they had different views on almost everything, including politics. However, they both joined the Irish Volunteers together in 1914.

Michael lied about his age as he was only thirteen. A short time later there was a split in the Irish Volunteer movement with the majority siding with John Redmond MP. George followed Redmond's line while Michael favoured Eoin McNeill's view that England's difficulty was Ireland's opportunity. The tension grew in the Sweeney household and eventually became unbearable. Finally, after a typical family row, George left home in 1916 and enlisted in the British Army. Our father, Hugh, the youngest brother of George, rarely mentioned his name to us, but when he did it was with great affection and sadness. Just once he told us the story of that fateful day George went off to take the 'King's shilling'. Our father ran after George and walked with him to Portobello Bridge. While they were tearfully embracing George slipped a half crown piece into Hugh's hand, turned and went away. Our father described being overwhelmed by a sense of shame that there had been a price on his love of his older brother. As George disappeared Hugh threw the coin into the canal. He was never to see his beloved brother again.

Michael's role models in history were Wolfe Tone, Robert Emmet and the Young Irelander, John Mitchel. He joined the Irish Volunteers in 1914, trained and drilled with the 4th Battalion in the Dublin Mountains a number of times weekly. He fought in the 1916 Rising under Eamon Ceannt and his second in command, Cathal Brugha, in the South Dublin Union, stationed at what is now St James's Hospital. He was then only fifteen and if not the youngest, he was certainly one of the youngest volunteers involved in the conflict. The small garrison of volunteers held out bravely for a week despite being heavily out-numbered and out-gunned in a fiercely contested battle. When they finally surrendered Cathal Brugha was carried on a stretcher and had numerous bullets lodged in his body. His leadership had made a lasting impression on the young volunteer Sweeney, who marched out proudly behind the stretcher with his hands held high above his head. Miraculously, Michael was not wounded, but there was a bullet hole in his volunteer's hat, which we were privileged to see and hold as young boys.[119]

The story of Michael Sweeney's part in the Irish War of Independence is fascinating and deserves to form part of a separate account about the less celebrated leaders in that war. Michael was a motor mechanic and gainfully employed, whilst a volunteer in the 4th Battalion. However, in December 1921 he gave up his job when chosen to go full time with the newly formed Active Service Unit (ASU). He was assigned to Section 4 as second in command to Gus Murphy. When Gus was killed on 24 March 1921 Michael was immediately promoted to Section Commander.

Shortly after the truce was signed on 11 July 1921 the Active Service Unit was disbanded and reformed with a new name, different structures and a changed agenda. It was to be known henceforth as 'The Guard' and all members were given officer rank. The purpose of the company was to protect the institutions of the state when it came into existence and would form the nucleus of a new National Army. The vast majority of the 'The Guard' favoured acceptance of the treaty, but Lieutenant Michael Sweeney and a small minority rejected it completely. His position in the new company was becoming increasingly untenable and he began drifting back to old companions in the 4th Battalion. On 19 February 1922 he was arrested along with six other men on suspicion that they were involved with robberies of military motor vehicles in Dublin. At 6.15pm on 10 April 1922, the second day of his appearance in court, the President closed the proceedings and members retired to consider their verdict. When the lorry escorting Michael Sweeney and his comrades reached the corner of Nassau Street and Grafton Street a scuffle broke out in the back of the lorry and Sweeney was shot dead from close range. The inquest was held at Jervis Street Hospital two days later and the verdict was accidental death. Lieutenant Michael Sweeney's coffin, draped in the tricolor, was taken to St Paul's Hall, attached to the Passionist monastery of Mount Argus, where he lay in state. His remains were taken to Glasnevin Cemetery, where in an impressive ceremony, Brigade-Commander, Oscar Traynor, gave the graveside oration. His nephews concluded:

> Private George Sweeney was killed in action, far away from home and family, in a Belgian battlefield. He has no grave, just his name inscribed on a memorial wall in a cemetery. For George there was no lying in state, no massive funeral procession, no graveside oration, no last post sounded by a bugler, no firing party and no grieving family present. As far as we are aware no member of George's immediate family has travelled to Belgium to pay their last respects.[120]

Chapter Five

Carrickmines and Foxrock

'A Soldier's Grave'
Then in the lull of midnight, gentle arms
Lifted him slowly down the slopes of death
Lest he should hear again the mad alarms
Of battle, dying moans, and painful breath.
And where the earth was soft for flowers we made
A grave for him that he might better rest.
So, Spring shall come and leave it seet arrayed,
And there the lark shall turn her dewy nest.[1]

–Francis Ledwidge

HISTORY AND ROLL OF HONOUR

Beatrice Elvery (later, Lady Glenavy) was one of the best known artists in Ireland. Her family moved from Bray to live in Carrickmines in 1888 and Beatrice was charmed with her new place of residence. She wrote: 'The country around Carrickmines was beautiful. We knew every field and lane in it! The best ponds for leeches, water beetles and newts: the best streams for minnows and sticklebacks. We knew the best places for primroses, blackberries and mushrooms.'[2] Her brother, 2nd Lt William M. Elvery, Royal Inniskilling Fusiliers, was wounded, but survived the Great War.

Carrickmines railway station was adjacent to the croquet and lawn tennis club owned by William Wilson, whose family home at Carrickmines House could be reached from the club along a path known locally as Waterman's Way. The local post office, managed by Esther Hackett, was situated in the valley close to Carrickmines River and adjacent to Mooney's farm. The farm land extended along each side of Glenamuck Road leading to Golden Ball. Anecdotal information says that Glenamuck Road is a 'famine' road and employment in road improvements may have been carried out during the Famine years to relieve impoverished victims. However, according to nineteenth-century maps the road was already in existence at the time of the Great Famine.[3] In more recent times Mooney's farm became well known as the site, where the foundations of Carrickmines Castle were uncovered. The castle was the scene of the 'Siege of Carrickmines' in 1642. Another field opposite the post office and alongside the Golf Lane was the site of the old Fair Green, where fairs were held on the first Wednesday of each month up to the middle of the nineteenth century. The Golf Lane led to William Wilson's farm and Carrickmines Golf Club. The river ran under the bridge and meandered alongside the gardens of Priorsland, a large Victorian house, which is said to have had a traditional prior's walk close by. This house was later to become the residence of well-known businessman and owner of Irish Independent Newspapers, T.V. Murphy, son of William Martin Murphy, the name mostly associated with the 1913 lockout in Dublin. The existing few labourers' cottages situated on the Ballyogan Road, close to the village, and a few more along the road in the direction of Kilgobbin, were there in 1914. These cottages are adjacent to a well-preserved section of the Pale ditch identified by Rob Goodbody.[4] A total of nine men and one woman from the village and townland of Carrickmines lost their lives during the Great War and at least three others served, but survived the conflict.

In the early nineteenth century, Foxrock was a stunning rural countryside situated between the mountains and the sea. When the Harcourt Street Railway line was built in 1854 and Foxrock railway station opened a few years later, this beautiful area of South County Dublin was within commuting distance of the city. The brothers, William and John Bentley, leased the lands of the Foxrock Estate from the Ecclesiastical Commissioners and Richard Whatley, the Church of Ireland Archbishop of Dublin, for the purpose of creating an affluent leafy suburb. The development of the village included the construction of a hotel and three roads – Brighton, Torquay and Westminster – which today are among the best known suburban roads in Ireland.

Due to a slower than expected take-up, the Bentley brothers got into financial difficulties and when they mortgaged their last piece of land in 1867 it signalled the end of their enterprise in the area. The Royal Exchange Assurance Company took over ownership of the Foxrock Estate and it was at this time that the hotel, which had become derelict, was converted into tenements catering for up to thirteen families. The Company was also responsible for constructing the village's first dwellings in 1901. They were known as Brighton and Orchard Cottages, from which five young men perished in the Great War. The cottages were rented to men and women who were available for gardening and domestic work in the large houses and as coachmen or dairymen in the Foxrock and Carrickmines area. In the period up to the outbreak of the Great War, locals showed great allegiance to the Royal Family. King Edward VII visited Leopardstown Racecourse in April 1904 and King George V made a visit in July 1911. Foxrock village was decorated with flags and coloured bunting for the occasion. This loyal support for the Royal family changed following the 1916 Easter Rising. During the war, people were encouraged to grow food, and Rathdown District Council sought land for the families living in the old hotel, but no land was made available by local land owners. Nevertheless, a small number of residents used the railway banks, where they also grazed their goats.[5]

Sir Horace Plunkett MP, PC, KCVO, lived close to the village. He was the younger son of Lord Dunsany, of Dunsany Castle, Co Meath and was elected Unionist MP for South County Dublin in the years between 1982, but lost his seat to the Nationalist candidate, J.J. Mooney in 1900. Sir Horace was an expert in agricultural cooperation and Vice President, Department of Agriculture and Technical Instruction, Ireland. He worked with dairy farmers in the south of Ireland where he formed most harmonious relationships with Christian denominations in his enlightened work for agricultural co-operation.[6] His house at Kilteragh, Foxrock, was burned down in 1923 by anti-treaty Republicans. On learning that his house had been destroyed, he said: 'It is sad but I can bear it. It is not so sad as if it had been a poor man's one roomed house.'[7]

A house can be rebuilt, but the destruction of so many books, papers and works of art was a great loss to the country. Plunkett said: 'I had too many things it is true; but I had records of real historical importance.' His collection, lost in the fire, included 'fifty paintings by George William Russell, (AE); twenty paintings by J.B. Yeats and one by Nathanial Hone, together with 1500 volumes of books and reports, many of them irreplaceable.'[8] His house at Foxrock was a well-known centre of hospitality where poets and wits met, together with those who were concerned to support Plunkett's plans and hopes for the agricultural development of Ireland. Just three days before he was murdered, Michael Collins visited Kilteragh in the company of Lady Lavery. Frequent guests to Kilteragh included, George Bernard Shaw, George Moore and George William Russell, who wrote under the pseudonym AE.[9] Sir Horace Plunkett was a member of the Senate; Chairman of Foxrock Golf Club; Trustee of St Brigid's National School, Foxrock, and Trustee of the Workman's Club, Kingstown. He was a cousin of Count George Plunkett of Golden Ball. A short time following the fire at Kilteragh, Horace Plunkett left Ireland to live in England. The fire was seen by many people as a meaningless act of revenge against a man who contributed so much to Irish agriculture. At the birth of a fragile new state, Ireland needed all the expertise it could muster and it could ill afford the loss of a man of Plunkett's calibre. Sir Horace Plunkett did not favour any one form of worship, but was deeply concerned about the people's welfare.

Foxrock Railway Station was situated in the village alongside Leopardstown Racecourse, which was completed in 1888. Two shops, McEvoy's, followed by Lynch's, were opened by residents in Brighton Cottages. Both families lost a relative in the Great War. Two other residents, Mrs Sharpe and Mrs Foran, opened tea rooms to cater for sightseers who travelled to Foxrock by train at weekends. The Findlater family, who lost four men in the war, opened its grocery shop in the village in 1904. The local post office was managed by the sub-postmistress, Elizabeth Byrne and the local garage was in the ownership of the Treacy family. Foxrock Golf Club, founded in 1889, was situated on the Torquay Road a short distance from the village.

Leopardstown Park Hospital was presented to the Ministry of Pensions in 1916 by the widow of James Talbot Power (Power's Distillery), and it opened the following year, as a hospital and home for the care and treatment of soldiers who had been disabled or injured during the Great War.[10]

Before he died, Brendan Reynolds related a story about his involvement in a game-shooting incident in the grounds of Leopardstown Park Hospital in the 1940s:

One day in the late 1940s, it was brought to my notice that a flock of wildfowl was frequenting a small lake situated behind the hospital. I set out with some friends early on a Saturday morning, across the racecourse to the lake where wildfowl were present in numbers. We began firing our guns, but almost immediately a man wearing a white coat came running towards us shouting: 'Stop! Stop! You fools, don't you know this is a Military Hospital; my patients are everywhere, diving for cover?' We had failed to take into account that the hospital was caring for many patients who were survivors of the Great War, suffering from the effects of shell shock. Apart from feeling foolish, we were very remorseful and promised that it would not happen again.[11]

FATHER AND SON KILLED IN THE TWO GREAT WARS
STEWART, Hugh DSO MC
Lieutenant-Colonel, 94th Field Ambulance Royal Army Medical Corps, in the 31st Division.

Previously attached to the 10th Field Ambulance in the 4th Division. He was killed, aged 38, while evacuating the wounded from an advanced dressing station, of which he was in charge at Strazeele on 12 April 1918. Stewart was at Outersteen, Merris and Strazeele on the morning of 12 April 1918, when 'the 93rd Brigade was driven by a very heavy counter-attack and 92nd Brigade had to fall back with it. Wounded soldiers in Outersteen and Merris were all cleared, when a space was found at a farm about a half-mile in behind Merris. At Strazeele, Lt-Col Stewart was killed with Lt Jibb and another soldier wounded. "It was terrible, everyone being blown to bits by shellfire".[12] His commanding officer wrote of Hugh's efficiency and sympathetic nature, which the latter had endeared him to the men: 'I was about to appoint him to command – casualty clearing station. I recently inspected his field ambulance, and came away so refreshed, feeling that I had seen something really efficient.'[13]

His grave is at B. 1. Borre Churchyard, France and he is commemorated on the Roll of Honour, Tullow Church of Ireland, Carrickmines; Hall of Honour, Trinity College, Dublin; Roll of Honour of the Royal Medical Corps in the Chapter House of Westminster Abbey and on the family grave in the south-west section of Dean's Grange Cemetery. He was awarded the Distinguished Service Order (DSO) and Military Cross (MC). 'His DSO was awarded in November 1916, but it is not clear in which engagements he achieved this distinction. One possibility is the Arras offensive in the spring of 1917, which was a major engagement for the 31st Division.'[14]

On 1 January 1915, Lt-Col Stewart was the first officer in the Royal Army Medical Corps to be awarded the Military Cross, and he received his decoration at

Buckingham Palace in March 1916. He was also 'Mentioned in Despatches' on four occasions; on 9 December 1914; 1 January 1916; 4 January 1917 and 29 May 1917.[15] His campaign awards were the 1914 Star, British War and Victory medals. His entire five piece medal group and bronze memorial plaque was auctioned off at Purdy and Sons Auctioneers, London, in April 2006.[16]

Hugh Stewart joined the Royal Medical Corps on 5 September 1905 with the rank of Lieutenant and served with the 10th Field Ambulance. He was promoted to Captain on 31 January 1909 with further promotion to Major on 15 October 1909, while he was with the 10th Field Ambulance. The 10th Field Ambulance was a regular army unit, which was to be part of the original British Expeditionary Force, but was held back in England at the last minute to counter any German invasion. Stewart arrived in France on 20 August 1914 and may have been involved in the Battles of Cateau, Marne and Messines in 1914. It appears from his Service Records that he was with the 2nd Field Ambulance on 9 November when he received promotion to Lieutenant-Colonel in 1915.

> It is impossible to say with certainty when he transferred to the 94th Field Ambulance, which was part of the 31st Division. However, it is likely that he left France for Egypt with the 31st Division on 7 December 1915, with Divisional HQ being established at Port Said on Christmas Eve. The last units arrived in Egypt on 23 January 1916. The Division took over the No 3 Sector of the Suez Canal defences and Divisional HQ moved to Kantara on 23 January1916. The stay in Egypt was short, and during the five days, 1st to 6th of March, the Division sailed to Marseilles for service on the Western Front. The 31st Division subsequently remained in France and Flanders and took part in the Battle of Albert, including the attack on Serre and the Battle of the Ancre.[17]

Hugh Stewart was the son of Capt Hugh Stewart and Harriet Emily Stewart (née St George) of Hatley, Kerrymount Avenue, Foxrock. His grandfather was the late Sir Hugh Stewart Bt, Ballygawley House, Co Tyrone. There were five children in the family; Mary Elizabeth, Agnes Grace, Harriet Amy, Hugh and Herbert St George. The three youngest children were born in Kilkenny city, while Mary was born in

Co Tyrone in 1876 and her sister Agnes was born in Dublin in 1877. Captain Hugh Stewart, formerly of the Cheshire Regiment, was governor of the prison service in Kilkenny in the years 1877 and 1900. When he retired the family resided, for a short time at Park Avenue, Pembroke East, Donnybrook, before moving out to live at Kerrymount Avenue, Foxrock. His residence was close to Cooldrinagh House the home of the famous playwright, Samuel Beckett. Captain Stewart died in 1909. His wife, Harriett, who retained a residence in Kilkenny, passed away in 1934.

Hugh junior was born in Kilkenny city on Good Friday, 15 April, 1881 and received his early education at Corrig School, Kingstown, before entering Trinity College. He took his degrees – MB, BCh, BAO – at Trinity and qualified as a medical practitioner in 1905. Hugh married Muriel Dalzell McKean in India in 1909 and they lived at 4, Rostrevor Terrace, Rathgar. The couple had three children. Their son, Major Hugh Dalzell Stewart, Second in Command ,West Yorkshire Regiment, 2nd Battalion, died of wounds received in action on 1 April 1941, while serving in the Second World War. He married Arlie Woodhead from Brisbane, Australia and the couple lived at 19, Zion Road, Rathgar. Major Stewart was buried in 1. C. 6. Keran War Cemetery, West of Asmara, Eritrea, Africa. He was predeceased by his mother Muriel.

The younger brother of Lieutenant-Colonel Stewart, Lieutenant Herbert St George Stewart, Royal Inniskilling Fusiliers, 6th Battalion, served in the Great War and survived the conflict. Herbert was born in Kilkenny in 1888, entered Trinity College in 1906 and enlisted in the army in 1914. He married Eileen Elizabeth Burberry of Hampshire, England, and they had one daughter, Barbara.

ALL FIVE WILSON SONS JOIN THE MILITARY, FOUR DIE IN UNIFORM
William Henry Wilson and Emily Charlotte Wilson (née Hone) had seven children: William Henry, Emily Constance, Eva Jane, Charles Robert, George Henry, John Hugh and Arthur Hone. Four sons enlisted in the British Army prior to the outbreak of the Great War and the eldest boy was already serving. Tragically, only one came home. William Wilson married a second time when his wife Emily died in 1914 aged 61. His marriage to Marcella Ester Barrett took place in 1915. Marcella was secretary of the Carrickmines Croquet / Tennis Club, and she died in 1926. William passed away in 1931 while living at 24, Newton Court, London and was interred in the churchyard at Kilternan Church of Ireland with his first wife, Emily, and their daughter, Constance

Mitchell. The stained-glass window in Tullow Church of Ireland, Carrickmines, designed by local artist Beatrice Elvery was erected by William Wilson and dedicated to three of his fallen sons. The theme of the stained glass is three knights in armour offering their swords to the Lord.

William Henry Wilson, a stockbroker with the Dublin firm of William Wilson & Sons, farmed extensively at Carrickmines and had a great love of sport. He formed Carrickmines Golf Club in 1900, was its president from 1923 until 1931, captain in 1904 and treasurer from 1900–1915.[18] It was also due to his generosity that Carrickmines Croquet / Lawn Tennis Club was established in 1903.

The eldest son, Lieutenant William Henry Wilson, Royal Warwickshire Regiment, died in India in 1905. Captain John Hugh Wilson, Royal Field Artillery was the only son to survive the war. When three sons were killed in action, representations were made to the appropriate authorities on behalf of Capt Wilson. As the last surviving male member of the family, he was withdrawn from the front lines on compassionate grounds in March 1918. It is very likely that his family took advantage of a ruling introduced by the British Government on 29 October 1917, which stated: 'When all sons, except one, have been killed in action, the remaining son is exempted from infantry.'[19] Second Lieutenant Wilson was promoted to full Lieutenant on 1st June 1916 and was granted the rank of acting Captain whilst commanding a section of a Divisional Ammunition Column from 12 October 1917.[20] On 2 September 1918 the London Gazette published the following: 'Lieutenant (acting Captain) J.H. Wilson relinquishes acting rank of Captain on alteration in posting, 30 Mar 1918.'[21] This latter entry was the one that caught the eye at first for the phrase: 'on alteration of posting'. This alteration meant he reverted to Lieutenant and by implication meant he gave up the role of commanding a section of a Divisional Ammunition Column. He was also posted, which meant that he was sent somewhere else possibly back to England before returning home to Ireland.[22]

Hugh Wilson was a stockbroker and managed the family business in the city while continuing to farm at Carrickmines. He was born on 22 September 1888, attended Aravon School in Bray, Co Wicklow and entered Trinity College, in 1906, where he took his agriculture degree in 1918, following his return from war. He married Victoria Alice Payne in November 1915 at St Saviour's Church, Paddington, London. Following Victoria's death in 1921 he married, as his second wife, Gwendolyn Alice Sherlock Richardson Oliver, of Doneraile, Co Cork in1929, and they lived at

Little Gate, Brighton Road, Carrickmines. There was further tragedy awaiting him when Gwendolyn passed away in 1955. He was not blessed with children in either marriage. In the 1950s, his herd of jersey cattle was one of the best known in the country, winning many first prizes at the annual RDS Spring Show in Ballsbridge, Dublin. Apart from his stockbroking business, he was also chairman of McKenzie's of Pearse Street, suppliers of agricultural machinery. Hugh Wilson continued his father's sporting interest in Carrickmines Croquet / Tennis Club and Carrickmines Golf Club. He served as president of the Golf Club for a ten-year period until his death, treasurer from 1922–1925 and served as club captain in 1928. He died while on holiday in the Canary Islands in May 1966 and was interred with his two wives in the churchyard at Kilternan Church of Ireland, Kilternan.

Hugh's sister, Emily Constance, married widower George Mitchell in 1909, and they lived at Greyhouse, Carrickmines. She served as Lady President of Carrickmines Golf Club from 1924 until her death in 1935 at age 55.[23] George Mitchell's son, Francis, by his first marriage to Anne Mitchell, also died in the Great War and his profile may be seen in Chapter Seven.

WILSON, George Henry MC
Major, 'D' Battery, 282nd Brigade Royal Field Artillery, in the 56th Division; Previously, 1/3rd London Regiment, Royal Field Artillery.

He died from the effects of gas poisoning, aged 27, at the Advanced Dressing Station situated at Minty Farm, Belgium, on 4 November 1917. On the day he died at Minty Farm, Langemarck-Poelcapelle, his 'D' Battery had 282 severely gassed and several casualties. The major engagement of the time was the second Battle of Passchendaele. Wilson's commanding officer wrote to his father: 'Your son performed his duties to my entire satisfaction; they were hard, calling for both courage and endurance, in neither of which he was ever lacking. He won for himself the respect and affection of all ranks.'[24]

His grave is at II. E. 12, Gwalia Cemetery, situated 8.5kms west of Ieper town centre, Belgium. He is commemorated on the Wilson Memorial and Great War Memorials, Tullow Church of Ireland, Carrickmines; Great War Memorial, Stock Exchange,

London; Hall of Honour, Trinity College; St Luke's Church, Kensington, London, and Aravon School War Memorial, Bray, Co Wicklow. The cemetery was named after Gwalia Farm and is situated 400 metres behind the farm. It was originally started in July 1917, in the period between the Battle of Messines and the third Battle of Ypres. The present-day owner of the farm, Paul Leichar, inherited the property from his parents. His grandparents were in possession of Gwalia Farm during the Great War, when the main barn was used as a hospital for the 134th Field Ambulances. Paul Leichar said that 'railway lines were constructed for the purpose of bringing casualties in and out of the base. Soldiers who died of wounds were shipped out at night under cover of darkness to avoid demoralising other wounded men.'[25] Major Wilson was awarded the Military Cross in May 1917 and his citation read as follows:

> For conspicuous gallantry and devotion to duty—on one occasion carrying two advances and bringing his guns into action in an exposed position with great skill and judgment, and carrying on harassing fire without being located by the enemy. He has repeatedly set an example to his men by his coolness and courage when his battery has been under heavy shell fire.[26]

He was 'Mentioned in Despatches' by Field-Marshal Douglas Haig, Commander-in-Chief of the British Armies in France, on 9 April 1917, and was awarded the 1915 Star, British War and Victory medals.

> At the outbreak of war George Wilson volunteered to join the London Brigade, Royal Field Artillery, which was a Territorial Force unit of part-time volunteer soldiers. His medal index card shows that he was with the 1/3rd London Regiment Royal Field Artillery. On the 25th February 1916 the artillery re-joined the London Division, re-numbered as the 56th Division. The 56th Infantry Division fought at 'Gommecourt' (1 July); The 'Battle of Ginchy' (9 September); the 'Battle of Flers-Courcelette' (15–22 September); the 'Battle of Morval' (25–27 September); in which the Division captured Combles; and the 'Battle of the Transloy Ridges' (11–29 October), which were all phases of the Somme 1916. As the war developed Wilson was promoted and may have served with different batteries, but at his death he was in

command of 'D' Battery, with 4.5 howitzers.[27]

Major Wilson developed a septic finger on his right hand and attended the General Western Hospital, Manchester on 22 November 1916, where he was considered unfit for duty. A serious problem with his finger had developed and it was said to be, 'worse than useless and constantly getting in the way.' When Major Wilson became anxious to have the finger amputated at his own expense, the Board recommended two months leave for the amputation, which took place at The Military Hospital, York, on 23 March 1917. Following his recovery he was posted to light duties for a period of one month before returning to the front line.[28]

George Wilson, born on 13 June 1890 at Carrickmines, was educated at Aravon School (1899–1902), Radley College, Abington, England (1903–1907) and he entered Trinity College in 1907. He joined the London Stock Exchange in 1911. His marriage to Clementina Mary Ellis, daughter of Sir Robert Ellis Cunliffe Knight, solicitor to the Board of Trade, took place on 16 July 1912 at the Holy Trinity Church, Brompton, London, and the couple lived at 43, Elm Park Gardens, London. They had one daughter, Clementina Anne, born at home on 24 August 1913. His wife was residing at 34, The Grove, Bolton, London, SW, in 1931 and became Mrs Heath when she remarried at Kensington in June 1933.[29] Prior to the outbreak of war George Wilson was a Trustee of Carrickmines Golf Club and a member of Carrickmines Croquet & Tennis Club.

WILSON, Arthur Hone

Lieutenant, 4th Battalion, attached 7th Battalion Royal Irish Fusiliers, 49th Brigade in the 16th (Irish) Division.

By 8pm on 11 November the battalion was at Varennes and on the 12th it drew combat stores. Then at 5.30pm on the same day the battalion marched to Englebelmer. From there it marched forward, platoon by platoon, to assembly trenches at Hamel via Martinsart and Mesnil. The night was now moon-lit and it was not very cold. Lieutenant Arthur Wilson and 2nd Lt N.C. Whitall were attached to the Brigade as liaison officers. Hot soup and rum were issued at 5am and at the same time trench coats were taken off and stacked in bundles in the trenches. The attack on the enemy trenches started at 6.25am on 13 November, but it quickly became confused in the morning fog. This battle for enemy trenches lasted until nightfall on the following day, the 14 November. Lieutenant Wilson was listed among the casualties as wounded in the advance at Beaucourt and following the amputation of a leg, he died, aged 21, four days later on 18 November 1916, in the General Hospital, Camiers, France.[30] His adjutant wrote: 'At the time he fell he was gallantly leading his company in an attack. He was most popular with both officers and men of his battalion and we all much deplore his death.' A brother officer saw him and stated: 'He was leading his company in the advance on Beaucourt and those who saw him say he was splendid and feared nothing and even when hit urged on his men who were all very fond of him.' A non-commissioned Officer wrote: 'Lt Wilson was every inch a true soldier. He was an extremely popular officer with all his men, and was always ready to do any kindness to any of us.'[31]

His grave is at I. B. 69. Etaples Military Cemetery, Etaples, France, and he is commemorated on the Wilson Memorial and Great War Memorial, Tullow Church of Ireland, Carrickmines; Hall of Honour, Trinity College; Great War Memorial, Tonbridge School in Kent, and Aravon School War Memorial in Bray, Co Wicklow. He was awarded the 1914–15 Star, British War and Victory medals.

He obtained a nomination for Sandhurst Military College, where he was gazetted to the Royal Fusiliers (City of London Regiment) on 17 February 1915, and posted to France on 9 June of the same year. He was wounded at Loos on 16 June 1915 and was promoted to lieutenant on 28 October 1915. The young officer spent time in hospital twice during that year with gunshot wounds to his legs and back. His injuries, obtained in July 1915, caused him to lose power in his lower limbs and he was invalided home where he was cared for by his family at Carrickmines House. He wrote to the War Office on the 19 July informing them that his leave of absence was over on the 28 July and he requested a medical board. Later in the year, on the 1 October 1915, he was in the Queen Alexandra Military Hospital with further gunshot wounds to his back. When he returned to the front in the following November, he was attached to the 7th Battalion, with whom he served until he died of wounds. The battalion was formed at Armagh in September 1914 as part of K2.[32]

Arthur was born on 30 June 1895 and was single. His early education was received at Aravon School, Bray, Co Wicklow, 1904–1908 and at Tonbridge School in Kent from 1908–1913. He entered Trinity College, Dublin, in 1913, where he was an undergraduate. Arthur was a member of Carrickmines Golf Club and Carrickmines Croquet & Tennis Club. His effects, sent to his father, included a book of poems and a religious emblem.

WILSON, Charles Robert MC

Second Lieutenant, 88th Company Machine Gun Corps (Infantry), 88th Infantry Brigade in the 29th Division. Secondary Regiment, 6th Battalion Royal Munster Fusiliers in the 29th Division.

He was killed in action, aged 31, on 24 May 1917. The 88th Company was at Monchy-le-Preux, south of the Scarpe River on 24/25 May 1917: '...with considerable aerial activity, in the afternoon, Major Morris and 2nd Lt Wilson started to go to the 9th Brigade. Unfortunately they ran into heavy enemy shelling and 2nd Lt Wilson was killed.'[33]

His grave is at I.E. 50. Level Crossing Cemetery, Fampoux, France. As a boy Charles slept within ear-shot of the old steam trains that passed by at the bottom of the garden of his home at Carrickmines House. Now he sleeps in his grave situated beside the railway line that runs through the village of Fampoux and facilitates trains that travel between Belgium and France.

He is commemorated on the Wilson Memorial and Great War Memorial, Tullow Church of Ireland, Carrickmines and the Great War Memorial, Radley College, England. Second Lieutenant Wilson was awarded the Military Cross early in May 1917, just before he was killed in action. His citation read: 'For conspicuous gallantry and devotion to duty. He maintained control of his guns throughout the whole operation in a very effective manner.' This was not published until after his death, but the Commonwealth War Graves Commission noted that he was aware that he had won the Military Cross before he was killed. Second Lieutenant Wilson may have won his award when in action at Monchy on 14 April 1917. 34 He was also awarded the British War and Victory medals.

Although he did not enter Trinity College as a student, Charles Wilson was a member of its OTC. He joined the army in 1915 and was posted to France on 9 December 1916. On the nights of 7 and 8 January 1916, the Division was evacuated from Gallipoli and all units returned to Egypt. It embarked in March and arrived in Marseilles and concentrated in the area east of Pont Remy. The Division remained on the Western Front for the remainder of the war.[35] Charles was born in Carrickmines on 10 June 1886 and attended Radley College in England. He was single and a member of Carrickmines Golf Club, where he held the position of Trustee and was its Honorary Secretary in 1911. His effects included a damaged wristwatch, pocket case and photo.

HALPIN, William Oswald

Captain, Royal Army Medical Corps, attached to the 4th (Queen's Own) Hussars as Regimental Medical Officer, in the 2nd Cavalry Division.

He died in Caix Military Hospital, France, on 10 August 1918, of wounds received on the previous day, while attending to a wounded soldier. He was aged 32. It was recorded in the war diary that a hostile aeroplane dropped a bomb on the regimental headquarters of the 4th Hussars on the previous day. 'On 9-10 August the 4th Hussars and 5th Lancers advanced and at 1.30pm "B" Squadron advanced and was delayed awhile until the infantry took Vrély. Enemy shelling was very heavy and resulted in Capt Halpin being killed and 8 other officers wounded before 2.30pm. There were also 50 other ranks killed and 27 wounded.'[36]

His grave is at III. BB. 8. Villers-Bretonneux Military Cemetery, Somme, France and he was the only member of the 4th (Queen's Own) Hussars to be buried in this cemetery. He is commemorated on the Roll of Honour at Tullow Church of Ireland, Carrickmines; Great War Memorials at St Andrews College, Booterstown; High School, Rathgar; Great War Memorial in the former Adelaide Hospital in Dublin, and the Hall of Honour, Trinity College. Captain Halpin was awarded the 1914 Star; British War and Victory medals.

He volunteered for service at the beginning of the war and received his commission in the Royal Army Medical Corps on 10 August 1914. The 4th Hussars were in Dublin during August 1914 as part of 3rd Cavalry Brigade in the Cavalry Division, and it moved to France on 6 September 1914, where Halpin was attached to the No 6 General Hospital. On completion of a year's service he was gazetted captain, and appointed medical officer with the 4th Hussars.[37]

He was the son of William Oswald Halpin and Anna Maria Halpin (née Burgess) of The Laurels, Torquay Road, Foxrock. 'His parents married on 2nd August 1881 at the Church of St Stephen, Dublin. William and Anna died in 1908 and 1933 respectively and were buried in the family plot at Mount Jerome Cemetery, Dublin. Anna Maria resided at 25, Holles Street, Dublin, but, was born at Tobinstown, Co

Carlow. The couple had two children, William Oswald and George.'[38]

William Oswald junior was born in Foxrock on 31 August, 1886 and received his early education at High School, Rathgar and St Andrew's College, Booterstown. He entered Trinity College in 1904, aged 17, and took his BA, MD, MB, B Ch and BAO degrees. 'The Foxrock man was appointed to Senior House Physician, Surgeon and SMO at the Metropolitan Hospital, Kingsland Row, London, for a period of two years before enlisting with the Royal Army Medical Corps. His last Will and Testament was made in January 1918 while on duty in France and was witnessed by two soldiers, one of whom was Pte Kane of the 4th Hussars. He bequeathed 550 guineas to his fiancée, Sybil Chamberlain of London, and the residue of his estate went to his brother, George. The sum of 550 guineas was not inconsiderable, and it is reasonable to assume that the couple were committed to each other as the war was nearing its conclusion in 1918.'[39]

His brother George was born in Foxrock in 1882 and died in England in 1958. 'He was educated at Wilson's Hospital School, Multyfarnham, Co Westmeath, High School, Rathgar, and graduated from Trinity College in 1908 with a BAO, B Ch, MD. He was a general practitioner based in Swallowfield, near Reading, at the time his brother, William, enlisted. George married Antoinette Berthe Ermerins from The Hague in Holland. They had two children; George Ermerins and Elizabeth Hester. Captain George Ermerins Halpin, Royal Army Service Corps, graduated from Cambridge University and was killed, aged 28, on 7 July 1942 while serving in the Second World War.'[40]

Relatives of Capt Halpin, who also died in the war include: Private Alfred Corrigan, South Irish Horse, killed on 19 June 1917 aged 22. He was the son of William and Susan Corrigan, of Garrettstown, Rathvilly, Co Carlow. Private Corrigan is buried in Grave XIX. A. 21, in Loos British Cemetery, France. Lance Corporal Albert Victor Ernest Corrigan, Canadian Infantry, British Columbia Regiment, 7th Battalion, was killed on 27 March 1917. He was the son of Thomas and Adelaide Corrigan, 118, East 59th Street, Chicago, USA and formerly of Killerig, Co Carlow. Lance Corporal Corrigan is commemorated on Screen Wall K. 737, Epsom Cemetery, England.[41] 'The wider Halpin family produced at least thirteen doctors, numerous sea captains, lawyers and engineers. Captain Halpin was the grandson and great-grandson of two very famous engineers, George Halpin senior and George Halpin junior.'[42]

The Irish historian, Turtle Bunbury, wrote: 'George senior was one of the most competent civil engineers operating in Ireland during the 19th century. He was an administrator of exceptional ability, praised in equal measure for the number of works he carried out and the intense perfectionism applied in each case. Following the death of Francis Tunstall in 1800, Dublin Corporation sought a new Inspector of Works to the Corporation for Preserving and Improving the Port of Dublin.'[43] Bill Webster, who is a relative of the family pointed out that 'George Halpin senior, at age 20 or 21, was appointed to the post of Inspector of Works to the Ballast Board and commenced his illustrious career with Dublin's ports and Ireland's lighthouses. George's wife Elizabeth, died in July 1850, and George collapsed and died suddenly while carrying out a lighthouse inspection in July 1854. The couple were buried at Mount Jerome Cemetery, where the headstone gives George's age as 75 years, at the time of death.'[44]

'His son, George Halpin junior, emerged to take up the challenge on 26th September 1830. He was a qualified civil engineer employed by the Board as Assistant Inspector of Works and Assistant Inspector of Lighthouses from June 1830. As such, George Halpin junior shared a good deal of the workload.'[45] 'In August 1847, the younger George was elected a full member of the Institution of Civil Engineers of Ireland, and in the years between 1834 and 1840, he was greatly involved in deepening the channels and building new quay walls east of the Custom House.'[46] 'George met Julia Villiers and they had nine children, but the couple did not marry straightaway and all the children were baptised Villiers. They only took the name Halpin in the 1860s, at an ailing George junior's request, when he and Julia were recorded in a legal document to have married. George Halpin Junior died in Dublin in 1869.'[47]

George junior was a first cousin of the famous, Captain Robert Charles Halpin of Wicklow. In 1868, before he reached the age of 40, Robert Charles Halpin FRGS was captain of the CS *Great Eastern*, and was responsible for connecting several of the world's continents by telegraph, laying nearly 30,000 miles of underwater cable. Today, Halpin's life and times is one of the important tourist attractions in Wicklow Town.[48]

MARTYR, John Francis

Captain, 1st Battalion, attached 6th Battalion, Royal Irish Rifles, 29th Brigade in the 10th (Irish) Division.

On the afternoon of 5 August the Irish Rifles sailed from Mundros and disembarked about midnight at Watson's Pier, Anzac Cove, where they moved into bivouacs in Shrapnel Gulley. The next day it was heavily shelled, resulting in many casualties and then the battalion moved to Rest Gulley. On 6 August it attacked and captured Rhododendron Ridge, but due to strong Turkish resistance and intolerable heat, it failed in its objectives at Chunuk Bair and Koja Chemen Tepe. However the next morning the northern edge of Chunuk Bair was carried after heavy fighting.[49] The battalion's war diary does not give details of the action, in which Capt Martyr was wounded, but, we know from the diary of Capt David Campbell MC that he was alive on the morning of the 9 August, he wrote: 'I overheard the CO and our Company Commander, Captain Martyr, discussing the possibility of attacking with two companies instead of two battalions...'[50] Captain Martyr was wounded on the 9 or 10 August and died, aged 33, aboard HMS *Canada* at 8pm on 11 August 1915. He was buried at sea in a service conducted by Reverend D.A. Reid. [51] Casualties for this period were: 3 officers and 42 other ranks killed, 18 officers and 274 other ranks wounded.

Captain Martyr is commemorated on the Helles Memorial, Turkey; War Memorial, Christ Church of Ireland, Bray, Co Wicklow and the War Memorial at Quinsborough Road, also in Bray. The Quinsborough Road War Memorial was erected by the people of Bray. He was awarded the 1914–15 Star, British War and Victory medals, which were sent to his wife, Evelyn, in 1921. He also served in the South African campaign in 1901 and 1902, where he was employed with the Mounted Infantry and awarded the Queen's South Africa medal with five clasps. Captain David Campbell MC wrote in his diary about a social occasion with Capt Martyr and his wife Evelyn in the Curragh Army Camp, Co Kildare, prior to embarking for England and finally Gallipoli:

> Early in the New Year a batch of promotions came through. All the regular lieutenants were made captains, including our Company Commander, J. F. Martyr. Like many of the others, he had been waiting over ten years for his captaincy. He also had been engaged to be married

for a number of years, but could not afford to do so. Now he wasted no time; he got married as soon as he became a captain and stayed with his wife at the Royal Oak Hotel, near the Royal Barracks. One evening he invited me and the other officers of his company to meet his wife. I don't think I saw such a devoted and happy pair. But, tragedy was close at hand, for he died of wounds after that fateful day on Gallipoli in August 1915, when the battalion went into action for the first time. We mourned the loss of a gallant officer and true friend. But what was our loss to that of his adoring wife who had waited so long for him?[52]

A brother officer wrote to his widow: 'Up to the last he was thinking of others. His life and death were those of a good and true man, and it is no lip service to say that he was the most popular officer in the Regiment. His honesty, kindness, and devotion to duty were obvious to everyone.'

And an old school fellow wrote:

> Two things stand out clearly in one's memories of John Martyr, known to us familiarly as 'Monkey.' First of all he was one of the clean, straight sort, with a natural hatred of all that was otherwise. Secondly he was universally popular, and his friendship was sought by old and young alike. He was a sportsman in the true sense of the word, and was seen at his best in a losing game. His ambitions had always centred on the army, and I am sure that, had the choice been given to him, he would have chosen to meet death in the way it came to him.[53]

Captain Martyr was born in Norwood, Surrey on 28 February 1882 and educated at King's School, Bruton, Somerset from 1895 to 1898. He was a keen sportsman and represented his school in cricket and football. He was gazetted 2nd lieutenant 1st Battalion, Royal Irish Rifles in May 1905, promoted lieutenant in April 1907 and appointed captain on 12 December 1914. The 6th Battalion was formed at Dublin in 1914 as part of KI and moved to the Curragh, Co Kildare in 1915. In May 1915 it moved to Hackwood Park (Basingstoke). The Battalion embarked at Liverpool and sailed to Gallipoli, via Mudros, on 7 July 1915; landing at Anzac Cove on 5 August 1915.[54]

He married Evelyn Violet Blake-Knox at Christ Church of Ireland, Bray, Co Wicklow on 25 November 1914 and following his departure to Gallipoli his wife resided at Springfield, Foxrock. He was the elder son of the late Peter Horace Martyr, barrister, and Amy Martyr. The father of the bride was the late Edward Ernest Blake-Knox and Evelyn's brother, Charles Blake Knox, acted as groomsman. Captain Martyr had two siblings; Horace Martyr and Miss L. Martyr, both of whom lived in London.

Thirteen years after her husband's death, Evelyn Martyr married Colonel Charles Evatt DSO in October 1928 at the Church of Ireland, Kill-of-the-Grange. Evatt, who had served in the war, purchased Kerrymount House, the former home of the late Arthur McMurrogh Murphy (the O'Morchoe) and Susan O'Morchoe. He re-named the house, Mount Louise. Colonel Evatt was Professor of Anatomy at the College of Surgeons in Dublin and a well-known personality in Dublin medical circles. He died in January 1941 and Evelyn passed away in October 1971.

CRAWFORD, Sydney George

Lieutenant, 3rd Battalion Royal Dublin Fusiliers, Secondary Regiment, Service No. 17/4350, South Irish Horse and Royal Irish Rifles.

He was drowned along with his sister, Letitia Harriet Hill, when on board the RMS *Leinster*, which was torpedoed by a German submarine fifteen miles due east of the North Wall, Dublin, on 10 October 1918.

> On the bridge of the *Leinster* Seaman Hugh Owen from Holyhead saw the second torpedo approaching from the port side. He pointed it out to Captain Birch, who shouted, 'Helm hard a-Port! Starboard full astern!' The intention was to swing the ship to starboard, to avoid the on-coming torpedo. Before the manoeuvre could be completed the torpedo struck the ship forward on the port side in the vicinity of the mailroom, where 22 postal sorters were at work. The torpedo's firing hammer struck the detonating cap. The resulting small explosion triggered the 160 kilograms of high explosive at the front of the torpedo. The exploding torpedo blew a hole in the port side of the ship, passed through the ship and blew a hole in the starboard side.[55]

Lieutenant Crawford's body was washed ashore on the west coast of Scotland six weeks after the tragedy and buried at Kirkbean Parish Churchyard, Kirkbean, Kirkcudbright, Scotland. He is commemorated with his sister, Letitia, on a Mural Tablet at St Brigid's Church of Ireland, Stillorgan, and the Dublin Boy Scouts Memorial, St Patrick's Cathedral, Dublin. He was awarded the 1914–15 Star, British War and Victory medals. His mother, Elizabeth, applied for his medals on 15 November 1921.

Sydney Crawford joined the South Irish Horse in September 1914, but in February 1915 he was discharged as medically unfit. However, in March 1915, he enlisted in the 7th Battalion, Royal Irish Rifles, with the rank of corporal. He saw action in the Loos and Hulluch sectors, served through numerous operations from December 1915, including, the Battle of the Somme, Passchendaele Ridge and the capture of Guillemont and Ginchy. Corporal Crawford was commissioned as a second lieutenant, and later was reassigned to the 3rd Battalion Royal Dublin Fusiliers, which was stationed in the Grimsby area. He learned of his promotion to full Lieutenant at his home in Stillorgan on the day before his death.[56]

Sydney, born on 25 August 1897, was the younger son of William Henry Crawford and Elizabeth Crawford of Carrickbawn, Torquay Road, Foxrock, and formerly of 26, Tipperstown, Stillorgan. The Crawfords had five children: Elizabeth, Sarah Jane, Letitia Harriet, Ernest Harold and Sydney George. Sidney and Letitia were on a visit home to see their sister, Sarah, who was unwell, and on the night of the tragedy they were accompanied by their parents on the journey to Kingstown to bid farewell. Letitia was the wife of Capt Valentine Hill of Brewery Road, Stillorgan, who survived the war.

CRONHELM, Arthur Geoffrey
Lieutenant, 23rd Training Squadron Royal Flying Corps. Secondary Regiment, 2nd and 22nd Battalion London Regiment.

He was killed in an accident, aged 23, on 6 September 1917 while flying a BE 2e 6294 with Capt R.G. McNaughton, who was injured. His aircraft collided with an Avro 504 flown by Lt Frank Lawrence Johnson of No 22 Training Squadron (formerly 5th Battalion, British West India Regiment), who was also killed.[57] His grave is at B. 23, Alexandria (Hadra) War Memorial Cemetery, Egypt and he is commemorated on the Great War Memorial, Christ's Hospital, Horsham and the Great War Memorial, St Matthias Church, Dublin, which was transferred to Christ Church, Leeson Park, Dublin. He was awarded the 1914–15 Star, British War and Victory medals.

Arthur Cronhelm had been in Chile, but returned home at the outbreak of war and obtained his commission on 22 February 1915. He fought in battles of Neuve Chapelle, Festubert, and Loos, where he was wounded. In November 1916 he transferred to the Royal Flying Corps.[58]

He was the son of Theodore and Mary Eleanor Cronhelm (née Williams), Craigend, Howth, who were married on 13 August 1884 at the Church of St Matthew, Irishtown. Theodore was a solicitor and practised at 19/21 Eustace Street, Dublin. He was a local preacher and leading Methodist layman. In the period 1923 to 1925 he lived at the The Tunnel, The Burnaby, Greystones, Co Wicklow, and then moved to live with his daughter, Mea, who also lived in Greystones. Theodore suffered from deafness and was killed, tragically, by a train at Greystones.[59] There were six children in the family; Newton Williams, Theodore Stuart, Richard Edward, Mea Matilda, Williams Coates and Arthur Geoffrey. The first two children were born when the family was residing at 29, Belgrave Road, Dublin.

Arthur was educated at Christ's Hospital, Horsham (1903–1910), where he was a member of the Cadet Corps and Bisley Reserve, and prior to joining the army he was employed as an insurance clerk. Having received his commission in 1915, he returned home to marry Anne Gladys Steen, on 11 November 1916, at Irishtown, Ringsend, and they lived at Verona, Kerrymount Avenue, Foxrock, the home of his father-in-law, David Millar Steen. There were no children in their brief marriage of eleven months.

Anne Gladys Cronhelm, married Mr John M. Semple, a physician in the East Africa Medical Service, in August 1921 at Tullow Church of Ireland, Carrickmines. Her father, David Millar Steen BL, described as, 'formerly of the Ceylon Civil Service' died during 1949 at his home, Mount Sandal, Carrickmines. Anne Gladys had two siblings, Francis and Robert.

The name 'Cronhelm' originated in Germany and goes back to the mid-sixteenth century. An army officer, Wilhelm Georg Otto von Cronhelm, was taken captive by the Spanish in Minorca and shipped back to Plymouth in the late 1700s. He elected to stay in England and one of his sons married into the Crosbie family and hence the move to Ireland. This family fought on both sides in the Great War.

Two Dublin cousins emigrated to Canada, where they enlisted in the Canadian Army and were both killed in action during the Great War: Gunner Edward William Arthur Cronhelm, Canadian Field Artillery, 12th and 3rd Brigades was killed in action on 8 May 1917, and was interred in grave III. A. 33. Barlin Communal Cemetery Extension, Pas de Calais, France. He was the son of the Reverend C. A. Cronhelm, BA and Jeannie Cronhelm (nee Ashmore) of Dublin. Private Henry Cronhelm Tobias, Canadian Infantry 2nd Battalion, (Eastern Ontario Regiment). He was the son of Matthew and Elizabeth Tobias of Burrow South, Howth, Co Dublin.[60]

HONE, Nathanial Frederick

Lieutenant, 3rd Battalion, attached 9th Battalion Royal Irish Rifles, 107th Brigade in the 36th (Ulster) Division.

He was killed in action, aged 18, on 1 July 1916 during the first day of the Battle of the Somme. An eye witness, Private J. Jamieson, 9th Battalion Royal Irish Rifles, of 92, Ewarts Road, Belfast, stated that '...on 1 July 1916 at Thiepval, Lt Hone was killed by a bomb (hand grenade) during the big advance.' However, despite the eyewitness account of his death, his mother found it very difficult to accept that her son was dead and she continued to make enquiries. The War Office wrote to Mrs Hone on 23 March 1917: 'Enquiries through the American Embassy have been without result. In view of the lapse of time since anything has been heard of this officer his name is put forward for presumption of death.' Mrs Hone informed the Army Council on 9 April 1917 that she had a report of a Royal Irish Rifles officer, whom, having been reported missing on 1 July 1917, was next heard of in Switzerland after Christmas.

The War Office responded as follows:

> I am directed to inform you that it is not confirmed that there exists, either in Germany or in the occupied territory camps, a situation in which British prisoners of war are prevented from writing to their relatives. No case has come under the notice of the Army Council in which a missing officer has been heard of for the first time after so long an interval. I am to ask if you will be good enough to forward the name of the officer of the Royal Irish Rifles, who, after being reported missing on the 1 July last, was next heard of from Switzerland some

weeks after Christmas. It is regretted that no hope can now be held out of his being alive. The Council, however, do not desire to proceed to the official acceptance of death against your wishes, and I am to ask you if it is your wish that no further action in this matter should be taken for the present?[61]

The *Evening Herald* carried a notice during September 1916 stating that Lt N.F. Hone, Royal Irish Rifles, was missing since an engagement on the 1 July 1916, and his mother, who resides at Greencroft, Carrickmines, would be grateful for news of him.[62]

Lieutenant Hone's body was eventually recovered and buried at VIII. A. 10. Tincourt New British Cemetery, Somme, France. He is commemorated on the Hone Memorial and the Roll of Honour at Tullow Church of Ireland, Carrickmines; Memorial Plaque 1914–1918, at St Columba's College, Rathfarnham; Great War Memorial, Aravon School Bray, Co Wicklow, and the Great War Memorial, Kilgobbin. He was awarded the British War and Victory medals. It was only a matter of hours following Hone's death that his close friend and comrade, Lt John Healy, of Blackrock, was killed in the same battle.

Nathanial was Lance Corporal in the OTC at St Columba's College, Rathfarnham, and joined the British Army on 16 March 1915. The 9th Battalion was formed in Belfast in September 1914 from the Belfast Volunteers. It moved to Ballykinlare, Co Down, and came under orders in July 1915. It then moved to Seaford and landed at Boulogne in October 1915.

He was born on 3 August 1897, at Grassmere, Gregory's Road, Colombo, Ceylon, the son of Nathaniel Matthew Hone and Lillian Gertrude Hone (née Bate) of Glenbourne, Ballyogan Road, Carrickmines. There were two boys in the family: Nathaniel Frederick and Terence, born in 1903. Nathaniel junior was educated at Aravon School, Bray, Co Wicklow, and St Columba's College, Rathfarnham. He was one of the leaders of the first Boy Scouts Group in Aravon along with his friend, Pat Sarsfield. The groups were called 'Cuckoos and Curlews'.[63] Nathanial was a member of Carrickmines Golf Club and played on the First XI St Columba's cricket team.

Nathanial senior, a retired tea planter, lived with his wife in Ceylon where he had shares in the Goodneston Tea Estate. Following the family's return to Europe it lived for a short time in Moseley, England, before moving to Dublin to reside at

Greencroft, Claremont Road, Carrickmines. In 1906 Nathaniel built a new family house, Glenbourne, on the Ballyogan Road, Carrickmines, where Lillian and her sons were residing at the time of her husband's death in December 1912. There is a letter from the War Office, on 23 March 1917, addressed to Lillian Hone, c/o Croquet Club, Carrickmines. This reflects the close relationship with the Wilson family of Carrickmines. Nathaniel senior was related to the sisters, Emily Charlotte Wilson (née Hone), Annie Mary Hone, and their brother, Charles Henry Hone. He also acted as godfather to the Wilsons' son, John Hugh. Henry William Wilson and Nathaniel Matthew Hone were founding members of Carrickmines Golf Club in 1900 and Nathaniel was its first Honorary Secretary, a position he held until his death.[64] His wife, Lillian had the honour of being the club's first Lady Captain from 1904 to 1906. Lillian's second marriage to John Samuel Dyas took place at Sandyford Parish Church on 23 October 1919. The Rector, Thomas Good presided and the sponsors were Annie Mary Hone and Lillian's son, Terence Bate-Hone.

TROUTON, Edmund Arthur

Lieutenant, 3rd Battalion, attached 9th Battalion Royal Enniskilling Fusiliers, 109th Brigade in the 36th (Ulster) Division.

Lieutenant Trouton joined the 3rd Battalion in Gallipoli, and having survived this disastrous campaign he was declared missing, aged 24, and presumed killed in action during the first day of the Battle of the Somme on 1 July 1916. The Enniskillings were detailed to attack the enemy position at Thiepval, and he was seen leading his men to capture the third enemy line. One of Trouton's men, Pte William Pelion, 9th Battalion, Royal Innniskilling Fusiliers, wrote:

On July 1st 1916, near Thiepval, I saw Lieutenant Trouton wounded by the same shell as I was. This was on the morning of July 1st before we reached the German trenches. Going towards Thiepval, he spoke to me but I do not know how badly he was wounded. He was alive when I last saw him. When I was taken back that afternoon I told the stretcher bearers about him. I was his servant; the ground was won.[65]

The attack on the first day was preceded by the most formidable artillery preparation employed as yet in the history of the war lasting seven days and seven nights. Lieutenant

Trouton's Battalion was allotted 'pride of place' in the attack about to be launched, being the leading battalion on the right of the Division. 'On its right was the 32nd Division and on the left the 10th Inniskillings, while the supporting battalion was the 11th Inniskillings. The objective was the point christened Lisnaskea in the German third line. At 7.15am the bugle sounded the assault. The two leading companies advanced immediately in perfect line followed by the supporting companies in artillery formation. The discipline maintained by all was magnificent, the advance being carried out as if it was a parade movement. On reaching the Sunken Road in no-mans-land heavy machine-gun fire and shell-fire was encountered; the former from the village of Thiepval, afterwards alluded to by German prisoners, as Thiepval Fort. The battalion began to thin, men falling by the score, but calm and deliberate advance still continued. On reaching the German "A" line those still standing swept on with irresistible determination.'[66] The casualties in the 9th Inniskillings for the first day of the Battle of the Somme, were 16 officers and 461 other ranks, including Lt Trouton.

Lieutenant Trouton is commemorated on the Thiepval Memorial, Somme, France; Great War Memorial and Trouton Memorial Window at the Church of Ireland, Kilternan; War Memorial Cloister and Roll of Honour at Winchester College; Great War Memorial, Bilton Grange School, Rugby; Great War Memorial, Trinity College, Cambridge and the Great War Memorial, Kilgobbin. He was awarded the 1915 Star, British War and Victory medals. Following the notice of his death his father wrote to the War Office:

> Second Lieutenant Edmund Trouton was reported missing on the 1st July, I take it that this is meant for my son who was promoted to full Lieutenant on 24 July 1915. Will you be so good as to direct that steps be taken to ascertain all facts connected with his disappearance and whether the circumstances of his case would point to the likelihood of his being a prisoner in the hands of the enemy? No doubt you are aware that he was attached to the 9th Battalion Royal Inniskilling Fusiliers.[67]

Edmund received his commission on 20 October 1914 and served in Gallipoli as machine-gun officer. Promotion to full lieutenant was announced on the 24 July 1915. He took part in the general assault of 21 August 1915 when his unit suffered very seriously and he was invalided home. When Lt Trouton recovered from dysentery at the Royal Free Hospital in London he attended a course at the Staff College, Camberley, before joining the 9th Battalion of his Regiment in France, in the spring of 1916.[68]

Edmund was born on 27 November 1891 at Orange, New Jersey, in the USA, and was the only child of Edmund Arthur Trouton CBE, who formerly resided at The Grange, Galloping Green, Stillorgan. It appears that his wife had passed away prior to 1901. Edmund junior was educated at Bilton Grange Preparatory School, Rugby, and Winchester College, England from 1905–1909. The school magazine at Winchester revealed that he was a member of the boat club, coxing both pairs and fours and he also participated in rowing. In 1907 he was part of the team that won the house gymnastics shield and he won the headmaster's silver medal in 1909.[69] On 25 June 1910 he was admitted to Trinity College, Cambridge, as an undergraduate, and while there, he achieved third-class passes in Special Examinations in Chemistry (1911–1912), History (1912–1913); he took his BA degree at Cambridge in 1913. The Trouton family had close ties with Kilternan, where they were parishioners at the Church of Ireland. The late Miss Rita Rutherfoord of Ballycorus, Kilternan, a great-granddaughter of Judge Edmund Darley, Fernhill, Kilgobbin, said that Edmund's aunt married a member of the Darley family. This may explain why in the 1911 census, Edmund, aged 19, was recorded with his father staying at the residence of Edward Saunders Darley in Fernhill, Newtown Little, Kilgobbin.

HAMILTON, Geoffrey Cecil Monck
Second Lieutenant, 8th Battalion Royal Dublin Fusiliers, 48th Brigade in the 16th (Irish) Division. Secondary Regiment, Service No.17/4350, Leinster Regiment.

He was killed in action, aged 21, on 7 September 1916, two days before the main attack on Ginchy. Colonel Bellingham wrote to his father on 19 December 1915: 'He was one of the most fearless officers I have ever met, and if anything was too brave. Had he lived he would have been recommended by me for his gallant behaviour in the face of the enemy.' Following his death, his father received a letter from the Company Captain informing him that he never received any of his son's personal effects, which he always had with him.[70]

His battalion's war diary for 7 September 1916 is missing, however, another account of the action at Ginchy on 5–10 September 1916 reveals that on the 5

September, two battalions of 48th Brigade and four battalions of 49th Brigade were under the command of Tipperary-born, Major-General William Hickie. The task of clearing the village was given to the depleted 16th (Irish) Division. Its two attacking Brigades (47th–48th) were supported on the right by the 56th Division's operation in Leuze and Bouleaux Woods. The loss of Ginchy deprived the Germans of their strategic observation posts overlooking the entire battlefield.[71]

His grave is at II. G. 5. Guillemont Road Cemetery, Albert, France, and he is commemorated on the Roll of Honour and the Hamilton Memorial at Tullow Church of Ireland, Carrickmines; the family tomb in Dean's Grange Cemetery; Hall of Honour, Trinity College and the Dublin Boy Scouts Memorial at St Patrick's Cathedral, Dublin. His father erected the Hamilton Memorial at Tullow Church of Ireland. The inscription reads: 'Blessed are the pure in heart for they shall see GOD.' He was awarded the 1914–15 Star, British War and Victory medals.

Geoffrey was born on 8 December 1894, the youngest son of Arthur Hamilton JP, solicitor, and Alma Hamilton (née Croker) of, Hollybrook, Foxrock. Eight children were born to the couple of whom seven survived infancy: Dorothy Alice Letitia, Alick Edward Croker, Rosalie Alma Georgiana, Elsie Marguerite Monck, Robin Arthur Vesey, Eric Richard Monck, Geoffrey Cecil Monck. Geoffrey was an undergraduate at Trinity College in 1913, but enlisted before completing his studies. He was attached to the Cadet Corps, 7th Leinster Regiment, based at Kilwort Camp in Co Cork on 10 March 1915 and earned his commission with the Royal Dublin Fusiliers on 29 June of the same year.

'Two Hamilton sisters remained unmarried and resided with their unmarried brother, Alick, at their parents' home in Foxrock. Alick was known locally as, "The Captain" and it was said that he had a wooden leg.'[72] The disability suggests that he may have fought in the Great War; however, there is no evidence that this was the case. He died in 1943, aged 65, and is interred in the family plot at Dean's Grange Cemetery. When the last remaining Hamilton sister died, the family residence was sold, and later demolished to accommodate a block of luxury apartments.

JOY, Frederick Charles Patrick
Second Lieutenant, 3rd Battalion, attached 2nd Battalion Royal Irish Rifles. Secondary Regiment, Service No 14168, Royal Dublin Fusiliers.

He was killed in action, aged 23, on 16 June 1915 in what is officially known as the 'first action' at Bellewaarde. The attack involved a bombardment at Neuve Chapelle and Bellewaarde Farm. 'On the day that 2nd Lt Joy was killed, "C" and "D" Companies, with very short notice, were called upon to attack. It possessed just as much spirit and dash as their early morning attack. Owing to heavy artillery fire, which soon developed, "B" Company was unable to follow "A" Company quickly. They were formed up on Cambridge Road, 250 yards behind, in preparation for another effort to get through, when they were, unfortunately, shelled by enfilade fire causing 30 or 40 casualties. The remainder of the company was then withdrawn and kept in battalion support for the rest of the day. During the day, from early morning to nightfall, the battalion was subjected to a terrific artillery bombardment. It was relieved at 1.29am having acquitted itself in a manner which was highly praised by the Corps Commander. Four officers were killed in the attack (including 2nd Lt Joy), 9 wounded and around 300 casualties from other ranks'.[73]

Corporal Robert Platt of the 2nd Royal Irish Rifles, wrote to his father about the battle in which 2nd Lt Joy lost his life. An extract read:

> Since last I wrote to you we were in a charge and it was awful. The battle took place on 16 June. It was even worse than the charge we made at Hill 60. The Brigade officer says 'the Rifles have made a name for themselves out here that will go down in history'. Sharp at three o'clock the order came down our lines to fix bayonets and to load our rifles and 10 minutes later down came the order to charge so we all rushed over the trench but a good few of our boys fell on the parapet as the Germans had their machine guns trained on us, but on we went and as one fell, another took his place. We arrived at the German trench and when it came to the steel they could not match us and I am proud to say that I put a few out with the bayonet myself. Although one does not think of it at the time, one does think of it after the excitement is over. We took over 200 prisoners and a couple of machine guns. The net result for this loss of life was 250 yards gained on a front of 800 yards. I sent home a German sword.[74]

Second Lieutenant Joy is commemorated on the British War Memorial, Menin Gate, Ieper, Belgium; Hall of Honour, Trinity College and was awarded the 1914–15 Star, British War and Victory medals. He enlisted in the Royal Dublin Fusiliers at Naas, Co Kildare, on 15 September 1914, and held the rank of private until he was discharged on appointment to a commission in the 7th Battalion Royal Dublin Fusiliers on 29 September 1914. On 1 April 1915 he was gazetted 2nd Lieutenant in the 3rd Battalion, Royal Irish Rifles and was promoted to full lieutenant on 29 September 1914. He was posted to France on 22 March 1915 and was transferred to the 2nd Battalion on 1 April 1915. His brother, Robert Cecil wrote to the War Office from his home in Stillorgan, 'I am in receipt of your wire telling me the grievous news of my brother, F.C.P. Joy, Royal Irish Rifles, having been killed on the 16 inst., I would like to have any details that are available, particularly, I would like to know where and how he was killed.' There was no evidence in the officer's original documents of a reply to his letter.[75]

He was the son of the late Robert Joy and Elizabeth Grace Joy (née Hayes) of Banbridge, Co Down. His father, who passed away in 1900, was a well-known citizen of Belfast, and it is said that the Joy family occupied an important place in the history of the city; the name remaining on one of the streets. There were eight children in the family: Robert Cecil, Arthur Holmes, Norah Margaret, Conway Hume, Frederick Charles, William Bruce, Dorothea Marie and George Noel. Frederick Joy was born in Banbridge, Co Down, on 12 March 1892 and educated at Highgate School in London, where he was a member of its OTC. He took his BA at Trinity College in 1912, and qualified as a chartered accountant. Before enlisting, he lived with his brother, Robert, at their home, Grove House, Stillorgan. Robert, a solicitor employed by the Bank of Ireland, was his sole executor.

Another brother, Major, Arthur Holmes Joy, Royal Navy, survived the war. He was a distinguished student at Queens College, Belfast, and took his medical degree, with first class honours, at the Royal University. He remained unmarried and died in 1940 at Salford, Lancashire, aged 56. Albert Bruce-Joy ARHA, RHA (1842–1924) the well-known portrait sculptor was related to the Joy family. Albert was born in Dublin and worked for four years under another Dublin-born sculptor, the eminent J.H. Foley. When the latter died in 1874, Bruce-Joy had an instant route to success by fulfilling his outstanding commissions. He rejected ARA-ship in 1878, but some 15 years later, accepted an RHA. During his career, he produced some 150 or so portrait busts, and a goodly number of full statues.[76]

BARRETT, Sophia Violet

VAD (VoluntaryAid Detachment), British Red Cross Society and the St John Carrickmines Ambulance Nursing Division. Sophia Violet Barrett was drowned, aged 34, on 10 October 1918, when she was aboard the RMS *Leinster,* which was torpedoed by the Germans off the Irish coast. She was returning to duty at No 2 Stationary Hospital, Abbeville, France, where she nursed wounded German prisoners. Violet, (as her family knew her) also served at No 6 General Hospital, Rouen. She was laid to rest at the churchyard in Kilternan Church of Ireland and is commemorated on the Commonwealth War Dead Memorial, Hollybrook Memorial, Southampton; Roll of Honour at the Tullow Church of Ireland, Carrickmines and the Church of Ireland, Kenagh, Co Longford. 'On Monday the 14 October her funeral procession, headed by a firing party of Hussars, left her final abode at Carrickmines House for Kilternan churchyard. Her coffin was carried in an ambulance loaned by the Royal Irish Automobile Club and was met at the graveyard by the Reverand Clarke, Rector of Tullow Parish, Carrickmines, who conducted the service. He was assisted by Reverent Arthur O'Morchoe, Rector of Kilternan, together with members of St John Ambulance Brigade (Carrickmines Men's Division) who acted as bearers.'[77] She was 'Mentioned in Despatches' by Sir Douglas Haig in his despatch of 7 November to the Secretary of State for War. Violet Barrett was related by marriage to the Wilson family, and was spending a short holiday at Carrickmines House in the company of her aunt, Marcella Wilson, (née Barrett), the second wife of William Henry Wilson. 'She was accompanied to the Carlisle Pier, Kingstown by her sister Elizabeth, who had travelled from her home in the Midlands to bid her farewell. On her return journey home Elizabeth learned of the tragedy in Longford railway station as she alighted from the train.'[78]

NELSON, Samuel Tyndall

Sergeant, Service No 106454, 1st Battalion (Saskatchewan Regiment), Canadian Mounted Rifles, Secondary Regiment, 7th Hussars.

Sergeant Tyndall died of gunshot wounds to the head, aged 37, on the 18 September 1916, at No 20 General Hospital, Camiers, France. There is no record of casualties on the 16, 17 or 18 September, and it may be assumed that he was wounded during the heavy fighting on the 15th and died in hospital three days later. The battalion carried out a raid on Mouquet Farm and suspected dugouts in that vicinity. As a result of the bombardment, rifle and machine gun fire, the two front-line companies suffered heavily, especially the right company. The total number of casualties during the tour was 70 officers and other ranks killed, 179 wounded and 11 missing.[79]

His grave is at X. E. 8A. Etaples Military Cemetery, France and he is commemorated on the Roll of Honour, Tullow Church of Ireland, Carrickmines, and page 141 of the First World War Canadian Book of Remembrance. His name is also inscribed on the family gravestone in the church graveyard at Kilternan Church of Ireland. He was awarded the 1915 Star, British War and Victory medals. Samuel Nelson served eight years in the 7th Hussars and also served with that Regiment in the South African Campaign, where he was awarded the Queen's medal with five bars.

He was the eldest son of William Joseph Nelson (land steward) and Annie Nelson of, Kerrymount Cottage, Foxrock, (known locally as Nelson's Lane). The Nelsons had six children, of whom five were named: Samuel Tyndall, William John, Elizabeth, Henrietta and Robert. William and Annie Nelson passed away in 1926 and 1931, respectively. Samuel Tyndall was born on 3 October 1880 and his stated occupation was farmer. He was a single man with fair complexion, blue eyes, brown hair and a tattoo: 'Hussars Cross Swords & Gun'. Samuel joined the Canadian Expeditionary Force on 1 December 1914, embarked for France on 16 April 1915, and was promoted to Sergeant on 5 August 1916.

His brother, Staff Sergeant William Nelson, Supply and Transport, attached to the Indian Army, also served in the war. William survived the war and according to the 1911 census, he was staying at his parents' home with his wife, Winifred. Winifred was born in India and they had one child who died in infancy.

YOUNG, William Matthew O'Grady

Sergeant, Service No 208, 7th Australian Light Horse, 'A' Squadron. Previously served in the Boer War, Service No 96954, 5th Company, Irish Imperial Yeomanry.

Sergeant Young died, aged 43, at the 1st Australian General Hospital, Cairo, on 28 December 1915 from a bullet wound to his chest. His battalion returned to Egypt on HMT *Caledonia,* arriving on 27 December 1915, and the next day his death occurred as a result of a bizarre accident. When orders to return any unused ammunition, rifles and magazines were being carried out, a shot rang out and Sgt Young, slumped to the ground wounded. At the same time, outside the sergeant's tent, Trooper Hubert Charles Rigby grasped his groin, staggered and also fell. A bullet had apparently passed through Sgt Young and then struck Rigby. They were rushed to hospital where Young died the next day and Rigby the following day. The bullet came from the rifle of L/Cpl Thomas McKnight Roberts of the 4th Australian Light Horse. A Court of Enquiry found no blame beyond that of an accident could be attributed to L/Cpl Robertson. This accident took place at the Racecourse Camp, Heliopolis in Egypt. Lance Corporal Rigby, attached to the 4th Light Horse, was born in Coleraine and lived in Victoria, Australia.[80] Sergeant Young's brother, Owen, was informed officially by Australian Imperial Force Headquarters of his death and burial on 10 April 1916. There were no personal effects in the kit of the deceased.

Sergeant Young's grave is at D. 238, Grave / Memorial, 1 Cairo War Memorial Cemetery, Al. Oahirah, Egypt, and he is commemorated on the War Memorial at Tullow Church of Ireland, Carrickmines, and the Hall of Honour, Trinity College. He was awarded the 1914 Star, British War and Victory medals.

William enlisted in October 1914, aged 42, having previously spent one year in the Imperial Yeomanry, six years in the South African Constabulary and served in the Boer War from 1899 to 1901. His squadron embarked from Sydney, New South Wales on board HMAT A33 *Ayrshire* on 20 December 1914. During his time serving in Gallipoli, he was wounded on three occasions in August 1915. He was promoted to temporary corporal 15 October 1915 and was promoted again to full corporal on 22 November 1915. While his recorded rank is corporal, an official document issued by the Australian Imperial Force, following his death stated that he carried the rank of sergeant.

Mr O.H. Windsor, 'The Museum', Cronula, near Sydney, Australia, wrote to the Base Records Office in Melbourne on 3 May 1916. In his letter he stated that Cpl Young's sister, Miss Grace Young of Ellesmere, Carrickmines, requested him to send on her brother's personal effects. Windsor requested assistance from the Record's Office to forward the goods to Dublin and offered to pay the shipping costs. In the response from Base Office, it stated that, the matter was being referred to the Assistant Adjutant-General, Victoria Barracks, Sydney, Australia.[81] His only brother, Owen Waller O'Grady Young, was recorded as his next-of-kin. William was the son of James Young BA, JP and Grace Young (née Waller O'Grady) of Harristown, Castlerea, Co Roscommon. James Young, a magistrate for Roscommon, was shot dead on his own avenue on the 2 June 1877 aged 43. Media reports at the time stated that he died from revolver shots to the head and back as he walked down his avenue to attend the petty sessions in the nearby town of Castlerea. The murderer got away but left a cap lying on the ground, which it was hoped would lead to the arrest of the culprit. The report stated that the cap was 'of the same style as those worn by numbers of the peasantry.' James Young left his home at 12.30pm on a Saturday and was found by his wife lying dead on the avenue at 2.30pm. It appears that this was not the first attempt on his life and he was made aware that he was in constant danger. James Young was described as an 'improving landlord' and a popular man in the area, with a 'fearless temper, and most upright character in all his dealings'.[82] Today, much of the demesne at Harristown is occupied by Castlerea prison.

His wife, Grace, was the daughter of the Honourable Waller O'Grady, QC of Castlegarde, Co Limerick, second son of Standish, 1st Viscount Guillamore. The seat of the O'Grady family from the mid-eighteenth century was acquired through marriage with a member of the Hayes family and the family house, near Croom in Co Limerick, is now in ruins.[83] Sometime following the death of her husband, Grace Young resided with her family at Ellesmere, Brighton Road, Carrickmines.

There were eight children in the Young family: Rosa Julia, Owen Waller, Grace Elizabeth, Phoebe Mary, Constance Katherine, William Matthew, Ida Ethel, and Evelyn. William was born on 18 April 1872 at Harristown in the parish of Kilkeevin near Castlerea, Co Roscommon. He was described as a farmer from Boggabri, New South Wales, Australia, and was educated at Wimborne School in England before entering Trinity College in 1891.

KELLY, Christopher

Lance Corporal, Service No 24975, 8th Battalion, Royal Dublin Fusiliers, 48th Brigade in the 16th (Irish) Division. He was killed in action, aged 27, at Rossignol Estaminet on 31 May 1917. His battalion's war diary for 31 May did not contain any information on activities for that day and his death may well have been due to gas poisoning at Hulluch on 29 April 1916. Further information of his last days in action is contained in the profile of L/Cpl Patrick Daniel O'Driscoll in Chapter Two.

His grave is at III. D. 15. La Laiterie Military Cemetery, Heuvelland, Belgium and he was awarded the British War and Victory medals. His medal index card revealed that 'he displayed great courage and initiative in engaging a portion of the enemy'.

His battalion was formed in September 1914 as part of K2 and it moved to Buttevant, Co Cork, followed by a further move, in June 1915, to Ballyhooley, Co

Cork. In September 1915 the battalion moved to England, going to Blackdown in September 1915, before landing at Le Havre in December 1915.

Christopher was baptised at St Brigid's Roman Catholic Church, Cabinteely, and lived with his parents, Thomas and Mary Kelly (née Brien) at 19, Grange Terrace, Dean's Grange, Foxrock. Prior to enlisting his work was described as 'van driver'. There were eight children in the family: Christopher, James, Mary Jane, Patrick, Thomas, Catherine, Alice and Margaret.

Christopher's brother, Patrick, was a Roman Catholic priest, and Danny Shannon of Cabinteely stated that Father Pat received a great reception on his return home to the parish of Cabinteely following a long period serving on the Foreign Missions. Another brother, Tommy, lived at the family home in Dean's Grange until his death.

BYRNE, Daniel
Private, Service No 4224, 6th Battalion, Connaught Rangers, 47th Brigade in the 16th (Irish) Division.

He was killed in action, aged 19, on 13 May 1916. On the 12 May at Loos, 'the enemy displayed unusual artillery activity which was spread along the Connaught Rangers front support and reserve trenches. The battalion's artillery reply was feeble. The difference being that the enemy was lavish in his use of all types of ammunition. The next day the Connaught Rangers weak artillery supply was crippling its efforts of maintaining an equal fight. The 7th Leinsters were on its right. It is recorded that there was bright moonlight during the night of 13/14 May 1916.'[84]

His grave is at I. H. 9. Dud Corner Cemetery, Loos, Northern France, and he was awarded the 1915 Star, British War and Victory medals. Daniel enlisted in Dublin on the 3 May 1915 with his friend, Dominick Reynolds, and was posted to France in 1915. Another friend and comrade, Pte Richard (Dick) Murphy of, The Hotel, Foxrock, who survived the war, sent a postcard from the front to Daniel's parents, which was signed, 'Your friend, Dick.' On one side of the postcard there was a photograph of the Roman Catholic Church, situated near Loos, and annotated on the reverse side he wrote the following words of consolation, 'Dear Mr Byrne, The picture of this chapel is the nearest mark I could get to where poor Dan is buried. The graveyard is about

300 yards to the left of it. I sent you this; it will be a little consolation to you and to his poor mother.'[85]

Daniel Byrne, born in Monkstown Farm, was the son of Thomas Byrne and Jane Byrne (née Horan) of 6, Brighton Cottages, Foxrock. Jane was born in Queens County (now Laois). There were seven children in the family: Elizabeth, Mary, John, Tom, Michael, Ada and Daniel. Daniel's niece, Nancy Corcoran, daughter of Mary Byrne, said at her Foxrock home that 'Daniel and Dominick Reynolds enlisted with the Connaught Rangers without getting permission from their parents and my grandparents were extremely upset when they learned that their 18-year-old son was going to war.'[86] Prior to enlisting, Daniel recorded that he worked at gardening.

COATES, William Alexander

Private, Service No 25145, 7th Battalion Royal Irish Regiment, 49th Infantry Brigade in the 16th (Irish) Division. Secondary Regiment, Service No 1495, South Irish Horse.

Private Coates took part in the Kaiser's Battle, sometimes referred to as the 'German Spring Offensive', which commenced on 21 March 1918. He was killed in action, aged 25, on 27 March 1918, the last day of the battle. The attack was preceded by heavy bombardments, gas and infiltration troops. By the end of the month over ninety men of the battalion were dead or dying. 'On 27 March 1918, at Morcourt and Cerisy, the enemy attacked in force. Held off frontally, but managed to get along its left flank by the valley. The battalion retired through Morcourt and Lamotte and took up a position to the east of Hamel Wood.'[87]

His grave is at XVI. E. 1. Villers-Bretonneux Military Cemetery, Somme, France and he is commemorated on the Roll of Honour at the Tullow, Church of Ireland, Carrickmines. He was awarded the 1914 Star, British War and Victory medals.

The South Irish Horse was formed in 1902 as the South of Ireland Imperial Yeomanry and disbanded in July 1922 along with five other famous Irish Regiments. It was at sometime, quartered at Leopardstown. Briefly, the regiment served as separate Divisional Cavalry Squadrons and then as 2nd Corps Cavalry Regiments. In September 1917 the officers and men of both regiments were retrained as infantry and formed the 7th (South Irish Horse) Battalion, Royal Irish Regiment.[88]

Private Coates was survived by his wife, Maude, and there were no children in their short marriage. He was son of Susan Coates and the late Alexander Coates of 2, Brighton Cottages, Foxrock. There were six children in the family: William, John, Rhoda, Alexander, Susan and Frank. His father, Alexander, was alive in 1911 but had passed away before his son's death. William Coates was born in 1892 and worked as a groom before enlisting in the South Irish Horse. Local historian, and well-known County Dublin lyric tenor, the late Joe Murphy, from Brennanstown Road, Cabinteely, said that he knew Susan Coates very well and she liked nothing better than reminiscing about her son and never tired of showing him the photographs taken on her visits to his grave in France. Every year until her death in May 1945, she laid a wreath at the Great War Memorial, Islandbridge. Susan Coates held the franchise for the distribution of morning and evening newspapers in the Foxrock and Carrickmines area.

William's brother, Private John Coates, South Irish Horse, survived the war. When his first wife died, John moved from Dublin to live in Cork, where he married a second time. Iris Coates, who lived with her grandmother in Foxrock, was his daughter from the first marriage.

HAYDEN, Stephen Joseph
Bombardier, Service No 31744, 'D' Battery, Royal Field Artillery, 4th Brigade in the 7th (Meerut) Division of the Indian Army.

He was killed in action, aged 31, in the area of Barleux, Assevillers via Estrees on 24 March 1918. At Horgny, Barleux Assevillers, seven aeroplanes (German), unmolested, circled over the batteries and one of the aeroplanes was brought down. It was here in this area of the Somme that Pte Hayden fell.[89]

His grave is at II. B. 41. Honnechy British Cemetery, Picardy, France and he was awarded the British War and Victory medals. Private Hayden's service record is not available and there is a paucity of information on his last days in action, however, we know that he did not see action until late 1915 or early 1916. The 4th Brigade, comprising numbers, 7, 14 and 66 batteries, served with the division in France, Mesopotamia and Palestine.[90]

Stephen Hayden was the son of Michael Hayden (building contractor) and

Margaret Hayden of 2, Springfield, Foxrock. The couple were married in 1873 and had nine children: Michael, John, William, Mary Anne, Stephen, Margaret, Patrick, Edward and Laurence. Prior to enlisting Stephen was a bricklayer and most likely worked in the family business.

Enda Cullen is a great-nephew of Stephen Hayden, and the following are extracts from his compelling story of an Irish soldier forgotten for nearly ninety years and finally discovered and commemorated by his family, he wrote:

'A Forgotten Soldier'
'Sean Hayden of Lambs Cross was the key man in this story. A keen local and family historian, my uncle Sean was fond of producing obscure documents and facts relating to times past. Examples of eclectic research included hand drawn but meticulously accurate maps. One Sunday night in 2004, my mother Bella handed me her brother's latest historical teaser. It was a copy of an official Irish census return for 1901. The house was Springfield, located at the top of Kill Lane in Foxrock. According to some, Springfield was built by my great grandfather. On that particular night he listed the members of his household by name and occupation. I followed his pen, recognising each of my great uncles and aunts, their names familiar from scraps of conversations overheard during my childhood.

Enda went on to mention that he had heard of Ned, Larry and Michael junior, who had left Ireland for New York around 1920 to work as masons on the grand stone buildings being erected at that time. Ned and Larry put down roots in America but Michael came back to Ireland:

> The instant my eyes fell upon his name, I asked:" Who is Stephen Hayden, scholar?" Bella didn't pause as she poured tea from her near empty teapot. "He never came back from the war" was all she replied. I am sure that I asked many questions about fourteen years old Stephen over the minutes that followed but with no meaningful response. I didn't appreciate what circumstances could have led to such an information vacuum about one of our own!'

It seems that Enda's mother, Bella, couldn't admit he had died in the war ... "he just hadn't come back." Whatever the reasons, Stephen was real and Enda wanted to know more about a forgotten life, rediscovered. In the summer of 2006 Sean Hayden's health was deteriorating and the family feared that his time with them might be limited. Enda told Bella that he was going to France with the intention of visiting his great-uncle's grave:

Only then I realised how important this quest had become for her and Sean in particular. Her enthusiasm for our visit was strong and compelling. As my family and I journeyed towards Stephen's resting place, we noted familiar names along the route. In my head these names triggered grainy black and white images of the mud and blood, trenches and barbed wire and of course, men "going over the top". My sense of these images was exclusively from books and television. How much more horrific must the reality have been? The cemetery in Honnechy is actually small by Great War standards. A few hundred graves in perhaps six or seven rows.

Today the place is peaceful, surrounded as it is by trees and farm land. Cows graze closely in green fields alongside and one could believe it was Ireland. The last headstone in the row marked the resting place of Bombardier S. J. Hayden, Royal Field Artillery. We spent some time with him and we were in no hurry to leave. After all, he had waited 88 years for his relatives to visit him. Copious amounts of photographs were taken and subsequently scanned for every detail by Bella. By this time Sean was in hospital and losing his grip on life. His daughter Catherine brought him the photographs and though he couldn't see them, Sean seemed well pleased. In August of 2007 and a year after Sean's passing, Bella surprised us all by announcing her wish to visit Stephen's grave. She was petrified of flying so this expedition was obviously important enough for her to push fear to one side. We sensed that this trip was one she'd wanted to do with Sean had he recovered from his illness. Now, she wanted to do it for Sean.

The Cullen / Reid / Hayden Honnechy expedition took place in August 2007. It was not too solemn an occasion either. There were plenty of laughs and wistful sighs as we gathered at Stephen's grave. We remembered him and in the silence of the place, I know we all remembered Sean. He was with us. Bella planted a Tricolour and claimed a piece of France for Sandyford. She also snipped a few cuttings off Stephen's own personal planting to take home.

All are now rooted and thriving in Irish soil. This journey gave my brother Philip and I an opportunity to spend a really special time with our mother. We were in unfamiliar emotional territory but collectively we were engaged in something that was bigger than ourselves. We also witnessed a wonderful love for her brother Sean, himself a man of great modesty, honesty and integrity; a giant. After 89 years lying in France among the fallen, Stephen has finally been recognised by his family. He's been claimed.' [91]

McEVOY, Patrick

Private, Service No 3/6172, 6th Battalion, Connaught Rangers, 47th Brigade in the 16th (Irish) Division.

He was killed in action, aged 29, on the first day of the Battle of Wijtschate, Messines Ridge on 7 June 1917. The Battle of Messines-Wijtschate and that of Passchendaele are inseparably linked because the first was the prologue to the latter. Both battles were fought by the same troops (British, Anzacs and Irish) under the same commanders (Haig, Plumer and Rupprecht von Bayern. 'At 3.10am on 7 June 1917 at Wijtschate, the 47th Infantry Brigade attacked with great success; all objectives being taken and numerous prisoners captured, while the casualties were light. The attack was opened at zero hour by the explosions of mines all along the 2nd Army front. At zero plus 15 seconds the first wave left own trench under cover of a creeping barrage. Seventy-five per cent of the guns on the army front being used for this barrage, the other twenty-five per cent opened intense fire on the enemy's battery positions.' [92]

'The 16th (Irish) and 36th (Ulster) Divisions fought alongside each other to capture the Belgian village of Wijtschate in a well planned attack in June 1917 at the Battle of Messines, but this did not prevent the two divisions meeting in mortal combat on the field of play. Two football matches took place in Loker on 29 April 1917, between the 6th Connaught Rangers and 9th Royal Irish Fusiliers. At the second match, who for the Ulstermen was unusual insofar as it was played on the Sabbath, a crowd of 3,000 was reported to have turned up to watch this match. The large attendance at the match gave concern to Colonel Rowland Fielding. Such a concentration of troops, he believed offered a prime target to German shellfire if they got news of the gathering. However, knowing something about the politics of Ireland and the interest this match had developed, Colonel Fielding's heart ruled his head on this occasion and he allowed the match to take place. It would have been a brave man to cancel it. German artillery or not this match was going to take place. For the record, the Ulstermen won both games two goals to nil.' [93] There was a great footballing tradition among the residents in Brighton Cottages, Foxrock, and it would not be at all surprising if Patrick McEvoy was involved in one or both games.

His grave is at B.7. Irish House Cemetery, Heuvelland, Belgium. The cemetery owes its name to a small farmhouse known to the troops in 1917 as 'Irish House'. There were deep dugouts here and at various times during the attack on Wytschaete, several battalions of the 16th (Irish) such as the 1st Munsters, 9th Royal Dublin Fusiliers and 6th Connaught Rangers used the dugouts at Irish House as their battle headquarters. [94] Private McEvoy was awarded the British War and Victory medals.

He was born in Finglas and resided with his family at 1, Brighton Cottages, Foxrock and worked as a gardener, when work was available. He was the second son of James McEvoy (gardener) with his first wife who passed away some time following the birth of their daughter, Mary, in 1899. James and his second wife, Ellen, had one child, Annie. There were five children in the family; James, Patrick, John, Mary and Annie. The McEvoys were the first family in Foxrock to open a grocery shop, which operated from their home. His brother, James (Jim), began his working life as a porter at Foxrock railway station and was promoted to signalman. Local history says that 'Jim was a "stickler" for good order within his small demesne perched up high on the Dublin end of the station.' In later years, Foxrock railway station gained a reputation for being spotlessly clean and beautifully landscaped with colourful flowerbeds on both platforms. The station won many first prizes for the best kept railway station on the Bray to Harcourt Street railway line.

MOONEY, Joseph

Private, Service No 7128, 1st Battalion, 'G' Company, Connaught Rangers. Formerly 3rd Battalion.

Private Mooney died in a Dublin hospital, aged 38, on 9 Feb 1921 from the mental and physical injuries inflicted on him while on active service in Mesopotamia. His grave is at 45. D. North, Dean's Grange Cemetery and he is commemorated on the Great War Memorial, Kilgobbin. He was awarded the British War and Victory medals.

Joseph enlisted on 4 January 1916 at Kinsale, Co Cork, and was attached to the 3rd (Special Reserve) Battalion of the Connaught Rangers, where he remained until October 1916. He was billeted in Ballydehob, Co Cork during May 1916. In October 1917, he was posted to the 1st Battalion Connaught Rangers that sailed to Basra,

Mesopotamia. He was in India during the period, February 1917 and August 1917, and again in February 1918 until August of the same year. His health was breaking down under the pressure of active service and his condition was described as 'general paralysis, aggravated by campaign service'. He was discharged from the Belfast War Hospital to a Dublin hospital on 16 August 1918, and discharged from the army in October 1918 as no longer physically fit for military service. [95]

Joseph married Elizabeth Donovan of Carrickmines at St Brigid's Roman Catholic Church, Cabinteely, on 31 August 1909 and the couple resided at their farm, Brennanstown Cottage, Carrickmines. In 1911, Elizabeth's mother and father were dead and she was living at Brennanstown Cottage, with Joseph and her sister, Anne. The couple had one son, Patrick John, born in 1912, who later became the owner of the family's main farm in Carrickmines village. Patrick married Christina Egan and they had two children, Patsy and Christina. Mooney's farm in the village is on the site of the seventeenth century Carrickmines Castle, where the 'Siege of Carrickmines' took place in 1642. The foundations of the castle were discovered in 2002 during the construction of the M50 south-eastern motorway, which runs through the farm in close proximity to the former Mooney residence. There was great controversy surrounding the discovery of the foundations and construction of the motorway was delayed for a year to allow about one hundred archaeologists carry out excavations on the site.

Records show that the Mooney family have been farming at Carrickmines for more than 200 years. In 1798, rowdy elements from the royal encampment at Lahaunstown, Cabinteely, raided the family home and threatened to set fire to the house and shoot James Mooney and his family. They were arrested and convicted. [96]

MURPHY, William

Private, Service No 5142, 1st Battalion, Irish Guards, 4th (Guards) Brigade in the 2nd Division.

He was reported missing in action, aged 20, presumed to have been killed in the Battle of Festubert at Cour l'Avoine Farm on Tuesday 18 May 1915. 'On this day it dawned in wreaths of driving rain and mist that wrapped the flats. The preliminary bombardment of Cour l'Avoine Farm was postponed at 8.45am for lack of good light.

From noon on, the enemy began to shell the battalion severely in its shallow trenches, and there were 40 casualties while they lay waiting orders. The attack began at 4.30pm. Cour l'Avoine was then so bombarded by heavy shell-fire that, as usual, it seemed that nothing in or around it could live.

But as soon as the attacking companies rose and showed over the ground-line, the hail of machine-gun fire re-opened, and for the next three hours the Irish suffered in the open and among the shell-holes, beaten down, as the other battalions had been before them, round the piled wreckage of Cour l'Avoine farm. Out of 24 officers at the beginning of the attack, only 8 came through on their feet, and only 2 were absolutely untouched. The battalion came through it all, defeated, held down at long range, but equable in temper and morale. Small wonder that in the cheerless dawn of the 19th their brigadier came and 'made some complimentary remarks to the men who were standing about.' At the end of the period, 22 men were killed, 284 wounded and 86 missing. [97]

Private Murphy is commemorated on the Le Touret Memorial, Le Touret, France and Great War Memorial Kilgobbin. He was awarded the 1914–1915 Star, British War and Victory medals. *The Evening Herald* on 22 November 1915 carried his photograph with a notice, 'His mother would be grateful for any information.' [98]

Relatives of soldiers, who were serving at Christmas 1914, are sometimes interested to know if they took part in the Christmas Truce of 1914. The 1st Irish Guards were not involved in spontaneous fraternisation with the Germans during the Christmas period of 1914. 'The Christmas truce of 1914 reached the battalion in severely modified form. They lay among a network of trenches, already many times fought over, with communications that led directly into the enemy's lines a couple of hundred yards away. So they spent Christmas Day, under occasional bombardment of heavy artillery, in exploring and establishing themselves as well as they might among these wet dreary works. Two officers and six men were wounded. Their comfort on that Christmas night was frost so that the men kept dry at least.' [99]

William Murphy was born in Foxrock, the son of Patrick and Alice Murphy of 54, Ballyogan Road, Carrickmines. There were eight children in the family; William, Mary, Michael, Patrick, James, Robert, Nell and Alice. William enlisted in Dublin on 7 September 1914.

William's mother, Alice, passed away in August 1925, two weeks after the death of her daughter, Mary, who was killed in a bicycle accident on Brennanstown Road, Cabinteely. Her husband, Patrick, died in February 1947. Michael's brother, Patrick,

OUT OF THE DARK

(known as 'Yaddy') was employed, for most of his working life, as greenkeeper with Carrickmines Golf Club and he lived locally with his wife, Bridget, who was also employed by the Golf Club. He would have been well acquainted with the four Wilson brothers, three of whom fell in the war. Today, William's nieces and nephews, Bernadette, Margaret, Mary, Frances, Patrick and Phelim, all live in south Dublin.

MURPHY, William

Private, Service No 4225, 5th Battalion Connaught Rangers, 29th Brigade in the 10th (Irish) Division. The battalion was placed under command of 197th Brigade in 66th (2nd East Lancashire) Division on 22 July 1918. Private Murphy survived the horrific Gallipoli and Salonika campaigns and was killed in action, aged 26, during the German offensive in Flanders, on 29 July 1918, just three months before the war ended.

His grave is at 11. B. 10. Godewaersvelde British Cemetery, Nord, France, and he is commemorated on the Great War Memorial, Kilgobbin. He was awarded the 1914–1915 Star; British War and Victory medals, which were sent to his mother in 1919.

William enlisted at Fermoy, Co Cork on 3 May 1915, was appointed acting corporal (in the field) and transferred to 'B' Company on 14 January 1916. A letter from the Infantry Record Office to his parents on 7 October 1916, informed them that their son was in the 32nd Stationary Hospital, Wimereux, St Nazaire (Australian Voluntary Hospital) suffering from influenza. On 14 October of the same year he suffered a relapse and returned to hospital with influenza. In March 1917, he joined the 6th Battalion, and three months later he was in England recovering from the effects of gas poisoning.[100]

The 10th (Irish) Division came into existence as a result of Army Order No 324, issued on 21 August 1914, which authorised the formation of the six new divisions. It was formed of volunteers, under the administration of Irish Command. After initial training at the regimental depots, the units of the division moved in 1915 to the Curragh, Co Kildare, where training in brigade strength began. In May 1915 the division moved to England and was concentrated around Basingstoke. It was inspected by Lord Kitchener at Hackwood Park on 28/29 May. [101] From 1915 to 1918 the division suffered a total of 9,363 officers and men killed, wounded or missing in action. William was born in Rathfarnham, the son of Patrick Murphy and Anne Murphy (née Donnelly) of 84, Ballyogan Road, Carrickmines. There were four children in the family; William, Mary, Kathleen and Margaret. His father, Patrick Murphy, was a native of Dunane, Co Wicklow and his mother was born in Barnacullia. He received detention on three occasions for minor offences and was deducted three days pay for having a dirty rifle on parade. His personal effects included a leather note case, shampoo, rosary beads and a family photo. [102] The young soldier was not related to his namesake and near neighbour, Pte William Murphy, Irish Guards of 54, Ballyogan Road.

REDMOND, John,

Private, Service No 17965, 5th Battalion Royal Irish Fusiliers, 31st Brigade in the 10th (Irish) Division.

He was killed in action during the battle for Kiretch Tepe Sirt at Gallipoli, aged 36, on 16 August 1915. On this day at Kiretch Tepe Sirt 'his battalion moved along Kiretch Tepe past Jephson's Post towards the Pimple to relieve the 6th Royal Irish Fusiliers, who had been badly mauled – the leading Company "A" going into action about 9.30am. The Royal Irish were at the receiving the end of very heavy fire all along the Ridge and at the Pimple. One Company was moved into a very shallow trench on the extreme left and the trench was bombed from Turkish trenches over the slope of hill, just 50 yards away. The Turks enfiladed by a platoon of "D" Company from Pimple but the fire could not be maintained owing to machine guns of enemy sweeping the top. There were many casualties during the day and there was great difficulty in bringing wounded soldiers out of action, due to lack of stretchers and the loss of a machine gun put out of action by bullet tearing the band casing. At 15.30pm the Turks attempted a bayonet charge but were driven back. The battalion remained in action until 8.30pm, when ordered to retire. The casualty list amounted to more than 370 officers and men killed, wounded and missing. [103]

Private Redmond is commemorated on the Helles Memorial, Turkey and the Great War Memorial, Kilgobbin. He was awarded the 1914 Star, British War and Victory medals. The battalion was formed at Armagh in August 1914 as part of the K1 army. On 11 July his battalion embarked for active service at Devonport on board RMS *Andania* arriving at the Aegean Islands of Lemnos and Mitylene. [104]

At Alexandria the men of the battalion were able to stretch their legs ashore, marching through the town to the strain of the pipes and drums. When dawn broke on the morning of 7 August 1915, they found that the ship was off to Suvla Bay surrounded by craft of every description and when the orders came to land, lighters came alongside at about 7.00am for the landing at 'C' Beach.

John was the son of James (deceased) and Bridget Redmond, both of whom were born in Co Wexford. The family lived at 94, Ballyogan Road, Carrickmines and had four children; Thomas, John, Bridget and Sarah. On the evening of the 1911 census, John was recorded with his brother Thomas and sister-in-law, Elizabeth, in a house on the Ballyogan Road, Carrickmines. *The Evening Herald* carried a report on Tuesday 30 November 1915 stating that Pte Redmond was missing since an engagement in Gallipoli on 15 August 1915, and, 'his sister would be grateful for any information concerning him.' [105]

REYNOLDS, Dominick

Private, Service No 4259, 6th Battalion Connaught Rangers, 47th Brigade in the 16th (Irish) Division, He was killed in action, aged 19, at Mazingarbe on 27 April 1916. 'At 5am on 27 April 1916 at Mazingarbe the enemy launched an attack accompanied by gas. The gas was very slightly felt by The Connaught Rangers' men in the huts. The enemy bombarded the battalion's huts from 5am to 7.30am and got some direct hits. The three men killed on this day were; 'L/Cpl Monk; Pte Reynolds and Pte Duane and 20 other ranks were wounded.' [106] Across the entire 16th (Irish) Division there were almost two thousand casualties of which, 1260 were gassed. It emerged that the respirators used by Allied Forces were ineffective and the production of a new more effective respirator was rushed ahead.

General Hickie ordered the strengthening of defences, especially wire. Blankets soaked in Vermorel, an anti-gas agent, were to cover entrances to all dug-outs. The Irish infantry opened fire, but under cover of gas and smoke, the Germans advanced through the saps close up to the Irish trenches before assaulting. The front-line trenches of the 16th Division were smashed, parapets were blown down, trenches filled in, material and equipment lay scattered all over the battlefield. Walking wounded and gas cases, blinded, choking and retching green bile, supported each other or leaning on fit friends, formed long lines down the choked and chaotic communication trenches making their painfully slow way back to the Regimental Aid Post before being evacuated to the Casualty Clearing Stations. Father Willie Doyle, Chaplain to the forces, wrote of one such incident:

'As I made my way slowly up the trench, feeling altogether "a poor thing", I stumbled across a young officer who had been badly gassed. He had got his helmet on, but was coughing and choking in a terrible way. "For God's sake", he cried, "Help me to tear of this helmet – I can't breathe. I am dying". [107]

His grave is at I. A. 6. Mazingarbe Communal Cemetery Extension, Pas de Calais, France and he was awarded 1915 Star, British War and Victory medals. His mother signed for the 1915 Star medal on 9 June 1920, and his father received the British War and Victory medals on 12 December 1922.

Dominick enlisted for the duration of the war on the 3 May 1915 with neighbour and friend, Daniel Byrne. In November 1916, his mother received his effects, one disc only, from the Infantry Record Office for No 12 District. Kathleen Reynolds replied immediately stating that she had received the 'disc' and added that she was greatly disappointed not to have received a large woollen scarf, knitted gloves, prayer book, wrist watch and rosary beads. Interestingly, she said, 'When Captain Stephen Gwynn came home he told me that all his things were collected immediately after his death. I would love to have them, for he was the best of sons and a very brave soldier.' [108]

The battalion was formed in Kilworth, Co Cork, in September 1914 as part of the K1 army. It moved to Blackdown barracks in Aldershot in September 1915 and landed in France on 18 December 1915. The late Brendan Reynolds related an amusing incident, involving Pte Reynolds, which took place in the trenches at the frontline:

The German and Allied trenches were a short distance apart and during a lull in fighting the Irish soldiers got the opportunity to shoot and kill a hare, which was passing between the two lines. The sudden return to shooting caused some German helmets to rise above the parapet to observe what was happening. Later that evening, under the cover of darkness, Dominick, probably because of his height (he was 5ft 2ins) was chosen to go out and retrieve the hare. He was gone some time before returning to his comrades and the relative safety of his trench. When his comrades enquired about the hare; Dominick retorted, 'The bloody Germans got there first – but the smell of hare soup was lovely'. [109]

Dominick was the son of William (Batty) Reynolds (gardener) and Kathleen Reynolds of 8, Brighton Cottages, Foxrock. There were seven children in the family; Thomas, Edward, Daniel, William, Dominick, Julia and Cathleen. Dominick was educated at St Brigid's National School, Cornelscourt, and employed as a gardener when work was available. Brendan Reynolds said, 'There were three families living in Brighton Cottages with the Reynolds surname, and each had a nickname. They were the brothers, Thomas (Gosh); William (Batty) and my father Edward (Panter). My father, who was not related to Thomas or William, earned his nickname because he was employed as a gardener with George William Panter of 'The Bawn', Kerrymount Avenue, Foxrock.'[110] His son, Lt-Col George Panter, a confirmed Unionist, served in the war and survived despite his left arm being shot off in air action. When George Panter retired from the army in 1935 he was elected member of parliament for the Mourne Division. He died in 1945.

Private Patrick Lynch, Royal Army Service Corps, 615th MT Company, of Brighton Cottages was a first cousin of Dominick Reynolds. There are unconfirmed reports from local Foxrock residents that he was accidently killed by a horse on Leopardstown racecourse during the time he was on leave. His grave is at W. U. 28. Dean's Grange Cemetery. [111]

TRACEY, Francis William
Private, Service No 5148, 1st Battalion Irish Guards, 4th (Guards) Brigade in the 2nd Division.

He was killed on 25 February 1915, aged 23, when his battalion was operating in the Cuinchy Area.

There was a plan afoot to receive a visit from the Prince of Wales, 'if the situation could be considered'. Towards the end of the month, on 25 February 1915, the Irish Guards finished their trench-cleanings and bricking-up, had buried all dead that could be got at, and word went around that, if the situation on 25 February could be considered 'healthy' the Prince of Wales would visit them. The Germans, perhaps on information received (for the back areas were thronged with spies), chose that day to be very active with a small gun, and a fresh trench linking up with the French on the

La Bassee Road had been made and was visible against some new fallen-snow, they shelled that too. For this reason the Prince was not taken quite up to the front line. The precaution was reasonable enough.

A few minutes after he had left a sector, judged to be comparatively safe, 2nd Lt T. Allen was killed by a shell, or bomb, and three privates were also killed and four wounded on that same day. The Irish Guards had no other casualties on 25 February, and it may be assumed that Pte Tracey was one of the three other ranks killed along with 2nd Lt Allen. The battalion had 128 officers and men killed or wounded in the month of February 1915.[112]

His grave is at II. H. D. 2. Cuinchy Communal Cemetery, France, and he was awarded the 1914–15 Star, British War and Victory medals. He enlisted in Dublin on 7 September 1914. Frances, (known as Billy) was born in Kingstown in 1892, the son of Francis Tracey (car proprietor), and Elizabeth Tracey of 14, Rochestown Avenue, Kill-of-the-Grange. In the 1911 census, Billy Tracey's occupation was recorded as barman. There were six children in the family: Mary Jane, Thomas, Elizabeth, Alexandra, Patrick and Francis.

Chapter Six

Brennanstown, Cabinteely and Shankill

HISTORY AND ROLL OF HONOUR

Brennanstown Road runs from Carrickmines Cross Roads through the beautiful and picturesque Druids Glen to Cabinteely village. In the early twentieth century the Barrington family owned an estate and farm in the Druids Glen. John Barrington built a tower in the 'turret field', so called by my grandfather, Michael Brophy, whose family lived on Brennanstown Road for more than a century. Barrington named the tower 'Tillietudlem', after the fictional castle in Sir Walter Scott's novel, *Old Mortality*. There was a stile alongside the gate leading to the tower, which operated as a right-of-way that led across the fields to Carrickmines Railway Station.

Great War casualties, Arthur Marrable and Archibald O'Farrell, lived within a hundred metres of the tower and it is very likely that they spent some leisure time around this magical place. Joseph Mooney and Thomas Slater, two more Brennanstown casualties of the war, also lived nearby and would have known the place very well. The tower was situated in the centre of 'Beckett country' and had the Carrickmines River running along its boundary with Barrington's Wood, where the family had a private cemetery. It was a favourite haunt of the young Samuel Beckett, when he sought a place of peace and tranquillity. Many years later, Barrington's Tower, which Beckett named 'Foley's Folly', featured in a number of his literary works. Sitting on the rocky bank at the tower, Beckett could see Carrickmines Golf Course, another of his favourite places, where he played golf for many years. Situated in the glen, off the Brennanstown Road, there is an important cromlech or Portal Tomb, but known locally as The Druids' Altar. 'In 1914 Cabinteely Village was partly in the parish of Killiney, but mainly in Tullow parish, and had a population of 160 inhabiting 40 houses in 1911.'[1] In the seventeenth century it was known as 'Cabansheala' and it seems certain that it got its name from a tavern or roadside inn, which was known as, Caban tSíle or Sheila's Cabin.

Captain Lionel Keith and his wife, Olga Keith, of Brennanstown House, offered the use of their residence for wounded soldiers, if it was found necessary. In the end the house became a War Hospital Supply Depot, where splints, bandages, dressings, crutches and other items were made. Arthur Hamilton JP of Hollybrook, Foxrock, father of war casualty, Geoffrey, was among those named as Magistrates attending the Petty Sessions Court in Cabinteely on alternate Wednesdays.[2]

Shankill was a small village partly in Killiney and Rathmichael parishes in the Rathdown Barony. It contained a few straggling houses and cabins. The village served two railway lines; the old Harcourt to Bray line (see Foxrock/Carrickmines) and the main line from Bray through Kingstown now (Dun Laoghaire), which followed the coast and is now serviced by the Dublin Area Rapid Transport (Dart).

Rathmichael, situated above Shankill, was a quiet undisturbed townland frequented by weekend tourists from the city, who enjoyed the beautiful countryside with views over Killiney Bay. Six officers who fell in the war are commemorated on the Great War Memorial at the Church of Ireland in Rathmichael.

SCOTT, John Davie DSO

Lieutenant-Colonel, 2nd Battalion, Royal Irish Regiment, 49th Brigade in the 16th (Irish) Division.

He was killed, aged 28, on 21 March 1918. 'The army was reorganised in February 1918 and some units were disbanded. The 6th Battalion Royal Irish Regiment was disbanded and seven officers and 396 other ranks were posted to the 2nd Battalion at Hamel, north-west of Cambrai on the 9 February 1918. In March 1918 the 16th (Irish) Division was responsible for defending the northern side of Cologne Valley north of St Quentin and deployed along a ridge centred on Ronssoy. The 2nd Battalion was in the forward sector of defence, based in the neighbouring village of Lempire. Before 21 March the 2nd Royal Irish Regiment had a strength of 18 officers and 514 men. When the German offensive began, there was a thick mist and the machine guns were ineffective. A heavy bombardment caused severe losses on the right flank of the 49th Brigade, exposing that flank when the enemy infantry advanced at about 9am. Within an hour and a half, the 49th Brigade had been virtually destroyed.

On the day he was killed Lieutenant-Colonel Scott ordered his headquarters personnel to man Rose Trench, a forward trench on the Red Line at the tip of the Lempire defences. Rose Trench became untenable when ammunition began to run out. The Royal Irish Regiment withdrew to Irish Trench and Lt-Col Scott was killed when the remnant came under incessant attack at 14.15pm. The 2nd Battalion Royal Irish Regiment recorded 78 men killed outright and by 30 March 1918, the battalion had been reduced to 1 officer and 31 other ranks.'[3]

His grave is at H. E. 23.Unicorn Cemetery, Vend'huile, Aisne, France, and he is commemorated on the War Memorial, Rathmichael Church of Ireland, Shankill, and the Memorial Plaque at St Columba's College, Rathfarnham. He won the Distinguished Service Order (DSO) on 1 January 1918: 'The term, "in the field", indicating that he was in contact with the enemy. This award was announced, apparently, in the King's New Year's Honours.'[4] Captain Scott was also 'Mentioned in Despatches' and awarded one emblem (oak leaf) noted on his medal index card. He was awarded the 1915 Star, British War and Victory medals, which were issued to his mother on 7 July 1922, while she was living at Kensington Gardens, London W2.[5]

On 18 September 1909 John Davie Scott was included in a list of 'Gentlemen Cadets' from the Royal Military Academy, Sandhurst Military College to be second lieutenants. He was admitted to the Indian Army and was promoted to lieutenant on 8 November 1915. In the summer of 1917 he rose from the rank of captain through major to lieutenant-colonel in three months and on 25 August 1917 he was commanding a battalion.[6]

Scott's Medical Sheet recorded on 6 November 1915 that he spent ten days in hospital at Salonika suffering with jaundice. His condition improved in December followed by a relapse suffering with stiffness and pain. He spent some more time in hospital in the Balkans on 21 January 1916 with lumbago problems. His health suffered a further setback when on 26 February 1916 he was declared unfit for duty and spent six weeks in a London hospital. On 14 April 1916, he was invalided to England from Malta and then to the Royal Hospital, Dublin, where he recovered sufficiently to do light office work before returning to the front.[7]

He was the son of Sir Lieutenant-Colonel Hopton B. Scott (deceased) and Alice Jane Lady Scott of Locksley, Shankill. Their portraits were painted by the well-known artist, Stephen Catterson Smith PRHA. There were twelve children in the family, of whom eight survived infancy; Alice Mary, Edith Margaret, Dora Cecil, George Ernest Blaine, Marjorie Ruth, John Davie, Anastasia and Florence. John Scott was educated at St Columba's College, Rathfarnham and played in its First XI Cricket team.

CABINTEELY PARENTS LOSE TWO SONS IN WAR

A retired army officer, Lt-Col Richard Hobart Morrison, late of 18th (QMO) Hussars and his wife, Louise Caroline Morrison, (née de Ricci) of Johnstown House, Cabinteely, lost two sons in the war. There were three children in the family: Richard Fielding, Robert Herman Grant and Charles Colquhoun Morrison.

MORRISON, Richard Fielding MC
Major, Commanding 'D' Battery Royal Field Artillery, 51st Brigade in the 3rd Division.

The evidence points to his being wounded in action in the village of Kemmel and the adjoining hill, Mont Kemmel, which was the scene of fierce fighting in the latter half of April 1918.[8] He died, aged 27, on 25 April 1918 at No 36 Casualty Clearing Station, Heilly (near Albert), France. A correspondent wrote: 'Universally popular with all who knew him, Major Morrison was a very keen soldier and a good sportsman. Anything he undertook to carry through he accomplished, if it was humanly possible to do so, and his battery was one of the most efficient both in gunnery and in its horses and turnout.'[9]

Mont Kemmel had been enveloped by the advancing hordes, and there was much hand-to-hand fighting in the village of Kemmel, where the Germans were clustering all round the lower slopes by 9am on Thursday, April 25. The French Garrison withdrew towards the summit, and sold their lives dearly. All that day the fate of Mont Kemmel was still in some doubt.[10] His father wrote to the War Office:

Received the following telegram from Mr A. Ferrier of Ash Hurst, Killiney, my son's father-in-law, stating, 'Letter from Taylor saying he was wounded when attending Fielding (i.e. Major R.F. Morrison) on Friday April 26, who had lost his foot, no anxiety. Please get confirmation from the War Office'. Reference these messages and the telephonic communication this afternoon with Colonel Vaughan, Southern Command Headquarters. Will you kindly cause enquiry to be made as to the facts and communicate by wire with me and also with Mr Ferrier as above. I am not sure as to whom the Taylor is, who is referred to as having attended my son on Friday, the day after he is reported to have died, but I presume he is a medical officer as the statement is made that there was no cause for anxiety.

When Lieutenant Colonel Morrison received no response to his urgent enquiry in early May he wrote to the War Office again on the 22 May. The retired Army Officer was furious at the failure of the War Office to respond, especially since his son's details appeared in the list furnished to the press some days before. He stated that it was fortunate that it was possible to ascertain, through private sources, full particulars of his son's death. The anguish suffered by his daughter-in-law, Jessie, whilst awaiting the official enquiry, was also mentioned. Major Morrison's widow, Jessie, wrote to the War Office on 11 May 1918 requesting information on all matters relating to her late husband's death. She asked where he was buried, whether any clergyman was with him at the end, and if he left any message for her or gave one to anyone else. She concluded: 'I want to have his coat and any clothes he wore last, sent to me. It is very strange that no one has written me a line, it's a poor reward after dying for one's country.' There was no indication in Major Morrison's original documents that his wife received his personal effects as requested, with the exception of his wrist watch and four badges, however, this does not mean that all his effects were not recovered and sent to his wife at a later date.[11]

His grave is at V.B. 21. Haringhe (Bandaghem) Military Cemetery, Poperinge, Belgium, and he is commemorated on the Great War Memorial at Wellington College, Berkshire; Morrison Memorial, Church of Ireland, Kill o' the Grange; First World War Memorial and the Morrison Memorial at St Matthias's Church of Ireland, Ballybrack and the Book of Remembrance, associated with the Royal Military

Academy, Woolwich, in the chapel at the Royal Military College, Sandhurst. The Morrison Memorial at St Matthias was erected by his wife, Jessie. He also won the Military Cross in July 1918:

> For conspicuous gallantry and devotion to duty. Whether in command of his battery or of the brigade, or acting as infantry liaison officer, he displayed coolness and resourcefulness of a very high order. Once, when his battery came under heavy shell fire and direct hits on the teams caused some confusion, his fine example and complete command of the situation at once restored order. His courage and fine leadership were conspicuous throughout.[12]

Other awards included, twice 'Mentioned in Despatches' in1915, and again before he died in 1918. He was also awarded the 1914 Star, British War and Victory medals. Morrison passed out at the head of the gunners' list, at the Royal Military Academy, Woolwich, obtaining the Tombs Memorial Prize in July 1910. He was posted to France with the 129th Battery Royal Field Artillery in August 1914 and served with the 3rd, 7th and 9th Divisions continuously. Morrison joined the 126th Howitzer Battery at Dundalk, going on service with it in August 1914, and receiving his 'baptism of fire' at Mons, and being present in all the subsequent fighting in which his 3rd Division took part. In 1915 he joined the Royal Horse Artillery and became Adjutant of his Brigade. On promotion to Captain in 1916 he was given command of a Battery Field Artillery, which he commanded till his death through all the battles on the Somme in 1916 and those of his batteries further successes in 1917, being wounded by a shell in October of that year. He was given the rank of acting-major in July1916 and promoted to major on 10 January 1917.[13]

Richard Morrison was born in Mhow, India, on 30 April 1890 and educated at Wellington College, Berkshire (Lynedoch, 1903–1907), where he captained the 'shooting eight'.[14] When he finished at Wellington College he entered the Royal Military Academy, Woolwich. He married Euphemia Jessie Ferrier in 1916 and the couple resided at 53, Eglinton Road, Donnybrook, and it appears that there were no children at this early stage of their marriage. Jessie Morrison was the elder daughter of Alexander F. Ferrier and Elizabeth K. Ferrier of Ash Hurst, Killiney. It is believed that Alexander Ferrier was a director of the well-known Dublin Company, Ferrier Pollock Co. Limited, wholesale warehousemen.

A granddaughter of Jessie Morrison, writing under the username of 'vcj' contacted the Great War Forum in 2009 seeking information on her grandmother's first husband, Lt-Col Morrison; this indicates that Jessie married again.[15]

SECOND SON LOST IN CONTROVERSIAL SUBMARINE DISASTER

MORRISON, Robert Herman Grant

Sub-Lieutenant, HMS Submarine *A7* Royal Navy. Sub-Lieutenant Morrison was drowned, aged 23, when his ship *A7*, a coastal submarine, was lost on 16 January 1914. On the morning of the tragedy the submarine *A7* was exercising in Whitsands Bay, near Plymouth. She dived to carry out a mock attack on her escorts and failed to resurface. Her crew of eleven officers and men were lost.

The flotilla assumed their attack positions and was ordered to dive to a predetermined depth and then resurface. It soon became apparent that it was in difficulties, when a large stream of bubbles appeared on the surface over the area where she had submerged. All the other submarines returned to the surface safely, but for the *A7* disaster had finally struck:

> The flotilla commander on board HMS *Pygmy* sped towards the scene and ordered tugs and salvage lighters dispatched from Devonport with all possible speed. For some reason however, nobody bothered putting a marker buoy down, so when the tugs arrived with sweeping gear they could not locate the stricken submarine. In the end the Navy spent five days continuously dragging the seabed before they found the *A7*. By the time divers were ready to go down to the submarine, everybody knew it was a futile gesture. The *A7s* crew had all perished.[16]

The news of yet another submarine disaster shocked the people of Plymouth so much that they set up a public fund for the widows and orphans of the unfortunate crew. The Royal Navy was roundly condemned on all sides for its incompetence, and suffered huge embarrassment at the hands of the National Press, who made sarcastic remarks about the inability of the navy to salvage their own submarines.

Meanwhile in Whitsands Bay the struggle to lift the *A7* from the clutches of a muddy seabed continued. Wires snapped, and capstans burnt out, but the *A7* just would not move. In the end the Navy, by now in danger of being buried by the abuse hurled at it by a vitriolic press, decided to leave well alone and contented themselves by holding a memorial service over the wreck-site, with a Royal Marine Guard firing a salute, and wreaths being tossed upon the calm, silent waters. Thus the *A7* became a fitting tomb for all her officers and crew, and today, one hundred years later, that is how she still remains.[17] It was reported in *The Times* newspaper on 13 March 1914 that:

> Instructions were received at Devonport yesterday from the Admiralty that submarine *A7*, which foundered in Whitsand Bay on 16 January is to be abandoned. The special salvage craft which had been engaged in the operations will leave for Sheerness today. On Thursday morning a memorial service for the eleven officers and men will be held on the cruiser *Forth*, parent ship of the Devonport Submarine Flotilla, at the scene of the disaster, and at the same time another service will be held in the chapel of the naval barracks at Devonport. It is probable that both the Devonport and Portsmouth Submarine Flotillas will be present at the service over the wreck, the Portsmouth Flotilla being on an instructional cruise in the neighbourhood of the port.[18]

WINSTON CHURCHILL OBLIGED TO ANSWER A QUESTION IN HOUSE OF COMMONS

Through the influence of his father, Lt-Col Richard Hobart Morrison, this tragedy became the subject of a question in the House of Commons on 26 February 1914 by Lord Charles Beresford, who asked the First Lord of the Admiralty whether he had any further information to give the House with regard to the sinking of the *A7* submarine, particularly with regard to the statements made that she had remained on the bottom for an hour a short time before the accident occurred. Winston Churchill replied:

> These statements have been closely investigated. The statement contained in the published letter of Colonel Morrison, father of Sub-Lieutenant Morrison, who lost his life in *A7*, to the effect that *A7* sunk to the bottom when exercising off Plymouth, and that it took over an

hour of hard work to get her to the surface again, is, according to all the information I have received, quite untrue. I am informed that Sub-Lieutenant Morrison was only present in *A7* during one exercise prior to Christmas, namely, on the 16 December. Three men who were then on duty in *A7* depose that she did not go below a depth of twenty feet on that day. Sub-Lieutenant Morrison joined His Majesty's ship *Onyx* on the 1 December, 1913, and the only other exercises in 'A' boats in which he took part prior to Christmas, were three dives in *A8*.

On one occasion, owing to a personal error, *A8* was over-trimmed, and dived to a depth of seventy-eight feet. The interval of time from the moment she dipped her periscope until she regained the surface did not exceed one minute. She did not touch the bottom; and diving at such a depth is not considered dangerous, in fact, it is frequently deliberately undertaken. The lieutenant commanding *A8,* and the whole crew of the vessel who have been examined, declare that on no other occasion did *A8* go below a depth of twenty feet. It is not for me to explain this apparent discrepancy; but it is possible that Colonel Morrison confused his son's account of his recent experiences in *A8* with some reference to an accident which occurred in that vessel four years ago, in 1910, when, owing to a personal error, *A8* sunk to a depth of about 200 feet, and remained there twenty minutes before she could be brought to the surface. Had she been fitted with the efficient pumps with which all the 'A' class are now fitted, she could have been brought up immediately.

Submarines have been on the bottom scores of times; but this incident in *A8* four years ago is the only occasion during diving exercises on which a British submarine, prior to the loss of *A7*, has remained there more than a few seconds longer than she wished. Statements similar to that in Colonel Morrison's letter were attributed in the Press to Mrs Wagstaff and Mrs Northam, widows of men who lost their lives in the *A7*. In addition to the three men already mentioned, three other seamen witnesses can also testify that *A7* had never dived below normal depth or remained on the bottom. The services of these six men cover the whole of the period during which Wagstaff and Northam served in *A7*.[19]

Sub-Lieutenant Morrison is commemorated on the Morrison Memorial, Kill o' the Grange, Church of Ireland, and the Memorial Obelisk in the Royal Naval Cemetery, Clayhall Road, Gosport. He was awarded the 1914 Star, British War and Victory medals. Robert Morrison enlisted on 15 January 1909 and served as midshipman until 30 May 1912 when he was promoted to sub-lieutenant. He was born in Dublin on 11 May 1891 and was unmarried.

SHANKILL FAMILY LOSE THREE SONS, 1914–1918

The Henley's were the third family in South County Dublin to endure the intolerable burden of losing three sons in uniform. Jeremiah and Isabella Henley of 'Glen View', Shankill, had five children: Alfred, Florence, Frederick Louis, Ernest Albert William and Henry Thomas. According to the baptismal register from Christ Church, Leeson Park, Dublin, Alfred was born in December 1885 when his parents were living at Ranelagh Road, Dublin, however, there was no further mention of him, and since the census in 1911 recorded that Isabella Henley gave birth to five children, of whom four were still living, it may be assumed that he died in infancy.

Frederick and Henry were killed in action. Ernest entered Trinity College and qualified as a medical doctor before emigrating to New Zealand where he joined the New Zealand Army Medical Corps. He was refused permission to serve overseas due to poor health, but remained in the army attached to the 2nd Reserve Battalion. His chronic ill health led to his early death in 1918. It was his intention to serve in the Great War, and despite not being killed in action, the author felt it was important to record him along with his fallen brothers.

Jeremiah who was Professor of Education at the Government Training College, died in February 1926, aged 82, and Isabella passed away in July 1939, aged 95. They were interred in Dean's Grange Cemetery with their daughter, Florence, who died in October 1962.

HENLEY, Ernest Albert William
Captain, Second Reserve Battalion New Zealand Army Medical Corps.

He died, aged 43, in Napier, New Zealand on 14 November 1918, and was buried in grave plot No 9, Interment No 1, Section 7, Park Island Cemetery, Napier, New Zealand. His large headstone is a beautifully crafted Celtic cross engraved with sprigs of shamrock. Captain Henley is commemorated on the Great War Memorial,

Rathmichael Church of Ireland, Shankill; Hall of Honour, Trinity College; Great War Memorial in the former Adelaide Hospital, Dublin, and the headstone of the family grave at Dean's Grange Cemetery. Following his graduation from Trinity College, he emigrated to New Zealand where he joined the New Zealand Army Medical Corps, however, because of poor health, he was not accepted for foreign service. He remained in the service until his death and was promoted to Captain in April 1915 as part of the 2nd Reserve Battalion. Ernest Henley was born in Co Wicklow in 1875 and entered Trinity College where he took his MB degree in 1901 and a MD degree in 1911. During his Arts course he obtained first-class honours in mathematics and experimental science. He also obtained a senior moderatorship and gold medal in experimental science. In Trinity College he won the scholarship in chemistry, physics, botany, and zoology in 1898, as well as first honours and prizes in physiology, materia medica, anatomy and forensic medicine. In 1900 he obtained the gold medal for operative surgery in the Royal College of Surgeons in Ireland, and in the following year he won the Hudson Scholarship and gold medal with first prizes in medicine, surgery, dermatology and gynaecology at the Adelaide Hospital, Dublin. Dr Henley was for a time resident physician and surgeon at the Adelaide Hospital and afterwards practised for a few months in Belfast. Ernest met his wife, Mary Fitzpatrick, in the Adelaide Hospital, Dublin, where she graduated in medical surgical and fever nursing. They emigrated to New Zealand in 1902 and married in the same year at St Michael's and All Angels, Christchurch. They settled down in New Zealand, residing at 10, Marine Parade, Napier, where they had two children, Norah Isobel and Wilton Ernest. Dr Henley was an honorary visiting surgeon at Napier Hospital and established the first x-ray service in the region. In 1911, he returned to Dublin with Mary and the two children to complete his Doctorate of Medicine (DM). Mary returned to Dublin again in 1920, two years after Ernest died, with the two children. During the family's stay in Dublin, Norah recounts the story of her lying in bed when a sniper moved across the skylight to position for target at a nearby barracks. Norah married William Bird and they had four children: William, John, Barrie and Chris. The first three were all doctors.

Their eldest child, Wilton, was educated at Wanganui Collegiate and played rugby for Otago University and Hawkes Bay. He went to London with his mother, Mary, and took up his Rhodes scholarship at Oxford in 1929, graduating with an MB and ChB in 1935 having completed his clinical years at St Mary's Hospital. Mary died in

London on 20 May 1936 and is buried at Marylebone Cemetery. During his time in London Wilton played rugby with Oxford University, St Mary's Hospital, Combined Universities and was selected for an Irish trial. He was an outstanding place kicker and contributed a long-range penalty in a 3-3 draw in one of the annual colours matches against Cambridge University. Wilton returned to New Zealand in 1939 and served in the New Zealand Army Medical Corps during the Second World War. He was in Italy and in the occupation forces in Japan and was awarded the MBE for his contribution during the war years and was recognised for services in post-graduate education. Wilton was a medical practitioner, who played an important role in the administration of the affairs of the college, hospital board and the fledgling school of medicine in the University of Auckland.

He married Wilhelmina Muriel Jean Barnes-Graham in 1935 and they had four children: Peter, Victoria, John and Patrick. Doctor John Henley MB, ChB is associate professor in the Department of Medicine and was mentioned in the Queen's Birthday Honours in 2009. He received, Officer of the New Zealand Order of Merit, (ONZM) for his services to medicine. His brother, Dr Patrick Henley MB, ChB is a physician with special interest in obstetric medicine.[20]

HENLEY, Frederick Louis

Second Lieutenant,13th Battalion, attached 11th Battalion Sherwood Foresters, (Notts and Derby Regiment), 70th Brigade in the 23rd Division.

Second Lieutenant Henley was killed, aged 33, in action on the Somme, France, on 1 October 1916. On the day that he died it was decided that the battalion's objective at Martinpuich and Flers le Sars, was to 'capture the Flers le Sars line on a front of over a mile with the 50th Division on the right of the 23rd Division. The battalion moved up at 9.15am to the assembly trenches. The objective for the battalion was two lines of hostile trenches in Flers le Sars line between the division boundaries on the right of the main Albert–Bapaume Road. The leading companies were to pass the first hostile line and take the second. The supporting company was to take and consolidate the first hostile line. At 3.15pm "A" &"D" Companies advanced in two waves under its own barrage, which lifted off the objective. The objectives were taken and consolidated. The battalion was in touch with its division on its right, but the battalion on its left failed to hold its objective, and lost touch. The 13th Battalion was relieved from the line during the evening and came back to bivouacs at Lozenge

Wood.' The losses for the 1 and 2 October were 3 officers, Capt R.J. Nichols, 2nd Lt F.L. Henley and 2nd Lt D.J. Thornton, together with twelve other ranks killed. The wounded included, 3 Officers and 137 other ranks and 15 missing.[21]

He is commemorated on the Thiepval Memorial, Somme, France; Hall of Honour, Trinity College; Great War Memorial, Rathmichael Church of Ireland, Shankill; Bishop Winnington Memorial Clock and inscription in the Creighton Hall, Kilburn; The Old Boys' Association Memorial to the 1914–1918 dead and the staff memorial tablets to F.L. Henley and A.J. Stuart, also in the Creighton Hall, Kilburn. The plaques were refurbished, the memorial clock repaired and today they look very well in a new location at Kilburn Library, about 300 yards from their original home in Kilburn Grammar School.[22] He is also remembered on the headstone of the family grave at Dean's Grange Cemetery. Second Lieutenant Henley was awarded the British War and Victory medals, which were sent to his sister, Florence, on 28 June 1922.

Frederick Henley served in the Officers Training Corps at the University of London and spent two years (1912–1914) in the Territorial Army. His original documents revealed that he enlisted in July 1915, but his medal index card does not include the 1915 Star medal indicating that he did not enter a theatre of war until early 1916. The battalion took part in the opening day of the Somme offensive on 1 July 1916 and suffered such grievous losses that it was relieved that night. The 11th Battalion returned to the bitter struggle in late July and again in October for the final attempt to break through the German rear position.

His sister, Florence, a music student, took responsibility for the administration of his estate and was unhappy with the handling of his affairs by the War Office. She wrote a letter to the War Office on 5 March 1917 informing the Secretary that her brother's personal effects were missing from the parcel, which included clothes and towels only. Miss Henley's expectation that all her brother's effects could be located from the heat of battle and returned to his family, may have been a little unrealistic, but nevertheless, her letter concluded:'…neither his pocket book, field glasses, revolver, watch, nor many other things – nothing personal of his, which we would so much desire to keep. It is hard that such a state of affairs would still exist – personal effects – which relatives so much prize, not returned to them. Can nothing be done?' In her second letter on 18 March 1918, she wrote:

It is with amazement I hear that there is no record of the recovery of my brother's body. In a letter from Colonel Watson of the 11th Battalion Sherwood Foresters, dated 4 October 1916, to my brother's friend, Mr J. Ware, he says – 'It is with very deep regret that I have to report his death. He was killed instantaneously, and we buried him close to where he fell.' A brother officer, 2nd Lt J.H. Lacy, stated that he was hit by a sniper and death was painless – and he was buried near the village of ... on ... (he thought) the 3 October. A wooden cross has or will be shortly erected. After these facts being sent to me, I should be glad of an immediate explanation of the statement in your letter that there is no record of the recovery of his body.[23]

Frederick Henley's early education was received privately and he entered Trinity College in 1902, where he received a BA degree in 1906 and an MA in 1912. He was appointed Senior Mathematics Master at the Kilburn Grammar School, Middlesex in 1910 and remained in this position until he enlisted in 1915. In 1914 he was living at 9, Brondesbury Park Mansions, Kilburn, London and was single at the time of his death.

HENLEY, Henry Thomas

Second Lieutenant, 7th Battalion Royal Irish Rifles, 48th Brigade in the 16th (Irish) Division.Previously, Service No 7/6558, Sergeant in the Royal Irish Rifles.

Second Lieutenant Henley was killed in action, aged 27, at Broadway Park Avenue on 8 March 1917. From 10am to 2.30pm on 8 March 1917 there was intermittent shell and trench mortar fire on the Irish Rifles front line and support lines, and at 3.30pm the enemy commenced a heavy trench mortar and artillery bombardment on the battalion. At 4.40pm, under cover of an intense barrage, the enemy attacked in three parties of about 50 men each. The right party was driven back by the Irish Rifles Lewis gun-fire, while the centre and left attacking parties entered their trenches, some of whom penetrated to Park Avenue. Once again, the enemy was driven back by centre attack within 15 minutes, leaving 3 dead and 4 wounded. The casualties included, 2nd Lt Henley killed, five officers wounded, seven other ranks killed, 39 wounded and missing.[24]

His grave is at N. 53. Kemmel Chateau Military Cemetery, France and he is commemorated on the Great War Memorial, Rathmichael Church of Ireland, Shankill; Great War Memorial at High School and Abbey School, Rathgar; Dublin Boy Scouts Memorial, St Patrick's Cathedral, Dublin and the headstone on the family grave, Dean's Grange Cemetery. He was awarded the Military Medal and a commission on 8 March 1916. The promotion became effective on 24 October 1916 when he was posted to his battalion. In a letter to Headquarters on 16 September the Lieutenant- Colonel, Officer Commanding 7th Battalion Royal Irish Rifles, wrote:

> Sergeant Henley has distinguished himself in action by keeping the men in hand and setting them to work at consolidation after all the officers of his company had become casualties. He commanded his men with great coolness and ability. I recommend that he may be promoted at once, without undergoing any further training at a cadet school or elsewhere.[25]

He was also awarded the British War and Victory medals. Henry Henley enlisted in Dublin on 20 May 1915 and when responding to the question on his attestation papers, 'what nationality', he stated, 'British by birth – Irish by nationality'.[26] His battalion was formed in Belfast in September 1914 as part of the K2 army and landed at Le Havre on 20 December 1915.

He was born on 17 July 1887, and educated at the Church of Ireland Training College, Model School and High School, all in Dublin. It was recorded in his original documents that his occupation was 'farmer'.

THREE SHANKILL BROTHERS SERVE,
TWO DIE WITHIN FORTY-EIGHT HOURS OF EACH OTHER

George Fletcher FGS, Administrative Head of the Technical Instruction Branch of the Department of Agriculture and Henrietta Maria Fletcher of Mona, Shankill, had six children: Arnold Lockart, George Kenneth, Donald Lockart, Gilbert, Constance and Linton. Donald died of wounds, aged 20, in 1917 followed in a matter of hours by the announcement that his brother, Arnold, died from wounds. A third brother, Reverend George Fletcher ASC, Royal Army Service Corps, was gazetted captain on 19 October 1914 and survived the war. He was a chaplain in the forces.

FLETCHER, Donald Lockart
Second Lieutenant, 4th Battalion, attached 6th Battalion Leinster Regiment, 29th Brigade in the 10th (Irish) Division.

He died from wounds, aged 20, in Salonika, Greece, on 28 April 1917. Second Lieutenant Fletcher was accidentally killed during training classes, whilst conducting tests of grenadiers. His father received the standard letter from the War Office when his son was exhumed, identified and re-interred.[27]

His grave is at VII. B. 14, Struma Military Cemetery, Thessalonika, Serres Town, Greece. He is commemorated on the War Memorial, Rathmichael Church of Ireland, Shankill; St Philip and St James Church, Blackrock; War Memorial at St Andrew's College, Booterstown; Great War Memorial at High School and Abbey School, Rathgar and the Hall of Honour, Trinity College. He was 'Mentioned in Despatches' in January 1915 and was awarded the British War and Victory medals.

It is stated in his original documents that he embarked for Salonika on 7 June 1916. He was first admitted to hospital on 26 June 1916 and discharged on 11 July 1916. On the 19 July he was admitted to hospital again, and discharged eleven days later. There were other visits to hospital during this period, including hospitalisation for a snakebite on 9 August 1916, malaria on 14 September and gastroenteritis on 16 November, all in 1916.[28]

Donald Fletcher was born on 15 January 1897 and educated at High School, Rathgar; St Andrew's College, Booterstown and he was an undergraduate at Trinity College in 1914, where he was a member of its OTC. His effects included; violin with bow, silver watch, leather wallet, writing case with letters and a revolver colt in holster with lanyard.[29]

FLETCHER, Arnold Lockart
Second Lieutenant,193rd Company, Machine Gun Corps, in the 56th Division.

Second Lieutenant Fletcher was admitted to the No 2 British Red Cross Hospital near Rouen, on 19 April 1917, suffering with severe leg wounds received on the previous day, near Wancourt, while fighting in the second Battle of Arras. He died on 30 April 1917, aged 28. The second Battle of Arras took place on the days between 9 April and 16 May 1917. 'The enemy advanced on 9 April at Achicourt and it appeared to be easy and over when 100 prisoners came in. Lieutenant Wilson and 2nd Lt Fletcher then reconnoitered the point over which they would have to advance, and observed much hesitation on the part of the London Scottish in deciding their direction; both flanks seeming to be in the air. They decided to move up in immediate support. At 7.30pm on 18 April, a message was received by his section that two guns were to proceed in order and in case of an enemy attack on Wancourt, to fire down the valley on their left flank. Fletcher's section was ordered to hold the position until definite information was obtained that the enemy had advanced up Wancourt Valley. It was during this action that Fletcher was wounded by a shell. The night was extremely dark and direction was very difficult to maintain.'[30]

His grave is at B. 6. 1, St Sever Cemetery, Rouen, France and he is commemorated on the War Memorial, Rathmichael Church of Ireland, Shankill; Plaque N Chancel, St Philip and St James Church, Blackrock; War Memorial at St Andrew's College, Botterstown; Great War Memorial, Royal Grammar School Worcester and the Hall of Honour, Trinity College. It was reported in his obituary that his gallant conduct won him a 'Mention in Despatches', however no record of the 'mention' could be confirmed by the author. He was awarded the British War and Victory medals. Arnold Fletcher joined the army on 22 May 1915 and was gazette 2nd Lieutenant on 15 March 1916. 'His effects included a fountain pen, stud, pipe and stamps.'[31]

He received his early education at St Andrew's College (1901–1902), attended the Royal Grammer School, until 1905 and entered Trinity College, where he received a BAI degree in 1909, a BA and MA in 1912. The *Worcesterian* for 1911 revealed that he was granted £50 by the Royal Society to complete his research in Dublin.

He was working on radioactive materials, on which he published a paper in January 1911. Arnold Fletcher had a distinguished university career and made a substantial contribution to scientific research.[32]

O'FARRELL, Archibald Hugh
Second Lieutenant, 1st Battalion Irish Guards, 1st Guards Brigade in the Guards Division.

Previously served in the ranks, Service No 12311, 1st Battalion Irish Guards. Second Lieutenant O'Farrell was killed in action, aged 19, at Stafford Alley on 27 September 1918 just six weeks before the war ended. His death took place on the same day, and in the same place, as fellow Cabinteely man, Pte Michael Byrne.

Kipling's Regimental History described how 2nd Lt O'Farrell was killed:

> None recall precisely how they reached the bottom of the Canal, but there were a few moments of blessed shelter ere they scrambled out and reformed on the far side. The shelling here was bad enough, but nothing to what they had survived. A veil of greasy smoke, patched with flame that did not glare, stood up behind them, and through the pall of it, in little knots, stumbled their supports, blinded, choking, gasping. In the direction of the attack, across a long stretch of broken rising ground, were more shells, but less thickly spaced, and craters of stinking earth and coloured chalks where our barrage had ripped out nests of machine-guns. Far off, to the left, creaming with yellow smoke in the morning light rose the sullen head of Bourlon Wood to which the Canadians were faithfully paying the debt contracted by the 2nd Battalion of the Irish Guards in the old days after Cambrai. At the crest of the ascent lay Saunders Keep, which marked the point where the Scots Guards would lie up and the Irish come through. Already the casualties had been severe. Captain Bence-Jones and 2nd Lieutenant Mathieson of No 2 Company were wounded at the Keep itself, and 2nd Lieutenant A.R. Boyle of No 1 earlier in the rush. The companies panted up, gapped and strung out. From the Keep the land sloped down to Stafford Alley, the battalion's first objective, just before Lieutenant Barry Close was killed. That day marked his coming of age.

Beyond the Alley the ground rose again, and here the Irish were first checked by some machine-gun fire that had escaped our barrages. Second Lieutenant O'Brien, No 3 Company, was hit at this point while getting his men forward. He had earned his Military Cross in May, and he died well. The next senior officer, 2nd Lt E.H. Burke, was away to the left in the thick of the smoke with a platoon that, like the rest, was fighting for its life; so 2nd Lt O'Farrell led on. He was hit not far from Stafford Alley, and while his wound was being bandaged by Sergeant Regan, hit again by a bullet that passing through the Sergeant's cap and a finger, entered O'Farrell's heart.

During the month, the battalion lost 2 officers killed; 7 wounded; 21 other ranks killed; 159 wounded, and 51 missing.[33]

His grave is at II. B. 1. Sanders Keep Military Cemetery, Graincourt-Les-Havrincourt, France, and he is commemorated on the Roll of Honour at Tullow Church of Ireland, Carrickmines and on the Holy Water Font, St Brigid's Roman Catholic Church, Cabinteely. He was awarded the British War and Victory medals, which were issued to his father on 22 February 1922.

Archibald O'Farrell enlisted in the ranks of the Irish Guards, on the 7 September 1917 at Whitehall, London. He was discharged to a Commission as 2nd lieutenant on the 29 January 1918 and transferred to an officer training battalion. On 10 June 1918 he joined the 1st Battalion, Divisional Headquarters, Bavincourt Chateau, France, and was immediately involved in the action.[34]

He was the only son of Sir Edward O'Farrell, KCB and Dorothy, Lady O'Farrell (née Bunbury) of, Busselton, Western Australia, and they lived at Cuilnagreine, Brennanstown Road, Cabinteely. There were two children in the family: Archibald Hugh, baptised at St Brigid's Roman Catholic Church, Cabinteely, and Margaret Bunbury born April 1903 and baptised at Tullow Church of Ireland, Carrickmines.

Following his retirement, Sir Edward and his family moved to England, and at the time of his death in August 1926, he was living at Sallygap, Crowborough, Sussex. Sir Edward, born in 1856 in Dublin, was a barrister and spent most of his life as registrar in the Land Commission. He was Assistant Under secretary for Ireland and was knighted in 1915 for his services. In his last Will and Testament he bequeathed £100 to his sister, Helen O'Farrell, Loreto Convent, Youghal, Co Cork, and also recorded his desire to be buried in a Roman Catholic Burial Ground.[35] Sir Edward was a keen golfer and had the distinction of being elected the first Captain of Carrickmines Golf Club in 1900.

In October 1917 the Protestant Archbishop of Dublin, The Right Reverend John Henry Bernard, recommended that after the war, a simple, dignified tablet should be erected in each Church of Ireland church bearing the names of all in the parish who died in the war. He hoped it would be permissible to list all the names, whether they were Churchmen, Methodists, Roman Catholics or Presbyterians. The ecumenical gesture made by the Archbishop fell on deaf ears, although his legal advisers were doubtful about the viability of his proposal. A plague was erected in the porch of St Brigid's Roman Catholic church, Cabinteely commemorating both, 2nd Lt Archibald O'Farrell, and his father, Sir Edward O'Farrell. It is very likely that 2nd Lt O'Farrell has the distinction of being the only fallen hero of the Great War, in Ireland, to be commemorated in a Roman Catholic church and a Church of Ireland church, situated in the same parish/district.

MARRABLE, Francis Arthur

Sergeant, Service No 14177, 7th Battalion, 'D' Company (the 'Pals'), Royal Dublin Fusiliers, 30th Brigade in the 10th (Irish) Division.

Sergeant Marrable arrived in Gallipoli on 7 August 1915 and, almost immediately, received serious wounds from which he died, aged 28, on homeward-bound transport on 18 August 1915. On 19 August 1915, an officer attached to the 'Pals' Company wrote home about the action on 15 August:

At last we are having a rest, so I can write a few lines to let you know what we are doing and how we are doing it. We landed at about 9am on Saturday, the 7th inst., under sharpest fire, and we had about 16 casualties in our battalion before we landed. There we found another division holding a line along the sea shore, where they were entrenched, after suffering pretty heavy losses. Our orders were to advance across the plain and take a line of hills about six miles away

– and then push on. Each one of my fellows had to carry, in addition to his equipment (say, 70lbs.), an extra burden of about 25 to 30 lbs.; we had no transport. The first part of our advance was across a neck of sand about 50 to100 yards wide, where the Turks had the range to an inch – this was where poor Frank Marrable got it, and how we got across the swamp I do not know.[36]

He is commemorated on the Helles Memorial, Turkey, Roll of Honour; St Brigid's Roman Catholic Church, Cabinteely, Tullow Church of Ireland, Carrickmines, and Great War Memorial, Aravon School, Bray, Co Wicklow. Sergeant Marrable was 'Mentioned in Despatches' and was awarded the 1914–15 Star, British War and Victory medals.

An article in the *Irish Times* on 11 September 1914 encouraging volunteers to enlist resulted in more than 200 Rugby Union players attending a meeting at Lansdowne Road, where they were addressed by F.H. Browning, the President of the Irish Rugby Football Union and Lieutenant-Colonel Geoffrey Downing DSO, who had been given command of the new Royal Dublin Fusiliers, 7th (Service) Battalion. The men were mostly of middle-class background, solicitors and barristers and many working in banks and insurance companies. In an article published by the *Irish Times* on 14 September 1914 Lieutenant-Colonel Downing wrote: 'After speaking to them for a few minutes they all, with one accord, elected to join the 7th Royal Dublin Fusiliers, and a more splendid set of young men I have hardly ever seen.'[37] The men who joined up that day became 'D' Company (the 'Pals').

Sergeant Marrable was a member of the 'Record Committee', which was chaired by Lt-Col Downing. 'In the beginning of December 1914 the Machine Gun Section was formed, for which 21 men were taken from "D" Company. They were put under the command of 2nd Lieutenant Douglas and Sergeant Weatherill, both from the "Pals" and the section was transferred to "B" Company. Though they were henceforth nominally "B" and were on the pay-roll as such, they always looked upon themselves as the "Pals" with "D" men, and when possible were always with them.' Among the twenty-one men chosen there were three south Dubliners: Lieutenant William McFerran (survived), Second Lieutenant Jasper Brett (died), and Sgt Francis Marrable (died). On 5 December 1914 they left the camp for Dublin and Woodbrook, where they were entertained by Lt Stanley Cochrane.[38]

Francis Marrable was the son of Arthur Marrable BL and Mary Ann Marrable (née Meigh), Druid Hill, Brennanstown Road, Cabinteely. There were three children in the family: Harold Trevor, Francis Arthur and Constance Irene. Ann Marrable died in 1918, aged 63, and Arthur married, his second wife, Violet Wrigley. Arthur passed away in 1946, aged 90 and when his second wife died in 1949 the family home was bought by the well-known horse trainer, the late Seamus McGrath and his wife Rosemary. The name of the property was changed to Tayanglett.

Francis Marrable, born in Co Kildare in 1887, was educated at Aravon School, Bray, Co Wicklow (1900–1905) and entered Trinity College in 1905. Prior to the outbreak of war he practised as a chartered accountant. 'His brother, Lieutenant Harold Trevor Marrable MD, Royal Army Medical Corps, enlisted in 1915 following the death of his brother. He married Constance Edith Clarke, with whom he had five children: Audrey May, Arthur Trevor, Ian Harold, Francis Dermot and Peter. Harold died in Godalming, Surrey in 1965 aged 84.'[39] His sister, Constance Irene remained unmarried and died at her home at St Valerie, Bray, Co Wicklow, in 1940.

HIGGINS, John

Acting Sergeant, Service No 5490, 2nd Battalion, Leinster Regiment, 88th Brigade in the 29th Division.

He died, aged 35, on 17 May 1918 from wounds received in active service. From early May, the Leinsters were in the front. The Germans shelled billets with high explosive gas shells, the effects of which left 13 dead and 15 wounded. On 11 May a gas shell burst on a billet resulting in 10 casualties in 'B' Company. It was here at this time that Sergeant Higgins was wounded. His wife, Elizabeth, received a letter from his chaplain, Father Ambrose McGrath CF on 4 June 1918:

> Your kind letter of 29 May reached me today. Your dear husband Sergeant John Higgins of the Leinsters was brought here by one of the officers of his unit in the very early hours of Friday morning 17 May in the midst of a bombing outburst on the surroundings. He had come down from the line suffering from a gunshot wound in his right leg. There was a loss of blood and he was in complete shock. His state was hopeless from the beginning and I just had time to give absolution. He died just after in my arms and is buried in Aire Communal Cemetery.

He was not conscious when admitted into hospital, the only signs of life were low groans. Please accept my deepest sympathy in your loss and may God have mercy upon his soul and give him eternal rest.[40]

His grave is at III. A. 13. Aire Communal Cemetery, which is situated fourteen kms south-east of St Omer, France. He was awarded the British War and Victory medals.

The Prince of Wales's Leinster Regiment was formerly the 109th Foot and became the 2nd Battalion. It returned from India in 1911 and was stationed in Cork in August 1914. On 1 February 1918 the battalion absorbed troops from the disbanded 7th Battalion. Then on 13 April 1918 it absorbed troops from the disbanded 6th Connaught Rangers. A further change came on 23 April 1918 when the battalion was transferred to the 88th Brigade in the 29th Division.[41] Ironically, on the day John Higgins died, an inter-battalion sports event took place with the Leinsters enjoying a victory over the Worcestershire Regiment by five events to three.

John Higgins was the husband of Elizabeth Higgins (née Rock) of Tubberbawn Cottage (or Tubberaboure Cottage), Cabinteely. It appears from family information that they had four children: James, Eileen, Leo and John, all born in Liverpool. John was recorded in the 1911 census living at 4, Emly Street, Bootle in Lancashire with his wife, Elizabeth, and son, James, aged one. He was working as a railway porter and when he was killed, Elizabeth took her family back to Ireland, but they got caught up in the civil war and decided to return to Liverpool.[42] John Higgins was the second eldest son of John and Ellen Higgins of Cloondara in the parish of Slieve, Killashee, Co Longford. There were eight children in the family, of whom seven survived infancy: Thomas, William, John, Mary Ann, Margaret, James and Christopher. Agricultural work was almost the only employment in Cloondara and all male members of the Higgins family worked in this sector, when employment was available.

BELL, Patrick

Private, Service No 5195, 1st Battalion, Irish Guards, 1st Guards Brigade in the Guards Division.

He was killed in action, aged 34, in the Battle of Cambrai on 5 December 1917. On 3 December 1917, the 1st Irish Guards, numbering 450 battle-strength, took over the 2nd Scots Guards' and half the 1st Grenadiers' line and were allotted what might be termed 'mixed samples' of trench. No 1 Company, for instance, held six hundred yards of superior wired line, evidently an old British reserve line, with the enemy dug in sixty yards away. No 3 Company on its right had a section mostly battered to bits and further weakened by an old communication trench running up to the enemy, which had to be blocked as soon as possible. No 2 Company was even less happily placed; for the enemy inhabited the actual continuation of their trench, so that they worked with their right flank grossly exposed. Two platoons of No 4 Company lay close behind No 2 Company. The men in the trenches froze; for the frost held day and night and enemy shelled the line at their will, with trench-mortars from near at hand and heavier stuff from the ridges beyond. Just before dawn on 5 December, they put down a very heavy mixed barrage behind the front line and a trench-mortar on the line itself, and then attacked the weak spots No 2 and No 3 Companies' position with armoured bombers. The casualties in the battalion were 1 officer, 4 other ranks killed; and about 30 wounded.[43]

He enlisted in Dublin on 9 September 1914, is commemorated on the Cambrai Memorial, Louverval, France, and was awarded the 1914–15 Star, British War and Victory medals. Patrick Bell was born in Cabinteely, on 6 July 1883 and baptised locally at St Brigid's Roman Catholic Church. He was the son of James Bell (van driver) and Catherine Bell (née Quinn) of Kilbogget, near Cabinteely. There were ten children in the family: Patrick, Elizabeth, Michael Edward, Matthew, John, Maria Anne, William Thomas, Brigit, Raphael and James. His nephews, William and the late Matthew Fitzgibbon lived in Cabinteely village, where the family had resided for more than a century. Patrick Bell's brother, Matthew, married Catherine Cassidy, who taught at St Brigid's National School, Cornelscourt, and also played the church organ at St Brigid's Roman Catholic Church in Cabinteely for many years until her death in 1941.

BYRNE, Michael James

Private, Service No 12273, 1st Battalion Irish Guards, Guards Brigade in the 1st Guards Division.

Private Byrne was killed in action at Stafford Alley on 27 September 1918, aged 20. His death took place on the same day and in the same place as fellow Cabinteely man, 2nd Lt. A. H. O'Farrell. The action in which Pte Byrne was killed may be viewed in the profile of 2nd Lt O'Farrell, earlier in this chapter.

His grave is at II. A. 10. Sanders Keep Military Cemetery, Graincourt-Les-Havrincourt, Pas de Calais, France and he was awarded British War and Victory medals. He enlisted in Dublin on the 17 August 1917. On 4 June 1918, he received fifty-six days' detention for fraudulently enlisting in the Army Service Corps whilst belonging to the Irish Guards. It was recorded in his attestation papers that he was a stableman and had no next-of-kin. He lived at 8, Cabinteely Village.[44] There is an unconfirmed report that he was an orphan in the custody of the Christian Brothers at Artane Industrial School, Dublin, in 1911.

BYRNE, Thomas
Gunner, Service No 283416, 256th Siege Battery Royal Garrison Artillery.

Gunner Byrne died, aged 39, at No 8 Casualty Clearing Station, France, on 31 March 1918, from the effects of a shell-wound to his chest. His wife received a telegram on 14 April 1918 informing her of his death.[45]

His grave is at VI. F.8. Duisans British Cemetery, Etrun, Pas de Calais, France and he was awarded the British Star and Victory medals. He enlisted at Fort Brockhurst, England, on 19 July 1916. The Royal Garrision Artillery, 256th Siege Battery, first arrived in France on 8 February 1917. Byrne's Medical Case Sheet states that he was in the General Hospital in Bologna suffering from myalgia on 19 December 1916 and was admitted to the same hospital on 8 January 1917 with acute bronchitis. On the 23 January 1917, he was invalided to England, and entered the General Hospital in Camberwell, London. He returned to the frontline following a period of recovery.[46]

Thomas Byrne was the husband of Alice Ann Byrne (née Polydore) of 'Ville Amphdsey', St Martins, Guernsey. They were married at Guernsey Registrar's Office on 30 April 1913 and had two children: Robert Frederick, born 1913, and Alice Ann, born 1915. Thomas Byrne was baptised in St Brigid's Roman Catholic Church, Cabinteely in 1881, and was the son of William Byrne; described as an 'engineer' on Pte Byrne's marriage certificate. In the early 1920s, Alice Byrne was living at Mount Durand, St Martins, Guernsey. Byrne's stated occupation before enlisting was 'fireman/stoker'. There were no details of parents, siblings or other family relatives on his Service Record and it was not possible to trace his family using other research tools. His effects, forwarded to his wife in July 1918, included two discs, wallet, letters, photos, cards, two pipes, pocket book, purse, three medal ribbons, match box, pouch, two razors in a case, glass mirror, steel mirror, knife and two flash lamps. He was 5ft 11ins in height.[47]

NOLAN, Patrick Joseph

Private, Service No 5196, 1st Battalion Irish Guards, Guards Brigade in the 1st Guards Division.

He was killed in action, aged 34, near Boyelles on 26 March 1918.

> The 25th March saw Béhagnies, Grévillers, Irles of the wired bastions, Miraumont, Pys, Courcelette, Contalmaison, Thiepval and myriad dead, and Poziéres of the Australians – the very hearts of the deadliest of the first fightings – overrun; and the question rose in men's minds whether the drive would end, as was intended, in the splitting apart of the French and British Armies. For what was happening north of the Somme was play to the situation south of it. By 26 March the tongue of the advancing tide had licked past Noyon and Roye and next day had encircled Montdidier. Meantime, our old Somme base on the Ancre, whence the great fights were fed and supplied from the hundred camps and dumps around Méaulte and the railway-sidings between Albert and Amiens, had passed into the enemy's hands. To all human appearance, the whole of our bitter year's effort was abolished, as though it had never been. The enemy had prepared, brought together, and struck at the time that best suited himself, with 73 Divisions against 37 British Divisions, the outcome was appalling defeat of the Irish Guard's arms.[48]

Thus it was during this time of the 'March Push' that Patrick Nolan was killed in action.

His grave is at III. K. 8. Bucquoy Road, Cemetery, Ficheux, Franc, and he was awarded the 1914–15 Star, British War and Victory medals. Patrick enlisted in Dublin on 9 September 1914 and his brother James, living in his parent's home in Lehaunstown, was recorded as his next-of-kin. He was 5ft 9in in height, with blue eyes and sandy hair.[49]

Patrick Nolan was born in Tinahely, Co Wicklow in 1884, the son of James and Mary Nolan, Lehaunstown, Cabinteely. The Nolans had nine children, seven of whom were James, Bridget, Patrick, Terence, Peter, Margaret and Ellen Mary. The 1911 census recorded Patrick at home with his parents, brother and sister, two nephews, James and Thomas Nolan and a niece, Mary Lynch. His brother, Peter, was married with five children and lived in Cabinteely.

Patrick Nolan's occupation was farm labourer prior to enlisting in the army. The family was related to Dominick Reynolds, and Patrick Lynch, of Brighton Cottages, Foxrock, both of whom also died during the Great War. In his contribution to the history of Foxrock and Cabinteely, the late Brendan Reynolds wrote: 'In the 1940s and 50s, Patrick's mother came to Foxrock Village from Lehaunstown in her donkey and cart, to visit the Lynch family. She would leave her donkey in the charge of a local boy until she went home and for this he got, 6d (six old pennies).'[50]

SLATER, Patrick Joseph
Private, Service No 18848, 6th Battalion Royal Dublin Fusiliers, 197th Brigade in the 66th Division. Previously, 30th Brigade in the 10th (Irish) Division.

Private Slater was killed in action, aged 24, on 8 October 1918, just a month before Armistice Day. He had survived the horrific Gallipoli campaign, especially the carnage that took place during the middle of August 1915. In September 1918 the Allies brought forward a large number of tanks in an attempt to break through the Hindenburg Line and Private Slater was killed after the line had been overwhelmed.

> The attack on 8 October by the right division of third army woke up the German artillery, and their counter-bombardment caught the 66th Division in the act of assembling and cut them up. The 5th Inniskillings and 6th Dublins, with the help of five tanks, had captured the strong-point, Marliches Farm and six field guns by 7.30am. The Dublins then took a fortified farm and captured 113 men, including two officers. Heavy shell-fire drove the Dublins out of the position and this was immediately followed by a strong counter-attack which was driven back by rapid fire. Repeated attacks to retake the farm failed, even after two tanks came forward to help. At 11.30am the Dublins recaptured the farm.[51]

A Private Gallagher of the 7th Dublins, from Kingstown, mentioned in a letter home that while lying wounded on the battlefield he was carried three miles to hospital on the back of a chap named 'Slater' from Cabinteely.[52] He is commemorated on the Vis-en-Artois Memorial, Arras Region, France, and he was awarded the 1914–15 Star, British War and Victory medals.

The battalion was formed at Naas in August 1914 as part of K1 and moved to Fermoy, Co Cork in September of the same year. Next it moved to the Curragh, and then to Basingstoke. The Dublins landed at Suvla Bay on 7 August 1915 and in early October 1915 it was evacuated via Mudros to Salonika. In September 1917 it went to Egypt for service in Palestine. On 3 July the battalion sailed from Alexandria, arriving at Taranto, Southern Italy, five days later and then moving by train to France.[53]

Patrick Slater was born on 11 December 1894 and was the son of John Slater and Jane Slater (née Molloy), Glendruid, Cabinteely. There were four children in the family: Patrick, Thomas, John and Francis.

His brother, Private Thomas Slater, Royal Dublin Fusiliers, also fought in the Great War and was twice taken prisoner by the Germans. His son, Father Jack Slater, who served as curate in the parish of Cabinteely for a number of years, said: 'Prior to the outbreak of war my uncle Patrick was engaged to be married to my mother, Mary O'Brien, however, following the end of war my father began going out with Mary and the rest is history.' He also said that the survivors of the Great War were not treated well and they rarely ever spoke about their war experiences or fallen relatives and friends. When Father Slater was asked to describe his father and uncle, he said: 'They were strong and brave men.'[54]

Chapter Seven

Blackrock, Newtownpark and Stillorgan

HISTORY AND ROLL OF HONOUR

In the early years of the twentieth century the towns of south-east Dublin were larger, more densely populated and wealthier than the villages and towns further inland. Blackrock Urban District Council, embracing Blackrock, Booterstown, Dean's Grange, part of Monkstown and Williamstown, was formed by the Blackrock Township Act of 1863. The area had a population of 9161 in 1911. The district was residential and one of the most fashionable suburbs in Dublin, studded with mansions and beautiful villas standing in their own grounds. The air was described as 'particularly soft and is much esteemed by invalids, some of the sheltered portions being nearly as mild in winter as the south of France'.[1]

Temple Hill Hospital for the limbless was one of two hospitals in Blackrock catering for wounded soldiers. The second was the Industrial School for Protestant boys at Carysfort Avenue, which was taken over by the British Army in 1917 following the mounting casualties on the Western Front. It remained open until the early 1930s when patients were transferred to Leopardstown Park Hospital, Foxrock.

The writer James Joyce lived in 23 Carysfort Avenue known as Leoville for one year in the early 1890s. Kevin O'Higgins (1892–1927) lived at Dunamase on Cross Avenue, Booterstown and was the Minister for Justice in the first government of the Irish Free State. Minister O'Higgins, a staunch pro-treaty supporter, was assassinated on the Booterstown end of Cross Avenue on his way to mass at his local parish church on 10 July 1927.

Newtownpark village consisted of thirty-six small dwellings at Annaville Avenue, fifteen dwellings of similar size at Orchard Avenue, and some dwellings in Yankey Terrace. Many of the young men in Newtownpark would have received their early education at the Sisters of Mercy, Carysfort Convent, Carysfort Avenue, Blackrock. Newtownpark Avenue was an elegant road that extended downhill towards the coast where it met the Stradbrook Road. It had many beautiful houses together with at least two dairy farms in the ownership of the Sutton and Acres families.Other residents on the road included, William P. Geoghegan JP and George Mitchell, both of whom lost sons in the war. 'The Young Ireland Fife and Drum Band, whose members included many Great War heroes, was a winner of the All-Ireland Championship 1910–11 and All-Ireland senior winners in 1911–12.'[2]

Stillorgan is either a Danish or Anglo Norman corruption of Teach Lorcan, 'the house or church of Lorcan (Laurence)', possibly signifying St Laurence O'Toole. The original Celtic name for Stillorgan was Athnakill – 'Place of the Church'. The village and parish were in the Rathdown Barony and comprised of an area of 610 acres, of which the village occupied six acres. In 1911 the population of the village was 415, inhabiting 101 houses, and the parish, which included the Foxrock area, had a population of 1558.[3] The Stillorgan Park Golf Club opened in 1908 and numbered among its members some men who fell in the Great War. When the club closed in 1917 many of its members joined the Castle Golf Club in Rathfarnham.

Talbot Lodge, Stillorgan, an eighteenth-century villa, was bought by the Sisters of Charity and doubled in size. It became the Linden Convalescent Home and was used as an Auxiliary Hospital and convalescent home for wounded soldiers during the Great War.

Sir William N. Orpen KBE, RA, RHA was born in Stillorgan on 27 November 1878 and lived at Oriel, Grove Avenue in Stillorgan. Orpen was drafted as an official British war artist in the Great War and was deeply affected by the suffering he witnessed in the trenches. He died in 1931, aged 53. Orpen said of Sir Douglas Haig, 'Never once, all the time I was in France, did I hear a "Tommy" say one word against Haig. Whenever it became my honour to be allowed to visit him, I always left feeling happier – feeling more sure that the fighting men being killed were not dying for nothing. One felt he knew, and would never allow them to suffer and die except for a final victory.'[4] Haig encouraged Orpen to expand his painting repertoire to include the varieties of characters on the front. 'He said "Why waste your time painting me? Go and paint the men. They're the fellows who are saving the world, and getting killed every day."'[5] Some modern military historians do not concur with this view of Haig. Lieutenant-Colonel P. Dwyer MB, MD, Royal Army Medical Corps, lived at Kilmacud House, Stillorgan and served in the Great War.

THREE BLACKROCK PILOT BROTHERS DIE IN WAR

Six children were born to Joseph Patrick Callaghan and Croasdella Cruess Callaghan (née Bolger) of Ferndene, Stradbrook, Blackrock. Their names were Joseph, Croasdella, Stanislaus, Eugene, Cedric and George. Three sons, Joseph, Eugene and Stanislaus, all pilots and unmarried, were killed during the war. Joseph Callaghan came from Strokestown, Co Roscommon and was the proprietor of the North City Co-operative Outfitting and Hat store at 9/10 North Earl Street, Dublin. Joseph Callaghan and Croasdella Cruess Callaghan died in 1935 and 1940 respectively and were interred in Dean's Grange Cemetery.

The family's Great War heroes were featured in the *Daily Mirror* of Tuesday 2 August 1918 and carried a photograph of all three brothers under the heading, 'Pro-Patria'. They were described as: 'The most united brothers who ever lived.'[6]

CALLAGHAN, Joseph Cruess MC

Major, Commander of No 87 Squadron, Royal Air Force. The Royal Flying Corps and the Royal Naval Air Service were amalgamated to form a new service, the Royal Air Force (RAF). Secondary Regiment, 7th Battalion Royal Munster Fusiliers.

Major Joseph Cruess Callaghan was known all over the United Kingdom and France as 'Casey the fighting pilot'. He launched a solo attack on a large formation of German fighters, estimated to number as many as twenty-five, on 2 July 1918, near Contay in France, during which he was killed when his plane was shot down in flames by German ace Lieutenant Franz Büchner.[7] Friends and comrades wrote to his parents:

I am afraid it is of little use to hold out any hope as to your son's fate.

I am afraid there is no doubt that he died the finest death that any man could die, fighting in the air against overwhelming odds. He was last seen fighting by himself against several German planes close in front of the lines. I cannot possibly express to you in these few lines the sympathy which all of us who knew him feel for you. He was one of the most gallant officers I ever met, and had that wonderful power of infusing those that served under him with the same spirit. His squadron worshiped him, and we all fully realise the terrible loss he will be to you.[8]

A second letter explained:

As Squadron Commander he was not expected to fly. When his squadron took to the air he had to remain below, so when they were back, he also flew above quite unprotected. 'Casey', for so he was called by all his friends, loved Stonyhurst and was devoted to the Jesuits. He was a man of not only extreme physical courage, but also great moral courage.

No one ever heard him say an unkind word. He was great in every way, for he was 6 feet 2 inches tall. His Military Cross was gained chiefly for his daring in night flying. Following fifteen months' service in France he obtained charge of one of the biggest teaching Squadrons in Scotland and was promoted to Major. But he was restless for active service, and his request to go to the front was acceded to. On three occasions when he went to see his mother, he flew from Scotland, over to Dublin in his aeroplane.[9]

His grave is at 123, Contay British Cemetery, Contay, Somme, France and he is commemorated on the War Memorial at Stonyhurst College. Major Cruess Callaghan was awarded the Military Cross for conspicuous gallantry in action. His citation read: 'He displayed marked courage and skill on several occasions in carrying out night bombing operations. On one occasion he extinguished a hostile searchlight.'[10] He was also awarded the British War and Victory medals, issued to his mother on 14 March 1921.

The following is a report from J.C. Callaghan's Manuscript Log Book for the 9

October 1916, when he held the rank of captain and won his Military Cross:

> Crossed line at 11.55pm at Gueudecourt. A number of red lamps in Le Transloy. Followed road from Bapaume to Cambrai. Reached Cambrai at 12.20am. Had a good look at Cambrai and found a train with steam up in station on east side of the town. At 12.25am dropped three 20lb Hales HE on train. A beauty. Hit train just behind engine. All lights immediately went out and AA guns and searchlights became very active. We hovered about for a few minutes and then dropped remaining three bombs on a railway line which is on the west of the station running parallel. The AA fire was hellish. A strong searchlight played on us from Sailly on the northern side of the Cambrai-Arras Road, so we dived on him and I gave him a drum of the best. The searchlight went out and another one got on us. We then returned and AA fire kept on us for a long time. We then got away from the searchlights although a number tried to pick us up. Over Hermies at12.45am a strong searchlight was looking for us so I opened fire on him. The drum was of tracers accidently [sic] and gave our position away. AA fire and searchlights followed us until 1 am when we re-crossed the line at Morval at 3,000 feet. Beautiful night and observation good.[11]

Joseph was living in Texas when the Great War began, but returned home to join the Royal Munster Fusiliers, where he was gazetted to the 7th Battalion on 1 September 1915 and transferred to the Royal Air Corps later in the same year.[12] 'He scored his first victory in 1916 flying an F E 2b, but was wounded in action on 31 July 1916.'[13] In December 1916 he suffered with a heart condition, 'accentuated by overuse of tobacco', and from the condition, ague, a fever/chill associated with malaria, which he had contracted two years previous. He received three months' sick leave, and was declared fit to resume service in early February 1917, when he was posted to Auxill School of Aerial Gunnery at Turnberry, Scotland. His promotion to full Captain came in the autumn of 1917, with further promotion to Major and Squadron Commander in December 1917.[14] In April 1918, he returned to combat flying a Sopwith Dolphin No D3671 and was commanding officer of the 87 Squadron. By the end of June, he had scored four more victories to become an ace.[15]

Joseph C. Callaghan was born at 1, Sloperton, Monkstown, on 4 March 1893, and attended Stonyhurst College in 1902. He joined the Royal Veterinary College of Ireland on his return to Dublin.

'Brother'
My brother: I'll never say those words.
Our mother had no sons – Words on someone else's tongue,
coupled with older or younger; brave or bullying.
Our mother's favourite. Our father's.

Was it he who taught us to kneel by our beds
and into the dark call to God?
God bless Mammy, God bless Daddy …
My father fathered five of us, all girls,
never cast a glance back to a non-existent brother.

Heads bowed, faces in our hands,
from the edge of memory – a shadow;
Three brothers, his soldier-brothers,
Joseph, Eugene, Stanie.[16]

–Louise C. Callaghan

CALLAGHAN, Stanislaus Cruess
Captain, 19th Squadron, Royal Army Flying Corps.

Captain Cruess Callaghan died, aged 21, as a result of an aeroplane accident in Canada on 27 June 1917. His body was interred at Berrie St Mary's, Roman Catholic Cemetery, Canada, and he is commemorated on the War Memorial at Belvedere College, Dublin, and the Great War Memorial at Stonyhurst College. He was awarded the British War and Victory medals.

Stan joined shortly after the outbreak of war and

was the first to wear the Observer's wing in the British Army. It was no surprise to those who knew him that he joined the Royal Flying Corps on 4 December 1915 at a time when flying was particularly dangerous. 'For some two years before joining up, he had studied wireless telegraphy, for which his smartness was especially suited. While he was learning to fly at Hendon, the authorities, discovering that he had expert knowledge of wireless and Morse Code, moved him at once to the Southern Command where he practised the artillery in ranging from aeroplane observation. Shortly afterwards, he was ordered to the front and attached to No 5 Squadron, which was stationed in the Ypres Salient.'[17]

'During the long struggle at Ypres, Stan rendered notable service in connection with the use of wireless as a means of signalling, which was then in its experimental stages. Twice, the sparking from his wireless apparatus ignited the petrol vapour and his machine caught fire. On the first occasion the pilot, in trying to increase his speed, got the machine into a spin but cleverly affecting some sort of "perch", he managed to bring it safely to earth. On the second occasion, however, they were flying low over enemy lines and before they could reach their aerodrome Stan's face and legs were burnt. No doubt the strain of such experiences had told upon his nerves and he was appointed to a less trying but no less important post of wireless "Equipment Officer" being the youngest to that position in the Flying Corps. His efficiency led to further promotion, for after fifteen months' service in France, he was ordered home at Easter 1916 and appointed Inspector of Wireless to the Northern Group with the new rank of captain.'[18]

'Before taking up his new post, he went home to Dublin on leave. Here a new experience awaited him, for he arrived in Dublin at the time of the revolution, was captured by Sinn Féiners, and kept a prisoner in the Four Courts for a week.' *The Belvederian* of that year describes what happened: 'He was motoring along the quay when he was held up and his motor car taken and he himself led to the Courts as a prisoner. He was treated well by the insurgents, but did not find his holiday much of a "rest".'[19]

Following a period of six months' valuable work with the Northern Group, he was transferred to the larger and more important post of Inspector of Wireless to the Southern Group. Finally, the precision, method and efficiency of all his work led to further recognition, and in June 1917 he obtained the post of Brigade Wireless Officer in the Imperial RFC in Canada. The day after his departure, news came of the death of his brother, Eugene, who had been 'missing' since 26 August 1916. A few days later he went to Camp Borden to assist in the installation of wireless. It was here, on 27 June, that he met with the fatal flying accident which ended his life and a career of valuable service.[20]

He was born on 4 December 1897; his education began at Stonyhurst College, Lancashire (1906–1910) and continued at Belvedere College, Dublin, when he was 13 years old. It was written in his college's memoirs that: 'In many ways "Stan" was a quite remarkable character. Sharp and quick-witted, full of fun and humour, he was one those who baffle the pedagogue, for his obvious talent would not or could not be brought to bear upon his books. He was fearless almost to recklessness, but a very generous nature, easily accessible, quick to respond, and loyal to his resolution.'[21]

CALLAGHAN, Eugene Cruess
Second Lieutenant, 19th Squadron, Royal Army Flying Corps.
He died when engaged in a bomb-dropping expedition on Sunday 27 August 1916 on the Bois d'Havrincourt, where he went missing. It is suspected that he landed, by mistake, on a German aerodrome. Ten months later the War Office pronounced that he was presumed dead aged 18. The day before, Saturday 26 August 1916, he flew his single-seater across the Channel to the Western Front where he was involved in fierce aerial combat with two enemy aircraft, bringing one down and damaging the other. The major in command of his squadron wrote: 'He had the makings of a splendid pilot, full of dash and energy – a regular thruster. I was quite expecting him to do something brilliant and get rewarded. He was one of the most popular youngsters in the mess, and we will all miss him very much.'[22]

Second Lieutenant Cruess Callaghan is commemorated at the Arras Flying Services Memorial, Pas de Calais, France; Hall of Honour, Trinity College; War Memorial, Belvedere College, and the War Memorial at Stonyhurst College. He was awarded the 1915 Star, British War and Victory medals.

Owen (as known to his family), was born in 1897. He commenced his education in 1906 at Stonyhurst College, in the company of his older brother Stan, and later attended Belvedere College, Dublin. When he finished at Belvedere, he entered Trinity College, but almost immediately joined the Royal Flying Corps. In his Stonyhurst College's memoirs it states that: 'Owen was a serious, thoughtful, and religious boy.'[23]

TWO MORE BLACKROCK BROTHERS PERISH IN WAR

Leslie and Arthur Callaghan, the sons of the late Thomas Prushaw Callaghan and Kate Margaret Callaghan (née Nickson), of 7, Grosvenor Terrace, Monkstown were killed in France during a two month period in 1917. Thomas P. Callaghan was the Assistant Irish Manager of the London North Western Railway. There were four children in the family, of whom three survived infancy: Leslie Wilfred, Arthur Nickson and Thomas Edmonds. Following the end of the war, Mrs Kate Callaghan moved to England and lived at Cannock Wood, Rugeley, Staffordshire.

The youngest son, Sapper Thomas Edmonds Callaghan, Royal Engineers, Tank Corps, followed his fallen brothers into the army on 16 April 1918, while still a student at Trinity College. He was posted to the 24th Tank Battalion at Wareham on 5 November 1918, less than a week before armistice. During his time in the army he was assigned to the motor cycle section, and on 26 June 1918 he was found guilty of riding a motor cycle in a manner that endangered the public; he was fined three days' pay. His early education was at Wesley College, Ballinteer.

CALLAGHAN, Leslie Wilfred
Captain, 8th Battalion West Yorkshire Regiment (Prince of Wales's Own), Leeds Rifles (Territorial), 146th Brigade in the 49th (West Riding) Division.

He was killed in action, aged 25, at Passchendaele, Flanders, on 9 October 1917. The following account of the battle, in which he died, did not mention Capt Callaghan by name: 'The rear company only arrived in assembly position for the attack west of Passchendale five minutes before zero. In spite of the difficulties of weather and ground conditions the battalion advanced under the barrage towards its objectives. All four companies for the first and second objectives led to high casualties among officers and NCOs. Much hostile machine-gun fire and sniping was encountered, and eventually the battalion dug itself in short of its first objective after an advance of about 300 yards. Out of the 23 officers who went in with the unit, eight were killed, eight were wounded, one was missing and 2, who remained on duty, wounded. There were 301 casualties amongst the other ranks on the night of the 10 October.'[24]

He is commemorated on the Tyne Cot Memorial, Belgium; Hall of Honour, Trinity College; Great War Memorial, Wesley College, Ballinteer; Great War Memorial, N Chancel, St Philip and St James Church of Ireland, Blackrock, and the Great War Memorial, Monkstown Church of Ireland. Captain Callaghan was awarded the 1915

Star, British War and Victory medals, which were issued to his brother, Thomas Edmond Callaghan, of 186, Haverstock Hill, Hampstead, on 22 March 1923.

He was gazetted 2nd Lieutenant on the 14 April 1915. The 1/8th Battalion, (Leeds Rifles) West Yorkshire Regiment, a territorial battalion, was at Carlton Barracks, Leeds in August 1914 when war broke out. On 10 August it moved to Selby, and later in the month to Strenshall. In late October 1914 it moved to York and in March 1915 it was at Gainsborough before proceeding to France, sailing from Folkestone on 15 April 1915 and landing at Boulogne with the 146th Brigade. [25]

Leslie Callaghan was born in 1892 and was educated at Wesley College and Trinity College, which he entered in 1909. He was unmarried and prior to enlisting he resided at Hollywood, Blackrock. His brother, Thomas, wrote to the War Office on 1 October 1919, informing the secretary that his father, Thomas P. Callaghan, had died in May 1918 leaving him next-of-kin. He also requested that gratuities for his two brothers should be remitted to him. In response to a letter from the War Office on 1 January 1920, seeking confirmation of next-of-kin, his brother Thomas, wrote: 'I wish to point out the spelling of my brother's second name is "WILFRID", otherwise the name and rank are correct.'[26]

CALLAGHAN, Arthur Nickson
Lieutenant, 14th Battalion, The King's (Liverpool Regiment), 65th Brigade in the 22nd Division.

He was killed in action, aged 24, at Pillar Hill in Salonika on 30 August 1917. On 29 August 1917 a patrol under Lt Callaghan reconnoitred ground east of Corne du Boise and met with resistance. The patrol was very well handled and led; there were no casualties. On the 30th the battalion was in the front line and bombardment continued. Hostile retaliation was vigorous and increased in volume. There was a heavy hostile barrage over whole battalion front. On the same day there was a successful raid on the enemy, inflicting casualties and bringing in 4 prisoners; 3 men slightly wounded. At about 11pm the enemy increased its volume of barrage and raided Jackson's Ravine – occupying the latter. Casualties included, Lt Callaghan killed and 4 other officers wounded. Other ranks suffered 1 killed and 16 wounded.[27]

His grave is at C. 576, Karasouli Military Cemetery, Polikastron, Pellis, Greece. He is commemorated in the Hall of Honour, Trinity College; Great War Memorial at Wesley College, Ballinteer and the Great War Memorial, N Chancel, St Philip and

St James Church of Ireland, Blackrock. Lieutenant Callaghan was 'Mentioned in Despatches' and awarded the 1915 Star, British War and Victory medals, which were issued to his mother, who was living in England.

He enlisted in early 1914 and was serving in Salonika in November 1915. The battalion was formed in October 1914 at Seaforth, Liverpool and landed at Boulogne on the 5 October 1915. It sailed from Marseilles, arriving in Salonika on 5 November 1915.[28]

Arthur Callaghan was educated at Wesley College and Trinity College, where he took his BA and LL B degrees in 1913. He was single.

EATON, Guy Wellesley MC

Captain, 8th Battalion Royal Irish Fusiliers, 49th Brigade in the 16th (Irish) Division.

Captain Eaton was killed in action, aged 26, on 6 September 1916 at Leuze Wood in the Battle of the Somme, France. The wood is situated in the Somme area close to the town of Combles and not far from Delville Wood, Guillemont and Montauban. His comrade and friend, Captain Thomas Fitzpatrick, former school friend from Kingstown, was killed in this battle also, and his profile may be read in Chapter Eight.

On 6 September 1916 at 2.30am a message was received from the 95th Brigade that the 15th Brigade was held up by wire and machine-gun fire. The message ordered a bombing party to go out down trench, running south-east from the wood in order to assist the 15th Brigade. This order was repeated to 'B' Company. At the same time a message to 'A' Company to take special precautions for the protection of their right flank. During the night the Irish Fusilier's 'heavies' directed their fire on the wood causing considerable casualties to its own men. This took place during the whole of the 6th and four messages were sent for them to lengthen range. A reply was received that no 'heavies' attached to the 5th Division were firing close to the front edge of the wood.

On visiting the wood at 8.30am it was found that the south-west end of the wood was being shelled and that the approach to the wood was under constant sniper fire, which caused numerous casualties. At 9am it was decided not to move Battalion Headquarters forward into the wood owing to the insecure state of the position and the difficulty of maintaining communications with the brigade from that forward position. A hostile patrol entered the wood from the east side at 10.30am, but was driven back by the Irish Fusiliers leaving 2 dead and 2 wounded. At 7.30pm the enemy made an organised counter attack on the front line. This attack came from the direction of Bouleaux and from the east side of the wood. He also attacked the north corner of the wood. The second line held the enemy back and finally drove him out of the wood. Then at 10.30pm the battalion was relieved by the 1st Battalion, London Scottish. Total casualties were 4 officers killed and 5 wounded. In the other ranks; 36 were killed, 95 wounded and 40 missing, believed to have been taken prisoners.[29]

His colonel, writing to Mrs Eaton, stated:

You will probably have received news from the War Office of the great loss that you and the battalion has sustained in the death of your son. He was hit about 7pm on the evening of the 6 September, and died about 3am this morning at battalion headquarters. His end was quite peaceful, I believe, and he was unconscious when brought to headquarters. I saw him when he was first brought in. I cannot tell you what a splendid soldier he was. He was most popular with officers and men alike, and his chief thoughts were for the welfare of his men and the regiment. At the time he received his wound he was holding a very difficult part of the line, and he succeeded in preventing the enemy making any appreciable advance.[30]

His heartbroken mother received a letter from the War Office on 16 February 1918, stating that her son was buried at a point about 500 yards south-east of Guillemont and west of Combles in France. However, the exact location of his grave is unknown and he is commemorated on the Thiepval Memorial, Somme, France; Town Memorial, War Memorial, St Andrew's College, Booterstown; St Mary's Church Memorial, Uttoxeter and Thomas Alleyne Grammar School War Memorial, Uttoxeter. He was awarded the Military Cross in 1916 and his citation read:

For conspicuous gallantry during a raid on the enemy's trenches. His party met with great difficulty in crossing the enemy's wire, but he himself, with a sergeant, entered their frontline. He shot two of the enemy with his revolver. On his return, hearing that another officer had been wounded and was missing, he went out and helped to bring him in under heavy fire.[31]

He was awarded the Certificate of Vellum. This award came from his Divisional Commander for a feat of great gallantry on 11 July 1916, the letter read: 'I have read with much pleasure the reports of your Regimental Commander and Brigade Commander regarding your gallant conduct and devotion to duty in the field on 11 July 1916, and have ordered your name and deed to be entered in the record of the Irish Division.'[32] He was also awarded the 1914–15 Star, British War and Victory medals.

In October 1916 the *Uttoxeter Advertiser* quoted extracts from a tribute which his friend Arjay, had written in *The Motor News*:

It is only when we receive news of the death of a friend or relative that we fully realise the widespread devastation and grief caused by this awful war. I have lost a good many friends and several relatives, but in no case was I so much affected as when I heard of Eaton's heroic exit. I knew him intimately, as boy and man. Even as he grew older, my affection, respect and admiration increased. He was one of the finest characters I have ever met, beloved in his family circle and by everyone who knew him, but more especially by his men, whose interests he put before his own. Eaton was wounded, but not very seriously. He refused, however, to leave his men, and with cheery words of encouragement urged them on. His example was infectious. The Huns were eventually hurled back.

Meanwhile, however, he had bled so much, and was in a state of collapse. He died early next morning of heart failure. If one of his men had been similarly wounded he would have received immediate attention, and would undoubtedly be convalescent by this time.[33]

Guy did not enter Trinity College, but was a member of its OTC, from which he was gazetted second lieutenant in the Royal Irish Fusiliers in 1914 and was promoted to captain on 1 February, 1915. His medical, which took place on 5 September 1914, recorded that he 5ft 11ins in height and weighed 149 lbs.[34] The 8th Royal Irish Fusiliers was formed at Armagh in September 1914 as part of the K2 army and then moved to Tipperary. In October 1916 it amalgamated and became the 7/8th Battalion.

Captain Eaton's mother, Florence, wrote the War Office on 3 October 1916 requesting an Application Form for pension. 'My son, Captain G.W. Eaton, was killed on the sixth of last month, in action in France. I was dependant on him for part of my income, my husband being dead also'. It is recorded that she did receive a pension. Her second son, Douglas, wrote to the War Office on 10 October 1916 to enquire on her behalf about Guy's personal effects, and confirming that a package was received: 'The package merely contained his clothes, field glasses and toilet requisites. She is anxious to know if the pocket book, prayer book, ring and wrist watch could be recovered, as they are particularly valuable to her.'[35] This was followed on 31 October 1916 by a letter from Mrs Eaton:

> I have been informed by the Chaplain attached to his battalion, that he forwarded all Captain Eaton's personal effects, including his letters etc. I shall be greatly obliged if you will have enquiries made as to whether this parcel reached the War Office. I greatly fear his personal effects have been lost in transit. His personal effects, as recorded in his original documents, included; purse containing newspaper cuttings, keys, button and a piece of steel.[36]

Guy was the third son of the late Richard Arthur Eaton (solicitor), who died in February 1915 and Florence Emily Eaton (née Tighe Mecredy). He was grandson of R.J. Eaton, RM of Mitchelstown, Co Cork, who died in 1895. There were five children in the family: Richard Netterville, Douglas Arthur Tighe, Hugh Bouchier, Guy Wellesley and Thomas Tighe Mandersforde. His parents, who were married in December 1882, lived at Maryville, Blackrock, and later at 27, Newtown Avenue, Blackrock. Guy was born on 20 July 1890 and educated at St Andrew's College, Booterstown, Cowbridge Grammar School, South Wales and London University, where it is recorded that he registered in October 1909 and took his examination in the arts in 1912. He was master at the Thomas Alleyne Grammar School at the outbreak of war.

EDWARD AND ANNIE LEE LOSE TWO SONS IN THE WAR

Edward Lee JP and Annie Lee (née Shackelton) of Bellevue, Blackrock, had nine children, of whom four survived infancy: Edward Shackleton, Robert Ernest, Joseph Bagnall and Alfred Tennyson. One of the deceased children was their only daughter, who died before the age of six months. Three of their four sons joined the British Army at the outset of war in 1914, two of them losing their lives. The youngest son, Tennyson, survived the war but was badly affected by his experience and the loss of his brothers.

Edward Lee was the proprietor of Edward Lee & Company Limited, a well known chain of retail drapery stores. His wife Annie was the aunt of another casualty of the war; 2nd Lt Richard Shackleton, whose profile may be seen in Chapter Eight. Edward Lee broke ranks with his fellow employers in the 1913 'Lockout', saying: 'the employers should withdraw the pledge requiring their employees to cease to belong to the Transport Workers' Union. To my way of thinking such a pledge is an unfair interference with the personal liberty of the workers.' Edward Lee also said: 'Men of capital ought to be ashamed to have it go out to the ends of the earth that so many families were each living in one room.'[37] He was the first employer to introduce a five-and-half-day working week.

The Lee's eldest son, Edward Shackleton, was born in Bray in April 1879, and attended Wesley College. He married Orynthia May Collings in London in 1921. When war broke out, Edward junior, who had very poor eyesight, stayed at home to help his father manage the business. He died in Dun Laoghaire in 1965, aged 86, and Orynthia passed away in 1972, aged 75.

Captain Alfred Tennyson Lee, 6th Battalion Royal Munster Fusiliers was born on 6 October 1892 and named after his mother's favourite poet, Alfred Lord Tennyson, who died on the day that he was born. He entered Trinity College in 1913, but enlisted in the forces soon after the outbreak of war. Tennyson received his commission in 1914, was promoted to lieutenant in 1915 and captain in 1917. In August 1915 he was badly wounded at Suvla, during the Gallipoli campaign, and following a period of recuperation he served in Italy in 1918. He survived the war and was demobilised in September 1919. Captain Lee was awarded the 1915 Star, British War and Victory medals, sent to his Dublin home at 76, Park Avenue, Sandymount on 17 December 1922. Tennyson married Winifred Cranwill, sister of Valentine and Thomas Cranwill, who died in the First and Second World Wars, respectively. They had two children, John Patrick Lee MB (deceased) and David Lee. Winifred and Tennyson died in April 1959 and April 1982, respectively. Tennyson was a member of Stillorgan Park Golf Club with his brothers, Edward and Robert. He is commemorated on the board in the porch at St Philip and St James Church of Ireland in Blackrock.

WAR CASUALTIES HAD TRAUMATIC EFFECT
ON MUCH RESPECTED MERCHANT FAMILY
Michael Lee, a great-grandson of Edward Lee, wrote about the effect on the family of losing two sons in the war and having a third son, who survived, but suffered greatly from his experience:

> I certainly feel that the Great War had a profound and lasting effect on the family. As with so many other families at that time, the war changed everything. My great-grandfather Edward Lee had risen from humble beginnings in Tyrrellspass, Co Westmeath, where the family were tenant farmers. With £100 given to him, I suspect by his mother Hannah (née Bagnall), he set off for Dublin to make his fortune. He married Annie Shackleton from Dungar, Roscrea in 1878 and they opened a drapery shop in Bray, Co Wicklow in 1885.
>
> My great-grandfather was very concerned for the welfare of the poor and was elected to Bray Urban District Council in 1903, where he was instrumental in having housing built for the working families of Bray. He was made a Justice of the Peace in 1906 and was known as a model employer, always concerned for his employees and fair in his dealings with them. His motto was 'a good day's pay for a good day's work'. In 1907 he was involved along with other merchants, in the setting up the Irish International Exhibition in Dublin, where he and Annie were presented to the King and Queen. Within one generation Edward Lee had attained wealth and position, with shops in Bray, Kingstown, Mary Street and Rathmines. The two eldest sons attended Wesley College, the younger two went to Epworth College in Rhyl,

and all entered Trinity College. The family were now living in a large house, Bellevue on Cross Avenue, Blackrock. My great-grandfather was always proud to say that he was a 'self made man'. During the 'Lock Out' in 1913, he broke ranks with William Martin Murphy and was the only employer to try and work out a settlement. He joined the ill-fated Peace Committee along with Tom Kettle and others.

The family were firm supporters of the British war effort. Edward Lee made his shop in Mary Street available to the Red Cross for collecting comforts for the troops and he was on the recruiting committee for the 10th (Commercial) Battalion, Royal Dublin Fusiliers. Meanwhile three of his sons joined the colours at the outset of hostilities. Robert Ernest Lee, a doctor, joined the Royal Army Medical Corps, and Joseph Bagnall Lee, a barrister, along with his younger brother Alfred Tennyson Lee, a student, joined the 6th Battalion, Royal Munster Fusiliers. On the 7th August 1915 the war came home to the Lee family in all its horror and sadness when Joe was killed at Suvla Bay, Gallipoli, and two days later Tennyson was wounded there also. One can imagine the sadness in the family at this time; however, many other families were going through the same horrors.

The war would continue for another three years and in October of 1918 Edward and Annie must have felt some relief that the war was coming to an end and that they had at least been spared two of their three soldier sons. However fate had one more terrible blow for the Lees, when Robert, who had survived four years on the Western Front, was drowned along with over 500 other souls when the RMS *Leinster* mail boat was torpedoed off Kingstown on the 10 October 1918, just one month and one day from the signing of the Armistice. This was the killer blow for Edward and Annie. All they had strived and worked for down through those years, bringing up four healthy sons, who in the future might make a difference to society, all this was lost. Lost too was the connection to Britain, a new political beginning was opening up for Ireland. I do think my great-grandfather was a supporter of Home Rule, but the stress and heartbreak of losing his two sons overshadowed everything else.

Edward was less involved in the business over the next few years and by 1926 he was spending much time in Tyrrellspass, where he was born. He was now suffering from terminal throat cancer, perhaps he needed to remember where the great adventure all began. All the shops, the meteoric rise in society for the family, what use was it without his beloved sons? He was a religious man and he did feel that he and Annie would meet his children again, 'we only trust in God that when our time comes we will meet our babes and our dear Joe and Ernest with all our loved ones, where there will be no more partings or death or sorrow–may we prove ourselves worthy.' But he was also a broken man and although he kept his hand in the business and a few other interests, I feel that he knew it was all over for him. I know that when my father was born in 1923, there was great joy in the family, another boy, but nothing was ever spoken of the lost boys in the family. Edward Lee died at his home in Blackrock in February 1927 and Annie lived there for another few years, often going into the garden and 'seeing' her beautiful boys beside her.

As a child I was always fascinated by the large sepia photos of the two handsome men in uniform, both looking so proud. I asked Dad who they were. All he would say was that they were his two uncles, Ernest and Joe. I don't think dad was told much about them; it was too painful for his father, Edward Shackleton Lee, to talk about his brothers. I think that he always felt somewhat guilty that they had died and he had lived. Tennyson too had been traumatised by Joe's death. It was said in the family that he had seen his brother being brought down dead. How could he tell his mother? Tennyson would suffer for the rest of his life. Annie died in 1938, seemingly a strong woman, but the tragedies must have been so painful for her too. The Lee family had burned bright for a short while at the beginning of the twentieth century, but by the end of the Great War the light had dimmed and it would never again attain the heights achieved by Edward and Annie.[38]

LEE, Robert Ernest
Captain, Royal Army Medical Corps.

He was drowned when the RMS *Leinster* was torpedoed by the German submarine, *UB-123,* off the Irish coast on 10 October 1918, aged 35. Michael Lee said that his great-uncle was travelling to England to stand as godfather to a child of a friend, before returning to duty in France. His body was recovered on 15 October 1918 and buried in the family plot at Dean's Grange Cemetery. He is commemorated on the Great War Memorial, St Philip's and St James Church, Church of Ireland, Blackrock; Great War Memorial, Baggot Street Hospital, Dublin; Great War Memorial, Wesley College, Dublin; Great War Memorial, Quinnsborough Road, Bray, Co Wicklow, and the Hall of Honour, Trinity College. 'Captain Lee was awarded the 1914–15 Star, British War and Victory medals. He was promoted to lieutenant in August 1914 and captain in 1915 following his gallantry and bravery under heavy fire at Hill 60, Ypres, Belgium.'[39]

Edward and Annie Lee received two letters from people associated with the disaster: 'I heard the other day in the Castle Hospital that your son just before losing his own life was instrumental in saving a brother officer's, who, with his arm in a metal splint would have been quite helpless had not your son taken care to fit on his life belt for him after the ship was first struck.'[40] An extract of a second letter from a Dublin doctor read: 'He was the man who did all earthly power could do to save my life. He adjusted my life belt with a smile on his face, when the ship was actually sinking. He spoke to me encouragingly, fastened my belt securely, and wished me luck.'[41]

Captain Lee's father, Edward, wrote to his son, Tennyson, still serving in the war:

> My Own Dear Boy Tennyson: – You will have seen no doubt from the papers the terrible tragedy which occurred to the Mail Boat yesterday. I fear our very dear and loved son Ernest is no more in this world. There is no account of him, dead or alive. He left by the boat. The Leinster was torpedoed on Thursday morning and she was sunk inside an hour. Oh the horror of it. Your poor mother is bearing up as well as can be expected but God alone knows the sorrow that we feel.[42]

Robert was born on 14 January 1883 and educated at Wesley College, and Trinity College, where he obtained his BA and MD degrees in 1910 and 1911. Prior to the outbreak of war, Dr Lee was house surgeon at Bootle Hospital, Liverpool for two years and resident medical officer of the Royal Hospital for Incurables in Donnybrook. He was a member of Stillorgan Park Golf Club.[43]

LEE, Joseph Bagnall
Lieutenant, 6th Battalion Royal Munster Fusiliers, 30th Brigade in the 10th (Irish) Division.

Lieutenant Lee arrived at Suvla Bay at noon on 7 August 1915 and was killed in action on the same day, aged 27. 'His official date of death on 8 August is incorrect.'[44] The battalion strength was 25 officers and 749 other ranks when it landed East of Ghazi Baba. War Diary records state that 'many lighters were running aground and officers and men were required to enter water waist deep and wade ashore'.[45]

A report in the *Irish Times* on Monday 6 September 1915 from a Methodist Minister, Reverend Robert Spence describes how he found Lt Lee lying face downward dead on the slopes of the Kiretch Tepe Sirt.

Sometimes we stumbled over the lifeless form of a brave fellow who had given his life for his country. One such incident brought home to me with tremendous force the gigantic tragedy of war. We were nearing the firing line, and somewhat apprehensive, when, close by, in the gathering light of the early dawn, I saw a man lying face downwards, motionless and lifeless. There had been all too many such incidents earlier but the form could not be recognised. On looking closely at the features, I found it was my good friend, Lt Lee, a young fellow whose successful college career promised a future of rare brilliance. Twenty-four hours before we were laughing and chatting together on the troopship, where he was so full of life and spirit. Now I was looking through tears on his lifeless body. A grave having been dug on our return from the firing line later, we laid his broken body in its final resting place, on a rocky slope over-looking the Aegean Sea, confident that by his very willingness to die for the cause of right, he had proved his title to that unending life 'when eternal morn shall rise and shadows end'.[46]

He is commemorated on the Helles Memorial, Turkey; Great War Memorial, St Philip and St James Church of Ireland, Blackrock; Barristers Memorial, Four Courts, Dublin; Bar Memorial, Royal Courts of Justice, Belfast; Great War Memorial, Quinnsborough Road, Bray, Co Wicklow, and the Hall of Honour, Trinity College. Lieutenant Lee was awarded the 1914–15 Star, British War and Victory medals. 'He received his commission on 5 September 1914 and was promoted to full lieutenant in 1915.'[47] His battalion was formed at Tralee in August 1914 as part of K1, and it was in the Curragh before moving to Basingstoke in May 1915. On 9 July 1915, his Royal Munster Battalion embarked at Liverpool and sailed to Gallipoli via Mudros.[48] He arrived at Suvla Bay with his younger brother, Tennyson, on 7 August 1915.

Joseph was born on 3 May 1888, educated at Epworth College, Rhyl, and Trinity College, where he took his BA degree in 1908, and LL D in 1914. He was a member of Bray Golf Club, Co Wicklow.

FOUR COGHLAN BROTHERS SERVE IN TWO WORLD WARS
Denis Coghlan (staff officer at the Board of Works) and Louisa Coghlan (née Kernan), of 17, Waltham Terrace, Blackrock had thirteen children, of whom twelve survived infancy: Joseph Patrick, Mary, Maureen, John (Jack), Francis James, Bernard, Leo, Sheelagh, Thomas, Anne, Daniel and Brid. All eight boys attended Blackrock College, while the girls were educated at Sion Hill Convent in Blackrock, and all but one child won a scholarship. Their grandson, Lt Noel Coghlan, described an incident following a visit by the Auxiliaries to the Coghlan home in Blackrock:

The Auxiliaries wished to take custody of some arms which the boys had brought back from the front, a not unreasonable initiative in the circumstances, but one to which my grandmother took the gravest exception, to the extent of picking up a live Mills bomb and threatening to pull the pin. In the negotiations that followed the Auxiliaries moderated their demands and departed with the rifles leaving the other weaponry (and the Mills bomb) behind. This, however, proved insufficient to appease my grandmother, a somewhat forceful lady, and she betook herself to Portobello Barracks where she related her sad and sorry story (duly exaggerated, no doubt) to the orderly officer; he in turn related it to the field officer of the day, who agreed that the honour of the regiment had been impugned, and gravely so. Thereupon a military truck duly set out to recover the confiscated weapons from the Auxiliaries and to impress upon the latter the finer points of military etiquette. The weapons were made safe by the regimental ordnance sergeant in the course of the following morning and in the afternoon a small military convoy wended its way to Waltham Terrace. Profuse apologies were forthcoming, and more to the point, the 'stolen' weapons were restored to my still simmering grandmother.

When Denis Coghlan passed away in 1926 Louisa decided to travel in America, where she visited her son, Francis, before moving on to other parts of country. After a number of years she returned to Dublin and lived with her daughter, Maureen, until her death in 1950.

Four brothers joined the British Army. Lieutenant Joseph Coghlan MC died when he received a fatal shot while wounded and being carried to a Dressing Station. His brother, Major John Coghlan MC, a celebrated officer of the Royal Irish Regiment, was attached to the Royal Tank Corps and survived. A younger brother, 2nd Lt Francis Coghlan, joined in 1918, but did not see any action and Major Bernard Coghlan, a medical doctor, served with the Kings African Rifles during the Second World War and survived.

COGHLAN, Joseph Patrick MC
Lieutenant, 228th Field Company Royal Engineers in the 39th Division.

Lieutenant Coghlan was mortally wounded, aged 27, in the advance at Tower Hamlets on 20 September 1917, and died before reaching the Dressing Station. His body was brought back to Camp, where it was interred in the cemetery at Voormezeele, on 23 September, by his battalion's Roman Catholic Chaplain. His Commanding Officer wrote to the family: 'As a stranger, I dare not attempt any word of sympathy; all I can do is, say how proud you should be of your boy. He was without exception, the finest subaltern I have met in France, as regards fearlessness and keenness in his work.'[49]

The action leading to his death on 20 September 1917 at Tower Hamlets, Flanders was described in the war diary: 'Lieutenant Coghlan MC, in charge of No 7 Unit, attacked Tower Hamlets Ridge. The attacking troops were held up temporarily by deadly machine gun fire about 200 yards in front of our front line. Lieutenant Coghlan was wounded and as he was being assisted to the dressing station, was wounded again, this time mortally. The attacking troops eventually drove out the hostile machine gunners and advanced to capture the Red Line.'[50]

FAMILY'S LINGERING DOUBT ABOUT HOW HE DIED

There were lingering doubts among family members about how he was killed. His nephew, Dublin-based District Justice Michael Coghlan stated: 'Although it was never confirmed by the War Office, there was a suggestion that he may have been killed by a bullet fired by one of his own men. Joe was a fearless officer and always very keen to get the job done. On occasions he risked his own life and those of his men by volunteering for very dangerous missions.'[51]

Another nephew, Noel Coghlan, who served as a junior subaltern (lieutenant) in 39th Regiment, Royal Artillery, wrote:

> The general view amongst his nearest and dearest, including his brother Jack, was that he was shot by his own men and indeed the

circumstantial evidence is strong. Whether this occurred at the wire, or when he was being evacuated to a forward dressing station is unclear.

The initial 'hit' at the wire is consistent with either explanation; the second and fatal 'hit' is more dubious. The official version is that he was the victim of a sniper. This is possible, snipers were occasionally active at night, but the balance of probability is against it. Most stretcher case casualties were the victims of shell fire, Joe would have been a low priority target and, in all probability, out of the range of any sniper.

When assessing the likelihood or otherwise of competing explanations one must take account of the circumstances which prevailed at the time. Joe died on the early hours of 20 September 1917, in short, at the latter end of what we know as Passchendaele. By that stage casualties were absolutely horrendous and life, that of one's opponents and one's comrades, was cheap. It was by no means unusual for an unpopular officer to be shot by his own men and, with a modicum of discretion; one's risk of detection was well nigh minimal. The soldiers whom Joe commanded were not, for the greater part, regulars, they were civilians in uniform, former miners and construction workers, sadly lacking in the 'theirs but to do and die' ethos of the late lamented regular army. They were urban animals, proletarians, not peasants, and as such were despicably innocent of that sense of deference to the officer class that led so many of their predecessors to the slaughter. They believed in survival, they were not collectors of medals. Joe would have been aware of the risks that might have followed from pressing his men too hard, but seemingly chose to ignore or at least discount them; he paid the price. I am personally convinced on the evidence available to me that he was killed by his own men.[52]

His grave is at I. K. 2, Voormezeele Enclosures No 1 and No 2 Ieper, Belgium. His name is recorded in the *Book of Remembrance* associated with the Royal Military Academy, Woolwich, in the chapel at the Royal Military College, Sandhurst, and he is commemorated on the Blackrock College Union website. Lieutenant Coghlan distinguished himself at Messines and won the Military Cross at Hollebeke on 31 July

1917, when he successfully stopped the German counter-attack. He was also awarded the British War and Victory medals. The citation for his MC stated:

> For conspicuous gallantry and devotion to duty when in charge of a wiring party in front of our line. The work was started in daylight under heavy machine-gun, rifle and shell fire, and, in spite of a number of casualties, he completed 800 yards of wire entanglement before dark. On subsequent occasions he has shown the same capacity for organisation and speed in carrying out his work.[53]

Joseph Coghlan entered the Regular Army as a Royal Engineer, having taken a high place in the entrance examination in June 1915, and passed with distinction through the Royal Military Academy, Woolwich, and the Military Engineering School in Chatham. On the 9 March 1916, he was appointed to a commission and posted to France on 19 October of the same year. He was through most of the heavy engagements near Ypres during the year.[54]

Joseph was born on 9 March 1892 in Blackrock. He was educated at Blackrock College as a day student (1900–1909), and entered University College Dublin(1909–1915). He was a brilliant student, gaining numerous prizes, honours, scholarships and exhibitions and graduated with a BA (honours), BE and MSc. His nephew, Noel Coghlan, wrote:

> According to my father: the masters would have been unusual at the time, and he was also prone to home experiments, not all of which ended happily. Joe was very conscious of his status as the eldest boy and behaved accordingly – his motto seemed to have been 'tremble and obey', an approach which I gather he carried with him into the army. As a former British officer I would have my doubts as to its wisdom – day to day disciplinary matters are best left to the NCOs, but that's another story. By all accounts he was a very driven man, determined to better himself and the army offered an evident route to that destination. His younger brother Jack was already with the Royal Irish Regiment and was no doubt another spur to enlistment.
>
> The family was mildly 'Home Rule' with suffragette leanings, read

the *Guardian* from time to time and, more regularly, London *Times* as well as taking a French paper, I suspect from context *Le Figaro* – in short the atmosphere parmi la famille Coghlan was one of self improvement or, as the Edwardians would have said, of 'getting on in life'. Joe set the pace in this endeavour.[55]

His younger brother, Major John Aloysius Coghlan, MC, Royal Irish Regiment, was attached to the Royal Tank Corps and was also decorated. He fought at the Battle of the Somme in 1916, at Cambria in 1917 and was awarded the Military Cross. His citation read:

> For conspicuous gallantry and devotion to duty in leading his section into action against the advancing enemy. On one occasion he advanced on foot in front of his sole remaining tank to within ten yards of the enemy, and enabled the tank to inflict heavy casualties. Throughout the day he set a fine example of leadership and courage. The 'D' Battalion tank, *Damon* was commanded throughout its final action by Major Coghlan.[56]

This last tank action would create a lasting legend in its own right that nobody could foresee, and the legend that is *Damon* and its long-gone tank crew still continues to grow. Noel Coghlan wrote:

> Jack, was an altogether different character to Joe. Kindly, gifted with sardonic humour and a strong idealistic streak, he was, in short, the life and soul of the party at all times and in all places. He got on well with his men; famously he carted his wounded driver back over a distance of several kilometres to a field dressing station after a disastrous encounter at Poelcapelle in October 1917 – one rather short officer trudging stoically along through mud, rain and shell fire with one very large and bloody trooper on his back and a two man escort of walking wounded. The driver survived, albeit minus one arm, and kept in touch with Jack long after he was discharged.[57]

Major Coghlan later narrated his experience on the 9 October 1917:

I had the honour to command the leading tank. We left St Julien in the middle of the night and under pouring rain. Each tank commander had to come out of his tank and walk before to scout the road. When the tank came forward, he had to dodge, to save himself from being crushed by the swinging colossus as it waddled from bomb-crater to bomb-crater. The felled trees were a nightmare. In an attempt to avoid one such tree trunk, my tank slipped into the ditch. With combined efforts and not without losing our precious unditching gear we managed to break free. Then, under infernal machine-gun fire, we had to clear the road of trees before we could continue; a lot of time was wasted. The day broke when we reached the first ruins of Poelcapelle, a mere three kilometres from our starting-point in St Julien. Captain Skinner, our section commander, boarded my tank and gave orders to shell the German cellars.

We had only started firing when the Germans struck home through the starboard-sponson. The enormous engine behind me saved me from death or injury; but the fuel tank exploded and I heard a shout; 'get out! Open the doors!' I grasped a fire extinguisher and was surprised that it worked so well – I had never used it before.

However, the right-hand side of the tank was blown to pieces and my sergeant and two gunners had lost their lives. On the left side, I found the rest of my crew in shock.

A few days later, we left for France where we would participate in the Battle of Cambrai. I was again allotted a tank the name 'Damon' and that made me feel good, for I had developed a liking for that name. When I received my first tank, with the presumptuousness of youth I wanted to call it 'Teddy Gerrard' after a young lady who at the time was a hit in the world of theatre. Unfortunately, the unromantic headquarters soon notified me that His Majesty's Land Ships should not be named after individuals from comedy; they suggested 'Damon' II (D29). And 'Damon' is the name that has inspired me up to today. I feel I had a friend in this name.[58]

Meanwhile, *Damon*, purchased from the War Office by the village Poelcapelle in 1919, remained at the scene of its destruction, half buried in the ground by the Zwan pub, until it was moved to a site more worthy of its fame in the market square some five years later. To the outrage of the villagers it was confiscated by the Germans in 1941. Happily, a new generation has constructed a beautiful red brick memorial to Lieutenant Coghlan and crew of *Damon II* and, more recently, has decided to create a full-sized replica of the tank which is now nearing completion and is destined to shortly resume its former place of honour on the market square. Each year the village commemorates the events of 9 October 1917, in a day-long ceremony on the Saturday closest to 9 October.

Major Coghlan married Mollie Donovan, daughter of Robert Donovan, one-time editor of the *Freeman's Journal*, and they had two children: Peter, who died tragically whilst a schoolboy and a daughter, Mrs Mary Ward, a medical doctor living in Oxford. John Coghlan was educated at Blackrock College (1907–1913) and returned in 1915 to study in the Castle. He died in Templeogue, Dublin, in 1963, and was survived by his widow, Mollie and daughter Mary, who, according to Noel Coghlan, 'had her father's looks and personality'.[59]

A third brother, 2nd Lieutenant Francis Coghlan, Connaught Rangers, survived the war. He was commissioned into the Connaught Rangers in 1918, but did not see action and was demobilised in 1919. Following a short period at home he emigrated to the USA where in 1963 he was employed by the Studebaker Motor Corporation, Ardsley, New York. He retired to Florida, and died in Petersburg in 1996.

The last brother to serve was Major Bernard Coghlan MD, King's African Rifles. Major Coghlan served as field surgeon in the East African campaign against the Italians in Ethiopia during the Second World War. He was born in 1899 and qualified as a doctor. According to his son, District Justice Michael Coghlan:

> As a student in the Royal College of Surgeons in Ireland he was arrested for drilling in the college grounds using a wooden rifle. The RIC was called and he was 'lifted' and sent to Crumlin Road Prison in Belfast, and at a later stage he was transferred to a prison in Wales, to keep him out of the way. He returned home to Dublin following his release from prison and passed his medical examinations. Upon the completion of his primary medical degree he was installed by the

Irish National Army as the superintendent of the military and civilian hospital in Boyle, for the duration of the Civil War in Ireland. It was this connection with the National Army and its commander Richard Mulcahy that caused him later difficulty when furthering his medical career in Ireland. He then moved on to Leeds/Bradford as a trainee general practitioner. He wished to return to Ireland to practice, but it became apparent, due to the political situation and as a result of his involvement and affiliations during the 'Troubles', that a job would not be forthcoming in Ireland.

My father subsequently took a degree in tropical medicine at Liverpool University and applied for a position in the British Colonial Service. He obtained a position on the Tanganyika/Uganda border researching the prevalence of malaria in that region. He was involved in tracing the Tsetse fly and its influence upon the carriage of the malaria disease from place to place. During this period of time there was understandably a high incidence of malaria amongst those working for the colonial service. As a result my father was employed on a six months on and six months off basis. After travelling home on a couple of occasions to Ireland he found that the country was so impoverished that his very presence alienated those friends and acquaintances with whom he met while on leave.

My father decided not to return home for some time there after, and went into a business partnership with another colonial servant in similar circumstances to himself.

Upon the outbreak of the Second World War in 1939, he was appointed acting major, seconded as a field surgeon to the King's African Rifles, and served in the East African campaign against the Italians in Ethiopia. When the war ended he was demobilised and served out the remainder of his twenty year contract in Uganda, where he became a medical director of local hospitals. Upon retiring, at age 49, he married my mother, Eileen Bennett, a librarian, and returned to Ireland where they purchased a general practice. Eileen was unhappy in Ireland, and in 1953 they sold the practice and returned to Africa, where he took up a position as general practitioner in Port Alfred in the Eastern Cape. My mother and I followed some six months later. Father was subsequently appointed Chief Officer for Health for the Grahamstown and surrounding area in 1955, and worked in that capacity until 1960 when the family returned to Ireland. In 1966 he resumed work taking up a position as ship's doctor with the Bibby Line operating from Liverpool to Singapore, completing two tours of duty before fully retiring. My mother passed away in 1980, and my father died in 1990, aged 90. They were interred in Dean's Grange Cemetery.[60]

FLEMING, Geoffrey Montagu Mason
Lieutenant, 2nd Battalion Bedfordshire Regiment, Royal Army Medical Corps, 21st Brigade, in the 7th Division, and later in the 26th Field Ambulance.

Lieutenant Fleming was killed, aged 35, by a shell while attending wounded soldiers at Windy Corner on 16 June 1915. His Colonel wrote: 'He was loyal and devoted to his profession and gallantly performed his duties with us. Lieutenant Fleming had endeared himself to all of us, and we all deplore his loss most sincerely.'[61]

His grave is at I. H. 12, Guards Cemetery, Windy Corner, Cuinchy, France, and he is commemorated on the Great War Memorial, formerly at St Matthias Church, Dublin, and now transferred to Christ Church, Leeson Park, Dublin; Hall of Honour, Trinity College; War Memorial from the former Adelaide Hospital, Dublin, and the Plaque, S chancel, St Philip and St James, Church of Ireland, Blackrock. He was awarded the 1914 Star, British War and Victory medals.

At the outbreak of war he was house surgeon at the Meath Hospital and the County Dublin Infirmary. He volunteered, was gazetted lieutenant with the Royal Army Medical Corps on 16 August 1914, and sent to Egypt to meet the Indian Troops, where he was attached to the Lahore Indian General Hospitals at Marseilles, Boulogne and Montreuil. At a later stage he joined the 26th Field Ambulance, and was involved in the attack on Fromelles on 9 and10 May 1915.[62]

Geoffrey Fleming was born at Wilton Lodge, Blackrock, on 8 February 1880, the only child of Alfred George Fleming and Marie M. Fleming of Beechfield, Blackrock. In the 1911 national census, the family was recorded living at 29, Sydney Avenue, Blackrock. His father, a native of Roscommon, was Deputy Chief Cashier with the Bank of Ireland, and his mother was born in France. Geoffrey was educated at Avoca School, Blackrock, before entering Trinity College, where he graduated with a Moderatorship in 1911, and obtained his MB and BCh degrees with honours in 1913.

HEALY, John Frederick

Lieutenant, 3rd Battalion, attached 9th Battalion Royal Irish Rifles, 107th Brigade in the 36th (Ulster) Division. Previously Service No 4/6536, Royal Irish Rifles.

He was killed, aged 19, early in the morning of the 3 July 1916, the third day of the Battle of the Somme. Lieutenant Healy, by all accounts, was a most capable officer and very much liked among his fellow officers and men. Following his death, some of his close friends and superior officers wrote to his parents. Fred E. Cox, an officer and friend, wrote to the family on 15 August 1916 with details of his last hours:

On the night of the 30 June to 1 July, the 9th with the 8th and 10th Battalions, marched up to their assembly trenches in Aveluy Wood. There they stayed until about 7am when they marched up to the forward assembly trenches in Thiepval Wood. The attack began about 7.30am and the 9th Battalion went over in support of the 109th Brigade very shortly afterwards. The Brigade had orders to go to 'C' line (the third), then they were to consolidate, and the 9th and the 10th were to go through them to 'D' line. Your son was of course leading his platoon in the first wave that went over. They did splendidly and got to their objective, and at once began consolidating. However, owing to the failure of the division, our flanks were unable hold our ground, and late on Saturday night withdrew to our own frontline. I saw your son about 10.30 that night – he came in to our Battalion HQ with some news. He had got through without a scratch and had done awfully good work. The rest of the night I believe he spent in helping people and on Sunday at 1.30am he was one of the officers from his battalion told to make a second attack with 350 men of the Brigade (all we could muster at the time). The purpose of this was to relieve and reinforce certain men of the brigade, who were having a hard time in 'A' line. He got over all right, and took charge of the men from his battalion – the second in command of the 9th being in charge of the whole thing. I have heard glowing accounts from everyone of his work there, and he was just mustering his men preparatory to going back after being relieved by men from a fresh division, when he was shot in the head. It was awful bad luck – for five more minutes would have seen him on the road to safety, but you can have the consolation, slight though it may be – of knowing that throughout the whole battle he showed great courage, and set a wonderful example to his men, and that his death was sudden and painless. As to Nat (Nathaniel Hone) I am sorry that I know nothing, but I will at once make enquiries and let you know the result.[63]

The Healy family, although heavily burdened by their own loss, still found time to enquire from Fred Cox about the plight of Jack's close friend, Nat Hone of Carrickmines, who was killed in action two days earlier. A couple of days before the commencement of the 'Big Push' on 1 July, Nat Hone photographed Jack during a break from action. He also photographed him holding his badly damaged rifle, which had been smashed by a shell.

Colonel H. Thompson, DSO, CMG, AMS, wrote, 'Our losses are very sad, 80 per cent from machine guns – ready to play on the men as they jumped out of the trench – many never got further than their own parapets – a sad waste of men equipped fully and trained for months and full of fight if only they could get at an army in the open hand to hand our men would wipe them out.' A letter from his Commanding Officer on 8 July 1916, stated: 'Your son was a great deal under my notice since he joined the battalion and I was always particularly struck by his soldierly qualities and Captain Sinclair, his Company Commander, who is wounded, thought very highly of him also; and often told me so. I can only deplore his loss both to you, my regiment, and the service in general.' The following is an extract from a letter sent by 2nd Lt R V Drought MC, another friend and fellow parishioner at St Philip and St James Church in Blackrock: 'It is with the deepest pain that I write you with regard to poor Jack's death. He was not only, I am glad to say a good pal of mine, but also a brother officer whom we were all proud to know. He went down like a man, and indeed I truly sympathise with you all in your great loss.'[64] A profile of 2nd Lt Drought MC may be viewed in this chapter.

Lieutenant Healy is commemorated on Special Memorial 2 Mill Road Cemetery, Thiepval, Somme, France; Healy Cross and Plaque, S Chancel, St Philip and St James Church of Ireland; Blackrock; Hall of Honour, Trinity College; Great War Memorial at Elstow School and Elstow Abbey in England, and on the headstone of his sister Emily's grave in Mount Jerome Cemetery, Harold's Cross, Dublin. The wooden cross on the 'Healy Cross and Plaque' at S Chancel, St Philip and St James Church, was first erected at Thiepval, Somme, France, to the memory of Lt Healy. He was awarded the British War and Victory medals, which were issued to his parents on 20 July 1923

Prior to being posted overseas, Lt Healy received a memorandum, on the 18 January 1916, from the Adjutant of 3rd Battalion Royal Irish Rifles, together with documents appertaining to the draft of forty other ranks proceeding under his command to join the 10th Battalion Royal Irish Rifles with the Expeditionary Force. The following is an extract from the communication:

> On arriving on the steamer at Southampton you will see that the equipment is hung on hooks provided for the purpose and post a man over these to prevent them being mixed with the equipment of other drafts. Your men are to be warned to have no lights on the steamer and no noise or cheering when entering the port. The sum of £2. 3s. 4d, which you have collected, will pay for a hot meal for the men for which you will make provision. The balance, after paying for this meal, will be expended as you think necessary.[65]

John was the son of George F. Healy (master printer) and Dorothea Healy (née Sullivan) of Peafield, Merrion Avenue, Blackrock. George Healy succeeded his uncle, Alderman George Frederick Healy in 1913 as a printer at G.F. Healy & Company Limited, 23, Ormond Quay, Dublin. There were four children in the family; Emily Dorothea, George Leonard, John Frederick and Euphemia Rose. John was born on 26 May 1897 and began his education at Avoca School in Blackrock, a small school founded in 1891. He later boarded at Elstow School, Bradford, where he was colour sergeant in its OTC. 'In the Michaelmas term, 1914, he was school captain in class Upper VI (Bunyan).'[66] He entered Trinity College in 1915, as an engineering student, but decided to enlist almost immediately. John's grandfather, Lt Colonel John Healey, of the 32nd Foot (later to become the Irish Rifles) changed his surname as that was the spelling on his commission appointment from Queen Victoria.[67]

McCORMICK, John Arthur Rice

Lieutenant, Nelson Battalion Royal Naval Volunteer Service, 2nd Brigade in the 63rd (Royal Naval) Division.

He was killed, aged 26, on Saturday 5 June 1915, in the third Battle of Krithia, while gallantly leading his men into action. Lieutenant McCormick joined the Royal Naval Volunteer Reserve in September 1914 and was attached to the Hawk Battalion before being transferred to the Nelson Battalion on 3 January 1915.

With more men than were required for service at sea, Winston Churchill MP, First Lord of the Admiralty, formed the Royal Naval Division in 1914. This was very unusual in that while it served on land, it maintained the traditions and customs of the navy. The new division sailed for Valetta in Malta on 28 February 1915 and set off for Lemnos, arriving there on 5 March 1915. When the first and second Battles of Krithia failed the Allied Command decided that a further assault should be made against the hill, and a third Battle of Krithia was planned for 4 June 1915. On the 4th the Collingwood, a sister battalion, suffered huge losses, but Lt McCormick of the Nelson Battalion, was one of the few officers to survive that awful day, only to lose his life the next day.[68] 'On 5 June 1915, 'D' Company of the Nelson Battalion advanced over the open and dug the celebrated Nelson Avenue. It was a fine piece of work, but it cost the lives of 4 officers and 76 men.'[69]

Lieutenant McCormick is commemorated on Special Memorial A. 40. Skew Bridge Cemetery, Turkey; Great War Memorial, Wesley College, Ballinteer and the Great War Memorial at Aravon School, Bray, Co Wicklow. He was awarded the 1915 Star, British War and Victory medals.

John McCormick was the only son of Thomas C. McCormick and Catherine McCormick, of Blackrock House, Newtown Avenue, Blackrock. Thomas McCormick was a Director of Tedcastle McCormick, Shipping Merchants. There were five children in the family: Mary Teresa (Minnie), John Arthur Rice, Kathleen, Violet and Ivy. John was educated Aravon School, Bray, Co Wicklow, Wesley College, Ballinteer and worked as an articled clerk prior to the outbreak of war. The profiles of other members of the wider McCormick family, who served in the Great War, may be seen in Chapter Eight.

MAHER, John Charles

Lieutenant, 2nd Battalion, Irish Guards, 4th Guards Brigade in the 31st Division.

Lieutenant John Maher was killed, aged 19, on 14 April, 1918. 'On 4 April 1918, at Chelers the accommodation trench was flooded and all had to walk through water half way up their thighs. About 280 pairs of long (thigh) gun boots were issued to the battalion. Men changed into these and left their marching boots in a ruined cottage behind the line before going into the trenches. Thus, some men were able to wade without getting wet. Sandbags and timber were carried up into the front line for repair of trenches, which were in very bad order. The parapets were not bullet proof, and were falling down due to recent rain.'[70]

Kipling's Regimental History gives a good account of Maher's last day in action:

On Saturday 13 April, the men, dead tired, dug in, as they could where they lay and the enemy – their rush to Hazebrouck and the sea barred by the dead of the Guards Brigade – left them alone. By the morning of the 14 April the Australians were in touch with the Guards left, which had straightened itself against the flanks of the Forest of Nieppe, leaving most of the Brigade casualties outside it. Those who could (they were not many) worked their way back to the Australian line in driblets. The Lewis-guns of the battalion – and this was pre-eminently a battle of Lewis-guns – blazed all that morning from behind what cover they had, at the general movement of the enemy between La Couronne and Verte Rue, which they had occupied. 'They was running about like ants, some one way, some the other – the way Jerry does when he's manoeuvring in the open. You can't mistake it; an' it means trouble'. An hour, however, elapsed ere our guns came in, when the Germans were seen bolting out of the place in every direction. A little before noon they bombarded heavily all along our front and towards the forest; then attacked the Guards salient once more, were once more beaten off by our Lewis-guns; slacked fire for an hour, then re-bombarded and demonstrated, rather than attacked, till they were checked for the afternoon. They drew off and shelled till dusk when the shelling died down and the Australians and a Gloucester Regiment relieved what was left of the 2nd Irish Guards and the Coldstream, after three days and three nights of fighting and digging during most of which time they were practically surrounded. The battalion's casualties were 27 killed, 100 missing and 123 wounded; 4 officers killed; Captain E.D. Dent, Acting Captain M.B. Levy; Lieutenants J.C. Maher, M.R. FitzGerald, and 3 wounded in the fighting.[71]

Lieutenant Maher was buried in grave III. B. 2, Aval Wood Military Cemetery, Vieux-Berquin, France and he is commemorated at the Royal Military College, Sandhurst and the Blackrock College Union website. He was awarded the British War and Victory medals.

A report at a Medical Board assembled at King George V Hospital, Dublin, on 2 March 1916, recorded that Lt Maher was in good health; 5ft 11ins in height, and 17 years old on his last birthday. In April 1916 he entered the Royal Military College at Sandhurst and was gazetted to the Irish Guards in October 1916. He was promoted to full lieutenant in February 1918.[72]

John was the son of William Stanislaus Maher and Maren Kristen Maher of Charleville, Killiney and later in 1918 at Greenwood, Blackrock. His mother came from Gathaab in Denmark. The couple had five children: John Charles, Matthias Aidan, Maurice, George Valentine and Louise. Lieutenant Maher's uncle, Matthias Aidan Maher MP, JP, died in 1901, a younger uncle, George Maurice, succeeded to the estates. George Maurice was unmarried and when he died in 1932, at the age of 85, he left the family property to his nephew, George Valentine, the brother of Lt Maher.

This ancient Gaelic family originated in Tipperary with territory situated at the foot of the Devil's Bit Mountain. The first of the Maher family to live at Ballinkeele was John Maher, born in Liverpool in 1801, who bought Ballinkeele House in 1825 and was responsible for building the present house in 1840. In 1935, the same John Maher built St Malachy's Roman Catholic Church in Ballinkeele. Almost all members of the family have been buried in the crypt beneath the church. The family have had a strong connection with the horse racing world, and in 1889 its mare 'Frigate' won the Grand National.[73]

John Charles was born in Vancouver BC on 17 November 1898, and received his education at St Michael's University School, Victoria BC from 1908 to 1914. His school's magazine, *Black and Red*, recorded that he joined as a day-boy in the September term 1908. He won a prize in mathematics when in the upper third form during 1911.[74] His school lost contact with John when he came to Ireland in 1914 and his name does not appear on the World War One Roll of Honour for the University School. The school has confirmed that this situation will be remedied in the near future. When his family returned to Ireland, John attended Blackrock College in 1914, before entering Sandhurst Military College.

The only girl in the family, Louise, married Owen John O'Hara, a son of Major Patrick O'Hara, and they resided in the historic country house, Mornington House in Co Westmeath. This house has been the O'Hara family home since 1858 and today is still furnished with much of the original furniture and family portraits.[75]

Lieutenant Maher's brother, Matthias Aidan Maher, also served in the Great War with the 1st South African Irish Regiment. This South African Irish Regiment was founded in September 1914. When he returned from war he married a South African, Myrtle Johanna Officer, of Johannesburg, and he died there in 1953 leaving one daughter, Maren Deirdre, who married Baron Lionel Van Dyck. This couple had one son, Maximillian Aidan, born in 1972.[76]

The late William John Maher (known to his family as John), lived with his family at Ballinkeele Country House. Sadly, John passed away in 2011 leaving his wife, Margaret Maher (née Hislop) and two children; Margaret Mary and James Valentine. Today, Ballinkeele Country House is a historic and private family home, offering luxury bed and breakfast accommodation.

MITCHELL, Francis Sidney
Lieutenant, 9th Battalion, attached Royal Sussex Regiment, Royal Army Medical Corps, 73rd Brigade in the 24th Division.

The Battalion moved to the Ypres Salient in February and took over trenches on the Bellewaarde Ridge near the hamlet of Hooge. It was here on 15 February 1916, while attending the wounded, that he was killed aged 26.[77]

His grave is at 26. I. H. 20, Menin Road South Military Cemetery, Ieper, Belgium and he is commemorated, on the Mitchell Window (No 6) at All Saints Church of Ireland, Carysfort Avenue, Blackrock; Hall of Honour, Trinity College, and the War

Memorial, Baggot Street Hospital, Dublin, where he was a student doctor. He was awarded the 1914–15 Star, British War and Victory medals.

The battalion was formed at Chichester in September 1914 as part of the K3 Army. It then moved to South Downs and went into billets in Portslade in December 1914. In April 1915 it moved to Shoreham and on to Woking in June. The battalion landed at Boulogne on 1 September 1915.[78]

He was the son of George Mitchell and the late Anne Mitchell, Ardlui, Newtownpark Avenue, Blackrock. There were three children in the family: George Douglas, Alan Gordon and Sidney Francis. In his second marriage, George Mitchell married Emily Constance Wilson, whose brothers – George, Arthur and Charles Wilson, of Carrickmines House – also fell in the war. George Mitchell was an importer of cigars and wine with a business address at 3, and 20, Sackville Street, Dublin. Prior to living at Ardlui, the family resided at Lisalea, Mount Merrion Avenue, Blackrock. George died on 8 November 1924.

Francis Mitchell entered Medical School at Trinity College, where he took his MA degree in 1912 and MB degree in 1915.

WELDRICK, George Joseph
Lieutenant, Royal Naval Reserve, HMS *Clan MacNaughton*.

Lieutenant George Weldrick was lost on active service in the North Atlantic on 3 February 1915, when his ship, HMS *Clan MacNaughton,* under the command of Commander Robert Jeffreys, was sunk while on patrol duty. Wreckage was found in the area and it was presumed that the *Clan MacNaughton* sank with the loss of 20 officers and 261 ratings.

The *Clan MacNaughton*, a pre-war merchant ship, was taken over by the Admiralty before the outbreak of war in 1914. Although never intended for the purpose she was then converted into a warship, which probably included mounted guns on deck that would have increased instability. The mixed crew hastily put together consisted of career Royal Navy officers, engineer officers, with Merchant Navy experience, and some career regular navy ratings. It also included mixed reservists (some from Newfoundland) and fifty boys just out of the training base at Shotly. Other members of the crew were inexperienced and unfamiliar with the ship and this may have contributed to the disaster. Another contributing factor was the terrible weather conditions reported in February 1915. Although some floating wreckage was found in the approximate area of her last known position, it was not possible to identify it, and her tragic end has remained a mystery.[79]

Lieutenant George Weldrick is commemorated on the Chatham Navel Memorial, Kent, England and he was awarded the 1914/15 Star, British War and Victory medals. At the age of 16 years George Weldrick was indentured apprentice with Messrs. James Cornfoot, London. He was appointed to a ship, *Beacon Rock*, in which he sailed from London to San Francisco on his first voyage. In 1903 he passed for second mate, in 1904 for first mate, obtained his Master's certificate in 1907 and was appointed a Master on the *Elder*, Dempster Line in 1908. Weldrick also held a pilot's certificate for Lagos, West Africa. He was forced to retire in the autumn of 1908, following an attack of malaria and ague. When he recovered from illness he was appointed as officer to the White Star and Orient Lines, and served on the SS *Bovic* and RMS *Celtic* before being gazetted to the Royal Naval Reserve as sub-lieutenant in 1913. Lieutenant Weldrick was a fellow of the Meteorological Society, and a member of the Imperial Merchant Service Guild.[80]

George Weldrick was born on 2 May 1883 at Idrone House, Blackrock, the son of John Francis Weldrick (publisher/literary editor) and Mary Ellen Weldrick (née Hart) of 12, Booterstown Avenue, Blackrock. He was educated at Blackrock College before going to sea. There were four children in the family: John Francis, George Joseph, Mary Elizabeth Clare and Brendan Charles Clare.[81]

DROUGHT, Robert Victor MC

Second Lieutenant, 3rd Battalion, attached 7th Battalion, Royal Irish Rifles, 48th Infantry Brigade in the 16th (Irish) Division.

His parents received a telegram on 27 May informing them that their son was wounded, but remained on duty. A further telegram arrived informing them that he received a gun-shot wound to the back on 8 June, from which he died aged 30, on 9 June 1917 at No 2 Casualty Clearing Station.[82] At 4am on 8 June at Wytschaete, the battalion moved forward to relieve the 47th Battalion on the Black and Blue Lines. At 11am 2nd Lt Drought was badly wounded at Wytschaete and died a few hours later.[83] A colonel in his battalion wrote to his parents:

He did so well at the Divisional School that he was kept on there for some time as the instructor. Since he came back he has done much good work, especially on one occasion when he entered the German lines at the head of a small party, and after a sharp fight, brought back a prisoner, and inflicted some loss to the enemy. On the day of his death I received intimation that he had been awarded the Military Cross. Such a fine soldier and a good sportsman is a great loss to us all, and we offer our most sincere sympathy to you and all his family.[84]

His grave is at III. C. 107. Bailleul Communal Cemetery Extension, France and he is commemorated on the Great War Memorial, Plaque N chancel, St Philip and St James Church of Ireland, Blackrock, and his parents' gravestone at Saint Fintan's Cemetery, Howth. He was awarded the Military Cross, 1914 Star, British War and Victory medals. The citation for his Military Cross read:

> For conspicuous gallantry and devotion to duty. He took part in a raid on the enemy trenches. Although stunned and slightly wounded he succeeded in bringing back a wounded prisoner and all his own casualties. He and another officer then went out again through the barrage to look for his men who had been left behind. Throughout he set a splendid example.[85]

Prior to enlisting he received a certificate of moral character from the Bishop of Kilaloe in early 1915. He was appointed to the special reserve of officers on 13 November 1915 while stationed at Portobello Barracks, Dublin, and was requested to report to the Commandant at Palace Barracks, Holywood, Co Down. On 19 December the 7th Battalion left Blackdown for Southampton, embarking at 4.30pm and arriving at Le Havre at 7.30am next day. It entrained that evening for Fouguereuil, in the coal-mining area.[86]

John G. Hammerton Esq. Solicitor, Northern Assurance Buildings, 39 Fleet Street, Dublin, acting on behalf of the Drought family, wrote to the Under Secretary for War on 2 August 1917 enclosing a Schedule of Assets, which amounted to approximately £800, and requested the usual certificate of exemption under the 'Killed in War Act' to the Estate Duty Office in Dublin. The letter concluded:

As I am writing to you, I have to draw your attention to the fact that 2nd Lt Drought resided with his parents, his father being a retired bank official with a small pension. The deceased had a very good position with excellent prospects in the Dunlop Rubber Company and made his parents a substantial allowance when he resided with them, £100per annum, whilst he was on active service and I shall be glad to know are there any arrears of pay due to Lt Drought and will his parents be entitled to any grant by reason of his death?[87]

Robert was the son of James Roe Drought (bank cashier) and Susanna Margaret Drought (née Young), of 17, Glenart Avenue, Blackrock. Susanna died in December 1918, aged 59, and James passed on in 1940. They were interred at Saint Fintan's Cemetery, Sutton, Co Dublin. There were four children in the family: James Young, Madeline Ethel, Robert Victor and Constance. Robert was born on 6 February 1887 and attended Avoca School, Blackrock (1898–1902). Prior to enlisting he worked as a representative for the Dunlop Rubber Company and was a well-known sportsman in Dublin. In his medical examination at the Military Hospital, Portobello Barracks, Dublin, it was recorded that he was a six feet in height. His personal effects included wrist watch with strap and guard, cap badge, pair of scissors in case, cigarette case, purse, knife and two pipes.[88]

He captained the Lansdowne FC, second XV and also played for the Lansdowne first XV. His other sports club memberships included Sandycove Lawn Tennis Club and Dublin Swimming Club.[89]

GEOGHEGAN, William George Richard
Second Lieutenant, 2nd Battalion, Royal Inniskilling Fusiliers, 96th Brigade in the 32nd Division.

Second Lieutenant Geoghegan died, aged 20, on 13 April 1917 from wounds received in a battle at Savy Wood four days earlier on the 9 April. His battalion's war diary for April 1917 at L'Epine-de-Dallon, Aisne, did not record the action, in which he was wounded, and it is a matter of speculation as to when he was hit. He spent his last days at the 36th Casualty Clearing Station at Heilly, Mericourt-l'Abbe, Somme, France.[90]

His grave is at I. C. 2. Cayeux Military Cemetery, Cayeux-en-Santerre, Somme,

France, and he is commemorated on the Geoghegan Window (No 4), All Saints Church of Ireland, Carysfort Avenue, Blackrock; the Great War Memorial in the chapel at Uppingham School, Rutland, and also on the memorial in its School House. Geoghegan received much of his officer training in Derry, Northern Ireland, and therefore is also commemorated on the Diamond War Memorial, in that city. He was awarded the British War and Victory medals, which his father received in November/ December 1921, when he was residing at Cray Hall, North Cray, Kent. William Geoghegan was appointed 2nd lieutenant (on probation) on 8 October 1915, but as a Cadet of the Officers Training Corps he may not have seen action until early 1916. His father received a letter from the War Office, stating:

> Second Lieutenant Geoghegan is buried at Cayeux French Military Cemetery. The grave has been registered in this office and is marked by a durable wooden cross with inscription bearing full details. The 2nd Inniskillings Battalion was in Dover in August 1914 as part of 12th Brigade in the 4th Division. It moved to Norfolk and landed at Le Havre on 22 August 1914 and was first to see action in the Battle of Le Cateau.[91]

He was the son of William Purser Geoghegan and Mary Elizabeth Geoghegan (née Stack), who were married in 1892 following the death of William's first wife, Frances Anne Geoghegan in 1890, aged 46. The Geoghegan family lived at Rockville, Newtownpark Avenue, Blackrock. William Purser had five children from his first marriage with Frances Anne; they were Esther, Robert Hugh, John Edward, Constance Rachel and Frederick William. The Purser/Geoghegan family had a long association with the Guinness Brewery going back to the early nineteenth century, and 2nd Lt William Geoghegan was employed with the firm before enlisting in the army. His father, William Purser, joined the Guinness Brewery, Dublin in 1859, at 16 years of age, as an apprentice brewer and became head brewer in 1880. In the early days of the firm, the Guinness Family and the Pursers appeared to have run the brewery. Following his retirement from the Guinness Brewery, he became interested in investing in British Columbia and purchased the firm, Urquhurt & Pither, wholesale liquor merchants. William Purser died in 1935, aged 91, while living at White House, Beckenham, Kent.[92]

William was born in Blackrock, on 7 February 1897 and attended Uppingham School, Rutland in England (1911–1915), where he was a prefect in the House School and passed the matriculation for Oxford College.[93] In the 1901 census, he was recorded, aged four, in the company of his 43-year-old maiden aunt, Cornelia Stack, at his parent's home in Newtownpark Avenue. The 1911 census reveals that at age 14, he was also recorded at home, in the company of his 22-year-old cousin, Janet Pearsall, and seven servants. His Regiment's Fund was the only benefactor in his last Will and Testament. Among his effects recovered was; a flask, cigarette case, tie pin and silk handkerchief.

His half-brother, Lieutenant-Commander Frederick William Geoghegan, Royal Naval Air Service, survived the war. Frederick was an engineer and married Gladys Celia Mason in Melbourne, Australia. He died in 1932, aged 48, at Marylebone, London and Gladys died in 1961 in Perth, Australia. The couple had one child.[94]

LELAND, John Henry Frederick
Second Lieutenant, 1/5 Battalion, Royal Welsh Fusiliers, 158th Brigade in the 53rd Welsh Division.

He was killed in action, aged 31, on 10 August 1915 the day following his arrival in Gallipoli. At Lala Baba and Scimitar Hill on 9 August 1915 his battalion sailed at 4.30am aboard HMS *Rowan* going via Imbros and disembarking at 'C' Beach at 6am. The battalion's strength was 26 officers and 811 other ranks. It proceeded to Lala Baba where it bivouacked for the night. Next day 10 August there was hot tea for the men at 4am. At 4.30am orders were received to attack. The battalion left bivouac at 4.45am in column of route, marching due east, 1/5 Royal Welsh Fusiliers leading. While crossing Salt Lake the enemy opened shrapnel fire. It passed through entrenching battalions of the 159th Brigade at 11.30am. The 5th Battalion suffered heavily on the 10 August and had three commanding officers killed in as many days. Eventually, the 5th and 6th Battalions were so depleted they had to merge until back up to strength some time later. At 5pm it opened fire on the enemy about 200 yards from the Turkish front line and later ordered to withdraw to 159th Brigade lines. Further attempts to take enemy positions during afternoon also failed. All reports of 158th Brigade's advance refer to lack of maps and confusion. Casualties were; Lt-Col B.E. Philips, Lt H.O. Williams, 2nd Lts R.C. Walton, J.H.F. Leland, F.P. Synnott, R.M. Mocatta and 13 other ranks killed; 6 officers, 116 other ranks wounded together with 39 missing.[95]

He is commemorated on the Helles Memorial, Turkey; Memorial Cross in the courtyard at St Philip and St James Church of Ireland, Blackrock; Barristers' Memorial, Four Courts, Dublin; Drogheda Great War Memorial, Co Louth; Great War Memorial at High School, Rathgar and Abbey School, Rathgar; Great War Memorial, St Andrews College, Booterstown; Memorial at the Courts of Justice, Belfast; Roll of Honour, Free and Accepted Masons of Ireland, Dublin, and Hall of Honour, Trinity College. He was awarded the 1915 Star, British War and Victory medals.

John Leland was a member of the Dublin University OTC before accepting a commission on 26 August 1914. His battalion sailed from Devonport on 19 July 1915 for Gallipoli, going via Imbros and disembarking at Suvla Bay on 9 August 1915.

His early education was received at St Andrew's College, Booterstown, and High School, Rathgar, before entering Trinity College, where he took his BA in 1907. He married Florence Mary Leland at Christ Church, Church of Ireland, Carysfort Avenue, Blackrock, on 9 March 1915, just five months before his death. John was the son of Henry Leland (retired accountant) and Laura Jane Leland (a native of Drogheda) of 6, Idrone Terrace, Blackrock. The couple had three children; John Henry, Henry William and Frederick William. His brother, Captain Frederick William Leland, Leinster Regiment, survived the war and died on 22 September 1943.

A FAMILY CONNECTION WITH THE GENERAL POST OFFICE AT THE TIME OF THE EASTER RISING

NORWAY, Frederick Hamilton

Second Lieutenant, 2nd Battalion, Duke of Cornwall's Light Infantry, 82nd Brigade in the 27th Division.

He died in hospital at Wimereux, aged 19, on 4 July 1915 from wounds received in action on 13 June 1915. An official report stated that, 'his battalion was in the trenches, near Ypres, for nineteen days under constant shell-fire, but later moved southwards to the salient of L'Epinette near Armentières. On 11 June he was warned by the Royal Engineers that the section of the trench held by his platoon had been successfully mined by the Germans and would probably be blown up at dawn. The section was not evacuated, and 2nd Lt Norway continued to hold it for thirty-six hours, until the mine was exploded early on 13 June. Twenty-four men of his platoon were killed or wounded, but he was unhurt. The explosion brought down the ruined walls and buried his sergeant and several men, whereupon he led a few men over the parapet, under heavy shell-fire, in order to dig them out, and was mortally wounded by a high explosive shell.'[96]

His colonel and captain wrote: 'I have noted the good work done by your son and when we are next asked to send in names, I shall forward his.' And his captain wrote: 'He proved one of the pluckiest youngsters and best workers I have ever come across. He was always ready to go out on patrol or on any job that had to be done in front of the trenches at night. He well deserves to be mentioned in despatches, and I hope it will be done in due time.' [97]

His grave is at III. O. 5. Wimereux Communal Cemetery and he is commemorated on the War Memorial at St Philip & St James Church of Ireland, Blackrock and on the panel of the Duke of Cornwall's Light Infantry in the chapel at the Royal Military College, Sandhurst. The promise from his superior officers that his name would be mentioned in the next despatch does not appear to have happened. He was awarded the 1915 Star, British War and Victory medals, which his father claimed in an application on 5 August 1921, when living with his wife at 23, Oakwood Court, Kensington, London.

Frederick applied for a commission in the new armies being formed by Kitchener, but failed the medical examination. 'He underwent a severe operation to remove a physical defect which impeded military service, before he could try again, however, his father decided that he should go for a commission in the regular army, because this would give him a career after war was over.'[98] He entered the Royal Military College at Sandhurst, by nomination, on 31 October 1914, and was gazetted to the 2nd Battalion, Duke of Cornwall's Light Infantry.[99] The battalion returned from Hong Kong in November 1914, moved to Winchester and landed at Le Havre, France, on 21 December 1914. It entrained for St Omar Arques and then marched to Wardrecques, where for the time being, it was relatively safe. Norway proceeded to Flanders in April 1915.

He was the son of Arthur Hamilton Norway and Mary Louisa Norway (née Gadsden), of South Hill, 91, Merrion Avenue, Blackrock. There were two children in the family, Frederick Hamilton and Nevil Shute. Arthur was born in Cornwall, worked as a civil servant in London and wrote travel books in his spare time. In 1912 he was appointed Secretary to the General Post Office in Ireland and according to his son, Nevil, their 'new social position in Ireland required a different house from the modern villa in a row that the family had lived in up till then'.[100] He leased South Hill in Blackrock, a rambling country house with thirteen acres where the Norways were happy for the two years prior to the outbreak of war. Everything changed when their son Frederick was killed in 1915. The happy memories with their two boys at South Hill were too much for Mary and Frederick to bear, and they took advantage of a break clause in the lease to give up the house.[101]

When the 1916 Easter Rising broke out on Monday 24 April 1916 the family was staying at the Hibernian Hotel. Although it was a bank holiday, Arthur Norway was in his office on the first floor of the post office, on Easter Monday morning, when he received a phone call from Sir Matthew Nathan, Under-Secretary of the Irish administration, asking him to go immediately to Dublin Castle. Thirty minutes later, rebels took the Post Office. A couple of days before the 'Rising' his son, Nevil, became anxious about the situation in Dublin and brought Fred's automatic pistol into the post office, urging his father that he keep it close to him. Arthur often wondered how he would have reacted had he been in his office when the rebels charged in the door. As the only armed person in the post office, would he have attempted to hold the rebels?

A short time before the General Post Office was seized, Nevil and his mother, Mary, arrived in Sackville Street (now O'Connell Street) on the way to meet Arthur for lunch. He sent his mother back to the hotel and went in search of his father, who was in Dublin Castle relatively safe from trouble.[102] Eventually, Arthur slipped out of Dublin Castle into a lane and got back to the Hibernian Hotel in Dawson Street, where his wife and son were anxiously waiting for him.

It is said that Arthur Norway was a liberal and generally seen to have behaved impartially in his position as Secretary of the General Post Office. However, he was resolute in his pursuit of seditious members of his staff. One senior member, P.S. O'Hegarty, Irish patriot, revolutionary, writer and at the time, postmaster at Queenstown (now Cobh), came in for special attention. O'Hegarty was posted to the postmastership of Whitechurch, Shropshire, for three years. He also dismissed O'Hegarty's brother, Sean, for refusing to accept a transfer to England. When the Rising was over it was found that only forty-eight out of seventeen thousand post office employees were disloyal. In his memoirs, *Irish Experiences in War*, published for the first time in 1990, Norway was critical of the government and administration in London for its complacent attitude towards the Irish Republican Brotherhood and Sinn Fein. The attitude appeared to be 'The country was quiet. Why should it not remain so?'[103] Arthur Hamilton Norway died in 1938.

Mary Norway made a 'joyful discovery' on 29 April 1916, when a large despatch-case came back from the Arthur's office containing her jewellery and three handkerchiefs sent to her by Frederick from Armentières with her initials worked on them. In one of four letters to her sister, Grace, who was living in England, she wrote: 'When I found them the relief was so great I sat with them in my hand and cried.' She also described the desolation in Dublin in the days following the Rising: 'If you look at pictures of Ypres or Louvain after the bombardment it will give you some idea of the scene'. She was distraught that everything belonging to Fred, stored in the office safe and cupboard, were lost, including his sword – 'our most precious possessions'. Mary Louisa Norway died in 1932.[104]

There is no doubting the bitterness felt by the British Government towards Irish Republicans for trying to take advantage of its heavy involvement in the war on different fronts. In Mary's second letter to her sister Grace, she wrote, 'It is difficult to think of the position without intense bitterness, though God knows it is the last thing one wishes for at such a time.' She also wrote that 'the only document stolen from among the official documents was Frederick's commission. Why, we cannot imagine, unless the fact that it bore the King's signature made it worthy of special insult and desecration.'[105]

Frederick was born in Brentford, Middlesex, on 31 October 1895 and entered Rugby School in 1909, where he had two abdominal operations and spent a great deal of time out of school. His father decided to remove him from school and bring him to Ireland. Later in 1912, he matriculated to Trinity College when only sixteen years.

He enjoyed South Hill, and his brother wrote: 'For Fred and myself, that house opened up new country pleasures we had hardly dreamed of. There was a pony to be ridden or driven in a trap, hay to be made and carted, and greenhouses to be walked through in wonder.' Frederick met the love of his live, Geraldine Fitzgerald, a ravishingly beautiful Irish girl, who wanted to go on stage. At age seventeen, he proposed to Geraldine on top of a Dublin bus and was kindly rejected. In later life, his brother, Nevil, speculated that 'she was the famous Irish actress, Geraldine Mary Fitzgerald, who played opposite Bette Davis in *Dark Victory*, and many other films, including, *Wuthering Heights*, *Watch on the Rhine* and *Ten North Frederick Street*'.[106] However, the film star, Geraldine Mary Fitzgerald, was born in November 1913 at Greystones, Co Wicklow, and we can now say with certainty that Fred's Geraldine was not the famous Irish actress.

Nevil spent the remainder of the Easter Rising as a stretcher bearer with the newly formed Royal Irish Automobile Club Ambulance Service. In 1918 he joined the Royal Military Academy and elected for the Royal Flying Corps, despite having a rather bad stammer. He spent nine months training as a gunner, which he enjoyed enormously. However, his stammer had become much worse and he failed his final medical examination before passing out as a commissioned officer, and was dismissed from the service. He tried three months treatment for his stammer in an attempt to get a commission in the newly formed, Royal Air Force, but was not accepted. In a final attempt to get to the front, he joined the ranks of the Suffolk Regiment and served as a private until the end of the war.[107]

He was a popular English novelist using Nevil Shute as his pen name and he wrote many well-known novels, including *A Town like Alice*. Nevil Shute Norway was also a successful aeronautical engineer, who by the age of thirteen had built several model aeroplanes of wood, glue, and paper with rubber motors, and knew something about longitudinal stability and negative tail incidence. He was one of the leading aeronautical engineers in Britain during the 1930s and a fellow of the Royal Aeronautical Society. Nevil established Airspeed Limited, an aircraft manufacturing company, in 1931, with fellow director, A.H. Tiltman, but left the company when he was bought out of Airspeed in 1939. Prior to leaving the aircraft manufacturing industry his novel, *What Happened to the Corbetts*, had been published. Nevil came back to South Hill for the last time in 1946, and was entertained by Michael Hannan and his family, who lived there from 1942 to 1964. He emigrated to Australia in 1950 and settled with his wife and two daughters on farmland in south-east Melbourne. Nevil died in 1960, following a stroke, and was survived by his wife, Francis Mary, and two daughters, Shirley and Heather Felicity.[108]

TRAGEDY FOR PARENTS: PROPRIETORS OF 'SMYTHS OF THE GREEN'
SMYTH, Donald Seymour
Second Lieutenant, 3rd Battalion, Royal Irish Regiment, attached 2nd Battalion, 8th Brigade in the 3rd Division.

He died from wounds, aged 20, on 19 October 1914 following action at Le Pilly, Aubers Ridge, France. 'At 3am on Thursday 17 September the battalion stood to arms. Artillery fire continued and 2 men were wounded. Heavy artillery fire was opened on

OUT OF THE DARK

the right trenches almost directly after they had been vacated. Captain Furnell and 6 officers arrived; Captain H.G. Gregorie; 2nd Lt J.R. Ross-Smyth, 3rd Battalion; 2nd Lt D.S. Smyth, 3rd Battalion; 2nd Lt P.E. Howard, 2nd Battalion, and 2nd Lt W.H. Flinn, 3rd Battalion.[109]

> On 19 October 1914 the 2nd Royal Irish Regiment stormed Le Pilly, a small bridge on the Aubers Ridge, which they held and entrenched. The British Commander completely underestimated the strength of the opposition and when five divisions of the German Army attacked the whole of the Allied line with large scale infantry assaults and heavy artillery, the Royal Irish were outnumbered three to one, and following a savage fight there were many casualties. When the battalion's ammunition ran out, its commander, Major E.H. Daniell, made the order to fix bayonets and to charge the enemy. Despite great bravery and determination, the situation was impossible, and resulted in 175 officers and men, of the 2nd Royal Irish Regiment, dead or missing on 19 and 20 October 1914.[110]

Second Lieutenant Smyth was numbered among those who were missing or killed. He was in 'A' Company commanded by Captain James Arnold Smithwick, from Kilkenny, who was badly wounded and transported to Germany as a prisoner of war. Captain Smithwick was involved in a prisoner swop and died from his wounds in London in 1915. He was buried in Foulkstown Cemetery, Kilkenny.[111]Following reports that 2nd Lt Smyth was wounded, his family had to endure the uncertainty that came when a loved one was missing. Was their son Donald dead, or wounded and taken prisoner? Mr Smyth wrote to War Office on 22 January 1915 outlining details of his son's last day in action, which must be assumed was received from an independent source:

> The battalion was sent to attack the village of Le Pilly on 19 October and succeeded in storming and capturing the village, but on the morning of the 20th the Germans came from another direction and cut off and captured, after great resistance, the rest of the Royal Irish. The French, who were on either side of the Royal Irish got orders to

retreat, but the Royal Irish got no order so had to cut their way on.[112]

On 5 June 1915 his parents received a letter from the War Office, which stated: The Military Secretary begs to inform you that the Commandant of the German Prison at Merseburg has sent to the War Office a copy of a statement made by L/Cpl Doyle, 2nd Royal Irish Regiment: 'During an attack on 19 October, 1914, at Le Pilly, France, 2nd Lt D.S. Smyth was wounded in the leg and shortly afterwards was killed by shrapnel shell as he lay on the ground.' In a reply on 8 June 1915, Mr Smyth wrote: 'I thank you for your letter but we do not accept the fact of our son's death on the evidence you give although it may be correct. We therefore do not want it published until corroborated.' Mr Smyth received another letter on 16 March 1916 from the War Office, which stated:

> I am commanded by the Army Council to inform you that they regret that no further report has been received concerning 2nd Lt D.S. Smyth, reported missing on 19/20 June 1914. Reference has been made to the Base concerning the report that he was 'wounded and a prisoner'. It is not possible now to state the precise grounds upon which this report was based, but in view of the fact that nothing further has been heard, it is regretted that it must now be regarded as incorrect. Before taking official action in the matter the Council will be obliged if you will confirm the fact that no further news of this officer has reached you. If that is the case, they will be regretfully constrained to conclude that he died on or since the 19 October 1914.[113]

Mr Smyth replied by return, confirming that no further news of his son had reached him and must conclude that his son died on that date. Despite the declaration by the War Office that they accepted 2nd Lt Smyth was killed in action on 19 October 1914, they were unable to issue a death certificate.[114]

Donald Smyth was a member of the DublinUniversity OTC for a period of three years, before joining the British Army. He embarked at Southampton on Friday 14 August 1914 and arrived at Boulogne the next day. On Sunday 16 August he was in billets at Aulnoye and on 23 August at Mons. His battalion retired from Audencourt on Wednesday 26 August and it was at Chauffry on Tuesday 8 September.[115]

He is commemorated on the Le Touret Memorial, Pas de Calais, France; St Philip and St James Church of Ireland, Blackrock; St Andrews College, Booterstown, and the Hall of Honour, Trinity College. Second Lieutenant Smyth was awarded the 1914 Star, British War and Victory medals.

He was the son of Edward Weber Smyth JP and Elizabeth Anna Smyth, of Cuil-min, 56, Sydney Avenue, Blackrock. There were four children in the family: Spencer, Weber, Reginald Osborn and Donald Seymour. Edward Weber Smyth was the proprietor of the well-known firm, Robert Smyth & Sons Limited (Smyth's of the Green), number 6 & 7, St Stephen's Green, Dublin. He owned other premises at number 1, 2 and 3, Westland Row; Ann's Lane and a lager beer store at number 5 St Stephen's Green. The family also had property situated near Birr, Co Offaly. Robert Smyth & Sons Limited was a private company and a long-established family business trading in tea and wine. Mr Smyth died in 1928 and his last Will and Testament reveals that his wife and sons held shares in the company. It appears that following his father's death, his son, Weber, took over as Chairman and Managing Director.[116]

Donald was born on 5 November 1893 and educated at St Stephen's Green School, Dublin and St Andrews College, Booterstown, before entering Trinity College in 1911. His brother, Reginald Osborn Smyth MD, Royal Army Medical Corps, qualified as a medical doctor, enlisted in the British Army and survived the war. He married Violet Butler Cranwill, a sister of Capt Valentine Arthur Butler Cranwill MC, who was killed in the war.

STEIN, John Francis
Second Lieutenant, 3rd Battalion, attached 2nd Battalion, Royal Irish Rifles, 74th Brigade in the 25th Division.

In a hurried letter from France to his mother, dated 13 October 1916, the Commanding Officer wrote: 'He was killed outright into 2nd Lt William Dobbin's arms by a shell that exploded in a skyline trench near Ovillers-la-Boisselle.' The tragedy occurred at Somme, France, on 28 September 1916. He was almost 30 years of age. The letter also mentioned that the young officer was a great friend of the chaplain, Reverend Father V. Gill, SJ, St Xavier's in Dublin.

There was no mention of his death in his battalion's war diary. Lieutenant W.P.L. Dobbin MC of Dunmurry, Co Antrim was killed on 21 March 1918.[117]

He was notified of his appointment to a commission as Second Lieutenant in the Special Reserve of Officers by the War Office on 29 June 1915. Prior to joining his unit he was selected to attend a class of instruction at the Queenstown Garrison, Cork Barracks, Cork, on 7 July 1915.[118]He inherited the 'Stein weak heart'. In Ireland he failed to pass two medical examinations and was deemed unfit for active military duty due to cardiac insufficiency. Nevertheless, he insisted on being sent to France. His nephew, John Stein Joyce, who lives in Germany, stated, that in Rouen his uncle once again turned down the opportunity offered him for medical reasons to accept safe service behind the frontlines. He also stated: 'My father claimed that John Stein's decision to abandon an engineering career in Canada was purely patriotic. Being a "Redmondite", he firmly believed that if the Irish joined the English against the Kaiser, the British Government would definitely grant Ireland Home Rule'.[119]

Mrs Stein telegraphed the War Office on 3 October 1916 requesting details of her son's death. The response two days later suggested that she should communicate directly with the officer commanding, 3rd Royal Irish Rifles, who might be in a better position to furnish her with some details. She wrote to the War Office again on 8 December 1916 requesting that her son's effects be forwarded to her as previously promised. His effects were received by the family.[120] Mr Stein Joyce has some of the memorabilia in his possession. These include a 'Campaign Compendium 1916' from which the first few sheets are ripped out. He presumes that his uncle used them to write his last letters to his family and also to his fiancée, May Lucas, who remained unmarried. He also has a canvass-backed map of Belgium, published by the German army staff, as well as a large portrait of his uncle in uniform painted in oil posthumously by his aunt, Caroline Scally, from a photograph by Lafayette.[121]

A letter to Mrs Stein on 19 June 1920 stated that:

It has been found necessary to exhume the bodies in certain areas. The body of Second Lieutenant J.F. Stein has therefore been removed from Paisley Avenue Cemetery and re-buried in Lonsdale Cemetery. You may rest assured that the work of re-burial has been carried out carefully and reverently, special arrangements having been made for the appropriate religious service to be held.[122]

His grave is at IX. E. 5, Lonsdale Cemetery, Authuile Wood, Aveluy, north-east of Albert, France, and he is commemorated on the Blackrock College Union website. He was awarded the British War and Victory medals.

John Francis Stein was the only son of Robert Francis and Mary Josephine Stein (née Macdonnell) of Woodview, Merrion Avenue, Blackrock. There were five children in the family; Mary Catherine, John Francis, Caroline Mary, Constance Mary Gertrude, Margaret Mary Alico. The girls received their secondary education at the English Sisters in Nymphenburg, near Munich, Germany.

John was born on 5 October 1885 and attended Blackrock College as a day student (1895–1896). His secondary education was received from 1899–1903 at the Benedictines in Windsor which became a Catholic boarding school for boys in October 1861 with the title of St Stanislaus College, Beaumont. When John Stein completed his studies at Beaumont, he attended the Royal College of Science in Dublin where he studied engineering. 'Soon after graduating he emigrated to Canada where he was employed by the Marconi Company in Montreal. He worked on the design, testing and commissioning of wireless telegraph relay stations which brought him to numerous sites scattered between Halifax and as far west as Saskatchewan.'[123]

John Stein's sister, Margaret Mary Alico, married Gordon F. Joyce and continued to live in Woodview, Blackrock. During the war she served as a VAD at the Linden Auxiliary Hospital, Blackrock, which was used as a convalescent home for wounded soldiers. Margaret was at Linden at the same time as Edie Lemass, sister of 2nd Lt Herbert Lemass, who also fell in the war. They were old girls of Sion Hill, Dominican Convent in Blackrock and represented Linden Auxiliary Hospital in a hockey match against the senior girls from their old school. The match finished in 2-2 draw.[124]

John F. Stein followed in the footsteps of his father and maternal grandfather who were both civil engineers. The latter, John Joseph Macdonnell worked as an assistant engineer for the Dublin to Kingstown Railway; the world's fourth steam railroad. He emigrated to England where he worked for the famous pioneer of railroad engineering, I.K. Brunel who nominated him in 1849 to be elected a member of the Institute of Civil Engineers. J.J. Macdonnell continued to work on railroad design and became known for the innovative 'Macdonnell Way' on the Bridgefort line. He also designed a train turntable with a 42ft diameter for the Bristol and Exeter Railway.

John F. Stein's father, Robert Francis Stein, graduated from Trinity College, Dublin and practised railroad engineering in India for many years before returning to Ireland to adopt the traditional Stein profession of malting and distilling. He took over the Rathstewart Malt House near Athy, Co Kildare from his father. It produced barley malt for Jameson's Distillery and the Guinness Brewery.

It all began in 1751 when the five sons of John Haig and Margaret Stein founded the Haig–Stein whisky distilling dynasty in Scotland and later in Ireland. The Haig and Stein families co-operated closely in business matters and at one time owned nearly all the distilleries in the Scottish Lowlands. Robert Stein (John F. Stein's grandfather) discovered that the alcohol in fermented wash could be driven off by steam, leading him to invent the continuous distilling method which he patented under the title 'The Patent Still' in 1826. Two such stills were installed in Haig distilleries in Scotland. A few years later an improved patent still resulted in the 'Stein Stills' being superseded by the 'Coffey Stills'.

An earlier John Stein established two distilleries in Dublin, one in Marrowbone Lane in partnership with his cousin, William Jameson, and the other in Bow Street with the latter's brother, John Jameson. In 1780, John Stein relinquished his stake in the Bow Street Distillery in order to concentrate on malting, which he carried out in various locations. The Bow Street Distillery thus became the John Jameson Distillery.[125]

LETT, Emily Sarah (survived)
Voluntary Aid Detachment (VAD), British Red Cross Society.

Emily Lett was born at Tomsallagh, Co Wexford in 1877, and trained at Sir Patrick Dunn's Hospital, Dublin. In 1911, she was recorded working as Matron in a hospital for the mentally ill at Finglas, Dublin. She was awarded the Royal Cross (second class) for outstanding service.

Emily Lett was the daughter of the late Pierce Lett of Tomsallagh, Ferns, Co Wexford and Sarah Catherine Lett (née Rudd), who, following the death of her husband, lived with two of her daughters at Idrone Terrace, Blackrock. There were seven children in the family: Katherine Lucy, William, Emily Sarah, Hannah Elizabeth, Alice Hester, Frances Susan and Pierce (Percy). Emily remained unmarried.[126]

KAVANAGH, Patrick

Company Quarter Master Sergeant, Service No 15567, 2nd Battalion, Royal Dublin Fusiliers, 48th Brigade in the 16th (Irish) Division.

The Second Battalion, Royal Dublin Fusiliers was in Gravesend and Harrow and landed in Boulogne on 22 August 1914. Company Quarter Master Sergeant Kavanagh was killed in action on the first day of the Kaiser's Battle, aged 33, on 21 March 1918. On this day the 2nd Dublins were operating in the Péronne area of the Somme. In the Kaiser's Battle at Lempire & Ronssoy on the 21 March 'the Germans attacked along the whole front at 11.15am. The mist prevented any observation. All companies were in their battle positions when the Germans reached Sandbag Alley, where they were held up by the companies in the Red Line.'[127]

Further information on the first day of the Kaiser's Battle reveals that 'the 2nd Dublins lost 117 soldiers more than double the losses from the first Battalion. Eighty per cent of those who died have no known graves, and are commemorated on the Pozières Memorial. The higher number of deaths in this battalion may have been caused by the fact that the German assault came from their flank and not from the front as anticipated. Their resistance gave more time to the 1st Dublins to withdraw before being surrounded.'[128]

He is commemorated on Pozières Memorial, Somme, France. The Pozières Memorial relates to the period of crisis in March and April 1918 when the Allied Fifth Army was driven back by overwhelming numbers across the former Somme battlefields. He was awarded the 1914–15 Star, British War and Victory medals.

Patrick was the son of Patrick and Elizabeth Kavanagh, Ardlui, Newtownpark Avenue, Blackrock. In 1911 the family residence was at 15, Stradbrook Road, Blackrock. There were five children born to the family of whom four survived infancy: Norah, Patrick, Catherine and Daniel. Patrick Kavanagh and his father worked locally as herdsmen.

DODD, William

Sergeant, Service No 11484, 2nd Battalion, Royal Dublin Fusiliers, 10th Brigade in the 4th Division and later the 48th Brigade in the 16th (Irish) Division.

Sergeant Dodd was killed in action, aged 23, in an attack on Redan Ridge, during the first day of the Battle of the Somme, 1 July 1916.

The 2nd Battalion Royal Dublin Fusiliers had 31 officers and 870 other ranks and were in the second wave of the attack on 1 July 1916. At 9am the battalion left its assembly trenches and advanced in the following formation; 'A', 'B' & 'C' Companies in four lines of platoons, each platoon in sections with the lines 100 yards apart. 'D' Company in reserve was 200 yards in rear of 45 Line – this company was in diamond formation, each company in columns of fours. Immediately after leaving assembly trenches, each line came under heavy enfilade fire from machine-guns in Beaumont Hamel and even the Reserve Company had casualties as they left Young Street. At 9.50am the order 'stand fast' was received, followed immediately by 'your battalion not to go beyond English front line trenches until further orders'. These messages were only delivered at the Dublins front line trenches and there it stopped. In the meantime the battalion had lost heavily, not only from machine-gun fire from Beaumont Hamel, but rifle and machine-gun fire from the German 1st line trenches. It had been impossible to stop all the platoons and some had got into the ground between the enemy and the Dublins trenches. All of these, without exception, became casualties, including 5 officers. At 12 noon orders as follows were received: 'You will attack the German trenches and consolidate line from point 86 to 88 inclusive. The Seaforth Highlanders are attacking north of the Redan. Point 59 is held by our own troops. The 29th Division are attacking Beaumont-Hamel at 12.30pm. Take care of your left flank as there are still some Germans in position opposite the Redan'. It was found impossible to collect more than 60 men, during the advance; out of 23 officers and 480 men going into action, 14 officers and 311 men had become casualties.[129]

Sergeant Dodd is commemorated on the Thiepval Memorial, Somme, France and he was awarded the 1914 Star, British War and Victory medals. William enlisted towards the end of 1911 and disembarked at Boulogne on 23 August 1914. He fought at Le Cateau in 1914, and was wounded and suffered gas poisoning during 1915. The 2nd Dublins were in Gravesend in August 1914 and the battalion moved to Harrow, before arriving in France.[130]

He was the eldest son of William Dodd and Margaret Dodd (née Golden) of 26, Annaville Avenue, Newtownpark, Blackrock. There were nine children in the family: Emily, William, Richard, Michael, Edward, Katie, Thomas, Joseph and George. William was born on 24 May 1893 and educated at the Sisters of Mercy, Carysfort Avenue, Blackrock. Sergeant Dodd was home on 26 January 1916 for his marriage to Catherine Dwyer of 6, St Mary's Street, Kingstown, which took place at St Michael's Roman Catholic Church, Kingstown. They had one boy, William, who died sometime following birth. William senior was a member of the hugely successful Young Ireland Fife and Drum Band from Newtownpark.[131]

His brother, Edward also enlisted in the British Army and was attached to the Cheshire Regiment. He was based in Dublin and became involved in stealing guns from the army for the IRA and when this activity was detected he was charged and sentenced to six months imprisonment. When he was released from jail he went full time as a pro-treaty member of the IRA before serving as an officer in the new Free State Army. He was the arresting officer of the anti-treaty IRA officer, Ernie O'Malley, when Free-State troops stormed a house in the Ballsbridge area of Dublin on 4 November 1922. In the shoot-out O'Malley was wounded, but drove the Free-Staters down the stairs, dropping their guns as they retreated. However, another column lead by Lt Dodd was nearby and he arrested the badly wounded O'Malley. In an extract of evidence in the case of Ernie O'Malley, Lt Dodd stated:

> I remember the morning of 4 November 1922, (last Saturday), I was in charge of a raiding party from Wellington Barracks, which raided [redacted] and I was proceeding as the operations there were finished. When I got opposite Aylesbury Road I heard some shooting

and turned the car back in the direction thereof, when I got opposite No 30, Aylesbury Road I saw six or seven soldiers lying across a wall firing towards the house from which the firing came. I rushed into the house (with two others), the first thing I saw was a wounded soldier at the bottom stairs. I went upstairs then and found a women (Miss Humphreys) lying wounded in the bed (wounded in jaw). I also found Lieutenant Keegan, Intelligence Officer, in charge of the other party, wounded (finger blown off) trying to open the secret chamber, I searched the top of the house and found the accused (Ernie O'Malley) had got out and down to the bottom of the garden, I rushed down stairs and when I got down there I found him lying wounded in a little passage way, he had a revolver and rifle by his side and there were empty cases around. I took up the rifle and revolver and there were three rounds in the magazine. I rang for an ambulance (Beggars Bush) and got him shifted to Wellington Barracks. I also got a wounded soldier and woman shifted to hospital. I searched the house and found three revolvers, three bombs (fully loaded), about 30 rounds of mixed ammunition, a lot of literature and documents were also found by me. I arrested the three women, Miss Humphreys, Miss Murphy and Madame O'Rahilly.[132]

In 1923 when government decided to downsize the army, Lt Dodd was one of the officers to mutiny. In the end he had to leave the Irish Army and subsequently emigrated to England, where he fell on hard times. He died alone and was buried in an unmarked pauper's grave. In recent years his family located the grave and erected a headstone.[133]

DOYLE, Christopher

Sergeant, Service No 11539, 2nd Battalion, Royal Dublin Fusiliers, 'C' Company, 10th Brigade in the 4th Division.

Sergeant Doyle was missing, presumed killed in action, aged 21, on 23 October 1916, during the final two months of the Battle of the Somme.

On 23 October 1916 at Gun Pits, Somme, there were 36 other ranks missing in action. The enemy was met within about 30 feet of Gun Pits when heavy machine-gun and rifle fire compelled the Dublin's leading lines to lie down, however, they crawled forward and bombed the Gun Pits and eventually got into them, where heavy hand-to-hand fighting ensued and it was the survival of the fittest. Congestion around Gun Pits was to a great extent the cause of heavy casualties, however, the majority of casualties were caused in the hand-to-hand fighting in the 'Pits' and by machine gunfire just before getting into them. The men had a hard time of it and underwent severe trials but throughout were cheerful and confident.[134]

Sergeant Doyle is commemorated on the Thiepval Memorial, Somme, France and he was awarded the1914–15 Star, British War and Victory medals. He was posted to France on 23 August 1914, and served there and in Flanders, Belgium, where he was twice wounded. Prior to serving in the Battle of the Somme he was reported to be in Egypt in early 1916. A notice, accompanied by Christopher's photograph, was carried by the *Evening Herald*, stating that he was missing following an engagement on 23 October 1916, and his parents would be grateful for news of him.[135] The 2nd Dublins were in Gravesend in August 1914 as part of the 10th Brigade in the 4th Division. The battalion moved to Harrow and landed in Boulogne on 22 August 1914. Following the death of Sgt Doyle, the battalion was transferred to the 48th Brigade in the 16th (Irish) Division.[136]

He was the son of John and Mary Doyle, Orchard Cottages, Newtownpark, Blackrock. There were ten children in the family, of whom five survived infancy:

Christopher, Sarah, Christina, Walter and Anne. On the evening of the census in April 1911, the family was recorded living at 3, Jolly's Lane, Stillorgan, and Christopher, aged 16, was working as a messenger boy. He was also a member of the local, Young Ireland Fife and Drum Band.

ARCHBOLD, Michael MM
Corporal, Service No 27247, 9th Battalion, Royal Dublin Fusiliers, 48th Brigade in the 16th (Irish) Division, Secondary Regiment, Service No 10973, Army Cyclist Corps.

He was killed, aged 23, on 16 August 1917, while engaged in a battle at the Bremen and Frezenberg Redoubts.

At 8pm on the 15 August, the battalion left Vlamertinghe area No 3 and marched to position on the Black Line. All companies reported in position by 11.30pm and Battalion Headquarters was established. During the whole night the enemy maintained intermittent bombardment of the Black Line; this was intensified and became a barrage at zero hour, which made it extremely difficult to cross the Black Line. The next day, 16 August, the battalion was in touch with 7th Royal Irish Rifles on its right and the 8th Royal Inniskillings at Low Farm, on its left and 2nd Royal Dublins, who were in support at the Frezenberg Redoubt. The 9th Dublins moved forward and the first wave of 'A' 'B' and 'C' Companies crossed the Black Line followed by their second waves with 'D' Company in support. At 7.30am a message was received from 2nd Lt Hickey of 'B' Company, saying that the battalion was held up and most of the assaulting waves killed or wounded. Flares, as arranged, were lit at zero plus 35 minutes, so the Strong Point referred to in 2nd Lt Hickey's message was assumed to be Bremen Redoubt, as at 5.40am the battalion should have been approaching this Strong Point at 6.30am. At 7.25am a pigeon message was sent to [redacted] repeating Lt Hickey's message. Following a situation report from CO 7th Royal

Irish Rifles that the battalion was held up, presumably, near Bremen Redoubt. At this point, 2nd Lt Martin and two other ranks, together with the runner who brought the message from 2nd Lt Hickey were sent out to ascertain the situation. The runners became casualties soon after leaving headquarters, but 2nd Lt Martin managed to get in touch with the battalion, however, on returning to headquarters, about two hours later, just twenty yards from HQ, he was shot through the head by a sniper, and died instantly. Any information this officer had must have been verbal because there were no written messages found on his body.

The action continued in this vein with the above-mentioned companies involved all night and the next day when there was an attempt to attack Borry Farm.[137]

Corporal Archbold is commemorated on the Tyne Cot Memorial. He won the Military Medal for gallantry in the field during the Battle of Ginchy on 9 September 1916 and was also awarded the 1915 Star, British War and Victory medals.[138] The Battle of Ginchy took place on 9 September 1916 when the 16th (Irish) Division captured the German-held village of Ginchy, and Lieutenant Tom Kettle was also killed. The War Office failed to make contact with the soldier's next-of-kin and this resulted in an application being made by the Dublin Medal Office on the 15 January 1922 to dispose of his medals.[139]

Michael Archbold enlisted on 7 September 1914 and was attached to the Army Cyclist Corps, but later transferred to the 9th Dublins. The battalion was formed in September 1914 as part of K2 and it moved to Blackdown Barracks in England in September 1915 before landing at Le Havre in December of the same year.[140]

He was born in Co Wicklow in 1894 and moved with his family to live in Blackrock, before 1911. He was the son of Mary Archbold, a widow, of 60, Brookfield Buildings, Blackrock. There were four children in the family: Mary, Michael, John and Edward. Prior to enlisting in the army, Michael was employed as a messenger in a local dairy shop.

BYRNE, Malachy

Private, Service No 7691, 1st Battalion, Irish Guards, 1st Guards Brigade in the Guards Division.

He died, aged 39, on 11 April 1918, from wounds received in action. It is not possible to determine precisely when Pte Byrne was wounded; it might have been some days earlier at his Bory St Martin camp, which was described as 'a scientifically constructed death-trap' or it may have taken place on 9 April when the enemy opened his second great thrust at the Lys Valley.[141]

Assuming that he received his wounds on the 9 April 1918, 'Kipling's Regimental History says that it was on the morning of the 9 April that the enemy opened his second great thrust on the Lys, and the three weeks fighting that all but wiped out the Ypres Salient won him Messines, Kemmel, Armentières, Neuve Eglise, Bailleul, Merville, and carried him towards the Channel Ports, within five miles of Hazebrouck.'[142]

His grave is at XXXIII. 6A. Etaples Military Cemetery, Pas de Calais, France, and he was awarded the 1915 Star, British War and Victory medals. He enlisted in Dublin, 9 April 1915. Malachy Byrne was born in Stillorgan in 1885 and married Alice Ryan, from Avoca, Co Wicklow in 1907. The couple lived at 28 Emmet Square, Williamstown, Blackrock, with their six children: Margaret, Mary, Edward John, Eileen, Malachy and Elizabeth Mary. He was the son of James Byrne (deceased) and Margaret Byrne (dairy keeper) of, Stillorgan, and he had two brothers, John and James. Malachy Byrne's occupation was described as groundsman prior to enlisting.

BYRNE, William

Private, Service No 3844, 6th Battalion Royal Irish Regiment, 47th Brigade, in the 16th (Irish) Division.

He was wounded at the Somme in the Battle of Guillemont and taken to the 5th Casualty Clearing Station before being removed to No 4 Stationery Hospital, St Omer, where he died on 7 September 1916. A letter notifying his parents of his death read as follows: 'It is my painful duty to inform you that a report this day has been received from the War Office notifying the death of Private William Byrne.'[143] It is not known when he was wounded, although information in his battalion's war diary suggests that it was very likely to have been during the attack on Guillemont on 3 September 1916. 'At 12.25pm the battalion advanced to the attack on Guillemont and Sunken Road, which latter was their final objective. The battalion went over the parapet with their pipes playing and the men went forward in excellent order. The final objective was in the battalion's hands at about 3pm and the line was consolidated and held in spite of counter attacks. Following heavy fighting 14 officers and 311 other ranks were casualties at the end of the day'.[144]

His grave is at 53, Plot 2. Row C. Corbie Communal Cemetery Extension, 15kms east of Amiens, France. The majority of graves in the extension are of officers and men who died of wounds in the 1916 Battle of the Somme. He was awarded the1915 Star, British War and Victory medals.

Following his death his parents received a letter from the War Office, which stated: 'No place to hold effects.' The personal effects, to which the letter referred included, clasp knife, purse, badge, religious medal, a photo, letters, pen in case, rosary beads and prayer book. William enlisted in Kingstown on 18 August 1915 and was posted to Cork for his initial training. He declared his age to be 19 years when enlisting, however, his stated age at death was 17 years! He was in hospital in Aldershot on 5 October 1915 with a problem described as 'vaccination wound'.[145] The battalion was formed at Clonmel on 6 September 1914 as part of the K2 Army and it embarked for France on 17 December 1915.

He was the son of James Byrne (general labourer) and Ellen Byrne, who lived in a private two-roomed house at 13, Georges Place, Blackrock. There were seven children in the family: James, William, Crisdina, Patrick, John, Lucy and Jane. William worked as a labourer and his brother, John, was a boot maker's apprentice at age 16.

DOYLE, Thomas Patrick

Private, Service No 43065, 8th Battalion Royal Irish Fusiliers, 49th Brigade in the 16th (Irish) Division. Secondary Regiment, Service No 7038, 3rd Battalion, Connaught Rangers.

Private Doyle was killed in action, aged 31, near Estaples on 6 September 1916. The action on his last day in service at Bouleaux Wood near the Ginchy/Combles road was described as follows: 'The 8th Irish Fusiliers, also with 5th Division, came into the line. Advancing along the Ginchy–Combles road, they entered Bouleaux Wood. But both their flanks were open, and throughout the 6 September they were heavily bombarded. Both Irish Fusilier Battalions reverted to command of the 49th Brigade that night. The 49th Brigade had suffered heavy losses under command of the 5th Division and received little credit for their share in advancing the British line on the right of Guillemont after the place had fallen.'[146]

His grave is at XXVI. E. 11/16, Serre Road Cemetery No 2, South of Arras, France, and he was awarded the British War and Victory medals, which were sent to his wife in December 1924. He enlisted in the Connaught Rangers on 3 March 1916 at Kingstown, and was transferred to 8th Royal Irish Fusiliers on 31 August 1916 when based at his depot in Kinsale, Co Cork. Understandably, his wife was not aware of his transfer to another regiment, just two weeks before he fell. Confused, she wrote to the Infantry Records Office in Dublin, following a letter informing her that he was attached to the Royal Irish Fusiliers, her letter read as follows:

> I received your form announcing my husband's death, but I cannot understand why it comes marked 'Royal Irish Fusiliers', he was not in that regiment. This is my third letter and I cannot claim a pension on that form. My husband was L/Cpl Thomas P. Doyle, No 7038, 3rd Connaught Rangers, attached to the 16th Infantry, when I last heard. Will you see to the matter for me and write back soon, as I am in suspense and have five babies to rear.[147]

His service record reveals that his wife was granted a pension. It is also noted that she understood her husband held the rank of Lance Corporal. His transfer to the Royal Irish Fusiliers on 31 August 1916, just two weeks before he died, may have had something to do with his lost stripe. An item in his record also points to him being admonished for overstaying his furlough, by a period of one day, on 11 April 1916, at a time when his wife was heavily pregnant with their fifth child.[148]

He married Margaret Byrne from Booterstown on the 21 October 1905, and they had five children: John, Tobias, Sylvester, Patrick and Ellen Mary who was born on 27 May 1916. Thomas lived with his family at 1, Gaskin's Cottages, Kilmacud Road, Stillorgan, until he moved to England, where they resided at 22, Bennett's Yard, West Town, Dewsbury. The War Office issued his scroll and medals to his wife on 19 October 1921, who had remarried and was known as Mrs Margaret Ingram, still living at her former address in Dewsbury.[149]

Thomas was the son of John Doyle (deceased) and Catherine Doyle of 13, Kilmacud Road, Stillorgan, and his siblings were Sylvester, Ellen, John, Margaret,

Patrick and June (half-sister). His record states that he was employed as a tramway cleaner prior to enlisting.

BOOTERSTOWN BROTHERS DIE IN FRANCE

'In France'
The silence of maternal hills
Is round me in my evening dreams;
And round me music-making rills
And mingling waves of pastoral streams.
Whatever way I turn I find
The path is old unto me still.
The hills of home are in my mind,
And there I wander as I will.[150]

–Francis Ledwidge

Peter Dwyer and Mary Dwyer (née Bly) of 23, Booterstown Avenue, passed away suddenly in circa 1900. They had four children: Maria, Hubert Patrick, Peter and James Joseph. The three boys lived for a time with friends in Barnacullia, following their parents passing.

DWYER, Hubert Patrick

Lance Corporal, Service No 10687, 7th Battalion, Duke of Cornwall's Light Infantry, 61st Brigade in 20th (Light) Division. Formerly 6th Battalion, 43rd Brigade in the 14th (Light) Division.

Lance Corporal Dwyer was with a raiding party that had been sent to rest at Chataeu-de-la-Haie when he was killed by a German bomb on 25 July 1918, aged 39. There was an enemy bomb dropped on Details Camp (Chataeu-de-la-Haie) causing 28 casualties, but it is not known if this was the bomb that killed him.[151] His body rests close to Zouave Valley at the western foot of Vimy Ridge where his brother, James, was killed in action the previous year. His grave is at XI. C. 1. Villers Station Cemetery, Villers-au-Bois, France, and he is commemorated on the Great War Memorial, Kilgobbin. He was awarded the 1915 Star, British War and Victory medals, which were claimed by his wife.

Lance Corporal Hugh Dwyer was posted to France on 22 May 1915 with the 6th Battalion, which was formed at Bodmin in August 1914 as part of K1 army. The battalion moved to Aldershot, but by November 1914 it was at temporary camp set up on Witley Common in Surrey. In February 1915 it moved back to Aldershot before landing at Boulogne.[152]Hugh (as he was known to his family) was twice wounded on 30 July 1915 and again on 16 September 1916 when attached to the 6th Battalion. He was born in Booterstown, on 7 December 1879 and emigrated to England following a short stay in Barnacullia. He married Beatrice Annie Quantrill at Marylebone, London in 1902, and the 1911 British census recorded Hugh and Beatrice at home at 9, Carlton Mews, Kilburn, with their four children, all born in Marylebone. Their names were Beatrice Elizabeth, Hubert James, Doris Louisa and Richard Peter. Following Hugh's death, Beatrice married, as her second husband, William Woods, at Bury St Edmonds in 1920 and they lived at Frizzles Green, Great Saxham, Bury St Edmunds, England.

DWYER, James Joseph
Private, Service No 808998, 50th Battalion, Canadian Infantry, (Alberta Regiment) in the 4th Canadian Division.

He was killed on 8 May 1917, aged 23, during action at Zouave Valley, which lies at the western foot of Vimy Ridge. While the War Diary for the 8 May1917, at Lievin and Zouave Valley, was rather faded, it was possible to glean some information about his last day in action. It stated that the 'wind was west-north-west, unsettled with rain and the ground sticky'. At 4am there was a barrage on the left of enemy's front and the Canadians retaliated. The enemy was quiet until 9.30am when it commenced on the Canadian front line with 'heavies' and trench mortars and retaliation was necessary. Then ensued artillery fire with occasional bursts of heavy fire and a good deal of enfilade machine-gun and rifle fire. The enemy's trench mortars were busy. Then the Germans bombarded the Canadian front line with trench mortars from 11am for about three hours. The casualties were 4 other ranks killed, which included Pte James Dwyer.[153]

He has no known grave, but is commemorated on the Vimy Memorial, Vimy, Pas de Calais, France; Great War Memorial, Kilgobbin, and the *First World War Book of Remembrance* in Canada. Private Dwyer was awarded the British War and Victory medals claimed by his wife and remain in the family today.

James Dwyer enlisted on 15 March 1916 and sailed to England from Halifax, Nova Scotia, on 22 August 1916, aboard the SS *Olympic*, arriving in Liverpool eight days later. He was transferred to the 21st Reserve Battalion, based at Seaford in Sussex, on 10 January 1917, and moved on again to join the 50th Battalion at Bramshott, Hampshire on 8 March 1917. On the 16 March 1917 he was posted to France and joined his unit at the front on 28 April 1917.[154]

He was born in Booterstown, on 4 February 1893 and in 1901 was recorded living with his brother, Peter at the home of Patrick Kelly in Barnacullia. In 1911, aged 18, he was living with the Rothery family in Barnacullia. He met Sophia Corbett of Kingston Cottage, Harold's Grange, Sandyford, and the couple planned to marry and begin a new life in Canada. James emigrated to Canada in 1914 to prepare for their new life together. He lived at 129-139 NW, Calgary and worked as a postman. However, the war interrupted their plans and on 15 March 1916 he enlisted in the Canadian Army for the duration of the war. When he arrived in England the army granted him leave to marry Sophie. The wedding ceremony took place at the Church of Assumption Sandyford, on 25 October 1916 and their sponsors were Michael Rothery and Sarah Kelly. The couple spent some time on honeymoon in England where Sophie remained living at 2, Lake Cottage, Whitley Park, Milford in Surrey.[155] When James was killed Sophie stayed in England for some time, before returning to Barnacullia in 1920. She did not remarry. Family history says that on her way home to Kingstown Harbour, on the mail boat, she encountered offensive and rowdy behaviour from a contingent of Black and Tans. Sophie confronted the 'Tans' and told them that her husband had fought and died fighting the Germans and that they should be more respectful to Irish passengers, who may also have relatives in the British Army.[156]

In James's last Will and Testament made on 3 March 1917, while attached to the 21st Reserve Battalion, and witnessed by Pte F.W. James and Pte Harry Hollas, he bequeathed his estate to Sophie.[157] The only consolation arising out of his brief loving relationship with Sophie was the birth of their daughter, Annie. Their grandchildren,

Drew (deceased), Sophia and Jim have kept alive the memory of James and Hugh Dwyer.

KEARNEY, John

Private, Service No 9384, 2nd Battalion, 4th Company, Irish Guards, 2nd Guards Brigade in the Guards Division.

He died, aged 23, on 1 August 1917 from wounds received in action. Although the date on which he was wounded is a matter of speculation, it is likely to have been in the area of the Yser Canal on 28 to 31 July. The division had its battle-patrols out and across the Canal on the night on the of 28 July, pressing forward gingerly, digging themselves in or improving existing 'slits' in the ground against shell-fire. On the 29th, all went well in the summer afternoon till a hostile aeroplane saw them filing across, and signalled a barrage which killed or wounded forty men. The next day, 30 July, the French on their left and the whole of the Fifth Army put down a half-hour barrage to find out where the enemy would pitch his reply. He retaliated on the outskirts of Boesinghe village and the east bank of the Canal, not realising to what extent we were across that obstacle. In the evening dusk the remaining two companies of the battalion slipped over and took up battle positions, in artillery ('pigtail') formation of half-platoons, behind No 1 and 2 Companies, who had shifted from their previous night's cover, and now lay out in two waves east of Yper Lea. By ten o'clock the whole of the Guards Division was in place. The 2nd and 3rd Guards Brigades were to launch the attack, and the 1st going through them, was to carry it home. A concrete dug-out in the abandoned German just north of the railway was used as a Battalion Headquarters. It was fairly impervious to anything to smaller than a 5ft 9ins, but naturally its one door faced toward the enemy and had no blind in front of it – a lack which was to cost us dearly. On 31 July 1917, the day opened, at 3.30am with a barrage of full diapason along the army front, followed on the Guards sector by three minutes of "a carefully prepared hate", during two special companies projected oil-drums throwing flame a hundred yards around, with thermit that burned everything it touched. His barrage in reply fell for nearly an hour on the east bank of the Canal. They had lost in the past three days, three officers and casualties in other ranks came to 280, in large part due to machine-gun fire.[158]

His grave is at II. J. 13. Dozinghem Military Cemetery, located to the north-west of Poperinge near Krombeke in Belgium and he was awarded the British War and Victory medals. John was born in Stillorgan in 1894, the son of Philip Kearney (gardener) and Esther Kearney (née Carty), of Ruby Lodge, Blackrock. Philip married Bridget Byrne on 12 October 1883 at the Roman Catholic Church, Little Bray, Co Wicklow, and they had six children: James, Philip, Daniel, Mary Bridget, Elizabeth and Mary Elizabeth. When Bridget died in 1891, aged 37, Philip married, his second wife, Esther Carty, with whom he had five children: John, Sarah, Mary, Esther and Patrick Leo. In 1884 Philip was the gardener at Glendruid, Cabinteely, owned by the Barrington family. He was also employed as gardener by Beaufield House, Stillorgan, before taking over as gardener at Ruby Lodge. Philip and his wives, Bridget and Esther, together with some of their children, were buried in Dean's Grange Cemetery.[159]

John's half-brother, Private Philip Kearney, 2nd Battalion Royal Irish Fusiliers, was born in Stillorgan in 1885 and served in Quetta, Balochistan (now Pakistan) before 1911. He married Kathleen Bourke and they had two children, Teresa and Patrick Philip. He appears to have interrupted his service, which may have been due to wounds or sickness, but enlisted again at the outbreak of the Great War, serving the full period from 1914–1918. When the Great War finished Philip was involved in the War of Independence and later in the Civil War, on the anti-treaty side. He worked as a railway porter and served in Heuston Station until his death in 1947. Philip and his wife, Kathleen were staunchly republican and they had a big influence on their son Patrick Philip, who was involved in raids on Army Barracks in Northern Ireland during the 1950s. However, having served a prison sentence Patrick Philip decided to quit the IRA and renounced all violence.[160]

McNALLY, Myles
Private, Service No 26442, 8th Battalion, 'D' Company, Royal Dublin Fusiliers, 48th Brigade in the 16th (Irish) Division.

He was killed in action, aged 32, on 8 August 1917 during the third Battle of Ypres, which commenced on 31 July 1917. 'At 3.30am on 8 August 1917 at Ypres, the battalion was relieved by the 7th Dublins, but the counter attack during relief caused casualties (including those of the 7th Dublins). At 8am the battalion passed Ecole on way out to Vlamertinghe No 3 Camp.'[161] Private McNally may have been among the casualties involved in the relief operation. He was in action in the Frezenberg sector of Flanders the week before Dalkey chaplain, Father Willie Doyle, was killed. The tactics employed at Passchendaele, in the Third Battle of Ypres are as controversial as those executed at the Battle of the Somme and the Gallipoli campaign.

His grave is at VI. A. 11. Brandhoek New Military Cemetery, Ieper, West-Vlaanderen, Belgium and he was awarded the British War and Victory medals. The battalion was formed in September 1914 as part of K2 army, and moved to Blackdown Barracks in England in September 1915. It landed at Le Havre in December 1915.

Myles was born on 16 September 1884, the son of the late James and Honoria McNally (née Kearney) of 23, Brookfield Terrace, Blackrock. There were five children in the family: William, James, Myles, Maria and Margarita. He married Catherine Mahon in 1913 and they had two children, Honor and Annie. Following his death, Catherine married again and had another child, Mary (Maisie). His grandchildren, Patrick and Catherine Kelly live in south Dublin, and have a very clear recollection of their mother Honor, talking about her father. They said that the family could never understand why he joined the British Army in 1916 at a time when he was enjoying a good position with the Department of Education at Marlborough Street, Dublin. A postcard from his children was found in Myles McNally's effects. The card, which was missing the postage stamp, read: 'Dear Daddy: Just a line hoping to find you are keeping alright as Annie and myself are longing to see you. I hope you will soon be home to take us to Oney Park as the weather here is splendid. God Bless. Love to dearest father from his little children, Honor and Annie.'[162]

MAHON, John

Private, Service No 10707, 1st Battalion Irish Guards, 1st Guards Brigade, in the Guards Division.

He was killed in action, aged 30, at Bermerain & La Croisette on 4 November 1918.

On 4 November, one week before the end of the war, 26 British Divisions moved forward on a 30 mile front from Oisy to north of Valenciennes, the whole strength of their artillery behind them. The battalion had marched from St Hilaire, in the usual small fine rain, on 2 November to billets in Bermerain and bivouacs nearby. It meant a ten mile tramp of the pre-duckboard era, in the midst of mired horse and lorry-transport, over country where the enemy had smashed every bridge and culvert, blocked all roads and pulling-out places with mine craters, and sown houses, old trenches and dug-outs with fanciful death-traps. The battalion went through the 2nd Grenadiers and continued into the dusk that was closing blind, hedge screened-country. The boggy-banked Aunelle had to be crossed on stretchers, through thick undergrowth, in a steep valley. Everything after that seemed to be orchards, high hedges, and sunk and raised roads, varied with soft bits of cultivation, or hopelessly muddled-up cul-de-sacs of farm tracks. Companies played blind-man's buff among the obstacles, in the pitch dark, as they hunted alternately for each other and the troops on their flanks. There was very heavy shelling on the three most advanced companies as well as on the Brigade Headquarters throughout the night. Casualties, all told, came to about twenty. The next morning amid much rejoicing by the inhabitants when, on coming out of their cellars they saw Allied troops again.[163]

It seems certain that Pte Mahon was one of the unlucky soldiers to have been killed in the fighting on the previous night, and it was especially poignant, given that the armistice was just days away. His grave is at I. 7. Villers-Pol Communal Cemetery Extension, Nord, France, and he was awarded the British War and Victory medals. He enlisted at Kingstown on 28 December 1915.

John was born on 2 March 1885 and was a member of the Young Ireland Fife and Drum Band prior to enlisting in the army. He was the son of James Mahon and Mary Mahon (née Noctor) of 2, Mason Cottages, Newtownpark in Blackrock. His father and mother, who were born in Co Wicklow, passed away in 1915 and 1919 respectively. There were seven children in the family: Mary (Polly), John, Patrick, James, Michael, Susanna and Thomas. Two other children, Elizabeth and William, died in infancy.

John's brother, Private Michael Mahon, also fought in the Great War and survived the conflict. He was home in Newtownpark for his mother's funeral in 1919.[164] The *Evening Herald* carried a photograph of Michael Mahon, stating that he was wounded in an engagement in France on 21 October 1914 and was in hospital in England.[165] When the war ended, Michael returned to England and the family lost touch with him. He was also a member of the Young Ireland Fife and Drum Band prior to enlisting in the army.

MANNING, William Joseph

Private, Service No 18865, 7th Battalion, 'D' Company, (the 'Pals'), Royal Dublin Fusiliers, 30th Brigade in the 10th (Irish) Division Secondary Regiment, Service No 13701, 4th Hussars.

The Balkan winter took its toll on the men with frostbite exposure just as did malaria, disease-bearing insects and dirty drinking water in the hot summer. Private Manning joined the 7th Dublins in August 1915 and served in Gallipoli before moving to Salonika, where he was invalided from Serbia suffering from frostbite, and was home in Dublin in time for the 1916 Easter Rising. He returned to the front line following recuperation and was killed, aged 24, on 3 October 1916.

On 3 October 1916 the 7th Royal Dublin Fusiliers were in the front line at the Greek village of Jenikoj (Yenikoi) to the north and the Struma River to the south a distance of about a mile and a half. The strength of the 7th Dublins was twenty eight officers and 741 other ranks. The 6th Dublins and 7th Munsters were in the firing line and the 7th Dublins with the 6th Munsters in support. Their objective was the village of Jenikoj. Crossing at the Jungle Island Bridge, the Dublins crossed the River Struma at 2.30am and working with the Munsters they took up their position 1,000 yards south west of Bala.

All hell was suddenly let loose at 5am and British big guns sent shell after shell into Jenikoj village. In the dim light of early dawn one could just discern the smoke rising from the houses set alight by our artillery fire. At 5.30am the village was easily seen, and troops moved up behind the artillery barrage. Two companies of Royal Irish Rifles were in the right of the first wave and two companies of the Royal Dublin Fusiliers on the left. Behind the leading waves came the Royal Dublin Fusiliers and a second Battalion of the Royal Munster Fusiliers, the former with orders to clear the village after the first wave had gone through, the latter to remain in support during the initial stages of the attack.

At dawn the battalions moved forward in waves and were allowed to reach the outskirts of the village without opposition. And then someone yelled, 'The Bulgars are running'. The Irish charged through the village with fixed bayonets and through to the other end. Jenikoj had fallen. The majority of the Bulgars and others emerged with hands held high waving white flags. The village was taken with only a few casualties. By 6.30am the 7th Dublins cleared the village and took up a position north of the village (along the Serres Road). The Bulgarian trenches at this point were about 450 yards away.[166]

During the day the enemy launched three heavy counter-attacks. The first two were stopped by artillery fire, which caused severe loss to them. At 12pm some of the 7th Dublins were killed by their own artillery. The Bulgar batteries opened up at 2pm, as they launched a new counter attack with fresh troops. The Dublins had more than their share, owing to the fact that the nature of the ground left them more exposed to shell fire. Meanwhile, the enemy infantry pushed forward for the attack with a reckless disregard for the heavy casualties they were incurring, both from the terrific barrage put up by the Allied artillery and the machine gun and rifle fire. At 3am on 4 October after nearly twenty-four hours continuous fighting, an exhausted 6th and 7th Dublins counter attacked the village and at 5.30am they re-occupied Jenikoj (Yenikoi) without opposition. A total of 385 men were killed, wounded or missing, of which 131 were 6th Dublins and 128 were 7th Dublins.[167]

His grave is at III. D. 14, Struma Military Cemetery, Greece. The Struma River flows through Bulgaria southward to the Greek frontier, then south-east into the Aegean Sea. From the Allied base at Salonika, a road ran north-east across the river to Serres, and it was this road that the right wing of the Allied army used for the movements of troops and supplies to the Struma front during the Salonika Campaign.[168] Private Manning was awarded the 1915 Star, British War and Victory medals.

He was born in Stillorgan, the son of James Manning (wine merchant) and Mary Manning of 4, Pembroke Road, Dublin. His father passed away in the period between 1901 and 1911. The family also lived for a time in Kingstown. There were six children in the family: Henry, Clare, William Joseph, Girlie, Emily and Angela. William was educated at Blackrock College (1901–1910), the National University of Ireland and worked with the Civil Service prior to enlisting.

PENDER, Joseph
Private, Service No 8477, 9th Battalion, Royal Dublin Fusiliers, 48th Brigade, in the 16th (Irish) Division.

Joseph Pender was another Dublin Fusilier to die from gas poisoning at Hulluch, France, on 27 April 1916. He was aged 18. His death took place at the time of the 1916

Easter Rising in his native Dublin. It was reported in 1996 that a Dublin Corporation housing maintenance team was working on a house in Brookfield, Blackrock, when it uncovered a British Army death certificate and a paper cutting in its attic, revealing that Pte Joseph Pender died on 27 April 1916 the day of the gas attack on Hulluch.[169] Father Willie Doyle from Dalkey, the Battalion's Chaplain, described this human tragedy:

> On paper every man with a helmet was as safe as I was from gas poisoning. But now it is evident many men despise the 'old German gas', some did not bother putting on their helmets, others had torn theirs, and others like myself had thrown them aside or lost them. From early morning till late at night I worked my way from trench to trench single handed the first day, with three regiments to look after and I could get no help. Many men died before I could reach them; others seemed just to live till I anointed them, and were gone before I could pass back. There they lay, scores of them (we lost 800, nearly all from gas) in the bottom of the trench, in every conceivable posture of human agony; the clothes torn off their bodies in a vain effort to breathe while from end to end of that valley of death came one long unceasing moan from the lips of brave men fighting and struggling for life.[170]

Private Pender is commemorated on the Loos Memorial, Pas de Calais, France, and he was awarded the British War and Victory medals. He enlisted in 1914 at age 16. The 9th Dublin Battalion was formed in September 1914 as part of K2 army. It moved to Blackdown Barracks in England during September 1915, and landed at Le Havre in December 1915.

Joseph was the son of Joseph Pender and Mary Ann Pender of 3, Murphy's Court, Blackrock. He was age 13 years on the evening of the 1911 census when he was recorded living with his father and step-mother, Jane Pender at 26, Brookfield Buildings, Blackrock. Following the death of Mary Ann, Joseph married Jane in1908. There were five children born in Joseph's first marriage to Mary Ann Pender; Annie, Essie, Mary Anne, Joseph and Mary Ellen.

STILLORGAN BROTHERS DIE, 1914–1918

ROCHE, Edmund Knight

Private, Service No 15411, 2nd Battalion, 'C' Company, Leinster Regiment (Royal Canadians), 88th Brigade in the 29th Division. Secondary Regiment, Service No 27700, Machine Gun Corps.

He was killed, aged 22, at Cheluvelt Wood, near Ypres, during the fourth Battle of Ypres, on 28 September 1918. On the day he died 'the 2nd Leinsters left assembly position at 12.45pm marched down the Menin Road; pipers playing and flags flying. Hence the battalion advanced on diamond formation to Cheluvelt where it concentrated. Casualties for the four days from 28 September to 2 October were 19 killed, 129 wounded and 10 missing.'[171]

His grave is at XIX. J. 13. Hooge Crater Cemetery, Ieper, (Ypres), Belgium and he is commemorated on the Great War Memorial, Clongowes Wood College, Co Kildare; Great War Memorial at Stoneyhurst College, and his family's headstone in Dean's Grange Cemetery. Private Roche was awarded the British War and Victory medals.

The Leinsters landed at St Nazaire, France, on 12 September 1914 and his Stonyhurst College record states that he was wounded on two occasions before being killed. He enlisted at Camberley, Surrey.

Edmund K. Roche, born in Stillorgan on 13 August 1895, was the son of the late Thomas Knight Roche and Mary Knight Roche of Halcyon, 29, Anglesey Road, Dublin. There were seven children in the family: Leo, Elizabeth, James, Eileen, Josephine, Gwendolyn and Edmund. Edmund and his siblings, Leo, Josephine and Eileen were born at their parent's original home, Avonmore House, Stillorgan. He was educated at Stonyhurst College (1908–1911) and Clongowes Wood College (1912–1914). His school record at Stonyhurst, St Mary's Hall (Old Stonyhurst-Hodder), the preparatory school to Stonyhurst College, states that he entered the school at age nine and was age thirteen when he arrived at the senior school. It also records that he began his education at Wicklow Convent School.[172]

His brother, Leo Knight Roche, is commemorated on his parents' headstone in Dean's Grange Cemetery, where it states that he was killed in Belgium on 28

December 1916, indicating that he may have served in the war also. No military record was available to indicate that he was a soldier. However, it is possible that Leo was a civilian serving in a hospital or ambulance unit.

Chapter Eight

Dalkey and Kingstown

HISTORY AND ROLL OF HONOUR

Dalkey Urban District had a population of 3536 in 1911. It was a parish and township in the Rathdown Barony and was at that time, as it is now, a picturesque situation on the south shore of Dublin Bay. It was protected by seven castles, one of which dates back to 1498 and was restored for the Town Hall in the early twentieth century.[1]

Kingstown was a seaport town, and the Royal Mail Packet Station of the metropolis to the parish of Monkstown, Dunleary, Kingstown and Rathdown barony. The town derived its name from King George IV who embarked here on 3 September 1821 when the harbour was also called the Royal Harbour of George IV, as was inscribed on a granite obelisk, surmounted by a crown, near the wharf, erected by the Harbour Commissioners to commemorate the occasion.[2] Queen Victoria visited Kingstown in 1849 and 1861.

The City of Dublin Company's Royal Mail steam packets, *Ulster, Munster, Leinster* and *Connaught*, started for Holyhead twice a day at 8.15am and 8.15pm. The Steamer of the London and North-Western Railway Company also started for Holyhead.[3] It was from here that the ill-fated *Leinster* sailed, with 771 passengers, on the evening of 10 October 1918, before being torpedoed by a German submarine resulting in 501 passengers losing their lives. The Royal Harbour, from which the town may be said to date its origin, was commenced in 1816. The population of the area, incorporating Glasthule, Glenageary, part of Monkstown and Sandycove, was 1694 in 1911.[4]

Kingstown was one of the wealthiest districts in Dublin and unemployment was slightly less of a problem for working-class people, when compared to the villages, towns and townlands situated inland. Among the well-known merchant families living in this district were the Dockrells, Findlaters and Martins.

BLACKROCK COLLEGE BROTHERS KILLED IN WAR

John Philip Butler JP and Mary Teresa Butler of Clonard, Killiney, had seven children: Constance, Richard, Marie Carmele, Mildred, Edmund William, Leonard William and Desmond. Two sons, Edmund and Leonard were killed in 1917 and 1918 respectively. John Philip Butler was a retired Wholesale Tea and Wine Merchant, who received his education at Blackrock College from 1866. He was elected President of its Past Pupils Union for 1913–1914.

BUTLER, Edmund William MC

Major, 5th & 10th Battalions, 2nd Life Guards attached Worcestershire Regiment, Secondary Regiment, 8th Battalion, Gloucestershire Regiment.

Major Butler died, aged 27, on 18 April 1918 at No 20 General Hospital, Camiers, France, from wounds received in an attack at Etaples in early April 1918.

> The Life Guards were in the frontline trenches from 2 April to the 10 April 1918 when nothing much was happening; perhaps it was the calm before the storm! At 3.30am on 10 April 1918 the battalion was bombarded for five hours before the enemy attacked and outflanked them. The battalion withdrew to a line near Stinking Farm and were eventually relieved on 12 April 1918.[5]

This may have been the action in which Major Butler was wounded. His original documents revealed that his mother wrote to the War Office on 9 April 1918 enquiring about his health, when reported that he was wounded. Six days later his father received a communication from the War Office informing him that he was permitted to visit his son at the hospital in Camier. The next day, he received details of his permit to visit his son and there is a reference to, 'embarking at Folkestone'.[6]

His grave is XVIII. J. 7. Étaples Military Cemetery, near Boulogne, France, and he is commemorated on the War Memorial, St Mary's Roman Catholic Church,

Haddington Road, Dublin; Glasnevin Cemetery, Dublin and the Blackrock College Union website. Major Butler was awarded the Military Cross and his citation read: 'For conspicuous gallantry and devotion to duty during an enemy attack. He commanded his battalion for four days with great ability, and was largely instrumental in holding up enemy attacks. He displayed fine courage, and set a splendid example to all ranks.'[7] He was 'Mentioned in Despatches', awarded by, Field-Marshall D. Haig on 7th November, 1917.[8] Major Butler was also awarded the 1914–15 Star, British War and Victory medals, which were issued to his father on 1 January 1920. He qualified for the 1914–15 Star medal by just five days.

Edmund Butler was born on 24 December 1891 and unmarried. He attended Blackrock College and joined the army on 7 November 1914 when his family was living at a temporary address; Russell Hotel, St Stephens Green, Dublin. He appears to have been commissioned into a reserve regiment of cavalry as a temporary (wartime only) second lieutenant and posted to the Reserve Regiment of the 2nd Life Guards of the Household Cavalry on 17th August 1915.[9]

The 2nd Life Guards Reserve Regiment had been raised at Windsor in August 1914 as a home-based reserve to feed the regiments abroad. He received the temporary rank of lieutenant while at Windsor and relinquished that rank on the day he was sent abroad. Officers 'relinquished' a rank when they were posted and where their posting did not require, or did not have the vacancy in seniority for, someone of a higher rank. They didn't relish losing their higher status as it could mean a loss of pay and allowances. So when he joined the 2nd Life Guards in France, they would only have been able to employ him as a second lieutenant until his seniority meant he could go higher. His army medal index card showed that he entered France on 27th December 1915, joining the 2nd Life Guards, who were already serving in France. He may not have spent much time with the Worcestershire Regiment, because he joined the Gloucestershire Regiment in December 1917. The 5th and 6th Battalions of the Worcestershire Regiment were training and reserve battalions, which, from August 1917, were based at Harwich. As they did not serve overseas there was no requirement for them to keep war diaries.[10]

Edmund Butler was listed under 'household cavalry' which would have placed him with the 2nd Life Guards when he was wounded at the time of the attack on the Messines-Wytschaete Ridge on 9 June 1917. In this attack he received multiple shrapnel wounds to his right side back, near the lung, right leg and right thigh, and was receiving treatment in the Officers' Hospital, Park Lane, London, for a period of six weeks. His treatment and rehabilitation continued at the Queen Alexandra's Red Cross Hospital for Officers (now the Eccles Hotel), Glengarriff, Co Cork.

> In relation to his recuperation in Glengarriff, it was War Office policy to allow soldiers to recuperate in a hospital nearer their home town, to allow their families to visit. During his time in Glengarriff, he applied for a 'wound gratuity' on 24 August. In a letter to the War Office he stated that he had been advised that his injuries were serious and would affect his subsequent career. In army medical parlance a 'severe' wound was one from which a soldier was expected to recover after hospital treatment. A 'very severe' wound (such as amputation) was one from which he would not fully recover. The payment of wound gratuities was at the discretion of the War Office on the recommendation of a medical examination board. He would then have been posted to the 5th Battalion Worcestershire Regiment, which moved from Plymouth to Harwich in the autumn of 1917. This posting would have given him the opportunity to get fit again and to provide troops, who were under training with the experience of an officer who had fought at the front.

Following his recovery, in October 1917, he transferred to the Worcestershire Regiment, 5th Battalion. He was promoted to acting Major while in second command of a battalion, on 6 January 1918. The battalion became embroiled in the retreat of 21–26 March on the Somme (Operation Michael), and Major Butler signed the war diary on 31 March 1918.[11]

BUTLER, Leonard William
Second Lieutenant, 4th Battalion, attached 7/8th Battalion, Royal Irish Fusiliers.
He was killed in action, aged 20, at Fontaine-les-Croisilles in the Battle of Cambria on 20 November 1917. His mother was notified by the Army Council on 27 November,

seven days after his death. In a letter to his parents, his Colonel stated that: 'He was bravery itself and was loved by all his officers and men.'[12]

> On 20 November 1917 at Fontaine-lés-Croisilles the battalion attacked the enemy. First objective was Tunnel Trench and second objective was Tunnel Support. At zero 6.20am his battalion's artillery barrage opened on Tunnel Trench lasting four minutes and it was lifted on to Tunnel Support. The battalion assembled without coming under any hostile shelling. Tunnel Trench was taken by 'A' Company without great opposition. 'B' Company on the left was held up for about three-quarters of an hour by a machine-gun post and suffered heavy casualties.

Tunnel Trench, as its names suggests was a tunnel measuring thirty or forty feet below ground with staircase access from the upper level. It had electric light, storage space, food, and ammunition. Following sniping by the enemy, all opposition was finally defeated by organised bombing parties and the whole of Tunnel Trench taken and consolidated. The enemy counter attacked four times, at 9.30am, 1.30pm, 2.30pm and 4.30pm, but an artillery barrage was put down on each occasion and attacks dispersed by the battalion's rifle and lewis gun-fire. There was a total of 106 casualties for the 20th, which included 2nd Lt Butler and a fellow officer.[13]

His grave is at II.C. 13., Croisilles British Cemetery, Arras Region, France, and he is commemorated on the War Memorial, St Mary's Roman Catholic Church, Haddington Road, Dublin, Great War Memorial, Downside College, Bath, and the Blackrock College Union website. He was awarded the British War and Victory medals, which were claimed by his father on 23 May 1921, when he was residing at 40, Fitzwilliam Place, Dublin.

Leonard Butler finished school in July 1915 and one month later was appointed to a temporary commission in the army. On 1 January 1916 he was admitted to the Queen Alexandra Military Hospital, London, suffering with tonsillitis. In early September 1916 he was in the 14th General Hospital, Boulogne, suffering with a severe case of trench fever, and on 20 September it was decided to send him to the King George Fifth Hospital in Dublin for further treatment. Despite having problems with muscle pains, he was passed fit and returned to the frontline three months later, on 28 December 1916. An inventory of his effects was recorded in his original documents. They included identity disc/chain, cigarette case, watch/case (glass gone), 2 x cloth stars, a simple prayer for soldiers and some correspondence.[14]

He was born on 8 November 1897, educated at Blackrock College and Downside (Roberts), the English Benedictine School at Bath, until July 1915. He was also a member of Downside's OTC. The young officer's father, John Butler, was the sole grantee of his son's estate and the firm of Brady Hayden, Solicitors, Molesworth Street, Dublin, was appointed to handle the administration.[15]

GALLANT 'OLYMPIAN' DIES FROM LINGERING WOUNDS IN 1924
DOCKRELL, George Shannon OBE
Major, 9th Battalion, Rifle Brigade, 42nd Brigade in the 14th (Light) Division.

Major Dockrell suffered badly from lingering shrapnel wounds received on 31 July 1915, and he died on 23 December 1924 at the Officers' Hospital, Richmond in Surrey. His superior officer stated, 'He was a gallant soldier, and was highly popular, with his fellow officers and those under his command.'[16]

His battalion's war diary for 31 July 1915 did not record when or how Dockrell was wounded, but it stated that: 'In the month of July, 5 officers were wounded, 41 other ranks killed and 194 other ranks wounded with 2 missing.' Lord Henniker and General Markham sent their compliments to the then, Lt Dockrell, when he was in hospital during 1915:

> Lord Henniker wishes me to tell you how on all sides your gallant bearing was admired, and how proud he is to have had you in his regiment. General Markham asked particularly for you and told the Colonel, how when wounded, your first thought was for the men. You were, he said, beloved by your men, and were, first and last a gentleman and, which is even better, a typical Rifle Brigade officer.[17]

Major Dockrell is commemorated on the Great War Memorial, Trent College, Nottingham, England and he was awarded the 1914–15 Star, British War and Victory medals. He was gazetted 2nd lieutenant in the 9th Rifle Brigade on 22nd December 1914, and promoted to lieutenant on 4th March 1915. He received further promotion to the rank of captain on 15 December 1918 and was demobilised in 1920 with the rank of major. He served on the staff during the last two years of the war.

The Rifle Brigade was formed at Winchester on 21 August 1914 as part of the K1 army. It moved to Aldershot before going on to Petworth in November, returning to Aldershot in February 1915 and landing at Boulogne in May 1915. The Rifle Brigade was also engaged at Hooge (German liquid fire attack) and Bellewaarde.[18]

George Dockrell was the son of Sir Maurice Edward Dockrell and Margaret Sarah, Lady Dockrell of Camolin, Monkstown. There were six children in the family: Thomas Edward, Henry Morgan, Maurice, George Shannon, Kenneth Brooks and Anne Dorothy. The family firm, Thomas Dockrell, Sons, & Company, Merchants and Contractors, was an old-established firm, its premises covering a large portion of the area lying between South Great George's, Drury, Lower Stephen and Fade Streets. The firm was leading suppliers of window glass, and well known as cement merchants, builders and furnishing ironmongers. Sir Maurice Dockrell died in 1929, aged 79, and Sarah Lady Dockrell passed away in 1926; they were interred in Dean's Grange Cemetery.

George Dockrell was born in Co Dublin in 1886 and married Helen Rebecca Robb. They are recorded in the 1921 Electoral Registers at their home address, 43, Eton Street, Camden, London. He was, in his time, the greatest swimmer that Ireland had ever produced. Dockrell showed great promise as a junior at Trent College, where he won most of the swimming medals offered for competition. Leaving school at 18 years, he spent the next two years in America, where he came into contact with C.M. Daniels, the world sprint champion, whose style he adopted. On his return to Ireland in 1906, he entered Trinity College, where he graduated. He introduced the 'crawl' stroke and dominated Irish swimming for the next six years. In 1912 he was selected for the British Olympic team. However, his most noteworthy success was in Paris in 1909 when he defeated the Belgian champion, Meyboom, for the 100 metres European Championship. Meyboom was the holder of the English Championship at the time.[19]

George Dockrell frequented the 'Forty Foot' in Sandycove and was remembered by a friend, L.A.G. Strong, in a poem that pays tribute to him and other swimmers of the day:

The Forty-Foot; Retrospect

DOCKRELL, Tallon, Tagert them
Were the days of mighty men !
Holmes, M'Guinness, Fawcett, Chute,
An Eldorado of the brute
Strength and grace of naked man:
Sure I am that no one can
Swim and dive the like of them. 'Club handicap. A' ye ready, Jem? ' '
Get ready! Go!' splash 'Wan!'
splash splat
(Jamesey M'Conkey's gone in flat!)
'Two ! Three ! and several splashes more
And quite a little crop at 'Four!'
George Holmes leaps in at thirty-eight
'Jasus, but there's a goin' gait!'
And Dockrell starts the last of all,
Dockrell, who with his foaming crawl,
Although there's men a length ahead,
Will win, or else will finish dead.
'He's jerked.' 'Bedam, he'll do it yet.'
' Glory to God, he has them bet ! '
' Up Dockrell ! ' And the old rocks ring
With praises of this glorious thing. Well, that's ten years ago and more,
And I am far from Kelly shore
And Ring Rock: no one that I love
Is left at all in Sandycove.
House sold, meadow and orchard gone,
And garden too, to build upon.
Dockrell, Tallon, Tagert where
Are the men I worshipped there?
Some still rub the pink flesh dry,
Some have laid their towels by.
Some go by the Round Tower still,

Some are passed to Hy Brasil,
Where Fawcett, he that dived and died,
Plunges in a fairer tide.

–L.A.G. Strong[20]

His brother, Major Maurice Henry Dockrell MD, Royal Army Medical Corps, (known to his family and friends as 'Morry') served in the Great War and survived the conflict. He married an Italian lady, Vera Exposito, before the onset of war. Vera was a Sinn Fein supporter and later mistress of an SS Commander in Florence. She was daughter of the Italian-born musical composer and pianist, Michele Exposito, who lived most of his professional life in Dublin. There were no children born to the couple. Dr Dockrell ended his career as ship's doctor, 'where the drink was both cheap and plentiful', and died at sea in 1953. Family history says that Richard Gordon, the English author, novelist, screenwriter and doctor, based a character on Maurice Dockrell in *Doctor at Sea*.

Dorothy, the only daughter, was born in 1891. She was a tragic figure, having contracted polio aged nine and later had a leg amputated. But, undaunted, this heroic lady, who was in constant pain, entered Trinity College, where she took degrees in Modern Languages, Law and Medicine. She died in 1976.[21]

WALDRON, Francis Fitzgerald

Major, First Commanding Officer of the 60th Squadron, Royal Flying Corps. Secondary Regiment, the 19th (Queens Alexandra's Own Royal) Hussars.

Major Waldron's wife received a telegram on 5 July1916 stating that he was reported missing on the 4th, but that this did not necessarily mean that he was wounded or killed. A further communication, signed by a captain at the 39th General Hospital, was received stating it was officially announced that he was killed on 3 July 1916. Major Waldron, known to his friends as 'Ferdy', was shot down in his Morane N Serial No A175, near Epinoy at 8.24am on 3 July 1916 and died of his wounds a short time afterwards. A note from Berlin on 23 January 1917, found in his original documents, gave details of how Major Waldron was killed and interred on the same day. The information in the note was forwarded to Waldron's wife on 1 March 1917. The German ace, Uffz Howe, flying a two-seater from FA5b, claimed that he brought down Major Waldron, but this was not confirmed.[22]

With reference to the 'Note Verbal' of the 5th ult PO No 14702 – The Foreign Office has the honour to inform the United States Embassy that according to the statement of the Mayor of Epinoz, Major F.F. Waldron of the Royal Flying Corps, Squadron 60, was brought down by a German aviator in the district of Epinoy on 3, July 1916. Having been disabled by wounds to his head, Major Waldron fell and thereby suffered severe internal injuries and expired in half an hour from that time. The corpse in two coffins made of oak were buried with Military honours in the cemetery at Epinoy on the evening of 3 July 1916.[23]

(Note: No information could be found to explain the reference to 'two coffins'.)

On 3 July 1916 'A' Flight of 60 Squadron set out on a dawn patrol in their Morane Bullets. With them was their Squadron Leader, 'Ferdy' Waldron, who despite his clear orders, insisted on trying to accomplish at least one mission a day over the lines with his men. He was accompanied by Capt Smith-Barry, Lieutenant Armstrong, Lieutenant Simpson and an 18-year-old novice, Second Lieutenant Harold Balfour. Balfour described what happened:

Both Armstrong and Simpson fell out, through engine trouble, before we reached Arras. Waldron led the remaining two along the Arras-Cambrai Road. We crossed at about 8,000 ft and just before reaching Cambrai we were at about 9000ft, when I suddenly saw a large formation of machines about our height coming from the sun towards us. There must have been at least twelve. They were two-seaters led by one Fokker (monoplane) and followed by two others. I am sure they were not contemplating 'war' at all, but 'Ferdy' pointed us towards them and led us straight in. My next impressions were rather mixed. I seemed to be surrounded by Huns in two-seaters. I can recollect looking down and seeing a Morane about 800ft below me going down in a slow spiral with a Fokker hovering above it following every turn. The Morane I watched gliding down under control, doing perfect turns, to about 2000ft, when I lost sight of it. After an indecisive combat with a Fokker, I turned for home, the two-seaters having disappeared. I landed at Vert Gallant and reported that 'Ferdy' had gone down under control. We all thought he was prisoner, but heard soon afterwards that he had landed safely but died of his wounds that night.[24]

The 60th Squadron was formed from the No1 Reserve Aero-plane Squadron at Gosport, and Major Waldron was its first Commanding Officer. Following Waldron's death, the squadron was taken over by another Irishman, Major Robert Smith-Barry, who was said to have been a great character, eccentric and a fine pilot. He was the first pilot to break both legs in an air crash. This happened near Amiens in the retreat from Mons.

Major Waldron's grave is at V.III. A. 26. H.A.C. Cemetery, Ecoust-St Mein, France. He was twice 'Mentioned in Despatches'. The first mention was by Field Marshall Sir John French, dated 8 October 1914 and the second came in a despatch from General Sir Douglas Haig in 1916, for gallant and distinguished service in the field.[25] He was awarded the 1914 Star, British War and Victory medals.

Before taking a commission, Francis Waldron stated in a letter to the Secretary at the War Office, London, that he would like a little time to consult with his father. He concluded by stating his personal preference for a commission was in the Royal Field Artillery. In November 1906 he obtained a regular commission from the militia and joined the 19th (Queen Alexandra's Own Royal) Hussars. He was gazetted 2nd lieutenant in the 11th Hussars in May 1907; took the rank of full lieutenant on 24 June 1910 and received further promotion to captain in June 1914. On 24 July 1912 he took his Royal Aeronautical Club certificate No 260 on a Bristol Biplane with the Bristol School at Brooklands and on 27 January 1913 he was appointed a flying officer with the Royal Flying Corp.[26]

In September 1913 the Royal Flying Corps took part in large-scale manoeuvres held throughout Britain and Ireland. The No 2 Squadron was assigned to take part in the exercises in Ireland. The deployment involved 12 officers, 14 NCOs and 92 men. Portable canvas hangers, spare engines, wings and other parts were carried on five lorries, six cars and six motorbikes, which travelled by sea from Stranraer in Scotland and made their way to Rathbane House, near Limerick. Seven aircraft were designated to take part in the exercises in Ireland, but mechanical difficulties resulted in only four making the initial flight to Limerick. Lieutenant 'Ferdy' Waldron was among the pilots of No 2 Squadron to arrive at Rathbane on 1 September 1913.

The pilots of the 2nd Squadron were billeted at Cruises Hotel, Limerick. On

2 September, during a series of practice flights, Waldron flew to the Curragh, Co Kildare and back to base in a BE 2A serial No 273. While flying a BE 2A serial No 225 on 8 September, he was forced to land two miles from the camp, but was able to continue after repairs to his engine. The army manoeuvres began the following day, with a simulated conflict between the Brown Army (5th Division) and the White Army (6th Division). Waldron was assigned to the Brown Army. At the conclusion of the exercises the squadron returned to Montrose in Scotland.[27]

When the Royal Flying Corps went to war Waldron was a flight commander with No 2 Squadron, having been promoted to that position on New Year's Day 1914. He was posted to the 60 Squadron just before it left for France on 28 May 1916. The late Dr Vincent Orange, who was a noted biographer of air force figures, wrote in the Oxford University Press that in April 1916 'Capt Smith-Barry was one of three old Etonians appointed as flight commanders in 60 Squadron, formed in France under another old Etonian, Ferdy Waldron.' Ferdy Waldron did not attend Eton College, nor is he commemorated on the college's Great War Memorial.[28]

Francis Waldron was the only son of Brigadier-General Francis Waldron CB, RH, RFA, and Helen Waldron (née Fitzgerald) of The Laurels, Kilmainham, Dublin and Melitta Lodge, Co Kildare. It appears that there were four children in the family: Francis Fitzgerald, Madeleine, Freda and Janet Cicily. Brigadier-General Waldron served with the Royal Artillery in the Boer War (1900–1902). 'At the Liddell Hart Centre for Military Archives at King's College, London, there is a letter from Lieutenant General Sir Arthur Singleton Wynne, Secretary of the Selection Board, War Office, regarding the appeal of Brigadier-General Waldron against his non-selection as Major-General, on 10 August 1910.'[29] Brigadier-General Waldron was appointed magistrate for the County of Kildare on 19 February 1913 and was handicapper to the Turf Club and INHC. At some time before he died in February 1932 he indicated that 'he did not want to be interred in Glasnevin Cemetery'.[30]

Francis Waldron was born in Melitta Lodge, Co Kildare, on 16 August 1886 and educated at Monkstown Park School, Kingstown, where they catered for boarders in the age bracket 9–14 years. He married Marjorie E. Waldron (née Sutherst) in January 1914 and lived at 66, George Street, Portman Square, London, before moving to Little Mill House, Montrose, Forfar, Scotland. Two months before his death Marjorie gave birth to their daughter, Patricia Ann Ursula, who was killed in an air raid during the Second World War. 'His effects received by his widow were ninety-two marks in a purse, photo and letters.'[31]

In 1926, Marjorie Waldron married Major Gerry Murland MC, who survived service in the First and Second World Wars. Major Murland was awarded the Military Cross in 1919 and was twice 'Mentioned in Despatches'. The Murland family had its roots in Co Down and owed its wealth to the Irish linen industry and the discovery of the wet spinning process in 1825. The couple lived in Suffolk until later in their lives, when they moved to sheltered accommodation. Gerry Murland died in 1980, aged 92, and Marjorie passed away a year later, aged 91.[32]

FOUR BATEMAN SONS AND ONLY DAUGHTER SERVE IN WAR, TWO SONS KILLED IN ACTION

John Godfrey Bateman LL D and Meloira Frances Emily Bateman (née Scanlan) of 26, Clarinda Park East, Kingstown, had seven children: Reginald John, Frances Emily, Ernest Maunsell, Edgar Noel, Arthur Cyril, John Victor and Godfrey; all born in Listowel, Co Kerry. Godfrey Bateman senior was born and lived in Co Kerry where he was employed as a schools inspector. When the family came to Dublin, they lived at 19, Northumberland Road for a short period of time before moving to reside in Kingstown. Meloira Frances was born in Limerick and died in February 1928, when living at 14, Adelaide Street, Dun Laoghaire. Her husband, John, died in July 1936 of pneumonia.

Captain Godfrey Bateman (survived), Royal Army Medical Corps enlisted in 1915, and served in France. At some point in the war he contracted trench nephritis and was sent home to recuperate. Godfrey entered Trinity College in 1910 and took his MB. He married Evelyn Lindsay and resided in Coleraine, where they had seven children. Godfrey died in 1942, aged 50.[33]

Major Edgar Noel Bateman OBE, Australian Army Medical Corps, attached to the 10th Light Horse Regiment. He was also a graduate of Trinity College and survived the Great War. Edgar enlisted in the Australian Army during January 1916 and lived in the Canberra area. He was promoted to Major in 1919 and when the war finished he resided at Mount Barker in Western Australia. In April 1920, Edgar married Olive Lillian Keown and the couple had two children, Barry and Betty. He was awarded the OBE for his work on malaria. Dr Bateman died of pneumonia in 1929, aged 40, and Olive, who remarried in her late 40s, died at Gwalia, West Australia, in 1990.[34]

Their sister, Frances Emily, served as a Voluntary Aid Detachment (VAD) in the British Red Cross Society and was 'Mentioned in Despatches' during the war. She married Henry Jermyn in 1919 and the couple resided at Merrion Avenue, Blackrock with their five children.[35]

BATEMAN, Arthur Cyril MC

Captain, Royal Army Medical Corps. Secondary Regiment, 7th Battalion, Cameron Highlanders.

He was killed in action, aged 27, on 28 March 1918. It was extremely difficult situation for any family, whose loved one was reported missing in action, but when the speculation extended over a long period of time it created an intolerable burden for everyone concerned. Such was the case of Capt Arthur Cyril Bateman. His father wrote to the War Office on 8 June 1918:

> You said in your last communication that you would institute enquiries through the Netherlands Government. Three other sons of mine are Captains with the Colours, two in war service and the third sick in hospital and my only daughter, a VAD, was mentioned by the War Office for her services. Please help us all you can, I have tried every conceivable way of tracing him. When recently examining his effects, his mother and sister found amongst them his identification disc, it was a silver one given to him by his sister as he had lost or mislaid his official one. Unfortunately, it looks as if he had no disc on, so unless he was able to speak, he might have died unidentified.[36]

He wrote again in 1918:

> I beg to enclose herewith a copy of a letter received from one of his chums, Captain Eric Lumley, Royal Army Medical Corps, who got six days leave in order to try and find out definite information as to the fate of my son. Though Captain Lumley's report is disappointing, yet it is by no means hopeless. The Boche by his low-minded spite in the ruthless destruction of identifying papers made Captain Lumley's journey nil as regards any possible results. As however, he reports that

there are no officers graves marked it follows that of the nine British officers' graves he saw at Douai, my son's was not one. There is a ray of hope here, though only negative.

Captain Lumley states that: 'Nobody had even taken records of Allied wounded who went through the Douai and Cambrai hospitals on their way to Germany.' It is therefore not impossible that my son is in some back German camp, and possibly with his health and perhaps memory too much injured to enable him to communicate with us?[37]

The War Office concluded: 'Apparently there is no evidence to show that Captain Bateman was ever at Douai, and it is therefore useless to press the German Government for further news, as experience has shown that it is no use making enquiries without some tangible evidence to go on.' The War Office wrote in November 1918:

With reference to your letter of the 13 October, concerning Capt A.C. Bateman MC, I am directed to inform you that in view of the statement reported to have been made by Pte Gillespie (15439), now a prisoner of war at Hameln in Germany, a communication has been addressed through diplomatic channels to the German Government enquiring whether any information regarding this officer can be given. The reply will be communicated to you when received, but cannot be expected for some considerable time. I am, however, at the same time to say that for the reasons stated in the last letter of 10th October, it is not possible to hold out any hope that Captain Bateman is still alive as a prisoner of war.[38]

The response to this communication from the Ministry of War in Berlin, did not reach the British War Office until 7 March 1919, and stated: 'The enquiries instituted regarding Captain A.C. Bateman have proved fruitless. Gillespie cannot be interrogated seeing that he has meanwhile been repatriated.'[39]

In the meantime, more tragic news was visited upon the family when their eldest son, Reginald, was killed on the 3 September 1918. As time went by doors were closing, one by one, on any hope that Arthur was still alive. A letter sent to his father from the British Red Cross and Order of St John, on behalf of the Earl of Lucan, informed him that they received the following information from another informant, A. Matthews (31640), 45th Royal Army Medical Corps: 'I found Capt Bateman on the cross-roads at Fenchy-Chapelle on 28 March and he had been shot through the lung. A stretcher-bearer stayed with the captain until he was picked up by the Germans. Captain Bateman was very weak.' The family received a further contribution from an unidentified informant:

> Captain Bateman and I were carried into a hut near the Tilloy cross-roads on the Cambrai Road, and had our wounds dressed. Captain Bateman, it grieves me to say was very seriously wounded in the region of the kidneys. I never saw him after he was removed from the hut. I think it is probable that he was carried to a place we used to call Fosse Caves, chalk caves under the remains of a farm on the Cambrai Road.[40]

The officer's parents may not have been surprised to receive the final communication from the War Office: 'The Army Council is regretfully constrained to conclude for official purposes that Capt Bateman is dead, and that his death occurred on or since 28th day of March 1918.'[41]

He is commemorated on the Pozières Memorial, near Albert, France; Roll of Honour, Trinity College; War Memorial, Dun Laoghaire Mariners Church and the Great War Memorial at Sir Patrick Dun's Hospital, Dublin. He won the Military Cross for conspicuous gallantry to duty at east of Ypres on 31 July 1917. His citation read: 'In repeatedly going round the front line and attending to the wounded, who had been lying out in some cases for two days. Although continually exposed to hostile sniping and machine gun fire, he displayed the utmost disregard of danger.'[42] He was also awarded the 1914–15 Star, British War and Victory medals.

Arthur Bateman entered Trinity College in 1910, took his MB in 1914 and joined the British Army in the same year. He was a medical student and his last address before joining the army was, Sir Patrick Duns Hospital, Dublin. 'Arthur was a fine cricket player and represented Ireland in a test against Scotland, played at Raeburn Place, Edinburgh on 10-12 of July 1913.'[43]

BATEMAN, Reginald John
Captain, 46th Battalion, Canadian Infantry
(Saskatchewan Regiment).

Captain Bateman was killed, aged 35, by a shell dropping at the entrance to Regimental Headquarters on 3 September1918 at Chalk Quarry. The incident took place during an assault on the Drocourt-Quéant Line, near the town of Dury. Reports of the situation were received from Capt Blair and Capt Bateman at about 3pm. On 3 September at 9.50am brigades were informed that they were going to advance and at 10am and at 12pm the battalion commenced to move forward in open formation and was established in Green Line at 12.10pm.[44] The 46th Battalion suffered 320 casualties but captured over 400 prisoners, including a German area commander, his assistant and medical staff and a large quantity of documents. The 46th Battalion was relieved on 4 September, following the death of Capt Bateman.[45]

Reginald Bateman enlisted in the ranks in the 28th Infantry Battalion on 26 October 1914, and following eleven months in training he served six months in the area around Ypres, Belgium. He was then invited by Walter Charles Murray, President of the University of Saskatchewan, to take command of the Saskatchewan Company of the 196th (Western Universities) Infantry Battalion. Bateman spent the summer and fall of 1916 in Canada, sat his officer's exams, and became a Major. Once in England, the 196th was broken up. He reverted from major to lieutenant so that he could see action again, and was posted to the 46th Infantry Battalion, arriving at the front in June1917. He was wounded in August 1917, but recovered and returned to the front line in the winter of the same year.[46]

He is commemorated on Vimy Memorial, Pas de Calais, France; Great War Memorial, Portora Royal School, Enniskillen, Co Fermanagh; Hall of Honour, Trinity College; War Memorial, Dun Laoghaire Mariners Church, and the Reginald Bateman, *Teacher and Soldier*, a memorial volume of selections from his lectures and other writings, which was published in London in 1922. Bateman's lecture notes are preserved in the Bateman fonds at the University of Saskatchewan, Saskatoon City, Canada. He was 'Mentioned in Despatches' and awarded the 1915 Star, British War and Victory medals.

Reginald Bateman was born on 12 October 1883 in Listowel Co Kerry, and received his early education at Portora Royal School, Co Fermanagh, before entering Trinity College, where he took his BA degree in 1906, having also received awards in English, French and Modern History. He took his MA degree in 1909 and was offered a position at the University of Saskatchewan in Saskatoon as its first professor of English; and one of the first four professors at the new university. In 1922 the University of Saskatchewan brought out a memorial volume in Bateman's honour, *Reginald Bateman, teacher and soldier*. The volume makes clear the kind of man and mind that went to war in 1914.

REGINALD BATEMAN: TEACHER AND SOLDIER

He was an idealist as a teacher. 'It is by Art and Art alone', he believed, 'that humanity progresses; progress in Science or in mere knowledge does not necessarily mean progress in any of those things in which man stands supreme above the rest of creation, those spiritual qualities which raise him to the level of the Divine'. The students he valued were those who could move in such rarefied air. Of all those he might teach, (Bateman taught 220 students in 1914) if a teacher inspired "even a single individual with a true desire for culture, his existence for that year is fully justified'.

Bateman went to war as an idealist too. On 25 October 1914 he addressed the Young Men's Christian Association at the university in a speech that was more extreme than any other pro-war speech delivered to Saskatoon from platform or pulpit in the war years. War, he said, 'is the one supreme, the only entirely adequate test of a nation's spiritual quality', and by punishing 'national depravity' war is 'the chief stimulus in the progress of mankind'. What is true of the nation is true of individuals: 'Is it not far better that they should feel a thrill of patriotism at the rude touch of war, and die striking a blow for freedom, than that they should live to a dishonoured old age, seeking beggarly gain'? War alone, said Bateman, keeps fully alive such virtues as courage, self-sacrifice, and honour, while a world without war would be 'enjoyed by a spineless and emasculated race of beings'.

Bateman followed his own beliefs and twice chose a lower rank so that he could go to war, once in 1917, but also in the winter of 1914–15. He had taken the officers' training course at Winnipeg, passed one examination, but refused to take the final because he would have had to resign from the 28th. He preferred to … 'not lose his chance of getting to the front at the earliest possible date'.

When Bateman returned to Saskatoon after his first tour of duty at the front, he was a different man, his idealism tempered by reality. He spoke well of the enemy, and summed up trench life as 'days of unendurable monotony and moments of indescribable fear'. He added two other aspects of war to that statement– the picturesque (he describes a night in the trenches) and the comic, where the breaking of a rum jar was a greater calamity to the men than their trench being shelled, and he listened happily to creative cursing. He had heard a ration party going to the front at night, 'wading through mud, plunging into holes, falling over broken trench mats, and I have heard with great pleasure the flow of language; it was immense, nothing like it is to be heard from any other troops in the world's history'. The idealistic professor had found the common touch, though with his customary hyperbole.

He was apparently well thought of as an officer. That he should command the University of Saskatchewan company was 'a very strong desire' of students. The authors of *The Suicide Battalion* say that he was 'considered one of the most popular officers in the 46th'. He was much honoured at the university by the book, but also by a scholarship in his name and by the Bateman professorship of English.

Reginald Bateman was in his life and writings a serious man. He had another side to him.While sitting his officer's examinations at Winnipeg so that he could take command of the Saskatchewan Company, Bateman received a new uniform. 'I have just received my uniform. It is a trifle loud. It is downstairs but I can still hear it calling me. I have posted a picket over it to prevent its escape, until the cleaning man arrives to take it in charge. I think it will go quietly'.[47]

IRISH INTERNATIONAL RUGBY PLAYER MORTALLY WOUNDED

BURGESS, Robert Balderston

Captain, Inland Water Transport, Royal Engineers. Secondary Regiment, Horse Transport Army Service Corps.

He died from wounds, aged 24, on 9 December 1915, at No 2 Casualty Clearing Station. In a statement made by Lt W.H. O'Brien on 13 December 1915, he wrote:

> I was with Capt Burgess about 1.30pm on 9 December; we were cycling ten yards apart through the Rue de Dunkerque when a shell burst between us and mortally wounded him. I assisted Capt Burgess into a house nearby and with the assistance of a French Gendarme obtained a stretcher-bearer, Cpl Matin SB, 10th Battalion, King's Own Yorkshire Light Infantry and another man who assisted me to carry Capt Burgess to the nearest Field Ambulance. From the time the shell burst to the arrival at the 64th Field Ambulance was three quarters of an hour.[48]

His grave is at II B. 63.Bailleul Communal Cemetery Extension (Nord), Bailleul, France and he is commemorated on the Barristers' Memorial, Four Courts, Dublin; War Memorial, Royal Courts of Justice, Belfast; Roll of Honour and Memorial, Portora Royal School, Enniskillen; Church of Ireland, Monkstown, for St John's, Mountown Memorial; Great War Memorial, St Stephen's Church, Dublin; Hall of Honour, Trinity College, and his parents' headstone in Dean's Grange Cemetery. He was awarded the 1915 Star, British War and Victory medals.

Robert enlisted in November 1914, and was transferred to the Royal Engineers, attached to the Inland Water Transport, on 6 March 1916. 'The First World War saw the founding of the Inland Water Transport Service in 1915, which operated barges on canals in France and Mesopotamia. Barges were used to carry bulky traffic of no great urgency travelling along the rivers and canals, and were also fitted out to carry the wounded.'[49] His kit and effects were handed over to his father by Lt R. Almack, Royal Engineers, when on leave in Dublin.[50]

Robert Burgess was the son of Henry Givens Burgess, Irish Manager of the London Midland and Scottish Railway Company, and Agnes Balderston Burgess (born in Scotland) of 12, Eglinton Park, Kingstown. Henry's first marriage to Ava Georgina Abbott produced two children, George Abbott and Sarah Frances Ethel.

When Ava died in 1883, Henry married Agnes Balderston in 1887 and they had three children; Robert Balderson, Helen Hamilton, Anna Givens. Henry was born at Finnoe House, Borrisokane, and Co Tipperary. This beautiful house with its long tree-lined entrance was, in recent times, lovingly restored by the late Tom Hayes and his wife Hilda. The ruined Church of Ireland church and small graveyard is situated on the former Burgess land about 100 metres from Finnoe House.

> Henry joined the Dublin and South Eastern Railway as a junior clerk in 1873. In 1878 he transferred to the London and North Western Railway, which also operated in Ireland. He remained in this position until 1923. During the First World War he served as Director-General of Transport, Shipping Controller, and Coal Controller in Ireland, in addition to his company responsibilities. Burgess was also a member of the Dublin Port and Docks Board, deputy chairman of the Dublin and South Eastern Railway Company, a member of the Unemployment Grants Committee in London, and a director of the Great Southern Railways. He was appointed to the Senate of the Irish Free State on its formation and appointed to the Privy Council of Ireland in the 1922 New Year Honours, for his wartime services, entitling him to the style 'The Right Honourable'. Henry Givens Burgess died at his country residence in Enniscorthy, Co Wexford, on 24 April 1937, while on a fishing holiday, and his wife died in 1945.[51]

Robert Burgess was born in Kingstown, on 25 December 1890 and attended Portora Royal School, Enniskillen in 1905, before entering Trinity College, where he took his BA degree in 1913. He was admitted, as a student, to King's Inns, Dublin in 1910 and was called to the Bar in 1914. The *Bray and South Dublin Herald* reported that 'he was known all over the country and popular to an unusual degree, by virtue of his bright, breezy manner and sterling qualities. The death of Capt Burgess will be deeply regretted.'[52]

Ten Irish Rugby Internationals were killed during the Great War. Robert Burgess was an outstanding rugby player with Portora School, Barbarians, Dublin University and Ireland. He won one international cap when he played for Ireland in a Rugby International against South Africa on 30 November 1912 and he was a keen golfer, playing as a member of Kingstown Golf Club (now Dun Laoghaire Golf Club).

TWO CRANWILL BROTHERS LOST AT WAR

Thomas Butler Cranwill (insurance executive) and Ellen Kate Helena Cranwill (née Blake) resided at 10, Mountpelier Parade, Monkstown and had six children: Helena Butler, Violet Dorothy, Valentine Arthur Butler, Thomas Philip Butler, Guy Butler and Winifred Maria Butler. Three sons served in the war: Valentine was killed; Philip, who served in the Merchant Navy, survived the Great War, but lost his life in the Second World War, and their brother, Guy, survived the conflict.

Three female members of the family also had connections with the two Great Wars. Helena was unmarried and died in December 1943. She lived in France for a time before working with the Admiralty in London during the Second World War. Her sister, Violet, a teacher, married Capt Reginald Osborne Smyth, Royal Army Medical Corps, who survived the Great War, and with whom she had two children. The third sister, Winifred Maria Butler, married Lt Tennyson Lee, who survived, but lost two brothers in the war. Winifred and Tennyson had two sons; John Patrick Lee MBA (deceased) and David Lee. Winifred and Tennyson died in April 1959 and April 1982, respectively.[53]

Their son, Captain Thomas Philip Butler Cranwill, Merchant Navy, survived the Great War despite being torpedoed on two occasions. He then served with the Clan Line in the Second World War, and was drowned on his birthday, aged 46, on the 16 August 1940 at 8.32 pm. His ship, SS *Clan Macphee*, was in convoy, OB-197, when hit by one torpedo from *U-30* and it sank about 350 miles west of North Uist, Outer Hebrides, with a loss of 67 from a total of 91 crew. He is commemorated on Tower Hill Memorial, London. Philip was educated at Kings Hospital School, Dublin, from 1905 to 1910.[54] A third brother, Lieutenant Guy Butler Cranwill, Indian Army, 2/3 Brahmans, survived the Great War. He was born in 1896 and educated at King's Hospital School, Dublin (1907–1913) and Queen Mary Grammar School, Walsall, England. Guy enlisted in 1914, served in the ranks with the 7th Dublins in Gallipoli during August 1915 and later was discharged to a commission on 27 March 1917. He wrote about his time at school:

Before the Great War began, we boys at King's Hospital used to be very interested in the various troops that occupied the Royal Barracks (now Collins Barracks). Some of us used to talk to soldiers from the English, Scottish and Welsh Regiments (when the headmaster was not looking) and we used to wonder why no Irish troops were ever stationed there.

The Royal Dublin Fusiliers enjoyed the distinction of being the 'City Regiment', and so were the only troops, I believe, who were allowed to march through Dublin with fixed bayonets. None of us ever expected to see a battalion of that regiment stationed in the Royal Barracks, and we would have laughed at the idea of being able to talk down to any of the school or staff as serving soldiers stationed there. The 7th Dublins were moved into the Royal Barracks early in 1915. Nearly two-thirds of the Irishmen in this battalion were enlisted in Dublin during 1914, and it contained one company, of whom the majority were either, past, present, or future intending members of various Dublin Rugby Football Clubs. This company, of about 275 men, contained several old boys from King's Hospital and other Irish Schools.[55]

Guy applied for his campaign medals in 1921 from an address in India, where he was still serving in 1926. He returned to Ireland and became a priest in the Church of Ireland. He married Dolly Hickson [*sic*], a widow with two children. The couple had no further children and Reverend Cranwill passed away in the pulpit of his church at Sutton Coldfield, near Birmingham, while conducting a service.[56]

CRANWILL, Valentine Arthur Butler MC
Captain, 2nd Battalion, East Lancashire Regiment. Secondary Regiment, Service No 21128S, 11th Battalion, Canadian 100th Regiment (Winnipeg Grenadiers).

Captain Cranwill was killed on 24 April 1918 in the Somme, France.

On this day at 3.20am the enemy commenced an intense bombardment of the battalion's front line village defenses and in the rear. Gas respirators had to be worn for about two hours. At about 7am the enemy attacked with tanks and broke through the divisional line up to the 9th Rifle Brigade front. The companies of the battalion held their ground, with heavy casualties, until 9.30am, when the tanks having outflanked them, they were forced to fall back, and a new line was taken up west of the village to prevent the enemy de-trenching. At this time 30 men only were available and about 20 Australian Infantry.[57]

It was in this battle, which went on all day until 8 pm that Capt Cranwill was killed.

His grave is at 14, Camon Communal Cemetery, Camon village, Somme, immediately east of Amiens. He is commemorated on the Great War Memorial, N Chancel, St Philip and St James Church of Ireland, Blackrock; Great War Memorial, Monkstown Church of Ireland, and the Great War Memorial, Kings Hospital College, Palmerstown, Dublin. Captain Cranwill won the Military Cross and his citation stated: 'For conspicuous gallantry and devotion to duty. He led his company throughout an attack with the greatest fearlessness and gallantry, moving about the line encouraging his men, with complete disregard of the enemy rifle and machine gun fire to which he was continually exposed. Later in the day he repelled two counter-attacks.'[58] He was also awarded the British War and Victory medals, which were sent to his father in July/August 1922.

Valentine Cranwill was born in Dublin on 19 October 1892 and was unmarried. He was educated at Kings Hospital School, Dublin and Waverly School in Birmingham from 1907–1909. Prior to enlisting he was employed as a stockbroker's clerk. He was a member of the OTC at Waverley School for a period of two years. His name was recorded on a British passenger list on the ship, *Royal Edward*, bound for Montreal on the 3 May 1911. It was here that he joined the Canadian 100th Regiment, (Winnipeg Grenadiers), 11th Battalion, on 23 September 1914, and his unit sailed for England on 4 October 1914. He was transferred to the 1st Canadian Contingent, and held the rank of Sergeant. On the 27 May 1915 he was discharged to a commission at Shorncliffe Military Camp in Kent. Cranwill was slightly wounded on 7 July 1916, but remained on duty. On 11 April 1917, he was in the 8th General Hospital, Rouen, suffering with trench fever. His father responded to the telegram from the War Office, stating that he was glad to see it was only a slight attack, and requested further information on his son's progress towards full health. Later in the month, his parents received news that he was discharged to the Reinforcement Depot. Following his son's death, Mr Cranwill wrote to the War Office on 26 July 1918, to confirm receipt of his son's effects. [59]

IRISH INTERNATIONAL RUGBY PLAYER KILLED BY SNIPER

DEANE, Ernest Cotton MC
Captain, 2nd Battalion, Leicestershire Regiment in the Royal Army Medical Corps.

He was killed by a bullet to the head, aged 28, north of Neuve Chapelle, on 25 September 1915, while returning from helping wounded men who were held up on German wire. 'At 5.30am on 25 September 1915 the battalion was in positions of readiness in accordance with orders in four lines opposite their objective with bombing parties, sandbag parties and carrying parties all arranged, and in position. At 6am the first line got over the parapet quickly followed by the second. The gas affected a number of Leicestershire men, and smoke caused a dense fog and direction was difficult. Casualties began at once and the third line was ordered out to fill up gaps. Owing to the thick smoke it seemed likely that gaps would occur on the flanks and at 6.07am the fourth line was sent with special instructions to maintain touch with the units on either flank. At about 6.10am the left were over the German parapet and the battalion's flag was seen flying on their lines. The left went forward with such a dash that they outstripped the 2nd and 8th Gurkhas. This caused a good many casualties including all the officers and most of the NCOs of 'A' Company. Undeterred the men went on, got over the uncut wire and reached the road. In the meantime the battalion's right had not fared so well. They went forward in good line under a heavy fire till held up by the German wire. A number of its men were collected in the ditch in front of the German wire waiting for developments.[60]

Captain Thomas Fitzpatrick, who also attended Corrig School, was killed on the same day at Leuze Wood and his profile may be viewed later in this chapter. The Senior Army Chaplin, Meerut Division, said of Ernest Deane: 'I have known him since he came to Meerut, some eighteen months ago, and remember how keen and pleased the dear lad was when he first received orders to proceed to the front. I know the regiment misses him dreadfully.'[61] Another officer wrote: 'Your son was straight, fearless, indefatigable, always cheery, and never anything else but conscientious and gallant. I was present at his funeral in the cemetery in the Rue-du-Bacqueret on Sunday, the 26th inst. – the day after he died gloriously.'[62] The Officer, Commanding the 2nd Battalion, wrote to his parents:

> He was the most gallant fellow I have ever met and we all loved him in the regiment, both officers and men. He was just part of us and the few of us left, mourn his loss very deeply. We had a big battle on the 25th and your son went out to help some wounded and got killed. I believe his death was instantaneous, but I am not sure as I was wounded myself, and had to be taken back. His body was recovered and buried by our Padre and I will give you the exact location of the cemetery afterwards.[63]

His grave is at II. D. 14. Rue-du-Bacquerot No 1 Military Cemetery, Levantie, France and he is commemorated on the Panel of the Leicestershire Regiment in the chapel at the Royal Military College, Sandhurst, and the Great War Memorial at the former Adelaide Hospital, Dublin. Captain Deane won the Military Cross and his citation read as follows:

> For conspicuous gallantry on 25 August 1915, near Farquissat. A standing patrol 100 yards in front of our line was bombed by the enemy at 10pm, the only notification being two loud bomb explosions. Captain Deane, without any knowledge of the enemy's strength, at once got over the parapet and ran by himself to the spot under rifle and machine-gun fire. Finding four wounded men, he returned for stretchers, and got them back into safety. This is not the first time Capt Deane's gallantry under fire had been brought to notice.[64]

He was also 'Mentioned in Despatches' and awarded the 1914–15 Star, British War and Victory medals. Ernest entered the Royal Military College at Sandhurst, was commissioned lieutenant and joined the Royal Army Medical Corps on 28 July 1911. He passed his examinations for captain with more than 90 per cent marks in 1913 and was promoted to that rank on 28 January 1915.[65]

He was the son of Thomas Stanley Deane (bank manager) and Aileen Annie Deane (née Byrne) of, 27 Cambridge Terrace, York Road, Kingstown, and for many years at 36, Main Street, Rathkeale, Co Limerick. Aileen Deane died in November 1927 and Thomas, passed away in September 1940 aged 88. They were interred at Dean's Grange Cemetery. There were five children in the family: Edward Stanley, Aileen Dora, Harold Kingston, Ernest Cotton and Norman Scarborough.

Ernest was born in Limerick on 4 May 1887 and his early education was at Corrig School, Kingstown. He took the licences of the Royal College of Physicians and Surgeons in 1909 at the Adelaide Hospital, Dublin and qualified MRCS (Eng), L, & LM, RCPS (Irel). 'Ernest played Rugby for Lansdowne FC and won one cap for Ireland in 1909 when his team lost 5-11 to England.'[66]

'Corrig School was established in 1875 and began its existence with two pupils at 26, Clarinda Park, before moving to 23, Corrig Avenue in 1878. The school won the Leinster Senior Schools Rugby Challenge Cup in 1889 and again in 1892. Eight former past men and two masters from Corrig School won international rugby caps playing for Ireland, before the outbreak of the Great War.'[67]

DOYLE, William Joseph Gabriel SJ MC
Captain, Army Chaplin's Department. In the 19 months at war, he served with the 8th Battalion Royal Irish Fusiliers; Royal Inniskilling Fusiliers; 8th & 9th Battalions Royal Dublin Fusiliers and 6th & 7th Battalions, Royal Irish Rifles.

Father William Doyle's life of immolation came to an end when he was killed by a shell, aged 44, on 17 August 1917. It occurred during action in the third Battle of Ypres, at Borry Farm on the Frezenburg Ridge, situated about 2kms from the village of Passchendaele. On 17 August 1917, toward the evening of a long and busy day, word came of a wounded officer lying in an exposed position. Father Doyle went out at once and found the officer in a shell crater. He gave the man his last sacraments, then half-dragged and half-carried him back into the line. As his runner was handing him a cup of water, a shell exploded nearby, instantly killing Father Doyle and three other officers.

Father Willie Doyle, Society of Jesus, the Catholic Chaplain attached to the 8th Dublins, met his death. Until that day he had seemed to his vast soldier flock the possessor almost of a charmed life. For months he walked and worked daily where the fighting was hottest and the dangers greatest, and he refused to be deterred from the standard of duty which he had assigned for himself by any thought of personal risk. By the law of averages alone, he should long previously have been swept into eternity; but the very recklessness of his approach to the terrors of the conflict appeared to turn the scythe away from him, so that death when at length it did come, struck him, as it were, *per accident,* killing him by a shell among a group of other men. Beyond the fact of his death-the death which he had looked undaunted in the face on so many occasions-that day was for Father Doyle much like other days: he gave his energy, every ounce of it, and his will and priestly power, to the tasks belonging to his chaplaincy, interpreted according to the highest canons of duty. A fellow Catholic, Sir Philip Gibbs, has recorded, so far as it is known, the story of his end:- 'All through the worst hours an Irish padre went about among the dead and dying, giving absolution to his boys. Once he came back to headquarters, but he would not take a bite of food or stay, though his friends urged him. He went back to the field to minister to those who were glad to see him bending over them in their last agony. Three men were killed by shell fire as he knelt beside them, and he was not touched-not touched until his own turn came. A shell burst close by, and the padre fell dead'.[58]

FATHER DOYLE WROTE OF HIS EXPERIENCES

As I came along the trench I could hear the men whisper, 'Here's the priest'. The faces which a moment before had been marked with the awful strain of the waiting lit up with pleasure. As I gave the absolution and the blessing of God on their work, I could not help thinking how many a poor fellow would soon be stretched lifeless a few paces from where he stood; and though I ought to be hardened by this time, I found it difficult to choke down the sadness which filled my heart. 'God bless you, Father, we're ready now', was reward enough for facing the danger, since every man realised that each moment was full of dreadful possibilities.

I don't think you will blame me when I tell you that more than once the words of Absolution stuck in my throat and the tears splashed down on the patient suffering faces of my poor boys as I leant down to anoint them.[69]

I found the dying lad – he was not much more – so tightly jammed into a corner of the trench that it was almost impossible to get him out. Both legs were smashed, one in two or three places, so his chances of life were small, and there were other injuries as well. What a harrowing picture that scene would have made. A splendid young soldier, married only a month they told me, lying there, pale and motionless in the mud and water with the life crushed out of him by a cruel shell. The stretcher bearers hard at work binding up as well as they may, his broken limbs; round about a group of silent 'Tommies' looking on and wondering when will their turn come. Peace for a moment seems to have taken possession of the battlefield, not a sound save the deep boom of some far-off gun and the stifled moans of the dying boy, while as if anxious to hide the scene, nature drops her soft mantle of snow on the living and dead alike.[70]

Father Doyle wrote about the 16th (Irish) Division:

The very night we handed over a portion of the front to another regiment – the Germans – how did they know of the change? – came over and captured the trenches, so we had to go back again. Still the unfortunate Irishmen could not be kept in the trenches forever. And on 25 August came the welcome order to move to the rear. Sudden and secret as the order was, the Germans knew all about it and put a board with the message, 'Good-bye, 16th Division, we shall give it hot to the English when they come'. The Irish did their work well in Loos; in the six months they did not lose a trench or a yard of ground; and out of the division of 20,000 over 15,000 men (including many sick and slightly wounded) had passed through the doctor's hands.[71]

SOME OF THE MANY TRIBUTES TO FATHER WILLIE DOYLE

Tributes were paid to his memory in the Press and sometimes in unaccustomed places. In the days following his death, Percival Phillips wrote in the *Daily Express* and *Morning Post*:

> The Orangemen will not forget a certain Catholic Chaplain who lies in a soldier's grave in that sinister plain beyond Ypres. He went forward and back over the battle-field with bullets whistling about him, seeking out the dying and kneeling in the mud beside them to give them absolution; walking with death with a smile on his face, watched by his men hundreds of Irishmen who lay in that bloody place. Each time he came back across the field he was begged to remain in comparative safety. Smilingly, he shook his head and went out again into the storm. He would not desert his boys in their agony. They remember him as a saint—they speak his name with tears.[72]

Major-General William Bernard Hickie of the British Army, who was born in Terryglass, Co Tipperary, wrote to Father Doyle:

> I have read with much pleasure the reports of your Regimental Commander and Brigade Commander regarding your conduct and devotion to duty in the field on 27 and 29 April and have ordered your name and deed to be entered in the Record of the Irish Division. The Major-General also wrote to his parents on 15 December 1917: He

was loved and reverenced by us all. His gallantry, self sacrifice and devotion to duty were all so well known and recognized. I think his was the most wonderful character that I have ever known.[73]

And a Presbyterian wrote:

God never made a nobler soul. Father Doyle was a good deal among us. We could not possibly agree with his religious opinions, but we simply worshipped him for other things. He didn't know the meaning of fear and he did not know what bigotry was. He was as ready to risk his life and take a drop of water to a wounded Ulsterman as to assist men of his own faith and regiment. If he risked his life looking after Ulster Protestant soldiers once, he did it a hundred times in the last few days. The Ulstermen felt his loss more keenly than anybody, and none were readier to show their marks of respect to the dead hero priest than were our Ulster Presbyterians.[74]

Frank Laird was an officer in the 8th Royal Dublin Fusiliers in 1917 and he wrote:

No account, however fragmentary, of the 8th (Dublins) would be complete without remembering our Roman Catholic padre, Father Doyle, a Dublin Jesuit. His name was known and loved through the whole Division for unexampled bravery and equal kindness. He wore the Military Cross gained on the Somme, and was recommended for the Victoria Cross for his extraordinary courage in the deadly area of Frezenburg in the Paschendaele offensive of August 1917, where he met his death. When shells dropped round, ordinary mortals took cover or an opposite direction. Father Doyle made for them to see was he wanted. One morning in the line I was standing watching the Communication Trench a short way down getting a nasty shelling. In a few minutes Father Doyle arrived smiling having just come through it on his usual visit to the front line, without his tin hat, which he could not be induced to wear, in fact it was with great difficulty that he was got to even carry a gas helmet. His gentlemanly, reserved manner with his quiet humour and pleasant conversation which often contained some canard such as that the French were going to give in next month, all made him very pleasant man to meet at any time, and most of all in a bad time. Is it any wonder that he was welcome in every mess, that the men worshiped the ground he trod in, and that he was worth several officers in any hot spot where endurance was tested to its height?[75]

Paddy Harte, former Fine Gael TD, said that:

My mother believed Father Doyle was a saint and told me stories of reported intercessions by him on behalf of people praying for help. Father Doyle was to emerge again as a significant influence much later in my life when I embarked on my first visit to the battlefields of the Western Front that led to the building of the Island of Ireland Peace Park and Round Tower in Messines, Flanders in 1998. In a strange twist of fate I was to discover that during the construction of the tower that the man, who I so closely associated with the horror of that war, had lost his life near the site of the Peace Park.[76]

Father Doyle's friend and fellow teacher from Belvedere, Father Frank Browne SJ (Chaplain To the Irish Guards) and well-known amateur photographer in later years, wrote on 15 August 1917, the day before Father Doyle was killed:

He is a marvel. They may talk of heroes and saints – they are hardly in it! I went back the other day to see the old Dubs, as I heard they were having – we'll say, a taste of the war. No one has yet been appointed to my place and Fr D. has done double work. So unpleasant were the conditions that the men had to be relieved frequently. Fr D. had no one to relieve him and so he stuck it out in the mud and the shells, the gas and the terror. Day after day he stuck out. I met the adjutant of one of my two battalions, who previously had only known Fr D. by sight. His first greeting to me was: 'Little Father Doyle (they all call him that, more in affection than anything else) deserves the VC more than any man that ever wore it. We cannot get him away from the "Line" while the men are there: he is in with his own and he is in with us. The men couldn't stick it half so well if he weren't there: if we give him an orderly, he sends the man back, he wears no tin hat and he is always so cheery.' Another officer, also a Protestant, said: 'Fr D. never rests. Night and day he is with us. He finds a dying or dead man, does all, comes back smiling, makes a little cross and goes out to bury him, and begins all over again.' I needn't say through all this, the conditions of ground and air and discomfort surpass anything that I ever dreamt of in the worst days of the Somme. My God preserve him and keep him. He doesn't want VCs or anything else, but it would be the proudest moment of my life, if I could only call him VC. So rooted is the prejudice against such as he, that one of his men here said to me –knowing what Father Knapp and Father Gwynn had done – 'Aren't our priests, Father, forbidden to take the VC'?[77]

Father Doyle's last letter to his father was written on 16 August 1917, the day before he was killed:

I have told you all my escapes, dearest father, because I think that what I have written will give you the same confidence which I feel that my old armchair in Heaven is not ready yet and I do not want you to be uneasy about me. I am all the better for these couple of days rest and am quite on my fighting legs again. Leave will be possible very shortly, I think, so I shall only say au revoir in view of an early meeting.[78]

Father Frank Browne identified his remains and assisted at his funeral on 18 August 1917 at Crossing of Roads. Today, the exact place of his grave is unknown. He is commemorated on the Tyne Cot Memorial, Belgium; War Memorial at Ratcliffe College, Leicester; Great War Memorial, Belvedere College, Dublin and the Great War Memorial at Clongowes Wood College, Co Kildare.

On Friday 12 November 1999 the *Guardian* reported on a request by a retired Belgian teacher to open a grave:

Father Doyle was recommended for the Victoria Cross–blocked by church authorities – and nominated for sainthood. But for 82 years no one has known where his body was buried. Now perhaps we will find out. On the eve of Remembrance Day, an 85-year-old Ypres woman has made a request to the Commonwealth War Graves Commission for the exhumation of an anonymous grave in a British war cemetery outside the Flemish town to establish whether it contains the remains of one of the army's most celebrated heroes. Denise Dael, a former school teacher, is convinced that Doyle's body should be located as a first step to commemorating his bravery and, perhaps, jogging the conscience of Pope John Paul II.[79]

The author requested the Commonwealth War Graves Commission to comment on this report and its explanation was understandable:

As you state the Reverend Doyle died during fighting on the Frezenburg Ridge on 16 August 1917. There are reports that he and several of his colleagues were buried near where they died but, despite several searches by the graves registration units, his grave was never found. It is possible that the grave and his remains were destroyed during subsequent fighting or that the grave became unmarked and he is one of thousands of casualties whose remains could not be identified and that he is buried in a war cemetery as an unknown soldier. He is therefore commemorated by name on the Tyne Cot Memorial to the missing. It is a fundamental principle of the Commission that war graves should not be disturbed unless they are under threat or for reasons of overriding public necessity and it is therefore our policy, supported by the Commission's member governments, not to exhume remains for the purpose of identification. Many such cases have therefore been routinely turned down. We do, however, receive cases to identify graves and when they are well supported by documentary evidence they are submitted for a final decision to the appropriate member government. I am aware that in the late 1990s a claim was made that the Reverend Doyle had been buried as an unidentified soldier but I understand that the claim was made on the basis of evidence from a medium who had pinpointed the alleged grave location in a séance. I am sure that you will appreciate that the Commission would wish to see more concrete evidence to support the identification and none was forthcoming in this case.[80]

Roman Catholics from different countries throughout the English-speaking world, who believe in sainthood, must wonder why the Vatican has never reacted to the very strong desire of Irish Roman Catholics to beatify Father Willie Doyle. They are entitled to ask if those responsible within the Irish church have any interest in promoting the sainthood cause of one of the holiest and bravest men that ever lived. Is it because being killed on a battlefield while wearing a British army uniform is too big an obstacle for the church to overcome?

Father Doyle was recommended for the Distinguished Service Order (DSO) at Wytschaete and the Victoria Cross (VC) at Frezenberg. He was awarded the Military Cross in January, 1917.[81] Many officers and men believed that he deserved the Victoria Cross and Distinguished Service Order for his bravery under fire, but despite the recommendations he was awarded the Military Cross only. Was Father Doyle denied these gallantry awards by the British military hierarchy, or was it the Jesuit Order who said, 'no more awards'?

In correspondence with the Jesuit Order in Ireland, a representative stated that it was unlikely that Jesuit priests were forbidden by the Order to take the Victory Cross. However, Brother Nigel Cave of Ratcliffe the Roman Catholic College, in Leicestershire, where Father Doyle was educated, informed the author that Father Doyle's brother, Father Charlie Doyle SJ, wrote a letter to the college's Father President stating that: 'The award of the Victoria Cross was blocked by the Archbishop of Westminster on the grounds that a priest in those circumstances was only doing his duty and therefore did not fall into this category of the award of a Victory Cross.'[82] He was also awarded the British War and Victory medals, together with a Parchment Certificate from 16th (Irish) Division.

Following Father Doyle's death there was correspondence between the War Office and Maxwell Weldon & Company, Solicitors of North Great Georges Street, Dublin, acting on behalf of the Jesuit Order in Ireland, expressing disagreement about the amount of compensation being paid to the Jesuit Order. A letter from solicitors to the

War Office on 24 October 1917 stated:

> We are in receipt of your letter of the 22 October and note the
> amount of balance in your hands. Is it not usual for compensation to
> be awarded in these cases? The deceased was a member of the Jesuit
> Order and the education of each of the members of that Order would
> at all events cost £1,000 as we have been informed by the Head of the
> Order in Ireland.[83]

In a further letter, the solicitors wrote that the gratuity in hand was £38:10:0 and
requested compensation; suggesting that 'a precedent had already been set.... as was
granted in the case of Reverend Father J. Gwynne, Ref: 1126 29/1.'[84]

Father Doyle's great-nephew, Hugh Cumiskey from Dublin, said that Father
Doyle's first choice was the Foreign Missions, but when he failed to get permission
from his Order he volunteered his services following the outbreak of war and was
gazetted in November 1915.[85]

William was the youngest of seven children to Hugh Doyle (Registrar of the
Dublin Bankruptcy Court) and Christina Mary Doyle (née Byrne) of Melrose,
Dalkey Avenue, Dalkey. In 1922, on the occasion of his retirement and 90th birthday,
Hugh Doyle, received a letter from Buckingham Palace:

> It has been brought to the notice of the King that you have just retired
> from your post as Chief Clerk in the Bankruptcy Court, Dublin,
> after completing 73 years of public service. His Majesty desires me to
> convey to you his congratulations on this unique record, coupled with
> the earnest hope that you may spend many years of well-earned rest in
> peace and happiness.[86]

The Doyle family lived in a large detached victorian residence, adjacent to the railway
line in Dalkey. The house stood in its own grounds surrounded by beautiful flower
gardens, tennis court and greenhouse. The property also contained a coach house and
gate-lodge. There were seven children in the family; Robert Joseph, Mary Christina,
Charles Thomas, Frederick, Angelina (Lena), Elizabeth and William Joseph Gabriel.

William Doyle was born in Dalkey on 3 March 1873 and joined his brother

Charlie with the Rosminians at Ratcliffe College, Leicestershire in September 1884, where he spent six enjoyable years. 'He took his vows of religion in 1893 and the following year he spent the first of two spells at Clongowes Wood College. Father Doyle left Clongowes in 1898, but returned in 1901 for a further period of two years. He founded and edited *The Clongownian* and also laboured in the Crescent College, Limerick and Belvedere College, Dublin. Father Doyle was ordained by the Archbishop of Dublin in 1907.'[87]

His brother, Charles, also attended Ratcliffe College, became a Jesuit and was a member of the Belvedere Community. Another brother, Frederick, joined the noviciate, but died in Rome, aged 28, on 10 March 1887, the eve of his ordination. Their sister, Mary Christina, became a nun when she joined the Sisters of Mercy at Rushbrooke in Cork.[88]

FINDLATER, Percival St George
Captain, 21st Division Train, Army Service Corps.

He was a cousin of Charles and Herbert Findlater whose profiles may be seen later in this chapter. Captain Percival Findlater was killed instantaneously by a shell, aged 36, on 28 March 1918.

His grave is at Molliens-au-Bois Communal Cemetery, near Amiens, France, and he is one of only six Commonwealth casualties in the cemetery. Captain Findlater is commemorated on the 1914–1919 Memorial at Christ Church, Ranelagh; the Memorial in the Kildare Street and University Club in St Stephen's Green and the statue over the grave of his parents in Mount Jerome Cemetery. He was 'Mentioned in Despatches' on 4 January 1917 and awarded the 1915 Star, British War and Victory medals, which were issued to his brother on 5 March 1923.[89]

Those attached to the Army Service Corps are often described as the 'unsung heroes' of the war. 'At peak, the Army Service Corps numbered an incredible 10,547 officers and 315,334 men. In addition there were tens of thousands of Indian, Egyptian, Chinese and other labourers, carriers and stores men, under orders of the regiment. Yet this vast, sprawling organisation – so vital to enabling the army to fight – merits just four mentions in the Official History of the Great War.'[90] Captain Findlater's Division was established in September 1914, as part of Army Order 388, authorising Kitchener's Third Army, K3. Advanced parties embarked for France on 2 September and the main body began to cross the Channel five days later.

Percy (as he was known to his family and friends) was born on 24 March 1882. He was the son of the late Sir William Huffington Findlater MP, DL, JP, and his second wife, Marion Hodges (née Park). His first wife, Mary Jane Wolfe died in 1877 and there were no children in this marriage. Sir William and Mary Lady Findlater resided at Fernhill, Killiney and had three children: William Alexander Victor, Percival St George and Muriel Dempster. He was a solicitor in his law firm, William Findlater & Company, and Director of Findlater's Mountjoy Brewery. William Findlater was knighted in 1896 when President of the Incorporated Law Society of Ireland and was Member of Parliament for Monaghan in the years 1880–1885. He died at his Killiney home in 1906 and his wife died in 1916. They were interred in Mount Jerome Cemetery with their daughter Muriel, who died aged 12, and Sir William's first wife, Mary.

Percy Findlater was educated at Strangeway's School, St Stephen's Green and subsequently at Elstree School, Hertfordshire and Harrow School, Middlesex, before entering Trinity College, where he took his BAI in 1905. He was unmarried. 'His brother, Lt-Col William Alexander Victor Findlater, Royal Irish Rifles, survived the Great War. He was educated at Harrow and Trinity College and married Lelia Blackwell in 1904. The couple resided in Kent with their two sons and three daughters.'[91]

FITZPATRICK, Thomas Gordon

Captain, 8th Battalion, Royal Irish Fusiliers, 49th Brigade in the 16th (Irish) Division.

Captain Fitzpatrick was killed, aged 35, at Leuze Wood, Somme, France, on 6 September 1916. He fell on the same day, and in the same battle as Capt Guy Eaton, a former school friend from Corrig School. Details of the action in which Capt Fitzpatrick lost his life may be seen in the profile of Capt Eaton in chapter seven. Captain Fitzpatrick's superior officer, Lt-Col S. Watson, wrote to his wife, Ethel Fitzpatrick, on 7 September 1916:

> You will probably have received news from the War Office informing you of your sad loss. I regret to say that your husband was killed yesterday when in command of his company in a very difficult situation. There is one consolation and that his end was absolutely instantaneous. A shell burst quite close to him, and he cannot have suffered at all. Your husband was one of my best officers and always

did his work splendidly, and he will be very difficult to replace. When I saw him the morning he was killed he was in a very difficult position and much depended on his actions. One of his chief considerations was the care and comfort of his men. He was very popular with officers and men.[92]

His grave is at Plot 36, Row D, 10. Serre Road Cemetery No 2 Serre, Somme, France and he is commemorated on the St Columba's Church World War One Memorial at the Multi-Denominational School, Ranelagh Road, Dublin and the 1914–1918 Memorial, Christ Church, Leeson Park, Dublin.

His wife, Ethel, received a letter from the War Office on 1 February 1917, stating that her husband was buried in Leuze Wood, about twelve hundred yards north-west of Combles Church. The grave was registered at the War Office and was marked by a durable wooden cross with an inscription bearing full particulars. However, another letter from the War Office on 16 July 1920, received by his wife through her solicitor, Malcomson & Law, 6, Dawson Street, Dublin, contained disturbing news about her husband's grave. In accordance with an agreement made with the French and Belgian Governments, all scattered graves had to be moved into regularly constituted cemeteries. The letter stated:

> I very much regret to have to inform you that when the grave was opened for this purpose, no body was found. The cross over the grave has now been erected in Cobles Communal Cemetery Extension, south of Bapaume, as a Memorial Cross. I would point out that, as you will readily understand, in many areas which have been under constant heavy shell fire, the whole surface of the ground has been so completely altered. The landmarks and grave registration marks have been obliterated. As a consequence the work of accurately tracing graves has been and is one of extreme difficulty.[93]

Readers will note that Capt Fitzpatrick's body was found at some later time and buried in Serre Road Cemetery, and his wife was notified of the discovery. He was 'Mentioned in Despatches', which came from Sir Douglas Haig, 'for gallant and distinguished service in the field' and he was awarded the 1914 Star, British War and

Victory medals, which were claimed on 19 March 1922, by his widow, Mrs Ethel Berry, Mount Pleasant Square, Ranelagh, who by this time had remarried.[94]

Thomas Fitzpatrick volunteered on the outbreak of war and was gazetted lieutenant, 8th Battalion Royal Irish Fusiliers on 25 September 1914. He was the third son of Reverend William Fitzpatrick, MA (TCD) and Ruffimire Fitzpatrick of 10 Glenageary Road, Kingstown. His father aged 82 and mother aged 60 were recorded living at their home in Glenageary in April 1901.

Thomas was born at Kingstown, on 11 December 1880 and educated at Corrig School, Kingstown. Immediately prior to the outbreak of war, Thomas Fitzpatrick was on the management staff of the London and North Western Railway in Dublin. He married Ethel Frances Macready early in 1900 at the Registry Office in Kingstown. Later in 1901 the couple and their daughter, Ailean, were living at Wavertree in Lancashire. They had nine children: Almeria Aileen Norah, William Gordon Caulfield, Ethel Doreen, Brian Desmond, Kathleen Sheela, Terence Diarmuid, Mary Patricia, Moira Deidre and John Miles. Ethel Fitzpatrick came back to live in Ireland about 1910 and her last two children were born at 12 Mount Pleasant Square, Ranelagh. She was left with nine children and clearly in financial difficulties. Her solicitors, Malcomson & Law, wrote to the War Office on 18 September 1916:

> Her case is an extremely sad one, as she is left with nine young children, whose sole support is now gone; the eldest child (a daughter) is now sixteen years of age. I would be obliged to hear from you as to the scale of pension the widow and children will be entitled to. We presume the highest scale will be applicable in this very sad case.[95]

Ethel Fitzpatrick received a gratuity of £250 and an annual pension of £100 and was married a second time to Arthur Berry. 'She resided at Beulah, 4, Glenageary Hill, Dun Laoghaire, and died at the Adelaide Hospital, Dublin, in August 1943.'[96]

LYNCH, Joseph Edward

Captain, 10th Battalion, Yorkshire Regiment, 62nd Brigade in the 21st Division. Secondary Regiment; 2nd Battalion, Royal Irish Fusiliers.

Captain Lynch's Battalion was almost straight away involved in the build up to the Battle of Loos, which opened on 25 September 1915. They arrived in the front-line trenches east of Loos at dusk on 25 September. Although shot through the wrist, he carried on and was killed in action, aged 35, on the first day of the Battle of Loos, France, on 25 September 1915. His battalion moved from Noeux-les-Mines to Vermelles to attack Hill 70, but there was no mention of his death in his battalion's war diary. The battle was noteworthy for the first use of poison gas by the British Army.[97]

On the day he was killed, 'the reserve 21st and 24th Divisions moved by a night march into the Loos valley. Progress was slow and exhausting (and these units had been on the move constantly for several days already). The Staff was unfamiliar with the ground; communication trenches were flooded and packed with men. Roads and tracks were jammed with transport going in both directions. There were few bridges across shattered trenches, and wire was still stretched across wide areas. Men were carrying extra supplies, equipment, rations and ammunition. At 1.20am, the Brigadiers of 24th Division met to consider their actions for the next morning.'[98]

'Marching to Vermelles and crossing the Bethune-Lens Road where for the first time the 10th Yorkshire Regiment came under shell fire and adopted an open formation. On the afternoon of Saturday the 25th and Sunday the 26th the battalion arrived at the front trenches, as then held by the 18th London Regiment. The Yorkshires enquired of the Londoners what they were doing, and they said they had decided to dig in for the night, so the Yorkshires did likewise, except two platoons of "D" Company who pushed on a little further.'[99] It was here that Captain Lynch was killed.

When he received the sad news, his father wrote to the War Office: 'Please say by whom and where this officer was buried?' A reply was received: 'Report has just been received from Army Headquarters in the Field, which states that the late Captain

Joseph E. Lynch was buried near Loos; Reference to map sheet 36, at square G.C.5. O.' His mother, Annie, also wrote to the War Office requesting details of the cross placed on her son's grave. A reply was received informing her that: 'Durable wooden crosses treated with creosote and legibly inscribed are already in position on, or in preparation, for all known graves carefully registered.' A further letter from his father to the War Office stated that no effects had been received and expressing regret that his son's watch, ring and field glasses had not been recovered. Subsequently, a letter from Cox's Shipping Agency Limited, stated that it had forwarded his 'field kit' No 16973, property of the late Capt Lynch, to his parents.[100]

Letter from J. Bernard Marshall, C.F:

> I am the priest to the 62nd Brigade, and first joined it at Holton Camp on July 1st. It is needless for me to tell you that he was a fine Catholic. Sunday by Sunday he led his men to Mass – a thing that many Catholic officers shirk – and I know that his constancy was of value to the men. They all spoke highly of him. He first received a wound to the wrist, but declined to go back to have it dressed. The work of the moment was too urgent. The shot that killed him went straight through his head, over his left eye. The doctor of the East Yorks happened to be with him at his death, and I have spoken to him. Death was speedy and he never spoke. The place where he fell was at the bottom of 'Hill 70'. And there he must be buried. Although I could not bury your son, I have not forgotten to offer Mass for him and remember him at the altar.[101]

His fellow officer, Capt V. Fowler received a letter from Capt Lynch's father, to which he immediately replied. The following is an extract from the letter:

> I can assure you that it is no trouble to me at all, I am glad to be able to tell you something, knowing what sorrow you will be in. Your son was first wounded in the wrist, just before entering the village of Loos and went on with us to the assault of Hill 70. It was growing dusk at this time. We charged past the troops who had attacked on the morning of Saturday, and it was during this charge that your son was fatally

wounded on the German side of our trenches. We however, got him in during the night, and laid him near the side of the Slag Heap at Loos Pylons. We ourselves were unable to bury any of our comrades, not even our CO and our 2nd in command, who both fell. He was in the best of spirits all the day before the action as in fact he always was. We had a good long march before going into action, but all the battalion did well, although wet through the rain. I am afraid I can give you no hope of being able to identify the grave. I should not like to tell you that our comrades are not buried yet but owing to the bombardment of Hill 70, where we laid our comrade, the burial parties have been unable to work, but I personally could almost exactly show you where he fell and where he was placed but that does not help you much. I only had the chance to say good bye to him about four miles before we went into action.[102]

Captain Fowler was also killed in action in June 1917 following his promotion to major.

Joseph Lynch enlisted in the army in 1905 and was gazetted as 2nd Lieutenant to the 2nd Battalion Royal Fusiliers, which was stationed in India at that time. While serving there he suffered from paratyphoid fever and was invalided home where shortly afterwards he retired from the service. On the outbreak of the First World War the temptation to rejoin the army proved too much and he was one of the first officers appointed to the 10th Battalion, Yorkshire Regiment, in September 1914. He was promoted to Captain on 3 April 1915.[103]

Captain Lynch is commemorated on the Loos Memorial, France; Hall of Honour, Trinity College, and the Great War Memorial, Clongowes Wood College, Co Kildare. Despite confirmation from the War Office that his body was buried and marked with durable wooden cross, Capt Lynch's grave was lost or blown up in the ensuing battles that took place in the area. He was awarded the 1915 Star, British War and Victory medals.

The battalion was formed at Richmond on 30 September 1914, as part of the K3 army and in October of the same year it was attached to 62nd Division. It moved to Berkhamsted and then to Halton Park near Tring. The battalion spent November 1914 to May 1915 in billets at Aylesbury before returning to Halton Park. It moved to Witley Camp in August 1915 and on 10 September 1915 it landed at Boulogne.[104]

Joseph was the son of Michael Palles Lynch JP BL and Annie Josephine Lynch of 4, Clifton Terrace, Monkstown. There were three children in the family, Joseph Edward, James Joseph and Michael Brian. Joseph was born in Monkstown on 26 April 1880 and educated at Clongowes Wood College, Co Kildare from 1892-1897. He entered Trinity College in 1898, from which he joined the army in 1905. He was well known in sporting circles in Dublin and got his colours in cricket at Dublin University in 1905; Joseph represented Ireland on two occasions, firstly playing against, 'All New York', on Staten Island and his second match was against 'Philadelphia'. He also played rugby on the first fifteen at Monkstown Football Club, and was a member of Killiney Golf Club and the Royal Irish Yacht Club.

SHIPPING FAMILY LOSES TWO SONS IN WAR

There were eight children in the family of Samuel Smith McCormick JP and Isabella Marie Emily McCormick (née Gardiner) of, Shandon, Monkstown. Their names were Winifred Eliza, John Gardiner, Francis, Hilgrove, Julie Rose, Eileen Marion, Norah and James Gardiner. Two McCormick sons of the three that fought in the Great War were killed in action during the months of October 1914 and May 1915. The third son, Hilgrove, survived. Samuel McCormick and Isabella Gardiner married at St Barnabas Church, Kensington, on 31 October 1883. Samuel died in May 1921, aged 76, and his wife Isabella died in 1951 aged 85. They were buried at Mount Jerome Cemetery. Samuel McCormick was Chairman of the shipping company, Tedcastle McCormick & Company in 1897. 'The Company's slack "nuts" proved a huge hit across the country, heating houses and driving steam lorries from Limerick to Letterkenny. The company's steamers berthed along City Quay at Sir John Rogerson's Quay. It is said that Republican members of the crews ran guns between 1916 and 1922. When Michael Collins secured de Valera's escape from Lincoln Gaol in 1919, it was a Tedcastle McCormick coal ship that escorted him back to Ireland.'[105]

Major Hilgrove McCormick MC, 3rd Battalion, attached 1st Battalion Leinster Regiment, survived the war. He was born on 5 September 1888, took his BA degree at Trinity College in 1910 and got his commission in August 1914. Major McCormick was twice 'Mentioned in Despatches' in 1914 and 1918 and awarded the Military Cross in July 1915 for gallantry in the field. He was a brave and gallant soldier and a colourful character in peacetime. His nephew, Professor John H.C. McCormick stated:

I really did not know my uncle 'Hilgie' very well. He was about a year younger than my father, who was always very protective of him – he had a webbed hand with only three separate fingers (which did not stop him becoming an Irish hockey international). He was always the most 'popular' member of the family, and I think a good party man – people remembered him years after. There is a famous anecdote (pre-war) about him dressing as a woman and prancing round Kilkee in drag with a parasol announcing he was my father's fiancée (at the time my father felt that this had ruined his own chances of ever getting married). He also borrowed my father's clothes a lot at the time, and always managed to look elegant (something my father never really achieved).

Hilgie had become secretary to the Duchy of Cornwall. The *Argus of Melbourne* (7 February 1936), mentions his arrival in Melbourne with his first wife, Margaret Hune Cliff, and also refers to him in his capacity of secretary of the Duchy of Cornwall, and as a personal friend of King Edward VIII. I know that he played squash a great deal with Edward and also that he deputised for him on a number of occasions – on one occasion at a rather high-church Church of England service where he found himself confronted with a lady who genuflected. Coming from a low-church background he misinterpreted this and bowed back to her before realising that she was looking at the altar and not at him. By the 1930s Hilgie's marriage fell apart – his wife had an affair (I think became pregnant, but also died of tuberculosis not long after). A divorce was hastily arranged and largely paid for by my grandmother, anxious to hush up the scandal. Within a very short space of time he married, Dorothy Strick – I think a sort of arranged marriage which did not allow for love – someone to look after him. The first wedding had been in St Margaret's, Westminster and obviously a 'society wedding' – I think the next was in a registry office. My grandparents arrived and greeted the bride with the name they had been given, only to be informed that her name was something else (presumably the runner-up). Hilgie and his wife then moved into a flat on the top-floor of my grandmother's house in Monkstown and he hardly emerged for the next 10 or more years – which explains why I hardly knew him or saw him. I really do not know how much it was a physical health problem (cancer) and how much that he had simply taken to the bottle'. Major Hilgrove McCormick MC died in January 1952.[106]

Their sister, Winifred Eliza married Captain A.T. Waters Taylor, 43rd Erinpura Regiment, 14th Division, Signals Company of the Indian Army, on 28 September 1916 at Garrison Church, Poona, India. In 1941 Captain and Mrs Taylor were residing at Moat House, Longdon, Rugeley, Staffordshire. Winifred died in the early1950s. The couple had two sons, John and James. John's granddaughter, Sophie Rutherford, married Alexander, Duke of Wellington.

Another sister, Julie Rose, was born in June 1890 and died in 1972. She took over Williamstown House and estate at Williamstown, Kells, Co Meath, when her brothers were killed in the war. Miss McCormick continued to run the estate with the help of her employees, which included Rosie Guerin and her husband, Michael, who was the gamekeeper at the estate. Professor McCormick, stated:

> In her later years she ceased to farm and in the 1960s a number of local farmers were anxious to grab land if they could. They managed to stir up some agitation and involved the Land Commission. At the very last moment my aunt sold the place to a farmer she had known for many years. She was an interesting person and a great friend of Anew McMaster. During the really difficult years of the 1930s she fed a lot of local people with soup made from boiling up bullock's heads (we found all the skulls subsequently!). She also seems to have been an avid Fine Gael supporter at the time – apparently wore a blue shirt for years after, and at some point in the 1930s emptied most of the furniture out of the house for a ball for General O'Duffy.[107]

First cousins of the family also served in the Great War: Lieutenant John Arthur Rice McCormick, Royal Naval Reserve, attached to the Nelson Battalion, was killed in action during the Gallipoli Campaign on 5 June 1915. His profile can be seen in chapter seven.

Second Lieutenant John Eric McCormick (survived), 3rd Battalion Leinster Regiment, of 3, Queen's Park, Blackrock, son of William O. McCormick, shipping executive, and Helena Jane McCormick. Second Lieutenant Victor Ormsby McCormick (survived), 3rd Battalion Leinster Regiment, believed to have been a brother of the above-mentioned, John Eric.

McCORMICK, John Hugh Gardiner

Captain, 4th Battalion, attached 2nd Battalion Royal Warwickshire Regiment, 22nd Brigade in the 7th Division.

Captain McCormick was reported wounded and missing on 19 October 1914, and following a period of five months, his parents learned that he died, aged 28, in a German hospital at Menin on the day he was reported missing. His battalion's war diary for 19 October 1914 did not mention the circumstances in which Capt McCormick was wounded and captured. It did however state that his battalion had moved at 5am to a wood at Veldmoek and at 5pm marched to Beccelare, where the battalion billeted for the night and marched off at 5am towards Menin. It attacked Didizeele, went through last named, but had to retire owing to the arrival of a German Division. The battalion retired to Zonnebeke and prepared for a battle in Zonnebeke district by entrenching.[108]

Letters in his original documents were more enlightening. His father wrote a letter on 3 November 1914 explaining to the War Office that he had received no response to three communications sent between 20 October 1914 and 29 October 1914, in which he enquired if there was any further information on his son. He did acknowledge that this was, 'undoubtedly due to extreme pressure of work'. Mr McCormick, who was pro-active in making enquiries about his son's fate using different sources, contacted the War Office again on 15 March 1915 with some further relevant information:

> Lieutenant Sommerville, now a prisoner in Germany, writes that on the date in question, Capt Taylor and my son, with No 5 and 6 Platoons of 'D' Company were some distance to the front leading the attack. Sommerville joined them later on with No 7 Platoon and meeting with

heavy shrapnel fire he sheltered with half the force on the right of a hedge whilst my son with his men took cover on the left. When the fire slackened Sommerville went to consult with Taylor and McCormick, but found no trace of them, so concluded that they had been captured.

Private Petcher stated to Colonel Pollock, Royal Army Medical Corps that, 'during the afternoon of 19 October 1914 my company was making an attack in the trenches outside Menin. We were lying down in a turnip field just after having made a rush forward. I was wounded. Next to me the Captain of the Company was lying and a little further along I saw Lt McCormick also lying on the ground. He seemed to be in great pain but I could not see where he was wounded. We were all captured by the Germans. I did not see Lt McCormick again. Finally, Lance Corporal Ward, "B" Company, of the Warwickshires told me that Lt McCormick was brought to the Convent Hospital at Menin and placed in a bed next to him. Shortly after L/Cpl Ward saw Lt McCormick being taken out of the ward in a stretcher but did not see him again and does not know what became of him. Lt McCormick's clothes were left in the ward'.[109]

Further confusion was placed in the minds of the McCormick family following an unofficial report from Pte Harris of the Warwickshires, who was in Stevens Hospital, Dublin, suffering from wounds received at the first Battle of Ypres on 21 October. He stated positively that he saw Lt McCormick 'alive and well on that day'. A further report from Pte Patterson of the Warwickshires stated that he saw Lt McCormick about the 27th October. Lieutenant McCormick appeared to be suffering from some injury to his foot and being unable to walk was doing mounted duty with the Transport Corps.[110]

The terrible anxiety for the family ended towards the end of April 1915, when Mr McCormick received a letter from Mr Gutmann, British Consulate at Geneva, to say that, the Commandant at Gustrow (Mecklenburg) informed him that Lt McCormick had been captured on 19th October and that he died from his wounds in a German Hospital the same day. In the words of Mr McCormick: 'I suppose we must take this as final.' The family was beginning to come to terms with the death of John, when, just weeks later, a second son, James, was killed in the Battle of Festubert.[111]

John McCormick was born on 4 April 1886 and was unmarried. He received his commission in 1906 and was promoted to Captain on 19 September 1914, before being posted to France a few weeks later. The battalion returned to England from Malta in August 1914 and landed at Zeebrugge on 6 October 1914. He is commemorated on the British War Memorial at Menin Gate, Ieper, Belgium and the Great War Memorial, Monkstown Church of Ireland. Captain McCormick was awarded the British War and Victory medals, which were sent to his father on 8 May 1919.

McCORMICK, James Gardiner

Lieutenant, 2nd Battalion Worcestershire Regiment, 100 Infantry Brigade in the 33rd Division.

He was killed in action, aged 21, on 16 May 1915 in the Battle of Festubert. A report from his commanding officer, read: 'He died, as he would have wished, at the head of his men whom he had led with the greatest gallantry and fell close to the German Works, which we had orders to take.'[112]

His battalion's war diary for the 16th did not reveal how he died, but stated that the battalion was in billets at Gorre and on the 15th it was in trenches at Festubert. A great deal of shelling took place in the village and all around the Battalion Reserve Company billets. His father wrote to the War Office on 21 May 1915: 'I have your telegram reporting my son Lieutenant J.G. McCormick, Worcester Regiment, as wounded and missing between 15th and 16th May. I shall feel most grateful if you can ascertain for me where he was last seen and how he was known to be wounded as this information would greatly facilitate my searching for him.'[113] He also enquired about the rank of his eldest son, John: 'In the Roll of Honour my son John H.G. McCormick is unofficially noticed as died from wounds, but he is described as "Lieutenant" although in the April Army List he is noted as having got promotion last September and he was gazetted as "Captain" in March. It does not much matter, but the error might be corrected in any subsequent notices.'

Mr McCormick wrote to the War Office on 12 June 1915, acknowledging receipt of Field Kit, the property of Lt J.G. McCormick:

> I have your favour of the 9th inst re personal effects of the late Lieutenant
> J.G. McCormick, the Worcestershire Regiment, and I return the Form

of Undertaking signed. My eldest son, Captain John H.G. McCormick, 2nd Royal Warwickshire Regiment, was killed on 19 October, but I have not received so far any notification as to his personal effects. I wrote to the Commanding Officer and the Adjutant of his Regiment soon after he was reported missing, but I never received a reply. I shall be obliged by your making enquiries.[114]

Lieutenant McCormick is commemorated on the Le Touret Memorial, France; Great War Memorial, Monkstown Church of Ireland and the Worcestershire Regiment panel in the chapel at the Royal Military College, Sandhurst. He was awarded the 1914–15 Star, British War and Victory medals. James McCormick was born 10 April 1894 in Blackrock and was educated at Cheltenham College, Gloucestershire. He entered the Royal Military College at Sandhurst in November 1912 and was unmarried.

WAR DEVASTATES MCKEEVER FAMILY

McKEEVER, Louis Lawrence MC
Captain, 1/4 Battalion Royal Army Medical Corps, 55th (South Scottish) Brigade, attached Royal Scots Fusiliers.

Lieutenant McKeever died, aged 26, from wounds received on Thursday 8 November 1917. It was towards the end of the third Battle of Gaza, also referred to as the Battle of Beersheba (then Biüssebi). The second Battle of Gaza, on 17–19 April, left the Turks in possession and the third Battle of Gaza began on 31 October, ending with the capture of the ruined and deserted city on 7 November 1917. His chaplain, Father A. Parisotti, wrote to his mother:

I was the priest actually present at Capt McKeever's death and will here tell you exactly what happened. We were on the march pursuing the retreating Turks. We had breakfast that morning about six, and marched for hours under more or less continual shrapnel fire. Captain

McKeever showed great courage riding at the end of the column encouraging waverers and helping the sick. It was a most trying time because we were marching straight into a narrow passage which the Turks were shelling and it was obvious there would be casualties.

We enjoyed a rest and had a bit of lunch. Then we moved forward to the attack. Captain McKeever fixed his dressing station in the safest spot he could find. It was behind a hillock big enough to hide his horse and mine with the medical pack pony. Had the doctor remained there, no doubt he would have come through safely enough. However, having made all his arrangements, he invited me to come with him to seek the wounded. We went out into the open and lay down getting what little shelter was available. The shells were coming over now good and thick and our men were massing for the charge just at the top of the hill in front of us. We decided we were doing no good there and moved nearer the dressing station behind a small mound. There again we lay down. I asked the doctor if this was 'good cover' he said it wasn't bad. We then fell to laughing and talking, Mac seems to have the faculty of making one forget the danger. At last the shelling stopped for a bit and so far no one had been hit; most of the shell shaving burst behind us. So Mac got up and said to me, 'come on padre, we will go up to the top of the ridge. The last wave is just going over and we shall be able to see the other side'. He meant we should be able to watch the charge on the enemy's trenches.

We both got up and he walked on ahead. Before we were well clear of the hummock, however, the guns began again. He was just a yard ahead of me and I called to him to lie flat, throwing myself down where I was still partly behind the hummock. He jumped for safety back behind the hummock and just as he threw himself down half on top of me, a HE shell burst and fragments struck us both. I was not wounded. With the help of an orderly I ripped his clothes off and bound up his two wounds, one on the leg and one in the shoulder. They looked so alright to me that I thought he was suffering from shell shock more than anything else. However, he seemed likely to collapse so at his request I gave him the last sacraments. He asked me to say goodbye for him to you and his friends in the regiment. However, I still could hardly believe he was dying. But he knew best. Then he became unconscious and I knew he was right. Having done all I could for him I began to look for a stretcher. At this moment the Colonel was being carried past and asked if I could do anything. He said no, and asked whom had I got behind the hummock. I said it was the doctor and I thought he was pretty bad. The Colonel then made the stretcher bearers put him down and told them to take Capt McKeever. The Colonel finally had to be brought in sitting side-saddle on a horse. I then did my best to get the doctor down to the ambulance, but it was no good; he died before we got half-way. He was not in any way mutilated and did not suffer much. It was quickly over and he was conscious just long enough to make himself ready for death. I buried him myself next morning. Should you ever be able after the war, to visit the spot, I can give you full directions.[115]

Colonel Allen Tweedie wrote to his mother:

I trust you will permit me to offer my very great sympathy with you and all your family in the loss of your son. He died yesterday from the result of wounds received during the occupation of the north bank of the Wadi Hessy for the success of which the battalion he was attached to – the 4th Royal Scots Fusiliers – was largely responsible. Ever since he joined the Division he has been most untiring, conscientious and capable in the performance of duties allotted to him. He never ceased to take a constant and continuous interest in everything that concerned the health and welfare of the men in his charge – I had the very greatest respect for him. In addition to all that I know it must mean to you, the Corps, Division and his immediate comrades have lost one of their most efficient medical officers and one of their very best friends.[115]

His grave is at II. A. 12, Gaza War Cemetery and he is commemorated on the War Memorial at Belvedere College, Dublin, and the Blackrock College Union website. Captain McKeever won the Military Cross and his citation stated: 'For conspicuous gallantry and devotion to duty during an engagement. Hearing that there was no medical officer in the front line, he went forward at once under an intense bombardment and remained in the front line all night attending to the wounded under continuous and violent shell-fire. He set a splendid example of courage and devotion to duty.'[117] He also was awarded the 1915 Star, British War and Victory medals, which were issued to his mother on 8 March 1922.

Louis McKeever was the son of Mary McKeever and the late Peter McKeever, of Plas Newydd, Killiney. There were eight children in the family; Eleanor, Elizabeth, Josephine Anne, Ernest, James, Louis Lawrence, Hilda Mabel and Robert Walter. 'Peter McKeever's father had a brick business in Collen, Co Louth, but he decided to move to Navan, Co Meath, where he farmed. When Peter came to live in Killiney he bought the Victoria Hotel and post office. It was here that he first met Mary, who was the postmistress. Peter was an entrepreneur, and saw the potential for tourism in this beautiful village. He operated a horse driven charabanc that took tourists on a return journey from Dalkey railway station to his hotel and nearby Sorrento Park. Peter passed away in 1887 and Mary continued to manage the business and rear her young family. She married a second time to William Maxwell (pharmacist), with an address at 11, Upper Killiney Road. However, tragedy visited her again in 1907 when William died'.[118] More than one hundred years later, William Maxwell's premises at 28, Castle Street, Dalkey, is still operating as Maxwell's Pharmacy, under different management.

Louis attended both CBC Glasthule and Blackrock College (1903–05) before going on to Belvedere College. When finished at Belvedere, he entered University College Dublin, and the 1911 census reveals that he was a medical student living with his brother James, a pharmacist, at 110, Townsend Street, Dublin, a licensed premises owned by his late father.

His brother, Sergeant Ernest McKeever, Cheshire Regiment, survived the war. Ernest, was gas poisoned at the Somme, resulting in health problems for the remainder of his life. He attended Blackrock College with his brothers. When the war ended he travelled to Australia, but after some time had elapsed his mother persuaded him to return home. He settled down, married Kathleen Griffith, and they resided at Glengarriff, Adelaide Road, Kingstown.[119] Ernest bought land in Sandycove, where he opened a market garden. Caroline Mullan, archivist at Blackrock College and a valued contributor to the book, was acquainted with the McKeever family. She said:

Mr McKeever ran a market garden in the 1950s at the back of Breffni Terrace on Sandycove Road where I grew up. A new housing development was built there about 2002. I remember we bought all our vegetables and fruit there and as children were given delicious little apples from their trees. I remember that Mr McKeever used to make a joke about his name, which I didn't understand as a child – 'my brother is Frank and I'm Ernest' – which meant nothing to me although I knew it was meant to be amusing.[120]

Their sister Josephine married Lt Henry Burke Close, Royal Dublin Fusiliers, of La Scala, Vico Road, Dalkey. His profile may be seen later in this chapter.

James, as stated above, was a pharmacist and proprietor of a chemist shop in Clare Street, Dublin from 1919 until he retired in 1971. He married Eva Monaghan and they had one child, Joan. James died in 1976 and Eva passed away in 1982. Robert Walter was the youngest son and qualified as a doctor, but died as a young man from the effects of tuberculosis.[121]

IMPRESSIVE CONTRIBUTION TO THE WAR EFFORT BY THE MARTIN FAMILY

MARTIN, Charles Andrew
Captain, 6th Battalion Royal Dublin Fusiliers, 30th Brigade in the 10th (Irish) Division.

Captain Martin was wounded twice on 6 December 1915 and taken prisoner of war by the Bulgarians. His death was recorded as having taken place on 8 December 1915, two days after his 21st birthday. On the 1 September 1915, 'his battalion arrived at Mudros with a fighting strength of 13 officers and 487 other ranks. It bivouacked for the night and remained at Camp Mudros. At 1am on 8 December, one French Battalion arrived and took up position on the left of the 7th Dublins. Reports sent out, reported all clear as far as Kajali Village. Therefore, '"A" and "C" Companies were sent forward to hold Crete River. Heavily shelled all day, two companies of 6th Royal

Munster Fusiliers, under Capt French, came to reinforce, bringing two machine guns. They took on right of Crete Simonet to guard flanks. "A" and "C" Companies heavily attacked from right flank but held on all forenoon. Many were unable to get away when Bulgars took the ridge. The battalion received orders to retire to Dedeli at 6 pm shortly before the Bulgars rushed the summit. It bivouacked at top of Dedeli in heavy fog.'[122]

While war diaries did not mention Capt Martin's capture, his original documents contained details of being wounded and left behind to be taken prisoner by the Bulgarians. On 20 December, a telegram was sent from the Secretary of the War Office informing his family that he was wounded on a date between the 5 and 11 December 1915. A further telegram was received with the news that he was now reported wounded and missing. This was the beginning of a long series of frustrating communications between Mrs Martin and the War Office bringing additional stress on all members of the family. On 4 January 1916, Mrs Martin received a letter from Major W.H. Whyte, Commanding 6th Royal Dublin Fusiliers:

> I have been intending to write and give you what particulars I could of your son, Lt C.A. Martin who I am sorry to say, was wounded on 8 December 1915 and is since missing. I did not write before because I still had hopes that we might be able to trace him through a French Ambulance or Hospital after my enquiries through our own had failed.[123]

A letter from Salona, received in London on 20 January 1916, stated:

> It has proved impossible to obtain certain news of Capt Charles Martin. He has not been admitted to any of the General Hospitals. Sergeant Sinnott of his company states that Capt Martin was wounded in the arm on the afternoon of Wednesday 6 December in the retirement from Gevgeli Ridge. He moved to the right of his company and was then wounded in the leg. The retirement continued and a number of wounded men were left on the field owing to lack of stretcher bearers. Sinnott was himself wounded but later he heard that Capt Martin was among those left behind.[124]

Following private enquiries by Mrs Martin, the Red Cross wrote to the War Office on 7 April 1916 seeking confirmation of a report from the American Ambassador that Capt Martin was taken prisoner. Mrs Martin wrote to the War Office on 16 June 1916 referring to the above-mentioned communications and stating that: 'Since then, you have given me no information.' She wrote again on 6 November 1916, referring to letters from various persons who might have been able to throw some light on his disappearance. She pleaded with the War Office: 'In view of the opinion, expressed in letters by his fellow officers and men, I would be glad, now that the anniversary is drawing near, if it could be officially reported that my son was killed in action on December 8th 1915.' A tribute from an unknown source sent to Mrs Martin on 3 July 1916 stated:

> I have made enquiries among the British prisoners in the hospitals in Sofia and found two men of your son's command, i.e. Privates Sayill and Upton. They tell me that in the battle of 7th and 8th December your son displayed the greatest coolness and bravery. On the morning of the 8th he received a severe bullet wound in the leg but not withstanding that remained at his post directing and encouraging his men until the Bulgarian bayonet charge in force made it impossible to hold out longer with the few available men under his command. Then he ordered all who were able, to retreat in good order. He helped some of the men out of the trench and called, 'Goodbye Boys'...[125]

The War Office forwarded a copy of a letter to Mrs Martin from Lt W.E. Gilliland, Norfolk Regiment, Prisoner of War Camp, Philippopolis, Bulgaria, dated 14 August 1917. The letter was addressed to his sisters:

> ...by the way you also ask about Charles Martin of Dublin Fusiliers; I have learned the following facts: He was hit in the arm and leg, but carried on, subsequently he was, as far as I can gather, hit in the stomach, lodging somewhere in the spine. He was picked up on 9 December by the Bulgarians, paralysed from the hips downwards. Everything was done for him but he died probably on 10 December. The above facts were given to me by a Bulgarian medical student, a

candidate officer, who attended to Capt Martin, doing all that was possible in the circumstances.[126]

Mrs Martin responded graciously and with great dignity on 30 September 1917, stating, '…although the details are so painful, I am glad to have authentic news of my son's death. As my son was in command of his company for some time before and during the action in which he lost his life, and was later on gazetted captain, I would be glad to know if he is entitled to this rank in obituary notices etc.? The response confirmed that he held the rank of "captain" at the time he was killed.'[127]

Captain Martin is commemorated on the Doiran Memorial, Greece; Great War Memorial, Downside English Benedictine School and the War Memorial, St Mary's Roman Catholic Church, Haddington Road, Dublin. He was awarded the Order of the White Eagle 5th Class (Serbia) and the 1914–15 Star, British War and Victory medals, which were issued to his mother on 2 March 1922.

The battalion was formed at Naas in August 1914 as part of the K1 army. Following its move to Basingstoke in May 1915, it embarked at Devonport and sailed for Gallipoli via Mytilene, landing at Suvla Bay on 7 August 1915. It moved via Mudros to Salonika in October 1915.[128] Captain Martin was wounded in Gallipoli on 9 August 1915, and a telegram sent to his mother on the 10th informed her that he was in hospital with a slight wound to his right arm. He recovered from this wound and arrived at Mustapha on 26 August 1915. On 8 September 1915 he was at Mudros, from where he re-joined his unit on 2 October 1915.[129]

Charles Martin was the son of Thomas Martin and Mary Martin (née Levins-Moore). The Martins were a wealthy middle-class Roman Catholic family with a thriving timber business, (T & C Martin). They owned a house on five acres of garden that included a summerhouse and tennis court at Greenbank, Carrickbrennan Road, Monkstown. Mary and Thomas Martin were married at St Andrews Roman Catholic Church, Westland Row, Dublin, on 16 April 1890, an occasion that was described as 'one of the most fashionable weddings of its time'.[130] The couple had twelve children: Thomas Shannon, Marie Helena, Charles Andrew, Ethel, Violet, Beatrice, Francis Leo, Richard Denis, John, Cecil Bernard, Desmond Leonard and Andrew Clement. 'In 1907 during the time that Mary Martin was pregnant with their son Andrew, her husband, Thomas, died from a gun-shot wound, believed to have been accidental. Mary died in August 1955 and was buried with her husband in Glasnevin Cemetery.'[131]

Charles was born at Mountown House, Kingstown, and educated at St Gregory's Roman Catholic College, Downside. He entered Trinity College in 1912, but discontinued his studies to go to war.

In the early months of 1916 Mrs Martin still hoped that one day her Charlie would walk up the long avenue to his home at Greenbank. She wrote a letter to him every day, which she hoped to give him on his return from war. Mrs Martin began: 'Since I heard you were missing as well as wounded, it occurred to me to write the diary in the form of a letter. We hope to hear from you soon. Till then I cannot communicate with you and later on when you read this you will know what has been happening.'[132] The diary ended on 25 May 1916, shortly before official notice was received that Charlie had been killed. The following extract is an interesting commentary on how one middle class Roman Catholic family reacted to the 1916 Easter Rising. The reader should take into account that when Mrs Martin wrote in her diary about the Easter Rising, as it was happening, she was relying on unconfirmed reports, rumours and here-say. On Easter Sunday, 23 April 1916 she wrote that it was a very beautiful Easter day, however the next day all hell broke loose in Dublin:

Monday 24 April 1916:
Ethel and Violet started off to go with Aunt Rita to Fairyhouse and had a very pleasant day till they got back to town, here they discovered, to their cost, a Sinn Fein Rising and Dublin was in a state of siege. The General Post Office, Westland Row Station, Four Courts etc. in occupation by the rebels. The furniture of these places thrown on the street. They were held up at several points and would not be allowed to approach St Dymphnas in the motor car. Jack Donelan undertook to drive the girls home. Rita had to brave a barricade and walk home. They got here without much further adventure, but did not know how he was going to get back with the car to St Dymphnas, as a lot of people had to give up their car and find their way home on foot. He got back safely after trying the Automobile Club and Thompsons to put up the car.

Tuesday 25th April 1916:

A very quiet, peaceful day, but we hear (no newspapers or mail) that the Sinn Feiners are still in possession of the GPO and Westland Row Station. They say that seven people have been killed and that the GPO has changed hands a couple of times. A ship came into Kingstown with some troops. We also hear that there were 'Risings' in Cork, Limerick, Belfast and Derry.

Wednesday 26th April 1916:

Still no authentic news, but it appears the Sinn Feiners still hold the city, although I believe Stephen's Green has been cleared. In the afternoon I went to the Tea Rooms. We had a good many soldiers and sailors, mostly North Staffordshire Regiment. This has been a glorious day, it is too terrible to think how it is being desecrated with murders and pillage, for of course the mob are looting the shops. We hear this evening that Liberty Hall has been levelled to the ground, also the *Herald* Office, which shows that there is a good deal of connection with the strike; Jacob's factory being one of the rebels strongholds. Troops and artillery have arrived in large numbers.

Thursday 27th April 1916:

We went up on the roof when going to bed and saw a very big fire blaze from the city. The troops are still arriving. Aunt Marie called up this evening to tell us she heard from Mr Ross that Joe and Paddy Barry were both in Mountjoy Prison. They found their way as far as Drogheda, and there, having no money, pawned their watches, got to town by motor, and were wandering around and were about there when an officer took them to Mountjoy.

Friday 28th April 1916:

A perfectly glorious day, Ethel and I were off to Mass where we met Jack and Leo on the avenue. After Mass we met Sir Valentine Grace. He was very anxious about his son who he expected would have been with the boys, but they told him he went on to Holyhead with Paddy Barry.

The reports today are that Boland's Bakery has been taken from the Sinn Feiners. Burke's Bottling Stores were burning and H. & J. Martins Timber Stores also. I was told this afternoon that T & C Martins had been burned. It is reported that Connolly, Countess Markievicz and Sheehy Skeffington had been shot. The boys marked out the tennis courts so I presume play will now begin for the season.

[Note: Sir Valentine Raymond Grace, was 5th Baronet (1877–1945).]

Saturday 29th April 1916:
Fighting still continuing as fierce as ever in Dublin and fires were seen during the night and one could hear the big guns. Ballsbridge, Haddington Road and Northumberland Road seem to be the hottest districts. Boland's Bakery, one of the Sinn Fein strongholds, has been taken by the military. This afternoon Uncle Tom rang up and reported all well out there, but there had been very heavy fighting at Parkgate Street, north side of town, also that there was trouble in the country districts.

Sunday 30th April 1916:
Still beautiful weather; we hear there is a truce in town and that most of the rebels have given in. Stephen's Green is cleared and the GPO, but that they still have Jacob's factory and the Four Courts, but that the rebellion is practically over as the leaders have surrendered unconditionally. The guns of the Kish were booming all day which gives some people the impression that the bombardment is still continuing. The pickets are getting more strict about letting you pass; one cannot get up to Kingstown even.

Monday 1st May 1916:
We are told that the fighting is practically over in town, but there is still some sniping in the Ballsbridge district. The leaders of Sinn Fein from Enniscorthy, who would surrender, if the rank and file were allowed to return to their homes and would not believe the leaders in Dublin

surrendered unconditionally. They were escorted to Dublin to see for themselves. A party of soldiers, about twenty, have taken position at the cross roads at our wicket gate, belonging to the Leicester Regiment. They are making a barricade across the road taking our carts etc. from the yard to form it.

Tuesday 2nd May 1916:
The night passed quite quietly. There was some rain towards morning but in the afternoon it cleared up quite as fine as ever. I went to Mass at Kingstown, then to the Town Hall to get a pass. Violet, who was wearing her St John's badge, was allowed in at once. She said she would try to get one for me, and succeeded in quite a short time, which was fortunate as there was a queue half way down Marine Road, three deep and it would take hours to get in, in your turn. A letter from Tommy (Lt Thomas Martin), April 16th, they are having quite a strenuous time training in the hills.[133]

Charles's brother, Lieutenant Thomas Patrick Shannon Martin, Connaught Rangers, survived the war. He entered Trinity College in 1912, and took his degree before going to war. He was badly wounded in Gallipoli and sent home to Ireland to convalesce. When the war finished he returned home and married Anne Mary (Dolly) Kenny; the couple lived in Sandymount and had no children. He joined the family firm as its Chief Executive/Chairman.[134]

Charles' sister, Marie Helena Martin, served in the war as a Voluntary Aid Detachment (VAD), attached to the British Red Cross. Marie was an extraordinary woman. She was born in Dublin in 1892, completed her education in England and Scotland, and was sent to a finishing school in Bonn. Marie applied to join the Red Cross in 1915, and was immediately accepted and sent for three months training to the Richmond Hospital in Dublin. She joined the hospital ship *Oxfordshire* and arrived in Malta's capital, Valletta, on the 22 October 1915. On arrival in Malta, she was assigned to a converted barracks on a peninsula overlooking St George's Bay about six or seven miles from Valletta.[135]

On 27 December, she received a distressing cable from her mother saying that the War Office notified her that Charlie had been wounded and was missing. Marie had hoped that he might arrive in Malta on one of the hospital ships, but this did not happen and finally on 29 December she had to write home saying that there was no news in Malta of Charlie's whereabouts. She spoke to officials from the War Office and then phoned Salonika, but the only news was that Charlie had been wounded between 5th and 11th December. Marie had met several men from Charlie's regiment, but the news was the same; he was wounded on the 7th and again on the 8th, after which he and about a hundred others went missing. She was distressed about Charlie's death and feeling homesick. With the evacuation of Gallipoli, work in Malta was very slack and when her six-month contract ended, she left Malta for home on 20 April 1916.[136]

A month later, she was again called up for service, this time at Hardelot in France. In June 1916 she left London with four young women and sailed to Boulogne in France before travelling on to the No 25 General Hospital for the British Expeditionary Forces at Hardelot. In one of the letters to her mother, she wrote:

> Tending men with terrible wounds and young soldiers with the effects of poison gas was difficult nursing. As their battle scars healed their mental scars would run much deeper. These men, who bared their souls for battle, anticipating their fate without any question, were now left with much time to reflect on all the mutilation of battle. They had seen friends' bodies ripped apart in battle, and their fate pulled into question, while the smell of death was all around them. Helping to heal these haunting memories was as much a part of nursing as treating their open wounds.

During her time at Hardelot she never failed to write home. In one letter, she thanked her mother for the tobacco 'such ripping stuff' saying she would, 'keep it for her Paddys'. On 8 November 1916 Marie arranged with the chaplain at Hardelot to have Mass celebrated in memory of Charlie, on the first anniversary of his death, or capture. Her six-month contract in France ended at Christmas 1916. [137]

Marie spent all of 1917 at home in Dublin. She had a boyfriend, Gerald Gartlan, known universally as 'Jimmy' who like her brothers also went to war. One day in 1917 in her local parish church at Monkstown, she prayed to know what God wanted to do with her life. She decided that she wanted to become a Sister rather than get married and have children of her own, because there were many people in need of being loved. She was not sure what exactly this implied. She wrote: 'Next day I went to meet my friend. I wore my new navy suit and white spats. I told him that for me marriage was out of the question.' Many years later, long after she had founded the Medical Missionaries of Mary, she confided that 'he was the person I most loved in the entire world'.

This decision must have surprised her family and many friends in the wide social circle to which Marie belonged. As an attractive daughter of a wealthy family, her position would have been noticed in the seasonal round of races, hunt balls and tennis parties. These social events had been part of the fabric of her young adult life before the war. Major-General Gerald Ian Gartlan CBE, DSO, MC, JP, DL, was attached to the Royal Irish Rifles and survived the war. He died in 1975, aged 86, while residing at Castle Park, Ardglass, Co Down and was survived by his wife Dorothy and two daughters.[138]

In 1918, Marie again volunteered to serve as a VAD in a Leeds hospital for war injured. Then, on New Year's Day of 1919, she sailed for England to get more nursing experience in a hospital there. At first she was with orthopaedic patients, but spent most of the time scrubbing and cleaning. Later she felt she got good experience with influenza and pneumonia in France and had become quite experienced with respiratory problems, nursing soldiers who had suffered gas poisoning. She also began a new midwifery course at Holles Street Hospital in Dublin, and qualified in February 1921.

Marie went to Nigeria where she witnessed at first hand the need for a medical congregation of religious sisters. Then came the years of ill health and other obstacles before eventually on 4 April 1937, she made her vows in a government hospital in Port Harcourt, Nigeria. At that moment Medical Missionaries of Mary (MMM) was born. She became known as mother Mary Martin. When she died in 1975, the congregation she founded had grown to 450 sisters. Today MMMs come from 18 different nationalities and work in 16 countries.[139]

Another brother, Andrew Clement Martin, Irish Guards, served and survived the Second World War. He took his degree from Trinity College and was the last Managing Director of the family firm, T. & C. Martin, before it closed down in the 1960s. He married his first cousin, Aileen Moore, of the well-known Co Louth family. The couple had no children.[140]

Ethel Martin, Voluntary Aid Detachment (VAD), British Red Cross, was sister of Marie. Lily Levins-Moore Voluntary Aid Detachment (VAD), British Red Cross, was a sister of Mrs Mary Martin and is believed to have served in Malta with her niece, Ethel.

THREE BROTHERS DIE AT WAR AS MILITARY
AND SPORTING FAMILY PAY HEAVY PRICE

The O'Brien Butler family was descended from the Barons of Dunboyne. Major Pierce O'Brien Butler, of Otranto Terrace, Kingstown, married Marcella (Ella) Hynes in 1875 and they had five children; Pierce Edmond, William Dunboyne, Charles Paget, James Eustace and Capel Desmond. Pierce died in 1902 during the Boer War, while Paget and Capel were killed in the Great War.

Major Pierce O'Brien Butler served with the 3rd West India Regiment in 1858, and fought in the China War in 1860, with the King's Royal Rifle Regiment Corps. He retired from the military in 1878 and died in 1912. His wife, Marcella, passed away in 1935 aged 84.[141]

Lieutenant Pierce Edmond O'Brien Butler, Army Service Corps, Royal Dublin Fusiliers and Enniskilling Fusiliers, died of dysentery at Wyndberg, Cape Town, South Africa on 15 January 1902, six weeks before the Boer War ended. He is commemorated on the Maitland War Memorial, South Africa and the War Memorial at Belvedere College, Dublin. Pierce (known as Piery) was born on 12 January 1877 and educated at Corrig School, then Clongowes Wood College, before finishing at Belvedere College. Although he was only five feet and six inches in height and weighted less than ten stone, Pierce was an outstanding rugby player, winning six international caps for Ireland playing at full back. His home club was Monkstown Football Club and in 1898/99 season he captained his team to victory over Lansdowne Football Club to win the Leinster Senior Cup. In the same season he helped the Irish team win the Triple Crown. He also excelled at cricket and played most of his games with the Civil Service Cricket Club. Pierce is credited with making an undefeated 157 runs in a victory over Sandymount – a club record at the time.[142]

O'BRIEN BUTLER, Charles Paget

Captain, Royal Army Medical Corps, attached to the 5th (Royal Irish) Lancers, part of the third Cavalry Brigade in the Cavalry Division.

Captain O'Brien Butler died of gunshot wounds to the abdomen, aged 33, on 31 October 1914, while trying to rescue wounded comrades. On 12 October during the 'race to the sea' the regiment was approaching the Mont des Cats near the French-Belgian border. The abbey was believed to have been fortified by the 3rd Bavarian Cavalry Division who had dug trenches across its front. The British Cavalry Brigade made up of the 5th Lancers, 16th Lancers and 4th Hussars were ordered forward (on foot) to occupy the abbey. This was successfully carried out only after heavy fighting. Amongst the German wounded was an oberleutnant of the Leid-Dragoner-Regeiment Nr 24: Prince Maximillian von Hesse (a great-grandson of Queen Victoria). As the medical officer attached to the 5th Lancers it fell to Paget O'Brien Butler to attend the wounded officer whose injuries were clearly mortal. Speaking in very good English the Prince offered Paget his gold watch in thanks for his efforts to save him. He died shortly afterwards and was originally buried within the abbey grounds by the 5th Lancers. In 1926 his body was removed back to Germany. Sometime following the death of Capt O'Brien Butler, his family returned the gold watch to the family of Prince Maximillian, living in Germany.

Over the next few days the 5th Lancers continued in the general advance towards Klein Zillebeke to the south-east of Ypres. The first Battle of Ypres had begun on19 October and the Germans were pressing with all their might against everything the British, French and Belgians could muster to close the remaining kilometres between them and the coast. The Lancers were forced with the rest of the brigade to a fighting retreat in the face of overwhelming numbers of German infantry. There were no rear lines of defence at this stage of the war and the troopers had to find cover as best they could as they retreated. Eventually the line was steadied, but Capt O'Brien Butler had become one of the day's victims – killed while attending to the wounded.[143]

Paget O'Brien Butler was commissioned into the Royal Army Medical Corps gaining the rank of lieutenant in 1907. He was posted to India, where he was promoted captain in 1911. His wife, Winifred, received a letter from the War Office on 30 January 1915 informing her that Capt O'Brien Butler was buried at the cemetery attached to Bailleul Church and the officiating clergyman was Reverend J.P. Maloney.

His brother, Captain Capel O'Brien Butler, sent a telegram to the War Office on 2 November 1914 requesting confirmation that Paget had been killed.[144]

His grave is at B.17. Bailleul, Communal Cemetery, France and he is commemor -ated on the War Memorial, Belvedere College, Dublin. He was 'Mentioned in Despatches' and awarded the Delhi Durbar Medal. The Delhi Durbar Medal was issued to commemorate King George Vs Coronation Durbar celebration in British India, in December 1911. About 25 per cent of officers and men present at Durbar ended up with the medal. He was also awarded the 1914 Star, British War and Victory medals.

Paget, who usually went by his middle name, was born on 18 July 1881 at 21, Crosthwaite Park West, Kingstown. He was educated at Belvedere College, Dublin, obtaining diplomas of LRCP & SI in 1905 and was the first Belvederian to lose his life in the Great War. 'He was a good rugby player while at Belvedere College, but his greatest talent was as a horseman. Paget was an outstanding amateur jockey and finished 5th in the Grand National of 1913 and travelled the whole country to take part in races. In 1907 he was on top of the list of amateur jockeys. About a year before his death he returned to Ireland and from twenty-five mounts, he had thirteen winning rides.' [145]

He married Winifred Mary O'Brien, daughter of Lt-Col Henry Joseph O'Brien, in October1908 and they resided at Weston, Queenstown, Co Cork. The couple had two children; Paget Terence and Pierce. Their elder son, Paget, who usually went by his middle name Terence, served in the Second World War. He was awarded the Military Cross and was twice 'Mentioned in Despatches'. Terence married Tyrell Frances O'Malley and died in 1952, without issue. His brother, Pierce, died at a very young age.[146]

O'BRIEN BUTLER, Capel Desmond MC
Captain, 6th Battalion Royal Irish Regiment, 47th Brigade in the 16th (Irish) Division.

He was killed in action, aged 27, during the Battle of Messines Ridge on 7 June 1917. The infantry moved swiftly against the remaining German bunkers and trenches and as Capt O'Brien Butler approached a concealed German 'pill box' he was hit and died instantly.[147] The young officer fought with other Roman Catholic troops from the 16th (Irish) Division alongside the Protestant troops of the 36th (Ulster) Division.

Earlier in the day, O'Brien Butler's comrade, Capt William Redmond, Member of Parliament for East Clare, died of wounds while leading his men to victory.

His grave is at X.74 Kemmel Château, Military Cemetery, Belgium and he is commemorated on the War Memorial at Belvedere College, Dublin. 'He won the Military Cross on 18 June 1917 and was awarded the British War and Victory medals.'[148] The 6th Royal Irish Regiment was formed in Clonmel on 6 September 1914 as part of the K2 army and it landed at Le Havre in December 1915.

His wife, Phyllis, wrote to the War Office on 29 November 1917:

> I applied some time ago for the gratuity due to my husband, the late Capt C.P. O'Brien Butler, killed on 4 June 1914. He wrote to me a few days before he was killed, that in the event of anything happening to him, I was to apply for the sum of £150, so many days pay for each year to the date of his death.[149]

Capel O'Brien Butler was born in Kingstown in 1889 and educated at Belvedere College. He married Phyllis Mary Jameson, daughter of Charles Jameson, in August 1914 at St Luke, Marylebone, London. They had no children. His effects included; watch (glass broken), dictionary, wallet, a photo in case and letters.[150]

BATE, Alfred Francis
Lieutenant, 2nd Battalion Leinster Regiment, 17th Brigade in the 6th Division. Secondary Regiment, 4th Battalion Royal Dublin Fusiliers.

Lieutenant Bate was killed, aged 22, near St Eloi, France on 14 March 1915. Six other ranks, all of whom had witnessed his death, were interviewed in hospital, where they were recovering from wounds. Two interviews were transcribed and are filed in his original documents. Private Gavin, 4693, Maritime Hospital, Boulogne on 9 April 1915, stated:

> This officer was over my platoon and he was killed by the side of me. He was in the dug-out for safety on 14 March at L'Epinette on the left of Houplines. The enemy was shelling our advanced positions after we had advanced two nights before. A piece of shrapnel came into the 'dug-out' and struck Lt Bate in the stomach. He asked for Lt Daley for

he wanted to say something to him but the lieutenant could not come down to him. A stretcher-bearer came but, Lt Bate died in ten minutes. He was taken to the Dressing Station that night, and he was buried in the cemetery about 200 yards from the Dressing Station that same night. I never saw his grave. He was in the best of spirits before he was hit. He called his servant into the 'dug-out' with him for safety. This officer was very well liked.[151]

Sergeant Melsop, 7103, Hospital Ship, Boulogne, on 19 May 1915, stated:

This officer was killed on March 14 at L'Epinette by a sniper while he was in the trench and was shot in the head and died shortly afterwards. He was buried by the officers in his regiment, who all turned out at his funeral and his grave is in the churchyard at Armentières this side of the dressing station facing the distillery. Lance Corporal Wilmour was buried with him in the same grave.[152]

A letter to the War Office from his father stated:

In my great grief I received this morning a letter dated 15th March from Major G.M. Balen-Smith, Commanding 2nd Leinster Regiment, informing me that my son was killed in action the previous day, 14th inst. I shall feel grateful for any detailed information as to the place and circumstances under which the tragedy occurred, and if there are any letters to my son or any little properties of his at the place where he was last billeted or in the trench where he was killed, which can be kindly secured and sent to me.[153]

His effects, which were recovered and forwarded to his father included, two letters, five blank postcards, leather purse, tobacco pouch and combined clasp knife.[154] Lieutenant Bate was a member of the OTC at Trinity College, before taking his commission in August 1914. The battalion was formed at Cork in August 1914 and moved to Cambridge on 18 August and then on to Newmarket, before landing at St Nazaire in France on 12 September 1914.

His grave is at A.18. Ferme Buterne Military Cemetery, Houplines, and he is commemorated on the Roll of Honour, Trinity College; World War One Memorial Plaque, Christ Church, Dun Laoghaire and the 1914–1918 Memorial Plaque, St Columba's College Chapel, Rathfarnham. He was awarded the 1914–15 Star, British War and Victory medals.

Alfred was the youngest son of Edward Reginald Bate (solicitor to the Post Office in Ireland) and the late Charlotte Frederica Bate (née Bell) of 2, Eden Park, Kingstown. He was born in Kingstown on 10 January 1893 and educated at Corrig School, Kingstown and St Columba's College, Rathfarnham, before entering Trinity College, where he took his BA degree in 1913. Alfred was also a law student at King's Inns, Dublin, and was preparing for a call to the Irish Bar. There were four children in his family; Edwin, Reginald, Edith Florence and Alfred Francis. Following the death of his mother, Charlotte, his father, Edward, married Marguerite Violet, and he died in December 1931.

CLOSE, Henry Burke
Lieutenant, 7th Battalion, attached 3rd & 4th (Reserve) Battalion Royal Dublin Fusiliers, Secondary Regiment, Service No 30466, 30th Brigade, 129th Battery Royal Field Artillery.

He died, aged 30, at the George V Hospital, Dublin, on 1 November 1918. The cause of death was myocarditis, diagnosed while serving at the front.

Henry Close enlisted on 3 April 1903, when residing at 45, Albert Road, Sandycove, and held the rank of bombardier, attached to the Royal Field Artillery Regiment. He was posted to Egypt in May 1903 and on 15 August 1904 he served in India. In September 1907 he was in Athlone, Co Westmeath, where very poor eyesight was causing concern. Following a consultation in Belfast it was found that his sight was very poor, and on 4 March 1911 at Dundalk, Co Louth, he was discharged permanently unfit for duty. His discharge papers stated that his conduct and character with the colours was exemplary and his work, as a battery clerk, gave every satisfaction over a period of four years. His personal effects included a silver cigarette case containing a ten shilling note, a tie pin and silver pencil.[155] His grave is at St Pauls's SB. 37. Glasnevin Cemetery, Dublin, and he was awarded the British War and Victory medals.

Henry's father, Henry P. Close, died in March 1900 and his mother, Frances, continued to live with her family at 107, Terenure, Dublin, until her move to La Scala, Vico Road, Killiney. She went to live in Portsmouth in 1922 and died there in the late 1930s or early 1940s. Nine children were born to the family of whom eight survived infancy. Their names were Charles Stratherne Langford, Henry Burke, Ulick, Alan Parker, Frances Mary, Richard Burke, Mary Lousia and Eveline.

Henry was born on 18 May 1883, at Rathmines in Dublin. He married Josephine Anne (née McKeever), a sister of Capt Louis McKeever MC, a doctor attached to the Royal Army Medical Corps, who fell in the war. Their wedding ceremony took place at the Roman Catholic Church, Ballybrack, on 29 August 1915, and the couple resided at Plas Newydd, Killiney. They had two children, Carmel Mary Teresa and Hilda Mary Henrietta.

Josephine's brother, Capt Louis McKeever MC is profiled earlier in this chapter. Noel Kidney, grandson of Lt Henry Burke Close, wrote the following essay about how he discovered the story of his grandfather:

THE PICTURE ON THE MANTELPIECE

My mother had never known her father. His faded photograph in British Army uniform sat on our mantelpiece beside a large bronze plaque inscribed, 'He died for honour and for valour.' Granny seldom spoke about her husband and his life, which even with the fertile imagination of a grandson seeking a mark of bravery or distinction at war remained something of a mystery.

A few years ago staying with friends in Kew in London I visited the National Archives. I knew his regiment and the date of his death and I was soon holding the service record of Captain Henry Burke Close of the Royal Dublin Fusiliers. This comprised of three yellowed document folders.

The first folder, to my surprise, told the story of a nineteen-year-old man from Dun Laoghaire who had joined the Army in England in 1897 as a gunner and remained there until 1911. Henry's father was a barrister living in Dublin, and we can only imagine what family upheaval caused him to leave home and enlist at such an early age. He emigrated briefly to Canada, returning to Dublin in 1914, when he met my grandmother. Three weeks after a marriage, unsupported by his family, he received a wartime commission as a lieutenant in the Royal Dublin Fusiliers and in early 1916 Henry was sent to the front in France and Belgium.

The second folder goes on to record Henry being invalided from the trenches to a Dublin hospital with gastroenteritis, a not uncommon and serious illness at the time. Documents in terse longhand, record over a period, medical board assessments of Henry as unfit for service. As his health improved he was assigned to training duties at Mullingar Barracks where my mother was born in 1917. The following year, now deemed fit again for active service, he again left Dublin for the front. He suffered a heart attack while embarking on a troopship and was returned to Dublin where he died at George V Hospital, Dublin, and the story goes, while playing poker.

The third folder contained letters exchanged between my grandmother, seeking a pension and the War Office in London. There is a sharp contrast between her pleading in tiny handwriting on both sides of small sheets of writing paper, seeking funds for food, clothing and medicines for her two daughters and the dispassionate adjudication of War Office officials. They took the view that her husband had died as a result of illness and not on active service and that she was not as a result entitled to a war widow's pension.

Yeats' 'terrible beauty' had been born and the world was changing. Henry's widow, now living with her two daughters in Dun Laoghaire without support from her husband's family, both distanced by the British War Office and unrecognised by the Irish Free State. By granny's account it was only with the timely and effective intervention, in late 1919, of Emmet Dalton, a friend of Henry's and a former officer in the British Army, was a modest pension secured. Three years later Dalton, on a summer's day in Béal na Bláth in 1922 was to hold the dying Michael Collins in his arms and later became a General in the Free State Army. Henry's story, which came to life for me looking through the yellowed folders in Kew, is one of thousands of Irishmen lost in the rapidly changing sands of that time. I now have some understanding as to why, in her fifty-four years as his widow, my grandmother left to our imagination the story of the man in the uniform on the mantelpiece.[156]

ANOTHER MONKSTOWN FAMILY LOSES TWO SONS

Reverend Canon John Clarence Dowse MA, rector of the Church of Ireland, Monkstown and his wife, Jane Henrietta Dowse (née Boxwell), lived at Seafield

Lodge, Monkstown. They had five children: John Cecil, Henry Harvey, Charles Edward, Edith Mary and Richard Victor. Their eldest son, Major-General John Cecil Alexander Dowse MC, MB, CBE, CB, Royal Army Medical Corps, took his MB degree at Trinity College in 1914 and immediately joined the Royal Army Medical Corps for service in France. While a lieutenant he was 'Mentioned in Despatches' by Viscount French and was awarded the Military Cross in 1916 with bar in 1918. He married Mabel Todd and they had one son, Peter, who served in the Royal Air Force during the Second World War. John played Rugby with Monkstown Football Club and won three caps for Ireland in the 1913–14 season, before the Five Nations Championship was interrupted for the duration of the war.

During the Second World War he became Inspector of Medical Forces in the Middle East, Commandant of the Royal Army Medical College in 1943, and was promoted to the position of Major-General. He was appointed CBE in 1942 and CB four years later. In 1948 the Grand Cross of the Order of the Phoenix was conferred on him by the King of the Hellenes, in recognition of distinguished service in the cause of the Allies. He was honorary surgeon to the King in the years, 1946 to 1950. Major-General Dowse retired from the army in 1949 and died in August 1964 leaving a widow, son Peter, and two grand-daughters, Jennifer and Wendy.[157]

Richard Victor, Royal Navy, also survived the war. Having spent two years of his medical training at Trinity College he decided to interrupt his studies and join the Navy where he spent another two years as surgeon probationer on HMS *Wincote*. At some stage following his appointment, the *Wincote* narrowly escaped being torpedoed in the English Channel. Later he was in Halifax, Nova Scotia, shortly after the explosion there, when one tenth of the city was devastated by a collision between a French steamer carrying 3000 tons of TNT and a Norwegian ship carrying relief supplies to Belgium. Richard was born June 1897 and his early education was at Trent College in Derbyshire, followed by entry to Trinity College, where he took his degrees. When war was over he returned to his medical studies and fully qualified as a doctor. He worked at the Adelaide Hospital in Dublin, while his wife, Ellen, was training at the nearby Orthopaedic Hospital and they became engaged. The couple had known each other since childhood and were married in 1924, having four children: Ellen Elizabeth, John Richard, Hugh Graham and David William James. In the early 1930s, Dr Dowse decided, like his brother, to specialise in midwifery and was assistant master in the Rotunda Hospital, Dublin, from 1934–1937. The Dowse family moved to Ceylon in 1938, where it lived for more than twenty years.

With the Second World War raging in Singapore and Ceylon, Ellen moved to Kenya with three of her children and lived for a time in Nairobi. Ellen returned to Ceylon for a short period, but when the war was over they settled in Kenya. In 1964 Dr Dowse moved with his family to Uganda for four years, where he was the doctor for Kilembe Copper Mines until he retired with ill-health in 1968. He returned to Ireland in 1969 and died at his home in Courtmacsherry, Co Cork in 1973, aged 76. Ellen died in 1977.[158]

The only girl in the family, Edith Mary, lived to be over 106 years and in the year 2000 President Mary McAleese presented a silver Millenium Medal to all those who had lived through three centuries.[159] A nephew of Reverend Canon Dowse, Lt William A.C. Dowse, 11th Battalion Cheshire Regiment, died at the Battle of the Somme on 3 July1916. He was the son of Dr Thomas J. Dowse and K.E. Dowes of 14, Lower George's Street, Wexford.

DOWSE, Henry Harvey

Lieutenant, 139th Squadron Royal Air Force. Secondary Regiment, 7th Battalion, 'D' Company, (the 'Pals') Royal Dublin Fusiliers.

Lieutenant Dowse died in hospital, aged 24, from pneumonia on 10 November 1918, just hours before the armistice. His death followed wounds received when flying as a gunner in a Bristol FE2B, which crash-landed, having been shot down over Italy on 30 October 1918.[160] His father, Reverend Canon Dowse, was about to deliver his thanksgiving sermon at the end of the war when he received a telegram informing him that a second son, Henry, had died on 10 November 1918.[161]

His grave is at II. A. 7. Staglieno Cemetery, Genoa, Italy and he is commemorated on the War Memorial, Monkstown Church of Ireland; Great War Memorial, Trent College, Derbyshire, and Hall of Honour, Trinity College. He was awarded the 1914–15 Star, British War and Victory medals.

Henry enlisted in the 'Pals' Battalion of the 7th Royal Dublin Fusiliers in 1914 with the rank of private and was later promoted to sergeant. On 7 September 1915, he was seriously wounded in the chest and invalided out of Gallipoli. When he recovered, he joined the Army Service Corps, but 'finding it too boring' (as his sister Edith recalls) he joined the Royal Flying Corps, later to become the Royal Air Force.[162] He received his commission on 13 February 1916 as second lieutenant and in the summer of

1917 he was promoted to full lieutenant. Henry Dowse began his education at Trent College, Derbyshire, and entered Trinity College in 1912, before joining the army. He was single.

DOWSE, Charles Edward

Lance Corporal, Service No 14185, 7th Battalion, 'D' Company, (the 'Pals') Royal Dublin Fusiliers, 30th Brigade in the 10th (Irish) Division.

On the 16 August his battalion made two counter attacks but their success was only temporary, the Turks being in great force. He was shot in the head and killed aged 21, while storming the Kiretch Tepe Sirt Ridge on 16 August 1915.[163] His brother, Richard said that: 'his height, 6ft 2ins, made him an easy target'. On the same day, 25 other 'Pals' of 'D' Company were killed in action and a further seventeen wounded.[164]

> The 6th and 7th Battalions of the Royal Dublin Fusiliers arrived off Suvla Beach, on the Gallipoli Peninsula before dawn on 7 August 1915 and the 'Pals' Company landed 239 men; nine days later 131 were dead. In spite of incredible bravery, the men could not compete against the superior number of Turks who, unlike them, were familiar with the terrain and the heat, and had excellent leadership. The Turks held the higher ground and picked off the soldiers easily as they advanced up the ridge with no cover.[165]

He is commemorated on the Helles Memorial, Turkey; Great War Memorial, Monkstown Church of Ireland and the Great War Memorial, Trent College, Derbyshire, England. Lance Corporal Dowse was awarded the 1914–15 Star, British War and Victory medals, which were sent to his father in March 1922.

Charles left school at Trent College, Derbyshire, in 1913, and when the call to arms came, he was staying with cousins in the country, learning the basics of farming with a view to emigrating to Canada and taking up the farming life there. He was a member of the OTC at Trent College and was single.[166]

GOODBODY, Owen Frederick

Lieutenant, 72nd Field Company, Royal Engineers in the 13th Division.

Lieutenant Goodbody contracted enteric fever while serving in Gallipoli in 1915 and was evacuated to Egypt where he died, aged 24, at the No 15 General Hospital on 20 October 1915. His family received a telegram from the Secretary of the War Office on 15 September 1915, which stated that: 'Lt Goodbody, was admitted to No 15 General Hospital, Alexandria, on 14 September 1915, with suspected enteric. Condition not serious. Progress will be reported.'[167]

His grave is at Q. 533, Alexandria (Chatby) Military War Memorial cemetery Chatby, Alexandria, Egypt and he is commemorated on the Roll of Honour, Trinity College, Dublin and the Great War Memorial Plaque, Heuston Station, Dublin. He was awarded the 1915 Star, British War and Victory medals.

Owen Goodbody received his commission with the Royal Engineers in November 1914. His original documents record that his effects included, silver wrist watch and a silver cigarette case. His father received a letter from the Military Secretary on 27 April 1916, which confirmed that his son was buried at Chatby Military Memorial Cemetery and that the Reverend A.J. Oliphant officiated.[168]

He was the son of Jonathan Goodbody (stockbroker), and Ellen P. Goodbody, of Pembroke House, Blackrock. There were six children in the family: Owen Frederick, Denis, Marjorie Ellen, Lydia Kathleen, Barclay Clibborn and Rachel Constance. His great-nephew, Rob Goodbody, stated:

> As Quakers, my family would always have stood against armed conflict and would not have joined the armed forces. Unfortunately, I never asked anyone in my grandparents' generation what was the family reaction to Owen joining up. My mother supposed that he joined to help in the defence of small nations, but as she was only married into the family she had no knowledge of it. My aunt told me that she never asked either, and was as puzzled as I am, though she believes that her grandmother was emotionally damaged by Owen's death and was never the same again. In Michael Goodbody's book on the history of the family he said that the older generation would have been against involvement in the armed forces, though less so in the younger generation. He cites a report of a recruitment meeting that had appeared in the *Irish Times,* and which listed three members of the family in attendance, including Owen's father, Jonathan Goodbody. This strongly suggests that Owen Goodbody's immediate family were in favour of recruitment.[169]

Owen was born in 1891, entered Trinity College, where he took his BAI degree in 1912, and was employed as an engineer with Great Southern Railways. He was unmarried and a member of Stillorgan Park Golf Club.

His brother, Denis Goodbody, Friends Ambulance Unit, 1914–1919, also served and survived the conflict. He was born in 1892 and was employed as a stockbroker in the family firm. Denis married Olive C. Wilkinson and they had five children. Rob Goodbody stated: 'My grandfather died in 1971 when I was 21 and I was not aware during his lifetime that he had served. In later years I gathered that he was quite traumatised by his experiences at Dunkirk, and he never spoke about it'.[170] The following explanation may be one of the reasons why Denis Goodbody was traumatised:

> The Friends' Ambulance Unit provided a large proportion of the staff at the Queen Alexandra Hospital, Malo-les-Bains, Dunkirk. It was a small hospital of 200 beds and they didn't take in wounded, but local sick of all nationalities and any accident cases in the local area. The hospital was subject to much enemy bombing during the war, particularly in September 1917 and again during the German Spring Offensive of March/April 1918, when it was evacuated (and with several Military Medals to the nursing staff). So I imagine that the problems were, in the main, related to enemy action from the air.[171]

ONLY SONS KILLED IN TWO WORLD WARS

JULIAN, Ernest Lawrence
Lieutenant, 7th Battalion, 'D' Company, (the 'Pals') Royal Dublin Fusiliers, 30th Brigade in the 10th (Irish) Division. Previously, Private, Service No 14248, Royal Dublin Fusiliers.

He was seriously wounded, when he was shot in the back during the attack on Chocolate Hill, on 7 August 1915, and died two days later, aged 36, aboard the hospital ship, HMHS *Valdivia*, in Gallipoli. Lieutenant Julian's servant, Private W.H. Pannell, wrote to his mother, Mrs Margaret Julian, on 23 August 1915, from the Mustapha Convalescent Hospital, Alexandria, Egypt, where he was recovering from a bullet wound:

I was your son's servant from the time he was in England, up to the time he was removed to the hospital ship, and I am writing to let you know how he was wounded, also how I disposed of his personal belongings, which I took charge of after he was hit. We landed early in the morning and advanced all day under heavy shell fire.

Lieutenant Julian was hit just before sundown, leading his platoon in the final rush which captured the first hill. He was shot through the body; the bullet entered below his heart and came out at the back of his shoulder. As we were so close to the enemy and under a heavy fire it was impossible to move him to the field hospital until after night fall, but everything possible was done to ease him by myself and Lt Clover. I myself, got a bullet in my foot just before Lt Julian was hit, but I was able to stay by him and give him what medical comforts we had with us. Before daylight on the 8th the stretcher bearers reached us, and we got him down to the beach where the ambulance people took him in charge. He was taken off to the hospital ship *Valdivia* where he died on the morning of the 9th. I myself, was taken to the hospital ship, *MacGilloary,* where I handed over Lt Julian's two revolvers, field glasses, wire cutters, haversack and pack, to the medical officer in charge, and later on in the day I was taken to the hospital ship, *Valdivia*. Lieutenant Julian's watches, money, personal property were taken charge of by the medical officer on the *Valdivia*. Lieutenant Julian was in great pain most of the time, but he retained his senses till after he got on the *Valdivia,* and even when lying wounded his whole thoughts were for his men that were lying wounded around him, he was a very popular officer and his loss will be much felt by the whole regiment. With deepest sympathy for yourself in your sad bereavement.[172]

On 7 August 1915 the battalion arrived at Salt Lake Bay at 4am. Half the battalion, under Major M.P.E. Lonsdale disembarked from a 'Lighter' at 7am, landing on 'C' Beach. During the trip, the battalion came under accurate shrapnel fire and there were a number of casualties. The other half of the battalion, under Lt-Col G. Downing, landed at 8.30am. Both half battalions came under heavy shrapnel fire on landing. The half under Major Lonsdale advanced to the south-east corner of Valli Babah. At this point both half battalions stacked their packs and advanced eastwards across the Spit under heavy fire from enemy shrapnel.

> Major Lonsdale's men continued eastwards for about one and half miles where they wheeled to the right and formed the firing line of the attack on Hill 53. In the meantime, the remainder of the battalion under Lt-Col Downing had also advanced and entered the attack. The battalion was subjected to heavy shrapnel and rifle fire through which it steadily and quickly advanced from one piece of cover to the next. Unfortunately, 'C' Company lost its commanding officer, Major C.H. Tippet (killed) and Lt Julian (seriously wounded).[173]

The officer's original documents contained copies of correspondence between the War Office and his mother, Mrs Margaret Julian, concerning the loss in transit of some of the officer's effects. It should be said that the War Office made every effort to locate the missing effects. The items, which included the officer's two revolvers, handed to the medical officer on the hospital ship, *Valdivia*, by his servant, Pte Pannell, were lost, although, Mrs Julian did receive other items of sentimental or intrinsic value. However, her sad, but gracious letter to Mr J.A. Corcoran, at the War Office on 11 March 1916, put an end to the search for the lost effects, she wrote:

> Thank you so much for your kind letter, I feel so very sorry for giving so much trouble and worry now, only for my own feelings, so I want to ask you not to worry yourselves any more. I received all items sent through Cox & Company quite safely, one came in a small sack, which I have returned by post. The only things which I have not got are the things which his servant gave up on the hospital ship. Ernie had three watches so there were two which he wore always. There was the presentation watch which is the only one I should have cared to have and the belt he wore always. I thought he might have had some letter or note of something he wished me to do.[174]

Following his death on the hospital ship, *Valdivia*, Lieutenant Julian was buried at sea and is commemorated on the Helles Memorial, Turkey; Hall of Honour, Trinity

College; Four Courts, Dublin; Plaque commemorating R.H. Cullinan and E.L. Julian at St Ann's Church of Ireland, Dublin and Great War Memorial in the Memorial Chapel, Charterhouse School, Godalming, Surrey. 'Following a bequest from his mother, the "Julian Prize" is awarded by the Law School, Trinity College, to the student achieving second place in the final examination for the undergraduate law degree.'[175]

He was awarded the 1915 Star, British War and Victory medals. His medals were sent to his mother in March 1922, when she was residing with her brother, Lieutenant- General Sir L.W. Parsons KCB, Heathrow, Surrey, Commander of the 16th (Irish) Division, in 1914–15, during the recruitment and training period.

Ernest Julian was a member of the OTC at Trinity College, and attested in Naas, Co Kildare on 18 September 1914. He was posted on 16 September 1914 and one week later he was discharged on appointment to a commission in the Royal Dublin Fusiliers.[176]

He was the youngest son of the late John Julian, crown solicitor for King's County, and Margaret Julian (née Parsons), of Drumbane, Birr, Co Offaly. When the couple retired they resided at Frankfort, Dundrum, and later, at 24, Crosthwaite Park East, Kingstown. The Julian's had two sons; Charles John and Ernest Laurence.

Ernest Julian was educated at Strangeways School, St Stephen's Green, Dublin and Charterhouse School, Godalming, Surrey, where the school's records reveal that he was in Lockites House, between Cricket Quarter (summer) 1894 and Cricket Quarter 1897. He was awarded both a junior and a senior scholarship.[177] He entered Trinity College, where he took his BA degree in 1897. Ernest was a classical scholar and Reid Professor of Criminal Law. Mrs Mary Robinson and Mrs Mary McAleese, former Presidents of Ireland, held the same Chair in the 1970s.

He rowed with the college's 1st VIII in 1900 and 1902 and was captain in 1901. In 1914, he won the Emerald Sculls competition using the name 'E.L. Souspierre'.[178] Ernest was unmarried. He had a fair complexion and was over six feet in height. The solicitor firm responsible for the administration of his estate was, A.&.L. Goodbody Solicitors, 30, College Green, Dublin.[179]

His elder brother, Lieutenant Charles John Julian, Royal Horse Artillery, 'O' Battery, served in the Boer War and died at Vryheid, KwaZulu-Natal Province, South Africa on 6 November 1901 from the effects of perityphlitis. His body was interred at Vryheid. He attended Charterhouse School, Godalming, Surrey, and his name was inscribed on its tablet in the War Memorial Cloister. Charles was born in July 1876 and he entered the Royal Artillery in 1896. He was promoted lieutenant in September 1899 and went out to South Africa, at the beginning of the war.[180]

LILLIS, Martin Michael Arthur
Lieutenant, 3rd Squadron Royal Flying Corps. Secondary Regiment, 1st & 2nd Battalion Royal Irish Regiment.

Lieutenant Martin Lillis died, aged 26, of multiple fractures following air-action on 11 April 1917. He was flying on artillery observation in his Morane Parasol, A 6722, with Air Mechanic Alexander Fyffe, as observer, when he was shot down near Langnicourt, situated north-east of Bapaume, by the German ace, Fritz Otto Bernert.[181] The details of his death were described by his commanding officer in a letter to his father:

> He was attacked by two enemy scouts and was fighting for some time before he was brought down. He and his observer were shot dead in the air. I had the honour to command your son. It is indeed a loss to us all to lose such an old comrade. The whole Flight joins me in sending our sincerest sympathy to you in your sad bereavement.[182]

His father, Thomas Lillis, on receiving the tragic news that his son was killed in action, sent a telegram to the War Office: 'Received announcement today from War Office, death in France of my son, Lt Lillis, Royal Flying Corps – most anxious – further details, and if possible to bring remains back.' A response from the War Office came on the 16 April 1917, informing Mr Lillis that it is not permitted by the French Government to bring the body of a deceased officer to England and the Military Secretary suggested to the writer that Mr Lillis should 'write to his son's Commanding Officer, who might be able to supply him with some particulars'. His effects were forwarded to Mr Lillis through the usual channels. The items included; prayer book, rosary, devotional emblems, cap badge, three regimental crests, pilot's badge, letters, snap-shots and cigarette case.[183]

Martin entered Sandhurst Military College in 1914, was nominated to a cadetship by Dublin University and appointed second lieutenant with the Royal Irish Regiment on 24 March 1915. Having trained for some months, he then transferred to the Royal Flying Corps on 30 December 1915, where he served until his death. He was posted to the front in France in January 1916 and served all through the Battle of the Somme.[184]

YOUNG PILOTS ILL-EQUIPPED TO FIGHT GERMANS

Major Robert Smith-Barry, an Irishman, took over the 60 Squadron when Major Francis Waldron was killed in 1916. 'Although considered a brilliant pilot himself, Smith-Barry was deeply concerned about some of the British recruits being pitched against highly trained German fighter squadrons, he said: "They have barely learned to fly. Let alone fight," he told Major General Hugh Trenchard. At one point, he refused point blank to send replacement pilots over the front line until they had more experience.'[185]

'British pilots arriving in Europe in 1915 and the first half of 1916 were having difficulty performing all the skills required of a fighting pilot: skills that, in theory, they should have been sufficiently trained in before heading to the continent. Many, if not most, could not operate their aircraft safely either in the air or on the ground, they could not engage in air-combat, they could not navigate, and they could not even undertake the task that had originally been seen as the airplane's primary role: artillery observation. By November 1916, as the Battle of the Somme drew to a close, it was clear that the Royal Flying Corps training programme was broken and badly in need of repair. The story of Lt Martin Lillis is one of many examples of young officers who were not trained properly before being allowed to operate an aircraft. Martin Lillis graduated from the Royal Flying Corps training programme in January 1916 with average–good marks in all categories and was posted to No 22 Squadron in France. However, less than a week after being posted, and after destroying two aircraft as a result of unsuccessful solo flights, Martin Lillis was transferred back to England to be retrained. In protest, his commanding officer wrote that "it was an error in judgement to allow him to graduate and that he was found [to be] unfit to take his duties in a service squadron as a pilot".[186]

Despite his lack of training and experience, his bravery and determination were never in doubt: 'on one occasion during the Somme battle, when 6,000 feet up over the German lines, the top of his engine was blown away, and he managed, with great skill, to volplane his machine back to safety'. He was reappointed on 17 March 1917, twenty-five days before being killed. Lieutenant Lillis proved his competence when he was reappointed and displayed enormous courage and skill throughout his service with the Royal Flying Corps and Royal Irish Regiment and deserves to be mentioned with honour along with the many Irish heroes of the Great War.

His grave is at VI. E. 25, Heilly Station Cemetery, Mericourt-L' Abbe, France and he is commemorated on War Memorial at Sandhurst Military College; Great War Memorial, Clongowes Wood College, Co Kildare; Memorial in the Four Courts, Dublin; Hall of Honour, Trinity College, and 'Collegian 1917, CBC at the Front,' the past pupils of Christian Brothers College, Cork. He was awarded the British War and Victory medals.

Martin Lillis was the son of Thomas Barry Lillis JP and Anne Victoria Lillis (née Goggin) of Carrig, Queenstown, Co Cork, and formerly of Glenville, Monkstown. Thomas, of Duntaheen, Fermoy, Cork, began his career with the Munster & Leinster Bank and rose to become its Managing Director. He was Vice President of the Institute of Bankers; Fellow of the Royal Archaeological Society of Ireland and Justice of the Peace for the city of Cork. Mr Charles Lillis, a grand-nephew of Lt Martin Lillis, said:

> Thomas Lillis was responsible for the banking house at 66, South Mall in Cork to be built as the headquarters of the Munster & Leinster Bank in 1915/16 and today his portrait hangs in the boardroom there. The marble columns used in the banking hall had been designed in circa 1840, to support a new organ loft in St Paul's Cathedral. The organ loft was never built and the contractor engaged to build 66, South Mall managed to locate the columns in a builder's yard and to incorporate them with two new columns, which they had made to match.[187]

Lieutenant Lillis's mother, Anne Victoria, was daughter of Cornelius Goggin, of St Brendans, Booterstown. The couple married in January 1876 and there were eleven children in the family, of whom ten survived infancy; Thomas Barry, Mary Kathleen, Francis James, Richard Joseph, William Philip, Helen Margaret, Martin Michael Arthur, Anne Cecilia, Clare Monica and Madeleine Ursula. The family were members of the Royal Cork Yacht Club.

Martin was born in Monkstown, Co Dublin on 27 September 1890, and his family moved to Cork where he continued his education at Christian Brothers College in October 1904. In 1906 he attended Clongowes Wood College, Co Kildare for a period of two years. On leaving Clongowes, he entered Trinity College, and took his BA in 1913 and LLB in 1914. He was called to the Irish Bar in 1914 and served on the Munster circuit.

Martin's brother, Francis James, married Clare Renee Wogan-Browne in 1914, when she reached the age of 21. Clare's father, Frank Wogan-Browne, was not in favour of the marriage, causing it to be delayed until Clare reached the age of 21 years. Francis was a keen polo player and hunter. Charles Lillis stated:

> My grandfather Francis was also the leading Roman Catholic stockbroker in Dublin from 1914 until the 1920s, when he sold his firm, Lillis & Harrington, to Dudgeons, the leading Protestant broker. The irony of this story is that the Dudgeon firm was eventually bought by Allied Irish Bank, co-founded by his father, Thomas Barry Lillis. Francis died from the effects of lung cancer in 1931 at the age of 50.[188]

Clare Wogan-Browne's brother, Lt John Hubert Wogan-Browne, was murdered by the IRA on 10 February 1922 as he emerged from the Hibernian Bank with £135. He got as far as the corner of Infirmary Road, opposite the Artillery Barracks, when two men alighted from a car and shot him. Newspaper reports stated that he fell dead on the footpath, when he was shot through the head, resisting attempts to grab his money. He was a prominent member of Lansdowne Football Club, for which he did excellent service, and was due to play for his club the next day. John was a splendid rugby three-quarter back and excelled in the field of athletics, where he won many prizes, especially as a half-miler. He served in France and Salonika during the Great War.[189]

Lieutenant Lillis's sister, Helen Margaret, married Surgeon Rear-Admiral Guy Leslie Buckerbridge, CB, OBE, RN, who joined the Royal Navy in 1903 and was appointed Rear-Admiral in 1932. They had two children, Commander John Buckeridge RN, (1915–1995) and daughter, Anthea.[190]

TYNDALL, Joseph Charles

Lieutenant, 2nd Battalion Royal Irish Rifles, 107th Brigade in the 36th Division. Secondary Regiment, 4th Battalion Royal Dublin Fusiliers.

Lieutenant Tyndall was killed in action, aged 22, at Kemmel, France, on 2 March 1915, following two weeks in the trenches. The official war diary for 2 March at Kemmel did not reveal how he was killed. Captain G.A. Burgoyne wrote on 19 February 1915: 'Last night I took some stores up to a blockhouse behind our lines and took Tyndall, a youngster from the Dublin Fusiliers, who had just joined us, with me. And on 3 March 1915: he wrote: Tyndall was killed yesterday. He stood and fired, some say two, others four, flares from the same spot and one after another. Either he was spotted by a sharpshooter or it was a stray bullet, but he was hit in the face, the bullet shattering his spinal cord in the neck.'[191] In the period, 1 January to 12 March, the battalion's casualties were 3 officers and 15 men killed and 78 wounded.[192]

Joseph Tyndall joined the 4th Battalion Special Reserve, Royal Dublin Fusiliers, on 17 October 1910 and was gazetted lieutenant on 20 April 1912. He then travelled to Australia, but returned home on the outbreak of war and proceeded to join his old regiment in January 1915. The young officer was transferred to the Royal Irish Rifles, 2nd Battalion, just before his death. Capt Burgoyne, wrote to the late officer's father informing him that he personally took an inventory of the kit of his son. His effects assembled and sent to his parents, included; gold wrist watch; silver cigarette case; silver march box; whistle; rosary beads; crucifix; bundle of letters, pictures and fur-lined gloves. It was also reported that he (Tyndall) was 'a soldier to his finger tips', and gave promise of a brilliant career.[193]

His grave is at A.1. Kemmel Chateau Military Cemetery, France and he is commemorated on his parents' gravestone in Dean's Grange Cemetery. He was awarded the 1915 Star, British War and Victory medals.

Joseph Tyndall was the second son of Joseph Patrick Tyndall (solicitor) and Ellen (Nellie) Tyndall (née Devane) of 2, Eaton Square, Monkstown, and previously at 84, Palmerston Road, Rathmines, Dublin. The family also resided for a time at 4, Trafalgar Terrace, Blackrock and Farmleigh, Stillorgan. Joseph Patrick died in 1916, aged 56, and his wife Ellen passed away in January 1940. There were ten children in the family, of whom nine survived infancy: William Ernest, Joseph Charles, Eustace John, Robert Johnston, Cecil Francis, Eileen Mary, Donald Alfred, Florence, Alexander.

Joseph was born at 27 Holles Street, Dublin, on 18 May 1892, and educated at Castleknock College, Co Dublin. His estate and administration was handled by his father's company; J.P. Tyndall Solicitors, 11 Fleet Street, Dublin.

His brother, Acting Major-General William Ernest Tyndall MC, CB, CBE, MB, KHS, Royal Army Medical Corps, survived the Great War and served in the Second World War. William Tyndall entered Trinity College and took his MB degree in 1914. He enlisted later in that year and served as a surgeon in France, receiving promotion to lieutenant and captain in 1915 and 1918. In September 1918 he was awarded the Military Cross for bravery in the field. Following the end of the Second World War in 1945 he was awarded, Commander of the Most Excellent Order of the British Empire (CBE).[194]He married Miss Helen Bianconi in 1918, before continuing his career in the army. He died on 20 March 1975 aged 83.

'The Irish in Gallipoli'
'Tis not for lust of glory, no new throne,
This thunder and this lightning of our power,
Wakens up frantic echoes…
We but war when war,
Serves Liberty and keeps a world at peace.[195]

–Francis Ledwidge

GALLANT YOUNG OFFICER AND RUGBY INTERNATIONAL STAR DIES TRAGICALLY

BRETT, Jasper Thomas
Second Lieutenant, 7th Battalion 'B' Company Royal Dublin Fusiliers, 30th Brigade in the 10th (Irish) Division. Previously, Service No 14160, 'D' Company (the 'Pals') Royal Dublin Fusiliers.

Second Lieutenant Jasper Brett was suffering from severe shell-shock and following treatment at the Latchmere Military Hospital, Richmond, Surrey, his father brought him home to Kingstown in January 1917. He left his home at 9pm on 4 February 1917 to go for a walk and later that day his body was discovered on the railway track in a tunnel near Dalkey, where he was struck by the 10.10pm train. He was aged 22. Jasper Brett was just one of the many young men whose lives were destroyed by the unimaginable brutality, inhumanity and trauma experienced during the Gallipoli and Salonika campaigns.

In the vast majority of cases, a man's breakdown following a trauma of this severity was not due to his own innate weakness.

The treatment for shell shock, known today as 'Post Traumatic Stress Disorder' (PTSD), was primitive at best, and even dangerous. The National Institute for Health and Clinical Excellence (NICE) highlights the difference:

> PTSD was recognised in the First World War in men who had been subjected to prolonged and intensive bombardment, including gas attacks. It was called 'shell-shock' and many soldiers on both sides were discharged to a pitiful existence with severe psychiatric problems. It was poorly managed and misunderstood and, in some instances, afflicted soldiers were executed as deserters.[196]

Shell-shock led to an unknown number of suicides in all armies not to mention the innumerable soldiers who suffered throughout their lives.

A battalion's war diary frequently gave a factual, but usually an impersonal account of day-to-day operations on the battlefield. However, letters home from men at the front could be more personal. In the letter to his parents in August 1915, 2nd Lt Brett gave an account of the action following his battalion's landing in Gallipoli that included information on friends and comrades, and the skirmishes in which they were involved. His letter came at the time of the mass slaughter of his comrades; a very sad period in the history of the Royal Dublin Fusiliers, especially the 7th Battalion (the 'Pals') of 'D' Company. Jasper Brett was a private when he wrote the following letter home, a matter of weeks before being discharged to a commission. He signed the letter, 'Your loving son, J.T. August 1915'.

> We received post this morning. There was a parcel with writing materials and a pack of cards from Mabel. Letters from Pater, Mater, Vi (Violet) and Flos (Florence). All were very welcome. Thanks ever so

much. We have been through it. I will sketch briefly what happened. As you know we called at Gibraltar, Alexandria, Malta, Lemnos and then we were a while at a place I will not mention. We had a march at Alexandria and two at this place. We stayed on the ex-Cunard Liner *Alaunia* all the time and were fairly happy in fact, I may say very happy. Then one morning we were inspected by Sir Ian Hamilton and next day got two days rations and went on to somewhat smaller steamers and proceeded up the Dardanelles where we arrived just at dawn. We landed under shell-fire and one man was killed and several wounded before we landed at all. We had to carry our machine guns. After a couple of hundred yards we abandoned our oil sheets, blankets and packs. We had to cross a stretch of heavy sand about 400 yards or so from where we left our packs, it seemed miles. They had the range perfectly and the casualties were heavy.

When one hears a shell screaming one falls flat; well I fell flat several times, and then one time when I did not, the ground was torn up in front of me; the man in front was wounded in the neck. Poor Marrable was killed on my right. (Sgt Francis Marrable, Brennanstown Road). Eventually we crossed this death-trap. We proceeded and some of the wounded were awful sights. Then when we had advanced nearly a mile we came under rifle fire and one cuddled down very close to the ground. We were with the fourth line of the 7th. Then we had to cross open fields swept by awful shrapnel fire. Colonel Downing says they used more shrapnel at this part of the fight than was used in the whole South African War. I was lying down with a fellow, actually touching him when he was hit in the hip and arm and the ground round me was all torn up, oh yes, it is hell on earth alright!! I got up and ran on straight and it was here I lost touch with the other fellows. They went to the left somewhat. Then I was behind a bush for a long time trying to find the others.

There were nine behind the bush and six were hit. A fellow beside me had his rifle broken by the nose of a shrapnel shell bursting through the bushes and it also wounded him slightly in the face, the nose dropped down beside me red hot. Towards dusk I made a dash to a well and got water. I saw one of our fellows carrying a gun with two others and I tried to find them but could not. All this time I was carrying two cases with oil cans and tools connected with the guns. I reported to Hamilton (Lt Ernest Hamilton), who was taking on a party of 'D' Company but he wouldn't take me saying with truth 'that the gun section would want my case', so I slept a little with Quartermaster Sergeant Miles of 'D' Company in a bit of a ditch. The cold was terrible (and in the day the heat is terrible). In the morning I met poor Darcus struggling along; he had been shot in the rear-end. We bound him up and put iodine (which we all have) on it as well as possible, Miles gave him a little whiskey he had and I gave him some biscuits and I think he would be alright.

He had been wounded at five the evening before and had crawled back. If you see any of the Darcus family and they have not heard anything tell them he had a clean wound, nothing broken, and that it is bound to heal up perfectly and do him no harm.

Our front line stormed an entrenched hill at the point of the bayonet. Darcus was shot within about 150 yards of their trenches. Poor Edward Millar (Sgt Edward Millar, Monkstown) led about half 'D' Company in grand style and then brought up and served out ammunition under fire. He was shot dead doing so and I believe he was recommended for the VC. Arti Crookshank also did great work. To resume my story, I then struck Henry Crookshank of our section and was proceeding up to his position, which was under a bank when I met Archie Douglas very happy having a wound in the soft part of his calf. He was smoking a cigarette and seemed in great form at getting out of it. That night the bank that Crookshank and I were under was shelled and two shells hit right into it, a spent bit hit me on the leg without doing any harm whatever. Next morning we were going up with 'B' Company to the firing line on the left when we were ordered up the hill. Crookshank, McFerran and I (Lt William McFerran, Kingstown) were trying to stick together, we got a bit in front of the rest of 'B' Company and then I said, 'I think we had better wait for "B" here'. A little bit further on in about half a minute a big shell blew up a huge cloud of dust and smoke and again if I had not said, "let's wait here"; we would not be going strong now. We were in the trenches six days and then were relieved at night. We were not in the first line trenches but holding the hill we took, which is called 'Dublin Hill'. We were often fired on here and fired our machine guns quite a lot. I had seven or eight shots at fellows going to a well about 1400 yards away, but did not hit any. Their snipers were sometimes very close up to us but did not get any of us.

I took a couple of messages, one up to the 8th Royal Irish in the firing line along the communication trench and another to our Brigade Headquarters, no danger in either. We are in general reserve now and are getting a rest. I have been very sick these two days with slight dysentery and I think I am getting better. Please circulate this letter as I may not be able to write anymore.[197]

At her London home, his sister, Mabel Brett, wrote to the Infantry Record Office in Exeter on 6 October 1915, informing the secretary that she had called to the War Office on the previous Saturday to make enquiries about her brother, Jasper. She stated: 'We have not heard from him since 31 August. At that time he had just come out of hospital. We have heard since, unofficially, that he is back in hospital with dysentery. We are very concerned to hear something definite and would be very grateful if you could let us know if he is in hospital.'[198]

His grave is at 26. J1. South, Dean's Grange, Cemetery, Co Dublin and he is commemorated on the Great War Memorial, Royal School, Armagh. He was awarded the 1915 Star, British War and Victory medals.

Jasper Brett, in company with many other rugby players, enlisted as a private in the Royal Dublin Fusiliers, 'D' Company of the 7th Battalion (the 'Pals') in September 1914. At the end of December 1914, he transferred to the Machine Gun Section of 'B' Company, with fellow south Dubs, William McFerran and Francis Marrable. Training in Ireland went on until the last day of April 1915, before the 7th Dublins sailed for Holyhead and from there travelled to Gallipoli via Basingstoke, where the battalion was inspected by Lord Kitchener at Hackwood Park on 1 June.[199]

While in Gallipoli Private Brett was recommended for a commission and was gazetted second lieutenant from 14 September 1915. He returned to service in

Salonika following a period in hospital suffering with enteritis. Then, in June 1916 he went to Malta, but soon after was sent back to England to receive treatment for severe shell-shock.[200]

He was the son of William Jasper Brett (solicitor) and Mary Eleanor Brett of 18, Crosthwaite Park, Kingstown. His father, William, died in 1921 and his mother, Eleanor, passed away in 1926. There were nine children in the family: Eleanor Mary, William, Louisa Matilda, Violet Martha, Mabel Georgina, Jasper Thomas, Florence Isabella, Constance Annabella and Robert Henry. Jasper was born in Dublin on 8 August 1895, and educated at Monkstown Park School, and Royal School, Armagh. When he left school he was apprenticed to his father, W.J. Brett, solicitor. He played rugby, on the wing, for Monkstown Park School; Armagh Royal School and Monkstown Football Club. Jasper Brett won one International Cap on 14 March 1914, when Wales beat Ireland 3-11 at the Balmoral Showgrounds, Belfast. He also played in Sir Stanley Cochrane's Cricket team, probably at Woodbrook, Co Dublin.

'THE CHARGE MADE BY THE CONNAUGHT RANGERS AT 'KABAK KUYU' WAS THE FINEST THING WE HAVE SEEN IN THE WAR': AUSTRALIAN CONVALESCENTS

BURKE, John Errol
Second Lieutenant, 5th Battalion Connaught Rangers, 29th Brigade in the 10th (Irish) Division.

Second Lieutenant Burke was killed, aged 25, gallantly leading a charge at Kabak Kuyu in Gallipoli on 21 August 1915. 'At Kabak Kuyu, all out attacks on the Turkish strong points on Hill 60 for the period August 21–28 resulted in very heavy casualties for the battalion.'[201] During the Gallipoli campaign the 5th Connaught Rangers suffered over 70 per cent casualties with 20 per cent fatalities. There were 686 officers and men killed, wounded or taken prisoner. Second Lieutenant Burke was buried where he fell and his Commanding officer wrote:

> He was very much liked by all of us, and he went out to the charge beaming with delight, and waved to me as he advanced to the gap where he charged the Turkish trenches. He fashioned and helped to bring great fame and glory to the regiment. We deeply grieve for so good a man's loss.[202]

The Reverend Father Thomas O'Connor, Military Chaplain, wrote to his mother:

> He went out bravely and cheerfully, at the head of the leading company in the charge. The name of the Connaught Rangers has been in everyone's mouth since then, and he will be remembered as one of the bravest of a fine lot of men who fell that day. Both he and his brother Frank, whose wound I saw, and who had a marvellous escape from death, were always an example to the men.[203]

The *Bray & South Dublin Herald* reported that a comrade wrote to his mother: 'He met his death beaming with delight, and helped to bring great fame on the regiment. Altogether, the charge of the Irish Division in Gallipoli has caused much sorrowing in Irish homes in South County Dublin, for so many of the brave fellows were killed or wounded there.'[204]

> On the 21 August, a short distance north of Damakjelik stood two wells called Kabak Kuyu. These wells were extremely valuable to the Turks, since they too, were short of water, and it was against them that the first stages of the attack were to be directed. There was, indeed, no object for which any man in the rank and file would more willingly fight in Gallipoli in August than a well. As the attack was not to be launched till 3pm on the 21st they had a long wait before them, but there was plenty to be done. After reconnaissance, orders were issued for the attack, and while they were being prepared, officers and men alike were receiving the consolations of religion. For the Church of England men, the Reverend J.W. Crozier celebrated Holy Communion, and Father O'Connor gave absolution to his flock. The bullets of snipers were whistling overhead and ploughed furrows through the ground as the men knelt in prayer and listened to the message of peace and comfort delivered by the tall khaki-clad figure. In a few hours they were to plunge into a hand-to-hand struggle with the old enemy of Christendom, and their pulses throbbed with the spirit of Tancred and Godfrey de Bouillon, as they fitted themselves to take their places in the last of the Crusades.

Here and there a man murmured a prayer or put up a hand to grasp his rosary, but for most part they waited silent and motionless till the order to advance was given. At last at 3.40pm the bombardment ceased, the word came, and the leading platoon rushed forward with a yell like hounds breaking covert. They were met with a roar of rifle fire, coming not only from the trench attacked, but also from Hill 60, and from snipers concealed in the scattered bushes.[205]

Platoon after platoon charged forward into the enemy's trenches and with bayonet in hand, they beat off the Turks.

The Turks stood their ground well, but succumbed to superior numbers. The whole of the trenches guarding the wells, together with the wells themselves, were now in the hands of the Connaught Rangers, who were the recipients of much praise and congratulations from Lieutenant General Sir W. Birdwood, Sir A. Godley and Major-General H.V. Cox.

More than three months later, Mr John Redmond MP was showing a party of Australian convalescents over the House of Commons, and asked them if they had seen anything of the 10th (Irish) Division? They replied that they had, and in their opinion the charge made by the Connaught Rangers at Kabak Kuyu was the finest thing they had seen in the war.[206]

At the outbreak of war John Burke volunteered his services and was gazetted second lieutenant in the 5th Connaught Rangers on 13 November 1914. In the absence of his late father, he was given a character reference by Colonel A.G. Beamish (rtd) of 1, Eglinton Park, Kingstown.

The 5th Battalion was formed in Dublin in August 1914 as part of Kitchener's first new army. It went to Hackworth Park, Basingstoke, Hampshire in May 1915 and it embarked at Devonport bound for Gallipoli in May 1915, arriving at Anzac Cove on 6th August 1915.[207]

ACCOUNT OF FIGHTING ON 21 AUGUST 1915 DISPUTED BY COMMANDING OFFICER OF THE 5TH CONNAUGHT RANGERS

For long periods following the end of the war, post mortems were still being conducted on the various battles that took place in Gallipoli during August 1915. Lieutenant-Colonel H.F.N. Jourdain, Commanding Officer of the 5th Battalion, Connaught Rangers, was in correspondence with Brigadier-General C.F. Aspinall-Oglander CB, CMG, DSO, on 11 February 1931, requesting that changes be made to the various accounts of the fighting on 21 August, the day that 2nd Lt John Burke was killed and his brother, Major Francis Burke, was badly wounded. The following extract from his letter will inform readers about his annoyance at the false claims made by a 'garrulous quarter master attached to the 10th Hants'.

I am afraid I have made a good many corrections in 31. I have admired the way you have worked in all the different sections in the Anzac August fighting, but candidly the 21st attack did not convey anything like the real thing to me. If when you have gone through it, and wish me to write it out plainer than the many notes I have put down, I will do so. Certainly it is necessary to condense the account, but the draft does not convey what the attack was, and the taking of Susak Kuyu was really done by the left company 'D' of my battalion long before the 10th Hants got near there.

I hope you will excuse my saying that when one reads the space allowed to some of the miserable fighting in Suvla and then to the small space allowed to August 21st and 27th which was successful from a standard, that we took our objectives. I think you will allow us a little more space, especially for the 21st August. I don't know who suggested that the 10th Hants took over after the attack on the 21st. This is quite incorrect and untrue absolutely. I kept a minute diary of every event, no one else did. They (10th Hants) did a small attack after dusk I believe behind the Australians on the right, and that fizzled out after Morley was wounded. A garrulous Quarter Master has got a perfectly untrue statement in *Bean's* book, but everyone says how devoid of truth it is. It is totally untrue; no Hants were near me during the 21st and 22nd August, or any other day. They were behind the Australians. The account in *Bean* is not only stupid, but it is all a fabrication of someone's disordered brain. We, i.e. 5th Battalion, were the only troops on the left of the New Zealanders in the line.[208]

Although his comrades buried 2nd Lt Burke where he fell his grave is unknown and he is commemorated on the Helles Memorial, Turkey. He was awarded the 1915 Star, British War and Victory medals. 'Second Lieutenant Burke disputed with Lt J.L. Fashorn of the Munsters, the claim to be the smallest officer in the 10th (Irish) Division.'[209]

John Burke was the son of Dominick Francis Burke SIRIC, JP and Frances (Fannie) Burke (née Burke) of 6, Royal Terrace East, Kingstown. There were six children in the family; Mary, Francis Charles, Louis, Hubert, John Errol and Dominick. 'Dominic senior was born in 1821 at Cahernagarry, Kilreekil, Co Galway, and was a retired 1st class Sub-Inspector, Royal Irish Constabulary. He was awarded the Constabulary Medal for defending the Tallaght RIC Barracks in Co Dublin, during the Fenian Rising on 30 April 1867. His wife Frances was the only daughter of Denis Burke of, Ballyduggan, Co Galway. Dominic and Frances died in 1904 and 1924 respectively, and were buried in Dean's Grange Cemetery, with their sons, Dominick junior (d. 1941) and Major Francis Charles Burke (d.1936).'[210]

John Burke was born on 5 June 1890 and was educated at the Presentation Brothers, Glasthule, and Skerries' Academy, Co Dublin. He was an accountant employed by the Royal Bank of Ireland at Kingstown. Burke was a keen sportsman and a member of many sporting clubs, including Dublin Bay Sailing Club, Wag Club and Lansdowne Football Club.[211]

His brother, Major Francis Charles Burke, Connaught Rangers, 5th Battalion, was severely wounded in the 1916 Easter Rising. He held the rank of captain in the Royal Irish Regiment in October 1914, before joining the Connaught Rangers, 5th Battalion, where he was promoted to major on 18 January 1918. Francis was born in December 1874, and served with the RIC prior to the outbreak of war.[212] The *Irish Independent*, dated 14 September 1915, informed its readers that Capt Francis Charles Burke was reported killed at the Kabak Kuyu wells, however, it was learned subsequently that he was making a good recovery in Guys Hospital, London, following a miraculous escape when he was shot through the head and legs on 21 August 1921, the same day that his brother was killed.[213] In a letter to the War Office, dated 19 April 1920 from his home in Gort, Co Galway, he applied for a wound pension, stating: 'I was severely wounded in August 1915 at Gallipoli and from the effects of that wound I have never completely recovered and was never passed fit for active service.'[214] Major Burke was gazetted out of the army in June 1918 to rejoin the Royal Irish Constabulary and was appointed temporary adjutant of the Phoenix Park Depot in April 1919.[215]

HITCHINS, Henry Mayne
Second Lieutenant, 7th Battalion, attached 48th Trench Mortar Battery Royal Irish Rifles. Secondary Regiment, 7th Battalion, Leinster Regiment.

Second Lieutenant Hitchins was killed in action, aged 36, on 18 August 1916. His battalion's war diary for 18 August does not reveal how he was killed, but in the period 15 to 28 August 1916 at Autille Wood, Aveluy, the battalion was in action each day. His chaplain wrote to his parents:

> It is only a short time ago since he saved the life of an officer who was bleeding to death from a wound. His coolness and resourcefulness under shell-fire were well known to us all, and we mourn one who was loved by all who knew him and especially the men of his battery.

In a letter to the War Office on 22 August 1916, his mother acknowledged the wire informing her of his death, and requested the name of his Colonel … 'so that I may write to him as to my boy's noble end.'[216]

His grave is at III. O. 4. Vermelles British Cemetery, France and he is commemorated on the Great War Memorial in St Patrick's Church of Ireland, Dalkey and the Bank of Ireland 1914–1918 War Memorial, Dublin. He was awarded the 1914–15 Star, British War and Victory medals. Henry Hitchins enlisted in the 7th Leinsters in October 1914 and later was commissioned second lieutenant in the Royal Irish Rifles. He was posted to France in December 1915.

His father wrote to the War Office on 29 October 1916 enquiring about his son's effects, stressing that the presentation watch and beautiful binoculars, or any relics, would be dearly prized. There was nothing in the deceased officer's original documents to suggest that his effects were recovered, although this does not mean that they were not received by the family at some later time. [217]

He was the son of Henry Hitchins, (chief clerk at the Treasury) and Mary Elizabeth Hitchins, of 39, Sandycove Road, Kingstown, and later at Charleville, Harbour Road, Dalkey. There were six children in the family; Henry Mayne, Louisa, Richard Mayne, William, Dorothy and Edith. Henry was born in Kingstown in 1880 and educated at Chesterfield School, Birr, Co Offaly, High School, Rathgar, and Trinity College. He joined the Bank of Ireland in April 1901 and worked as a bank cashier in the Belfast Branch. His brother, Captain Richard Mayne Hitchins, was attached to The King's (Liverpool) Regiment and survived the war.

LEMASS, Herbert Justin
Second Lieutenant, 2nd Battalion Royal Dublin Fusiliers, 10th Brigade in the 4th Division.

Second Lieutenant Herbert Lemass died, aged 19, on 23 October 1916 from wounds received in action at Gun Pits, Somme. On this day at Gun Pits, Somme:

Everything was ready for advance soon after dawn on the 23rd, but no movement took place until the afternoon. The objective having been carefully pointed out, the battalion at 2.30pm 'went over the top' in four waves and doubled up to the English artillery barrage; the companies on the right, being some distance in rear of those on the left, had some way to double before they were able to get up in line, but they got forward in sufficient time to escape the enemy barrage. No opposition was encountered until within ten yards of the Gun Pits, when a heavy machine-gun and rifle fire were met, compelling the leading lines to lie down. They, however, managed to crawl forward and bomb the Gun Pits, and eventually got into them, where very desperate hand-to-hand fighting ensued. The Gun Pits were strongly built and were armed with four machine guns; three of these here were destroyed, and one was taken by the battalion.

'C' Company, led by Capt Patterson, went right through and over the Gun Pits and on to Strong Point, which was greatly damaged by shell-fire, but 'C' Company, pushing on, established a line some little distance beyond the Gun Pits. Two other companies, 'A' and 'B' remained on the Gun Pits, thoroughly cleared them and all surrounding shell-holes. 'D' Company on the right had somewhat lost connection, but a platoon on the right regained touch with the Rifle Brigade, while three remaining platoons, changing their direction quarter left, made for the Gun Pits also. This movement caused a gap in the line of about a hundred yards, led to considerable congestion at this point, and engendered many casualties; but probably the majority of these were sustained in the above mentioned hand to hand fighting, or were the result of heavy machine-gun fire. Considerable fighting took place before the whole of the Gun Pits, Strong Point, and the line of shell-holes were held and consolidated, and the third lines dug and joined up in front of Strong Point. During the battle, 2nd Lt Lemass, 2nd Lt Doran, 2nd Lt Killingley and 14 non-commissioned officers and men were killed.[218]

His grave is at XVII. K. 1, Caterpillar Valley Cemetery, Longueval, Somme, France, and he is commemorated in the Hall of Honour, Trinity College; Great War Memorial at Sandhurst College, Surrey; Blackrock College Union website and his parents' gravestone at Dean's Grange Cemetery. He was awarded the British War and Victory medals. The Second Battalion, Royal Dublin Fusiliers was transferred to the 48th Brigade in 16th (Irish) Division on 15 November 1916, three weeks after the death of 2nd Lt Lemass.

Herbert Lemass was the son of Dr Peter Edmund Lemass LSO (Secretary at the Department of Education) and Maria Patricia Lemass (née Scanlan) of 3, Clifton Terrace, Monkstown. Six children were born to the Lemass family, of whom five survived infancy: Gertrude Mary, Edwin Stephen, Edith Ursula, Herbert Justin and Maria Angela. Peter and Maria Lemass died in 1928 and 1932 respectively, and they were buried in Dean's Grange Cemetery with their daughter, Gertrude.

Herbert Lemass was educated at Blackrock College (1908–1913) and Catholic University School, Dublin. He entered Trinity College in 1913, where he joined the

Medical School. Prior to joining the army he was a member of the Dublin University OTC and in August 1915 he entered Sandhurst Military College, as a cadet, and was granted a permanent commission in the Regular Army in December 1915. Lemass was gazetted to the Royal Dublin Fusiliers and sent to France in June 1916.[219]

His brother, Captain Edwin Stephen Lemass, Royal Army Service Corps, survived the war. He had a brilliant career at Trinity College, was called to the Irish Bar at the age of 22, and practised for some time on the North West Circuit. Family history says that 'when he returned home from the war, the IRA warned him to leave the country'.[220] Edwin joined the Colonial Service and went to live in Tangier, Morocco. He was stationed in Cairo for many years and then moved to Alexandria, where he was one of the leading personalities. Judge Lemass was interested in the reorganisation of the courts in Egypt. He did not return to live in Ireland, but according to his second cousin, Owen Lemass, he did come home to see his sisters. Owen said: 'He generally came to us for a meal and as children our only interest was the range of foreign stamps he could supply for our collection. His Honour Judge Lemass was married to an Italian lady and died in April 1970.'[221]

At the time that Herbert, aged 19, and Edwin, aged 21, were in the trenches on the Western Front, their second cousin, Seán Lemass, aged 17, was fighting the British in the General Post Office during the 1916 Easter Rising. Seán Lemass became one of the most prominent Irish politicians of the twentieth century, serving as Taoiseach from 1959 until 1966. He may have had his cousins in mind in February, 1966, on the occasion of the 50th anniversary of the 1916 Easter Rising, when he was the first Fianna Fail leader to make a positive statement about Irishmen who fought in the Great War, he said: 'In later years it was common – and I was also guilty in this respect – to question the motives of those who joined the new British Armies at the outbreak of the war, but it must in their honour and in fairness to their memory, be said, that they were motivated by the highest purpose.'[222]

Their sister, Edith Ursula (Edie) Lemass served as a Voluntary Aid Detachment (VAD), with the British Red Cross Society. She was attached to the Linden Auxiliary Hospital for officers, situated at Stillorgan, and was mentioned in a despatch by the Chairman of the Joint War Committee to the Secretary of State for War, for valuable nursing services rendered in connection with the War. Following the end of war she became an actress, performing in Dublin's Abbey Theatre and at other venues in Dublin, and also found time to teach elocution.[223]

It was reported in the magazine of the Dominican Convent School in Blackrock, that a team from Sion Hill drew two-goals-all against a hockey team composed of volunteer nurses (VADs) from Linden Convalescent Hospital for officers, six of whom were old girls: Hilda O'Reilly, Agnes and Hilda McDermott, Una Minch, Pearlie Stein and Edie Lemass.[224] Pearlie Stein and Edie Lemass both lost brothers in the Great War.

McFARLAND, Francis John Elliott MC
Second Lieutenant, 4th Battalion Royal Irish Fusiliers. Secondary Regiment, Service No 2207, 5th and 9th Battalions North Irish Horse.

On 22 July 1918, following a raid at Shody Farm in the neighbourhood of Meulehouck near Bailleul, 2nd Lt McFarland did not return and was reported missing in action. He was aged 33. In February 1919 the family may have hoped that he would return with released prisoners of war. When no solid information was forthcoming from the War Office, his sisters, Frances Longworth-Dames and Emily Hardy supported by her husband, Major Hardy, advertised in the press and wrote directly to soldiers still serving in their brother's unit in France. Their initiative brought a response, when in March 1919, Cpl David Clarke MM of the 9th Royal Irish Rifles, with an address at Maytown Terrace, Bessbrook, Co Armagh, wrote with what appeared then to be good news. The report stated that a German document had been found containing the names of 2nd Lt McFarland, an officer named Radcliffe, and a couple of privates. An extract from his letter concluded:

> Your brother was captured on a raid in July and since that we captured a German document and it gives his name on it and another officer named Ratcliffe and a couple of men that is about all the news of him that I can give you. It was sent around to each Platoon Sergeant and read out to the men. They did not kill him. I am only too glad to give you all that I know about him hoping he will soon turn up.[225]

An extract from another letter written by Cpl Clarke gave further hope that he was still alive in a German Prisoner-of-War Camp, it read: 'I could not tell you where the document has gone to. I saw the document myself and I am almost sure your brother is living and well and I am certain sure that you will hear from him before long.' The following extract is taken from a report from Sgt Lockhard, which stated:

> Having seen your advertisement in The *Evening Telegraph* of 2nd Lt McFarland, I was with him about the latter end of July when my company were out on a raid one night and 2nd Lt McFarland came out with us too, but he shouldn't have been with us as he belonged to another company. But he came and done splendid work. When our company got word to retire we came back in the usual way but it wasn't till a few hours after I found 2nd Lt McFarland was missing along with a few more, and there was a party out looking for them, but couldn't get anyone. So I never saw him anymore, so he must have been taken prisoner.[226]

A couple of nights afterwards a strong rumour went round the battalion that 2nd Lt McFarland's body had been found and buried by the Inniskillings. The place of this raid was in an area between Bailleul and Kemmel Hill. Another report from Pte Taylor stated:

> In reply to your advertisement in the paper, I would like to let you know something about 2nd Lt McFarland. We were to make a raid on a post at Bailleul ('B' Company). That night when we were going out 2nd Lt McFarland came after us, and said he wanted to go. Well he went without a shell helmet or revolver. I saw him pull a gunman out of a hedge, and I also saw him up to the time we had to come back to our own lines but he was supposed to be taken prisoner, but I don't believe it for there was one officer found two nights after by the Inniskillings lying dead in no man's land. I never saw him so could not say who it was. Second Lieutenant McFarland came to our battalion from the 2nd battalion, and he proved to be one of the finest officers we ever had. We also lost another the same night, Mr Ratcliffe, but he is a prisoner of

war. This is all, but I hope you will find out something better.[227]
In a letter from the Army Council to his sister, Emily Harding on 19 March 1919, it stated:

> I enclose a leaflet showing the steps taken to trace missing officers and men and I am to say that so far as the evidence in the possession of the Army Council goes there is unfortunately no ground for believing that an officer could be a prisoner of war for so long a time without news of him being received. They regret therefore, that it will be necessary for them to consider whether they must not now conclude that this officer is dead.[228]

Their hope was justified, for they had three replies. But unfortunately, the stories these soldiers told were ambiguous and to some extent contradictory. Nevertheless, some of the evidence led the family to suppose that Elliott had been taken prisoner, and therefore might still be alive. The family then pestered the War Office to follow up certain leads that the soldiers' stories had supplied. Individual members of the family each wrote asking the War Office to do something. They got the Red Cross and other service organisations to do the same. But in the end, no further information was forthcoming. So reluctantly, fourteen months after the initial bad news, the family accepted that Elliott was dead.[229]

He is commemorated on Panel 140 to 141, Tyne Cot Memorial, Belgium; Hall of Honour, Trinity College, and his parents' grave in Carnmoney Cemetery, Belfast. Second Lieutenant McFarland was wounded in a skirmish with Turkish forces on 10 March 1918 and was recommended for the Military Cross on 15 November 1918. His citation read, 'For conspicuous gallantry and devotion to duty. Though wounded early in a difficult position under heavy machine gun fire, he continued to encourage his platoon. Wounded again, he stayed till the situation was cleared.'[230] He was also awarded the British War and Victory medals.

His mother received a letter from the War Office in October 1919 enquiring how she wished to receive his posthumously awarded Military Cross. The letter stated: 'Do you want it publicly presented to you on his Majesty's behalf on a parade of troops by a General Officer Commanding at a convenient Military Centre, or whether you wish it to be sent to you by post, or will you call for it at the War Office?'[231] In her profound grief, there was only one real option, she requested that the award be posted to her.

Elliott (as his family knew him) enlisted in the ranks with the North Irish Horse on 28 June 1916 and was posted to France in November 1916. In February 1917 he returned to England to train for a commission at Lichfield, and was gazetted to the Royal Irish Fusiliers on 31 July 1917. He left Ireland on 5 November 1917 and was posted to Egypt with the 4th Battalion, but was attached to the 5th Battalion, where he took part in General Allenby's successful campaign, driving the Turkish forces out of Palestine and Syria. It was here that he was wounded and following a period of recuperation he was posted to France on 2 June 1918 with the 9th Battalion.[232]

Elliott was the son of Dr Frank McFarland and Mary Georgina (née Elliott) of Dunloe House, Carrickbrennan Road, Monkstown. His father, who passed away in 1912, was a Surgeon Major with the Royal Army Medical Corps, stationed in India, and his mother was the daughter of a Dublin solicitor. The McFarlands had six children: Edward William, Francis John Elliott, Mary, Frances Longworth-Dames, Emily Caroline Hardy and Lucinda Annie.

He was born on the Antrim Road, Belfast, on 11 August 1885 and may have been educated privately prior to entering Trinity College in 1903. Here, he graduated with BA and BAI degrees in 1908 and 1909. 'On finishing college he entered the colonial service where he served for a period of three years in West Africa. His eldest brother, Edward, had enlisted in the Army Chaplains' Department and he probably found himself under pressure from the families of other Irish Protestants whose young males had joined the British army, many of whom had already perished. Elliott enlisted.'[233] He drafted a letter to his mother a short time before he died which was deposited with his regimental command, and would be available to be posted to his family in the event of his death. The following is an extract:

> If you ever read this, which I feel sure you won't as I don't think I will
> be killed. I do hope you will all do your very best not to fret too much.
> I am not afraid to die – and I know that will be a comfort to you all – I
> have not seen many men dead, but I saw a certain number in Palestine
> and the more I think about it, the more convinced I am that this life is
> nothing to what will come and I know when afterwards we look back
> on sorrow like death we will see that we were wrong to fret. Darlings
> (Mother, Nie, May, Dim, Toby and Teddie) I wish I could express how

I do love you all, and how happy you have all made my life, and how much I think of your goodness to me and your great unselfishness and generosity. Thank you all – oh so much. I know how much you all love me and that makes me happy.[234]

His family were quite unable to follow his wishes about 'not fretting'. They were devastated by their grief. Elliott's bedroom was turned into a kind of shrine. No one ever slept in it afterwards and all his belongings were left there untouched. A trunk under his bed still had his dinner jacket and starched shirt and cuff-links and other items in it for my mother, Alice, and her sister, Dorothy, to deal with. I have (and use) his silver cuff-links engraved with his initials EMcF; probably a 21st birthday present; paltry remains from a life destroyed in 'this awful war'. The medal was duly framed and hung in the drawing room of Dunloe, together with a tinted photograph of Elliott in his army uniform. It was still hanging there in 1963, when I helped Alice and Dorothy clear the house after Elliott's last surviving sister, Carrie (Dim to Elliott) had to go into a nursing home.[235]

Elliott's brother, Captain Edward William McFarland MC, Chaplain, 4th Class, Army Chaplains' Department survived the war and was awarded the Military Cross for bravery in the field. 'He was nine years older than Elliott and graduated from Trinity College with BA and MA degrees. When war finished he served as rector of Derryvullan, Co Fermanagh and married Beryl Grey, with whom he had one daughter.'[236] He died in 1946 and is mentioned in the *University of Dublin – War List 1922*.

Emily Caroline married Major Arthur Hardy, late 5th Battalion, Royal Irish Rifles, who died in 1931, and Emily passed away in 1939. They resided at Seafield, Booterstown.

THREE McFERRAN BROTHERS SERVE IN WAR

McFERRAN, Thomas Malcolm
Second Lieutenant, 1st Squadron Royal Flying Corps. Secondary Regiment, Royal Dublin Fusiliers – General List.

In 1917, the average life expectancy of a pilot arriving at the front was three weeks. Second Lieutenant Thomas McFerran was killed in action, aged 19, on 21 June 1917, when he was shot down while operating his Nieuport 17 single-seater B3495, two kms north-east of Becelaere in Belgium. When he was reported missing his family began investigations to ascertain if he was killed or taken a prisoner of war. One report, dated 20 October 1917, from the Prisoners of War Department, London, stated:

The following entry appeared on a list of British air losses occurring in June 1917, which was published in the *Norddeutsche Allgemeine Zeitung* on 17 July 1917. 'Nieuport one-seater B3495 (name of occupant) Jaerrat. Prisoner. In view of the foregoing it would appear that some definite information as to this officer's fate should be in possession of the German Authorities, and I am to request that a communication may be addressed through diplomatic channels to the German Government asking if such information can be given'.[237]

The following letter from the War Office to Mr McFerran on 22 October 1917 may have caused some confusion in the minds of his family, it stated:

In reply to your letter of 3 October 1917, and previous correspondence concerning Lt T.M. McFerran, I am directed to inform you that as this officer was flying in a machine No B.3495 when reported missing there can be no doubt that the statement in the *Norddeutsche Allgemeine Zeitung* communicated to you, was intended to refer to him. It has, however, been found that errors have occasionally occurred in the statements to the fate of officers included in the lists of British air losses published in the German press, and there can be no doubt that an error has occurred in this case.[238]

Mr McFerran wrote to the War Office on 24 October 1917, acknowledging an earlier communication and stating: 'Now that Becelaere is well within our lines I should be glad to know if there is an authority in or near that place that would have enquiries or search made for any record of my son or for his grave?' A letter from the War Office on 1 January 1920, stated: 'I am to add that it is regretted that no report as to the location of the officer's grave has yet been received by the Director General, Graves Registration and Enquiries.' This letter also stated that a report from a German officer concerning the death of Lt McFerran had been received from the German government and would be forwarded to Mr McFerran. When this letter was received by the family it put an end to the speculation about the young officer's fate. The German officer, Ludger Wewer, wrote:

> I was myself at the place where he was shot down, and ascertained the identity of the occupant as Lt McFerran. Lieutenant McFerran was dead; the cause of death was clearly an instantaneous shot through the heart. The roof of his skull was knocked off by the impact. The dead man was clean-shaven and apparently youthful. He was shot down after a short combat at the height of 3000 metres. The corpse was carried away in my presence on the wagon of a corps. I have no information as to its whereabouts, but presume that it was interred in a military cemetery in the neighbourhood.[239]

Second Lieutenant McFerran is commemorated on the Arras Flying Services Memorial, 1914–1918; Windows, Presbyterian Church, York Road, Dun Laoghaire; Great War Memorial, Campbell College, Belfast and the Roll of Honour, Trinity College. He was awarded the British War and Victory medals, which were claimed by his father on 20 May 1922.

Thomas McFerran was a cadet in the OTC at Dublin University, where his record of service form, dated 17 April 1916, stated that he had 'completed an intensive course of training satisfactorily. Bearing and word of command, excellent. Should make a good officer.' While still a student at Trinity College, aged 18 years, he enlisted in the army at the Curragh, Co Kildare on 25 May 1916, and was posted to the Officer Cadet Battalion. On 25 September 1916, he was appointed to a temporary commission on probation on the general list.[240]

He was the son of William McFerran (solicitor) and Kathleen Chalmers McFerran, of Pier View, Sandycove, Kingstown. William died in October 1932, aged 71, and was buried at Dean's Grange Cemetery with his wife Kathleen, who died in May 1905. There were seven children in the family: Isabella Matilda, Kathleen, Eileen Chalmers, James Stanley, Ian Alexander, Thomas Malcolm and William Robert.

Thomas was born at 3, Elton Park, Kingstown, on 30 September 1897 and educated at Campbell College, Belfast, before entering Trinity College, in 1914. However, he postponed his studies to join the colours.

His brother, Lt James Stanley McFerran, 7th Battalion, Royal Dublin Fusiliers, survived the horrific fighting in Gallipoli and the remainder of the war. He is commemorated on the 1914–1918 Roll of Honour at the Presbyterian Church, York Road, Dun Laoghaire. James McFerran set up a milk bottling plant in Australia, where he lived with his wife, Agnes, and adopted daughter, Mary Therese. He died in April 1999, aged 100.[241]

A third son, Lt William Robert McFerran, 7th Battalion 'D' Company (the 'Pals') Royal Dublin Fusiliers, survived the war. He enlisted in the ranks with the 'pals' and was discharged to a commission on 14 September 1915. William McFerran received his early education at Campbell College, Belfast, before entering Trinity College in 1913. Following the war he practised as a solicitor, and was proprietor of the firm, H. & W. Stanley, Dublin. He resided at The Peak, Killiney. William was commissioned in September 1914 and like his brother James, survived the Gallipoli, Serbia and Salonika campaigns. He was mentioned in a letter home by fellow Kingstown comrade, 2nd Lt Jasper Brett, in August 1915. 'William married Nellie Vaughan Simmendinger in 1938 and they had one son, Neil Vaughan, who lives in Belfast'.[242]

William died in May 1973 and was buried at Dean's Grange Cemetery. He is commemorated on The 1914–1918 Roll of Honour, Presbyterian Church, York Road, Dun Laoghaire.

NESBITT, William Charles

Second Lieutenant, 6th Battalion Royal Dublin Fusiliers, 30th Brigade in the 10th (Irish) Division.

Second Lieutenant Nesbitt was killed in action, aged 40, at Suvla Bay, Turkey, on 16 August 1915.

> At Kiretch Tepe Sirt on the 15 August 1915, Lady Day in Ireland, began with divine services. Canon McLean celebrated Holy Communion for Protestants in a marquee of a field ambulance, and Father Murphy of the 6th & 7th Dublins said Mass and gave general absolution in the open air, his vestments making a splash of colour. At 12.10pm the attack began and later that day, in the darkness, the 6th Dublins and 5th Royal Irish Pioneers came into the line and remnants of the 7th Dublins, 6th Munsters and 5th Irish Fusiliers fell back. All night the fight carried on relentlessly and mercilessly, but the line held. The 6th Dublins lost two of their best officers, Capt Richards, and 2nd Lt W. Nesbitt.[243]

It was said that, 'W. Nesbitt, a young officer of the 6th Dublins, who, though junior in rank, had made a tremendous impression by his character, and had earned the name of "the soul of the battalion".'[244] 'After nightfall of the 16th, as Irish soldiers withdrew still farther from their more exposed positions, one young Dublin Fusilier, Corporal Bryan, a stretcher-bearer and a drummer with the regimental band, stayed behind and spent hours in vain in the darkness looking for the corpse of a much-respected officer from "C" Company, called Nesbitt.'[245]

Second Lieutenant Nesbitt has no known grave, but his name is commemorated on the Helles Memorial, Turkey, and the Blackrock College Union website. There is a letter in the Blackrock College archives confirming his death and stating that he had taken part in three or four actions and had won honours by his brave conduct under fire.[246] However, the information on his medal index card does not indicate that he was decorated beyond the campaign medals. He was awarded the 1914–15 Star, British War and Victory medals, which were sent to his wife on 1 March 1922.

William was born on 14 January 1875, the only son of the late William Nesbitt and Jane Nesbitt, Dove House, Blackrock. He was educated at Blackrock College, and prior to joining the British Army he was chief cashier at the Alliance Gas Company. William was also a member of the Finance, Works, Library and Technical Committees of the Blackrock Council. In his original documents, there is a copy of a reference from Thomas Clarke JP, Chairman of Blackrock Urban Council, and Chairman of the County Dublin Irish Volunteers, with an address at 29, Belgrave Square, Monkstown.[247] He married Mary Farrell at the Most Sacred Heart Roman Catholic Church, Donnybrook on 1 June 1895 and the couple lived at 8, Crosthwaite Park South, Kingstown. The witnesses attending the wedding ceremony were Hugh Kiernan and Frances Hariland. In the 1901 census William was recorded living at 108 Castle Avenue, Pembroke West, Dublin, with his young wife and his mother, Jane Nesbitt. Ten years later, in the 1911 census, the couple were living at 45, Booterstown Avenue, Blackrock. There were no children recorded in the marriage at this time.

William Nesbitt joined the British Army on 10 December 1914 and was appointed to a temporary commission. His battalion was formed at Naas in August 1914, and moved to the Curragh, before transferring to Basingstoke in May 1915. It landed off Suvla Beach, on the Gallipoli Peninsula, before dawn, on 7 August 1915.[248]

Nesbitt's original documents revealed that his effects included a bank pass book and two pieces of private correspondence.[249]

ORR, Walter Leslie
Second Lieutenant, 4th Battalion, attached 2nd Battalion Royal Irish Rifles.

His mother received a telegram from the War Office on 29 September 1915 informing her that her son was killed in action, aged 25, on a date between the 25th and 27th. The official date of his death was deemed to be the 25 September 1915.[250]

> At 3.50am his battalion's artillery bombarded the front. Four mines were exploded on the night, but the attack was held up by wire and machine-gun fire. At about 4.30am 'C' Company in support went up to reinforce the attacking companies. This was seen to have penetrated the enemy's line. At 6am some of the men could still be seen in the enemy's trenches, but after that hour nothing further could be seen of them and although parties volunteered to go forward to find out what was going on, none succeeded in getting definite information. This

attack, in which 2nd Lt Orr was missing and assumed to have been killed in action, was carried out with the greatest determination and gallantry. Casualties were 11 officers wounded or missing, 46 other ranks killed and 300 other ranks wounded or missing.[251]

Walter joined his brother, Alexander Harman, who had a rubber planting business in the Federal Malay States. During his time there he enlisted in the Malaya State Volunteer Rifles for a period of two years. On returning to Ireland he enlisted in the army at the outbreak of war and received a commission in the Royal Irish Rifles. He left for the front in July 1915.[252]

Second Lieutenant Orr is commemorated on the Great War Memorial, Menin Gate, Ieper; Great War Memorial at St Philip and St James Church of Ireland, Blackrock, and the Roll of Honour, Trinity College. He was awarded the 1915 Star, British War and Victory medals.

Walter was the youngest son of Fingal Harman Orr (a mineral water manufacturer) and Constance Emelie Orr (née Moyers) of 25, Longford Terrace, Kingstown. He was born on 6 April 1890 at 6, Knapton Terrace, Kingstown, and educated at Avoca School, Blackrock, before entering Trinity College in 1908. He was unmarried. His father died in 1905 and his mother passed away in 1945, aged 82. There were six children in the family; George Lambert, Alexandra Harman, Ada Mary, Adrian William Fielder, Constance Clara and Walter Leslie.

Walter's nephew, Sir David Orr, was one of the most successful Irishmen in Britain in the second half of the 20th Century. From 1974 to 1982 he was chairman and chief executive of the giant Anglo Dutch conglomerate Unilever Company. He went from the High School to Trinity College before joining the Royal Ulster Rifles in 1941. He later transferred to the Indian Army and served with the Madras Sappers in the fierce campaign against the Japanese for the re-conquest of Burma in 1944–45. Orr won the Military Cross on two occasions for gallantry in the field. He maintained an Irish connection as a member of the court of the Bank of Ireland and first joint chairman with Dr T.K. Whitaker of Encounter, established by Charles Haughey and Margaret Thatcher in 1981, and charged to organise conferences for the exchange of ideas on cultural and social issues between Britain and Ireland. He was Chancellor of Queen's University, Belfast.[253]

Other members of the wider Orr family to serve in the war included: Private Alexander William Burrell Orr, Royal Fusiliers, 20th Battalion, who was a first cousin of Walter Orr. He was killed in action on 4 February 1916 and was buried at Cambrin Churchyard Extension, France. Burrell, as he was known to his family, was born in 1896 at Powerscourt, Enniskerry, Co Wicklow and lived there with his parents, Cecil and Theresa, until the early part of the twentieth century when the family moved to Staffordshire. However, he entered Trinity College in 1914 and his name is commemorated in the Hall of Honour; Major John Arthur H. Waters, Royal Army Service Corps. Major Waters, of Woodview, Stillorgan, married Rachel Orr, a cousin of Walter Orr. They had one son, Sub-Lieutenant Samuel A.W. Waters, Royal Naval Voluntary Reserve, who served and was killed aboard HMS *Implacable* on 27 October 1944, while taking part in anti-shipping operations off Norway, during the Second World War; Lieutenant Austin 'Bunny' Orr, London Irish Rifles was Walter's first cousin (once removed). He was killed in action on 18 July 1943 and is buried at the Cantania War Cemetery, Sicily, Italy. Austin Orr was the son of Augustine Thwaites Orr, a mineral water manufacturer, and the family lived at 19 Sydney Avenue, Blackrock.[254]

SHACKLETON, Richard

Second Lieutenant, 8th Battalion North Staffordshire Regiment, 57th Brigade in the 19th (Western Division). Secondary Regiment, Service No 6072, Sergeant in the 4th & 8th Hussars.

He was killed in action, aged 24, at Messines Ridge on 8 June 1917. His parents received a telegram from the Army Council, dated 6 June 1917, informing them that their son was killed in action. Following an enquiry by his father, a second telegram was received on 26 June 1917, stating that 2nd Lt Shackleton, previously reported killed, was now reported wounded and missing on 8 June 1917. Some time later, Sergeant Peg made a statement from the Base Hospital in Leicester, which was forwarded to his parents: 'On 8 June at Messines informant went out with 2nd Lt Shackleton on a fighting patrol and returned and then he took another party, including Pte Goodesson. Second Lieutenant Shackleton was shot by a German sniper and left on the parapet dying. Private Goodesson was wounded and doesn't know where he is now.'[255]

The casualties during this action were about 140 all ranks, which included 1 officer killed (Lt R. Shackleton); 6 wounded; 18 other ranks killed; 108 wounded and 7 missing.[256]

Second Lieutenant Shackleton is commemorated on the World War I Memorial, Christ Church of Ireland, Dun Laoghaire, and the Mariner's Church War Memorial, Dun Laoghaire. He was awarded the 1914 Star, British War and Victory medals, which were sent to his parents on 15 March 1922.

Richard enlisted in the Corps of Hussars of the line, at Richmond Barracks, Dublin, on 5 August 1910, and was attached to the 4th Regiment. He transferred to the 8th Hussars on 27 January 1912 and was promoted to Corporal on 18 July 1915. On the 29 September 1915 he was admitted to No 23 Hospital at Étaples, but was fit to join Base Depot on 28 October before returning to his regiment on 20 November 1915. He was sent to the 4th Army School on a Bayonet Fighting Course on 25 February 1916 and on 16 December 1916 he was promoted acting sergeant. But the young Roscrea soldier was back again at Army School on 22 January 1917, where he was discharged to a commission on 8 April 1917 just two months before being killed.[257]

The battalion, to which he was gazetted in 1912, was formed at Lichfield on 18 September 1914 as part of K2 and came under orders of the 57th Brigade in the 19th (Western) Division. In February 1918 it transferred to the 56th Brigade in the same division.[258]

Richard was born in Roscrea, Co Tipperary, in 1893 and was single. He was the son of Abraham Shackleton (farmer and land steward) and Ellen Shackleton (née Woods) of, Gortnagowna, Roscrea, Co Tipperary. Nine children were born to the family of whom six survived infancy: George, Anne, Abraham, William Richard, Thomas and Florence.

He was a nephew of Annie Lee, mother of Robert and Joseph Lee, Blackrock, who also died in the Great War. Richard was employed with Hannigan & Shackleton, as a drapers' assistant at its store in Kingstown, and he lived with his sister, Anne Jolly, in Mountown, Kingstown.[259] In 1925 his father died, and his sister, Mrs C.T. (Anne) Jolly of Kingstown, wrote to the War Office on 11 March, on behalf of her mother, requesting that his medals and kit, belonging to the Hussars, be forwarded to her as he 'had little items from home that he wished us to have'. The response of, 26 March 1925, stated that: 'the whole of the personal effects received belonging to

2nd Lt Shackleton was despatched in August 1917 to the late officer's father, Mr A. Shackleton, residing at Gortnagowna, Roscrea, Co. Tipperary. In view of the length of time that has elapsed since the death of the late officer, it is feared that no further effects will be forthcoming.'[260]

MONKSTOWN FAMILY OFFER OUTSTANDING SERVICE TO THE WAR EFFORT

Fitzadam Millar and Georgina Millar (née Westby) had ten children: Mary Georgina, Constance Geraldine, Henry James, George McGregor, Ernest Westby, Eileen Isabela, Adelaide Florence, Edward Chaytor, Fitzadam and Marguerite Flora. They were married in 1876 at the Church of Ireland, Monkstown and the family resided at Windsor House, Monkstown. Three sons served in the war and one, Edward Chaytor, was killed.

Major George McGregor Millar OBE, RIAMC, Indian Medical Service, survived the war despite being wounded in July 1917. He was born in 1880, married Christina Helen Rennie in 1928 and died in 1962. [261]

Commander Fitzadam Millar DSC (Distinguished Service Cross), Royal Navy, was born in 1889 and survived the war also. He was married three times (1) Frances Louise Lewarne, (2) Violet Marian Trouton and (3) Kay Bevan. [262]

The eldest brother, Henry James, was born in 1878 and married Helen Christine Piper in 1906. He was Director of the Bank of Ireland 1923–30; Governor of the Bank of Ireland 1930–32, and Managing Director of Messrs A. Millar & Company Limited, Wholesale Tea, Wine and Spirit merchants, (established 1843), Thomas Street, Dublin. Henry Millar played lock-forward for Monkstown Rugby Football Club and won four caps for Ireland in the1904–05 season. When his playing career finished he was elected President of the Leinster Branch Irish Rugby Football Union in 1923–24, and President of the Rugby Football Union in the 1928–29 season.[263]

A sister, Eileen Isabela, was born in 1884 and died 1956. She married Lt-Col Leighton Marlow Stevens DSO, 2nd Battalion Worcestershire Regiment, who died in 1965. [264]

Their sister, Adelaide Florence was born in 1886 and died in 1976. She married Captain Frederick Falkiner Standish Smithwick, chaplain to the Forces in the Great War. This was Frederick's second marriage, following the death of his first wife, Violet Irene Odlum, who died in 1922. 'Frederick Falkiner Standish Smithwick, who also attended Corrig School, was a remarkable man; he won two caps in 1889 playing rugby for Ireland, at the age of 17. The games were played in Belfast and Limerick against Scotland and Wales, and Ireland lost both games.' During his service in the war he was 'Mentioned in Despatches' three times, ending his wartime career as Assistant Chaplain-General, South-Eastern Command, before becoming Precentor at Killaloe Cathedral.[265]

MILLAR, Edward Chaytor

Sergeant, Service No 14645, 7th Battalion, 'D' Company, (the 'Pals') Royal Dublin Fusiliers, 30th Brigade in the 10th (Irish) Division.

He was killed in action, aged 29, at Suvla Bay, Gallipoli on 9 August 1915, while urging men of another regiment to 'stand firm'. Shortly before Captain Poole-Hickman was killed he made special mention of Millar's gallantry. 'On 9 August the battalion on the right ran out of ammunition, and "D" Company of the 7th Royal Dublin Fusiliers was called upon to supply them. Captain Tobin, with 60 men, was sent to bring up 20,000 rounds. When Tobin and his party got up they found the ammunition had been very urgently required and he and his men went farther up right into the firing-line with a portion of it.'[266] It was here that Sergeant Edward Millar was killed while gallantly assisting another unit to reorganise, for which he and Sergeant Burrowes received a special mention.

> Few episodes in the battle annals of the British Empire can match the nine-month Gallipoli campaign for waste of life of the rank and file, for valour, suffering, endurance and loyalty on land, sea and, for the first time, in the air and for indecision and incompetence in the leadership and ill-luck in the military sphere. The two contending sides fought face to face and chest to chest and died like the flies that fed on their unburied bodies.[267]

Second Lieutenant Jasper Brett, mentioned in a letter home that 'Edward Millar led about half "D" Company in grand style and then brought up and served out ammunition under fire. He was shot dead doing so I think he was recommended for the Victoria Cross.' Sergeant Millar was not recommended for the Victoria Cross or even the Military medal.

His Company Commander wrote to his mother: 'I deeply sympathise with you and yours in the bereavement you have sustained through the death of poor Edward. As a friend and comrade in arms his loss to me is indeed great. A more gallant gentleman never met a more gallant death. The company, which he loved and by which he was beloved, join with me in this expression of regret.'[268] Family history says that 'one of his brothers-in-law was working in the War Office when the news came through of his death in action, which was "leaked" to the family, causing considerable upset'.[269] Another of Millar's comrades, L/Cpl Arnold Moss, born in Kilgobbin, also died in this battle.

Edward Millar is commemorated on the Helles Memorial, Turkey; War Memorial, Monkstown Church of Ireland and the Hall of Honour, Trinity College. He was 'Mentioned in Despatches' by Sir Ian Hamilton for, 'gallant and distinguished services in the field' [270] and was also awarded the 1915 Star, British War and Victory medals.

He joined the Irish Rugby Football Union Volunteer Corps and on 14 September, with more than 200 men, enlisted in the Royal Dublin Fusilier 7th Battalion, 'D' Company (the 'Pals'). Millar was immediately promoted Sergeant. 'His only effect remaining today is a Royal Dublin Fusilier crested cigarette case.'[271] The battalion was formed in Naas in August 1914 as part of the K1 army. Finally, the 6th and 7th Battalions of the Royal Dublin Fusiliers landed off Suvla Beach, on the Gallipoli Peninsula, before dawn, on 7 August 1915.[272]

Edward Millar was born on 6 June 1887, educated at Corrig School, Kingstown, before entering Trinity College in 1906. When college finished he worked as a mercantile clerk in the wines and spirits warehouse of the family vintner firm of Millar & Company. He was a talented sportsman and excelled in college where he rowed with the Trinity junior eights for two seasons, and played on the first team at Monkstown Football Club in the 1913–14 season. It was reported that most of his team mates on the Monkstown 1st XV were serving with him in 'D' Company. 'There was a Dublin University Boat Club race called the "Millar Fours", the name of which was changed relatively recently'.[273] His uncle, Richard Chaytor Millar, a partner in the firm, Millar & Symes, was the architect of the Knox Memorial Hall, Monkstown, which opened in 1904.[274] Sergeant Millar was unmarried.

TWO BROTHERS OF WELL-KNOWN MERCHANT FAMILY
KILLED IN GALLIPOLI AND FRANCE

John and Mary Findlater of Melbeach, Monkstown, had eleven children, of whom five died in infancy, including twin sons who died on the day of their birth in 1875. The surviving children were Adam Seaton, John, Alexander, William; Charles Arthur, and Herbert Snowden. Three brothers, Captain Findlater, Charles and Herbert, joined the British Army for the duration of the war, but tragically, Alex was the only son to survive. Seven members of the wider Findlater family went to war and only three returned home; one with a limb missing.

Captain Alexander Findlater DSO, Royal Army Medical Corps, attached 1st London Mounted Brigade, Field Ambulance survived the war. He entered Trinity College, where he took his BA in 1885 and MD in 1886. Alex married Emily Anna Donnelly and when qualified as a doctor, he began practising in Alborough, Yorkshire, where their only child, Helen, was born. He joined up with the Royal Army Medical Corps, at age 54 years, and was immediately posted to Gallipoli. Captain Findlater was awarded the Distinguished Service Order, (DSO) 'For conspicuous gallantry and devotion to duty on several occasions, notably on 29 September 1915, at Chocolate Hill, Gallipoli Peninsula. Here Captain Findlater crossed over two hundred yards of open country under very heavy shellfire to render aid to two wounded men. He saved the life of one, but the other was beyond help.' [275] Captain Findlater was also 'Mentioned in Despatches'. In a letter home on 27 August 1915, Doctor Alex (as he was known to all) wrote in reference to his fallen brother: 'Am writing this in a dug-out, a hole in the ground on the side of the hill. Believe me, have left no stone unturned to find out all about Herbert and do not give up hope.' [276] Doctor Alex died in 1931, leaving his wife Emily and daughter, Helen.

FINDLATER, Charles Arthur
Lance Sergeant, Service No 14646, 10th Battalion Royal Dublin Fusiliers, 190th Brigade in the 63rd (Royal Naval) Division. Secondary Regiment, 7th Battalion, 'D' Company, (the 'Pals') Royal Dublin Fusiliers.

He was killed, aged 46, on 13 November 1916. On this day, 35 other ranks were killed, 57 missing and 132 wounded. The *Evening Mail,* dated 12 December 1916, published the story of his death:

Charles Findlater was killed in action on 13 November 1916 in the big battle on the Somme front, in which his regiment, the Dublin Fusiliers, took so glorious a part. The attack took place in appalling conditions that foreshadowed the horrors of Ypres the next year. German snipers made it their business to shoot the officers and many were hit. Nevertheless; the Dubliners were able to take all their objectives. However; about one hundred Dublin Fusiliers died that day. Charles who was in his forty-seventh year was not the kind of man to plead his years when his services were needed. Those who served with him at the front described him as a splendid soldier. In the ordinary course, his duty would have kept him behind. He asked permission to go 'over the lid', as the parapet is called, with his comrades, and the service for which he volunteered cost him his life.[277]

The 7th Dublins departed from the North Wall, Dublin, on 30 April 1915, on its way to Basingstoke in England for further training. The battalion arrived in Suvla Bay, Gallipoli, on 7 August 1915. Not one man embarking in Dublin on that day could have imagined that six months later only 79 out of the original 'D' Company of 239 would leave Gallipoli alive. While attached to the 7th Dublins, L/Sgt Findlater was wounded in Gallipoli and returned to England for treatment and a period of recuperation, before joining the 10th Dublins and returning to the front line in France.

His grave is at VI. J. 7. Tincourt New British Cemetery, Somme, France, and he is commemorated on the Great War Memorial at High School, Rathgar; Great War Memorial, Royal School, Armagh and the Hall of Honour, Trinity College. He was awarded the 1915 Star, British War and Victory medals.

Charles Findlater decided to enlist despite being above the upper age limit of 44. 'Volunteers had to meet the same physical criteria as the peace time regulars, but men with previous service in the army could be accepted up to the age of 45. Since proof of age was not necessary to enlist, there were many recorded instances of underage and overage men being accepted into the service.'[278]

The brothers, Charles and Herbert, were part of the 7th Dublins group that left camp on the morning of 5 December 1914 for Woodbrook, where they were entertained by Lieutenant Stanley Cochrane.[279]

In April 1911 the census recorded Charles Findlater living at home with his seventy-eight-year-old mother, Mary Findlater, at 4, Albany Avenue. He was educated at High School and Royal School Armagh before entering Trinity College in 1889. Charles was associated with the family firm, after which he turned his attention to engineering. In 1902 he went to South Africa and worked as an engineer in Johannesburg. On returning home he became interested in the cycle trade and was later associated with the development of the motor car industry in Dublin. He was a well known sportsman, and numbered among his many sporting activities was the gymnastic team of the Sackville Hall Club. He also won a number of long-distance cycling races in the Irish Road Club. Charlie (as he was known to his family and friends) was a member of the Monkstown Rugby Football Club and he distinguished himself in the keenly competitive days of the Dublin Swimming Club. [280]

FINDLATER, Herbert Snowden

Lance Corporal, Service No 14198, 7th Battalion, 'D' Company, (the 'Pals') Royal Dublin Fusiliers, 30th Brigade in the 10th (Irish) Division.

He was reported missing, presumed to have been killed in action, aged 43, on 16 August 1915. It was Major Harrison, who had been with 'A' Company on the right of the line, sent word that 'D' Company should be brought in to further reinforce the left. When they came they were told that the only chance they had of keeping the hill was to charge the bombers. Almost every soldier in the charge was killed or wounded.[281] Lance Corporal Findlater was among the men who followed the Major.

One of his comrades wrote to his brother, Willie Findlater:

> It was a mad-man's charge, but on the other side a very brave one – we were relieved at six that evening by the 5th Royal Irish Fusiliers. It was a hard job fighting and ducking from five in the morning until six in the evening and the only thing to keep our spirits up was an odd song and a smoke from a Woodbine – that was how poor Findlater went.[282]

When the report of a soldier wounded and missing in action was communicated to his family, it created the most agonising distress imaginable. The final outcome of L/Cpl Findlater's plight remained in doubt for some time despite the presence of his brother, Capt Alex Findlater, who was also serving in Gallipoli at the time, and doing everything possible to find Herbert. In the end, it was an affidavit sworn by his platoon commander, Capt Ernest Hamilton, that put an end to the speculation. Hamilton was in command of Findlater's platoon on that fateful morning, and he painted a distressing picture of his comrade's last moments:

> On the morning of 16 August 1915, I was stationed with my Company behind a ridge somewhere in Gallipoli and at about 5am, just shortly after dawn broke, a charge was ordered over the ridge and down the hill towards the Turks who were in a very strong position about 80 to 100 yards away from us; my company charged in two lots of about 80 men each, I (this deponent) having charge of the second lot, which included the said Herbert Snowden Findlater. Immediately we went over the ridge a most severe machine-gun fire was poured into us together with a fierce shell-fire. We had to go through a gap immediately over the ridge and then into the open towards the Turks. When I was crossing said ridge a shell burst close beside me and I was blown back again behind the ridge and wounded, but still possessed consciousness and, on looking up to see how the charge was progressing, I found that every man in both lots of my company was either lying on the ground dead or wounded. I remained in the ridge and a second party came up to take the place that our company had left and we held the ridge for about three hours and were then relieved by another regiment.

The ground in front of the ridge mentioned by me and where the casualties in the said charge took place was never re-taken by us, and for three hours during which we held the ridge after the charge the entire ground was most heavily shelled and a constant machine gun-fire swept over it, making it impossible, as I verily believe, for anyone to survive who was on the ground during the said shelling and fire.[283]

'Lieutenant Hamilton was bright and extremely handsome. However, the appalling horrors of war turned him into a chronic alcoholic and he was subsequently court-martialled and dismissed from the service. He returned to Ireland but never continued his medical studies … Perhaps those who did not return were the lucky ones.'[284]

Lance Corporal Herbert Findlater is commemorated on the Helles Memorial, Turkey; Great War Memorial, Royal School, Armagh; World War I Memorial Plaque at Christ Church of Ireland, Dun Laoghaire; Great War Memorial, Four Courts, Dublin and the Roll of Honour, Trinity College. He was awarded the 1915 Star, British War and Victory medals.

'He married Evelyn Maxwell Thompson in 1904 and they resided at 22, Clarinda Park East, Kingstown. They had two children: Herbert Maxwell, who graduated at Cambridge and spent a lifetime teaching at Pangbourne Nautical College, Reading; and John Godfrey, who settled in Canada.' John Godfrey Findlater was attached to the Royal Canadian Air Force and fought in the Second World War. When the war finished he became a Minister of the Episcopal Church.[285]

'Herbert was born in Dublin in 1873 and educated at Strangeway's School, St Stephen's Green and Trinity College, where he took his degrees, BA in 1895 and MA in 1898. He qualified as a solicitor in Sir William Findlater's office and attended Findlater and Empire Theatre meetings as the family solicitor. He was a member of the Royal Irish Yacht Club and an accomplished amateur actor. Like his brothers, he was a keen sportsman and a founder member of the Monkstown Hockey Club in 1895. Today, his grandson, Alex John Maxwell Findlater, lives in Edinburgh, Scotland.'[286]

BUTLER, William Percy

Lance Corporal, Service No 26187, 10th Battalion, 'C' Company, Royal Dublin Fusiliers, 190th Brigade in the 63rd (Royal Naval) Division.

He received severe wounds while in action at Gavrelle and died the next day, aged 20, on 24 April 1917, at No 19 Casualty Clearing Station. His Platoon Commander wrote to his parents: 'Your son was a thoroughly reliable soldier, in whom his officers had every confidence, and his loss is much felt by his comrades in the battalion, amongst whom he was popular.' And a comrade wrote: 'No man ever had a better chum – he was always the same – even under the most trying circumstances he never grumbled.'[287]

His grave is at IV. C. 41. Duisans British Cemetery, Etrun, France and he is commemorated on the World War I Memorial Plaque and Roll of Honour in Dun Laoghaire Christ Church, and Memorial Tablet in the hallway of the old Bank of Ireland. Lance-Corporal Butler was awarded the British War and Victory medals. He enlisted in February 1916 at Kingstown, and served in Dublin during the Easter Rising. He was sent to France in August 1916.

William was the son of William John Butler, MA, Librarian at Trinity College, and Georgina (Nina) Butler (née Elliott) of 36, York Road, Kingstown. His grandfather was John Kempston Butler of Clonmel. There were three children in the family; William Percy, Meta Letitia and Robert O'Neill. He attended Corrig School, Kingstown, and joined the Bank of Ireland in April 1915. William's younger brother, Captain Robert O'Neill Butler, Pioneer Corps, was killed in the Second World War and is buried in Pietermaritzburg (Fort Napier) Cemetery, South Africa. He was married to Elinor O'Neill Butler, of New York City, USA and his name is commemorated on the World War two Plaque at Christ Church of Ireland, Dun Laoghaire.

KEEGAN-COMISKEY, Patrick

Private, Service No 9574, 9th Battalion Royal Dublin Fusiliers, 48th Brigade in the 16th (Irish) Division.

Private Keegan-Comiskey was killed in action, aged 17, on 9 September 1916, during an assault by his battalion on the German positions in the village of Ginchy on the River Somme during the Battle of Ginchy.

Ginchy village, a mass of shattered masonry and shell-holes by late summer 1916, had been a key objective for the 7th Division in the important attack of 3 September. It was not taken and in the days immediately following, repeatedly defied British assaults, a further concerted attempt on Ginchy was planned for the afternoon of Saturday 9 September. The task of clearing the village was given to the depleted 16th (Irish) Division. Its two attacking brigades (47th and 48th) were supported on the right by 56th Division's operations in Leuze and Bouleaux Woods.

At 4.45pm Pte Keegan-Comiskey with his battalion in the 48th Brigade rushed towards Ginchy from the south-west, but were instantly halted by a ferocious German barrage. Two minutes later, the 47th Brigade's attack (from the south) was immediately cut down by close-range machine-gun fire. In wet conditions, bad light and the confusion of the assault elements, the 1st Royal Munster Fusiliers veered to the flank and there, confronted by the enemy, resolutely drove the Germans back; pressing on, the 48th Brigade troops were through the village by 5.30pm and gains consolidated. The attack was characterised by dash, turmoil and heavy casualties.[288]

Private Keegan-Comiskey was among the 66 casualties, who were killed or wounded at the same place and on the same day as Lieutenant Tom Kettle, known to his men as, 'Captain Tom'. He shared with his comrades an extraordinary tribute from Tom Kettle, who wrote in a letter to his brother: 'I have never seen anything in my life so beautiful as the clean and so to say radiant valour of my Dublin Fusiliers. There is something divine in men like that.'[289]

Private Keegan-Comiskey is commemorated on the Thiepval Memorial, France and he was awarded the British War and Victory medals. The 9th Dublins was formed in September 1914 as part of the K2 army. It moved from Ballyhooley in Co Cork to Blackdown Camp, Surrey, in September 1915, and landed at Le Havre in France during December 1915.

Patrick (Patsy as he was known to his family) was born on 29 May 1899, the son of Thomas Comiskey and Mary Comiskey (née Keegan) of 6, Bentley Villas, Kingstown. There were four children in the family; Patrick, Brigid, James and Margaret. Thomas wanted to take his family to America to begin a new life, unfortunately, Mary's mother died in childbirth and she refused to leave her father to fend for his young ones, so it was decided, like so many other families before them that Thomas would go and prepare the way for the extended family. Thomas left for Boston in 1906 and Mary stayed in Kingstown to rear her brothers Mike and Edward and her own children Patsy, Brigid and Jimmy. In 1914–15, Thomas returned from America to exert some control on his runaway son, Patsy, who tried on several occasions to enlist in the British Army. During his time at home, Mary became pregnant and their fourth child, Margaret, was born.[290]

Lieutenant Matt Comiskey (rtd.) wrote of his uncle:

> At the outbreak of war Patsy and his younger brother, Jimmy, were 15 and 12 respectively. They could catch buckets full of herring when they shoaled into the corner of the harbour, and replenish the traditional barrels of pickled fish outside the back door of the houses of Kingstown at that time. They knew the going rate for working one of the many coal boats that used the small quays near the west side of the harbour, and how hard it was to shovel out a hold until you had 'floored' it out. All this knowledge was gleaned from the men who stood on the corner of Cumberland Street waiting for an incoming vessel. They knew the Blackmore and Shortall families, who owned the moorings in the harbour and stood in the stern of their dinghies like gondoliers to skull the yacht owners out to their boats for a fee. They also knew of the practice of 'hobbling', when the seafaring men of Kingstown would read up the shipping notices and would sail as far south as Arklow or

north to Rockabill, to put a grappling hook onto a vessel bound for Dublin to claim the right to secure the vessel alongside in the port, or sometimes even to pilot it up the river.

Patsy eventually succeeded in enlisting in the army in late 1915 or early 1916. My Father died in 1980 without ever talking about his family and all we had of Patsy, was a photograph in my grandmother's home of a young soldier and inside the framed picture were two military medals. When I was going to Belgium and France in 1998 for the opening of the Irish Peace Park in Messines and to visit some of the battle fields, I contacted the Commonwealth War Graves Commission for information on Patrick Comiskey but to no avail. On my next visit with a group from the Irish Naval Association, I decided to request information on Patrick Keegan, and this time I received a perfect match with Mary Comiskey as next-of-kin. With Patsy's father in America, he was often addressed by neighbours as 'Keegan' (his grandfather's name) instead of his correct surname, 'Comiskey', hence the name, Keegan-Comiskey. When we arrived to lay our wreaths from the Comiskey family and the Naval Association at the Thiepval Memorial, where he is remembered, I was asked to say a few words. I did not expect this to bother me, but when I thought of Mary receiving that telegram with her husband in America, I found it difficult to speak. The day we arrived there was the 9 September, the day on which Patsy died in 1916, and the year, 1999, was the centenary of his birth.[291]

TWO MORE KINGSTOWN BROTHERS KILLED IN THE WAR

Two Kelly brothers joined on the same day and both were killed in 1914. Thomas and James Kelly enlisted in the Irish Guards on 2 February 1904 and were part of the British Expeditionary Force that departed for France on the 12 August 1914. They were the sons of Peter and Mary Kelly of 34, Convent Road, Dunleary. The Kelly's had eight children: Thomas, James, Julia, Patrick, Henry, Peter, John and William. Peter Kelly, a grand-nephew of Thomas and James Kelly, remembers his great-aunt, Julia Treacy (nee Kelly) who lived at Convent Road, Dun Laoghaire. His great-uncle, John was harbour master in Dun Laoghaire and lived in a house near the harbour, locally named, 'The Depot' [sic].[292]

KELLY, Thomas

Private, Service No 1889, 1st Battalion Irish Guards, 4th (Guards) Brigade in the 2nd Division.

He died on 9 November 1914, aged 34, from wounds received while engaged in the first Battle of Ypres at Zillebeke Wood, south-east of Ypres, Belgium. There is no way of knowing when Thomas Kelly was wounded, although it is very likely to have occurred during fighting on dates between the 6 and 9 November 1914. Private James Robinson was killed on 6 November and details of the action on that day may be seen in his profile in Chapter Two. It was unlikely that he was wounded on 7 November, but the next day, which was a quiet one, the remnants of the battalion were made into two shrunken companies. There were intermittent burst of shelling from French 75s on the right and German heavies; the enemy eighty yards distant. On 9 November the battalion of four platoons, three in the firing line and one in reserve, was relieved by the South Wales Borderers, drew supplies and men at Brigade Headquarters, moved back through Zillebeke and marched into bivouacs near a farm south of the Ypres – Zonnebeke Road, where they settled down with some Oxford Light Infantry in deep trenches and dug-outs which had been dug by the French.[293]

Family history says that he was killed in a bayonet charge. His great-grandson, Peter Kelly said: 'As a boy I was friendly with the son of a printer, who had survived the Great War, and I was a frequent visitor to his home. His father told me many stories about the war and also said that he saw my great-grandfather, Thomas, lying dead on top of a number of dead bodies.'[294]

His grave is at I.L. 17. Poperinghe Old Military Cemetery, Belgium and he was awarded the 1914 Star, British War and Victory medals. Thomas enlisted in London on 2 February 1904 and then embarked on the P & O, SS *Novara* at Southampton on 12 August 1914. They arrived at Le Havre, France, the next day and after resting, headed for the Belgian border and Mons. They were accompanied on board the *Novara* by seven comrades from Golden Ball, Dundrum and Carrickmines, all of whom lost their lives during the first nine days of November 1914 in the first Battle of Ypres.

Thomas was the husband of Mary A. Kelly of 18, Cross Avenue, Kingstown. They had four children: Peter, John, James and Mary Julia. He was 5ft 10ins in height, had dark brown hair, hazel eyes and a fresh complexion.

KELLY, James

Private, Service No 1888, 1st Battalion Irish Guards, 4th (Guards) Brigade in the 2nd Division.

He was killed in action, aged 30, at the start of the Battle of the Aisne on 14 September 1914.

> The battalion left its bivouac at 6am on 14 September 1914, crossed the pontoon bridge at Pont Darcy by 10am and advanced to Soupir. The order of march was advanced ... 2nd Grenadiers, head of main body, 3rd Coldstream, then Irish Guards, then 2nd Coldstream. The advance was checked at the Ridge Point 197, and marched through the village of Soupir. The column was shelled and the battalion took shelter under the wall of the chateau. The Coldstream were ordered to attack the ridge at Cour la Soupir Farm with the Irish Guards in support.[295] It was at Soupir, with his battalion under heavy fire, that James Kelly fell.

He is commemorated at La Ferte-sous-Jouarre Memorial, Seine-et-Marne, France and was awarded the 1914 Star, British War and Victory medals. James enlisted in London on 2 February 1904, embarked on the P & O, SS *Novara* at Southampton on 12 August 1914 with his brother and other ranks from South County Dublin, who are profiled in the book, arriving at Le Havre the next day. He was single, 5ft 8ins in height, with light brown hair, hazel eyes and a fresh complexion.

McCLATCHIE, Richard

Able Seaman, Service No 209542, HMS *Goliath*, Royal Navy.

He was lost at sea, aged 31, on 13 May 1915, when his ship HMS *Goliath* was sunk by a Turkish torpedo-boat destroyer. In 1914, his ageing battleship *Goliath* was dispatched to the East Indies for escort duties, but was transferred to the Dardanelles in April 1915 to support the landings around Cape Helles.

> In the early hours of 13 May, while anchored in Morto Bay, a Turkish torpedo-boat destroyer crept towards the *Goliath* hidden by a dense fog. At 1.15am three dull thuds were heard on *Cornwallis*, another ship anchored some distance away, and then the cries of men struggling in the water. The *Goliath* quickly turned turtle and sank within two

minutes, trapping hundreds of men below. Some 570 men were lost from her crew of 800. Some days later, Winston Churchill announced in the House of Commons that he had just heard from the admiral commanding in the Dardanelles that HM battleship, *Goliath,* was sunk in a torpedo attack on Wednesday while protecting the French flank, just inside the straits.[296]

He is commemorated on the Plymouth Naval Memorial and Great War Memorial, Monkstown Church of Ireland. McClatchie was awarded the 1914 Star, British War and Victory medals. He enlisted at Devonport on 22 January 1902, aged 18, for a period of twelve years and signed up for a further period of service on 22 January 1914. He joined *Goliath* from *Majestic* in July 1914. During his thirteen years in the Royal Navy he also served on the; *Black Prince, Minotaur, Agincourt, Colossus, Resolution, Vivid 1, Bulwark, Defiance, Halcyon, Trafalgar* and *Argyll.* He was described as, 'leading torpedo man', and received a ten shillings gratuity on 1 December 1912, for his work in recruiting volunteers.'[297]

Richard was the son of William McClatchie and Isabella Deakers. There were five children in the family: Margaret, Martha, Ellen, Richard and George. William was born in Co Meath and was living in Clonmel in 1883. In 1901 he was living with his family at 8, Stoneview Place, Kingstown, and in 1911 the family had moved to 9, Finnstown, Lucan, Co Dublin. William, who was employed as a gardener, died in 1919, aged 68, while the date of death of his wife, Isabella, is unknown.[298]

Richard McClatchie was born in Clonmel, Co Tipperary on 22 January 1884. His Service Record states that he worked as an errand boy prior to enlisting and was 5ft 4ins in height with dark brown hair and grey eyes. His mother, Isabelle, was recorded as next-of-kin.[299]

MAHONY, Bernard

Stoker (first class), Service No SS/116196, HMS *Raglan*, Royal Navy.

He was killed in action, aged 22, when his ship HMS *Raglan* was attacked on 20 January 1918 near Imbros Island, Turkey. In his research of the Dardanelles, Gerard Mahony of Killiney, retired seaman and a great-nephew of Bernard Mahony stated: 'Bernard was killed by a shell which landed next to him as he was ordered to abandon ship. His ship was attacked by the German battle cruiser, *Goeben* and the light cruiser, *Breslau*. Following numerous hits she eventually sank at 8.15am with the loss of 127 men from a crew of 220.'[300] A report from the Ministry of Defence, stated:

> Highly secret preparations were being made for *Goeben* and *Breslau* to attack British ships in their Aegean bases and to destroy any vessels on patrol. In the half-light of the early morning of 20 January, the two ships slipped out of the Dardanelles. The lookouts on Mavro Island failed to spot the enemy ships in the poor visibility before sunrise on that misty winter Sunday morning. The destroyer *Lizard*, patrolling north-east of Imbros, was the first to sight them at 7.20am, the *Breslau* steaming ahead of *Goeben*. Owing to enemy wireless jamming, it was several minutes before she could get in visual contact with *Raglan* and flash 'GOBLO', the signal that was out. Almost simultaneously, *Raglan* sighted the ship herself, as did the net drifters and shore lookouts. *Breslau's* fourth salvo included a lucky shot that hit *Raglan's* 'spotting top' killing the gunnery officer, wounding Capt Broome and wrecking the control gear. Now the *Breslau* had the range, she began firing rapid salvoes, knocking out the six-inch ammunition supply party.[301]

The 14-inch gun was reloaded and ready to go into local control when a hit from the *Goeben* pierced the tall armoured barbette and killed a number of the gun crew. The First Lieutenant, who had been in the turret, came out, saw the carnage and unable to see the CO ordered the ship to be abandoned at anchor. The *Raglan* lost

117 sailors. The monitor M28, which was close to the *Raglan*, blew up fifteen minutes later following further shelling by *Breslau*.[302] With two British destroyers, *Tigress* and *Lizard* in pursuit, the German ships continued heading south toward Lemons Island. The ships rounded Cape Kephalo and were driven into a British minefield where *Breslau* was sunk, killing 208 men. *Goeben* turned back and attempted to tow *Breslau* to safety, until it too suffered severe damage after striking several mines and was forced to run aground near Chanak (now Cannanakale) in the Dardanelles.[303]

He is commemorated on the Chatham Naval Memorial, England and was awarded the 1914 Star, British War and Victory medals, claimed by his mother. A report into the sinking of the two British ships gives an insight into how the hierarchy in the British armed forces assessed the loss of life in relation to the overall strategic gain; bearing in mind that 135 men died on its two vessels, it read: 'Nonetheless, the outcome was on balance favourable to the British, although not fully appreciated at the time. The two German ships had long been a potential menace to British forces, especially the vessels supplying the Salonika Army. Now, one was sunk, the other damaged, for the loss of two relatively expendable British vessels.'[304]

Bernard Mahony joined the Royal Navy at Devonport on 27 October 1914 and was promoted to stoker 1st class on 1 October 1915. He had previously served on the destroyers, *Miranda, Lookout* and the cruiser *Chatham*. The young sailor was posted to the *Raglan* on 21 August 1916 and in early 1917 his ship was engaged in shelling enemy positions in the Mediterranean. During the summer months of 1917 she came under attack from the Peninsula, and by bombing attacks from enemy planes. On 27 August 1917, he was transferred to the cruiser, *Europa*, a depot ship, but returned to the *Raglan* three weeks later. The *Raglan* arrived at Kusu Bay, Imbros Island, near the entrance to the Dardanelles on the 26 December 1917 where he spent his last few weeks.[305]

He was the son of Edward Mahony (a carpenter and boat builder) and Mary Anne Mahony (née McAuley) of 55, Patrick Street, Kingstown. There were ten children in the family: Catherine, Christopher, Joseph, Edward, Winifred, Mary Anne, Cornelius, Bernard, Agnes Elizabeth and Josephine Mary.

The Mahony family have a proud tradition in boat building and seafaring. Gerard Mahony stated that his great-grandfather, Edward, and his great-uncle, Edward, set-up the family boat building business circa 1910 in a yard situated beside the family home. A grand-niece of Bernard Mahony, Roseleen Whelan, who lives in the old family home, said: 'The boat building business stayed in the family for many years until the late 1960s, and the boat yard was sold in the 1970s.'[306]

Bernard was born on 31 October 1895 and at age 15 years he was working as a telegraph messenger, but prior to enlisting he was employed as a boatman. Bernard's address, according to Commonwealth War Graves Commission's records, was Mossoloe House, Cabinteely. As there was no Mossoloe House in Cabinteely it is now confirmed that it was Monaloe House, the address of his brother Edward, who lived there with his wife and son.

WEAFER, John Joseph

Private, Service No 25225, 8th Battalion Royal Inniskilling Fusiliers, 49th Brigade in the 16th (Irish) Division.

Private John Weafer (Jack as he was known to his family) died, aged 26, in a field hospital near the front during the Battle of Hulluch on 29 April 1916. It is not known when he was wounded, but it is possible that it was on the night of the 27th when the Royal Inniskillling Fusiliers suffered a heavily concentrated German chlorine gas attack near the German-held village of Hulluch, a mile north of Loos. 'On the morning of Thursday 27 April 1916, a storm of high-explosive and gas shells fell into the Irish positions. The brunt of the attack fell on the 48th and 49th Brigades; the 47th was in reserve. Minutes later German engineers opened the taps on 3,800 chlorine gas cylinders and the gentle easterly breeze carried the deadly gas deep into the Irish positions. Before the gas had cleared the Germans launched a very strong infantry attack on the Irish position and after fierce hand-to-hand fighting, were repulsed.' The war diary report for 29th April, the day of this death, stated that 'at 3.45am the enemy liberated gas and immediately started heavy shelling on the front and support lines. Gas came over in two clouds, the first of a greenish colour, the second of a yellowish creamy colour.'[307] His great-nephew, John Weafer, of Glasthule, has a keen interest in the history of the Great War, and has some thoughts about how Jack might have died:

> What were Jack's wounds? Were they as described by the poet Wilfred Owen in a stanza of that magnificent poem *Dulce et Decorum est?* – I hope not, or was he lying on a stretcher in the field hospital, comatose and unaware of the horror all around? – I hope so. About the same

time that my great-uncle received his fatal wounds, his Enniscorthy kinsman, Capt Tom Weafer, National Volunteers, commanding the Hibernian Bank outpost, diagonally across the street from the GPO at the corner of Lower Abbey Street, was shot dead aged 26. He died in the *Irish Times* paper store in Lower Abbey Street, now Madigan's pub.[308]

Private Jack Weafer is commemorated on Panel 60, Loos Memorial, France and he was awarded the British War and Victory medals. Although he enlisted late in 1914 he did not experience action until the end of 1915 or early 1916. 'His battalion was formed at Omagh in October 1914 as part of the K2 army. It moved to Tipperary and then to Finner Camp, Co Donegal, in August 1915. The battalion moved to Woking in England, before sailing for France in February 1916.'[309]

He was the son of Frank Weafer, a building contractor, and Elizabeth Weafer of 73, Glasthule, Kingstown. There were ten children in the family: Rose Anne, Richard, John Joseph, James, Thomas, Michael, Henry, Laurence Edward, Francis and Elizabeth. Their father, Frank Weafer, was a mason bricklayer from Enniscorthy, Co Wexford, and his joinery works and offices were situated at 72, Glasthule Road and the family lived next door at 73, Glasthule Road. He also had a premises at Weafer's Stone Yard, on Adelaide Road, Glasthule. Frank died in 1929 and his wife, Elizabeth, had already passed away at the time of Jack's death. John Weafer stated:

A few years ago I discovered a gully trap cover inscribed 'Frank Weafer, Contractor, Glasthule, 1911'. I also inherited a watercolour from my late uncle Michael, painted by Frank senior. It was a painting of houses built by him at Spencer Villas, Glenageary. The painting is inscribed, '9, 20 and 21 Spencer Villas, F. Weafer, December 18, 1916'. My grandfather not only built houses but also designed them, and the watercolour has a distinctive architectural feel about it. I was told that there were many gully trap cover moulds containing Frank Weafer's name, dated 1910-1920, indicating that there may have been a building boom in Kingstown at that time. Their sons, Francis and Henry, closed the family firm in the 1940s.[310]

John Weafer added:

> Jack was an outstanding swimmer and one of his favourite swims
> was from Sandycove Point to the elbow of the east pier and back to
> Sandycove before breakfast. Before he enlisted, he was employed
> as mason bricklayer in his father's building business. What made
> my great-uncles join up in 1914? Was it admiration for gallant little
> Belgium standing up to the might of imperial Germany? I know that in
> those days Glasthule boys had a reputation as scrappers, but mixing it
> with the central powers!! Why Jack picked the Inniskillings rather than
> the Dublins, Munsters, Leinsters or Connaught Rangers, I will never
> know. I also wonder why my great-uncles joined the British forces at
> all. Their father, Frank Weafer, was a successful builder in the Urban
> District of Kingstown and his sons were all craftsmen. Their rates of
> pay would have been many times the pittance paid to private soldiers,
> so whatever reason they joined the army, I think we can discount
> the economic one. He concluded: My father, Francis, was one of the
> three named casualties of the 'Nazi Blitz' of 20th December 1940 on
> Glasthule; the Weafers of Glasthule have a couple of old scores to settle
> with Germany![311]

Three of Jack's brothers also served in the British forces and survived. Sapper Michael Weafer enlisted in the Royal Engineers, 17th Field Company, on 1 August 1901, aged 18. He married Bridget Byrne at the Roman Catholic Church, Ballybrack in September 1908. Michael was in hospital on two occasions in 1916 and in April 1917, and was discharged from the army as no longer physically fit for war duty. He was awarded the 1914–15 Star, British War and Victory medals. In 1917, Michael and Bridget had four children: Rosanna, Alice Christina, Michael Joseph and Bridget.[312]

James Weafer served in the Royal Air Corps, fought in German East Africa and survived the war. James married Ann Collins, who lived opposite Weafer's Stone Yard on Adelaide Road. Prior to the outbreak of war he was employed as a carpenter in his father's firm. He played football with Edenville (Soccer) and was goalkeeper in the Edenville side that won the Metropolitan Cup in 1912. Ann's brother, John Collins, was gassed at the Battle of the Somme.[313]

A third brother, Francis Weafer, enlisted in September 1907, at Chatham, aged 20. He was attached to the Dismounted Branch of the Corps of Hussars on the Line until 1908, when he transferred to the Royal Engineers. He did not serve in the Great War. Francis married Elizabeth Nolan in 1910 and lived in Kingstown. The couple had eight children. In their service records, Francis and Michael were credited with being skilled bricklayers.[314]

Peter Brennan, the well-known sculptor, artist and potter, was a nephew of the Weafer boys and in 1966, Peter and his wife, Helena, also an accomplished potter, were the first in Ireland to exhibit hand-thrown stoneware and porcelain.[315]

Notes

PREFACE

1. Alfred O'Rahilly, *Father William Doyle, SJ, MC*, p.255.
    With thanks to Pearson Publishing, London and proprietor of title, St Francis Xavier's Church, Upper Gardiner Street, Dublin.

CHAPTER ONE

1. *Freeman's Journal* on 1 January 1915 and copied by the *Dumfries & Galloway Standard*.
2. *Kilkenny Journal*, September 1918.
3. Dan McPartland, writing for The Irish Cultural Society of the Garden City Area, *Irish Soldiers in the British Army*.
4. www.living history.ie phpBB, creating communities, bringing history to life. By Lordedward, 3 May 2008.
5. Brian McGinn, 'The Fighting Irish'. Brian McGinn passed away in 2005.
6. Courtesy of Mal Murray. Reference is made to the quotation in 'The History of the Royal Munster Fusiliers', Vol III, p.51, in an 'introduction' to Sir Ian Hamilton's despatches.
7. Published in the *Evening Herald* on 22 April 1916.
8. Alex Findlater, *Findlaters: The Story of a Dublin Merchant Family*, p.251.
9. Seamus Dun and T.G. Fraser, *Europe and Ethnicity World War I and Contemporary Ethnic Conflict*.
10. A speech Delivered by John Redmond on 23 Nov. 1915, London 1915; cited in Boyce, p.284.
11. Seán Connolly, Royal Dublin Fusiliers Association.
12. Tom Kettle's widow, Mary Sheehy Kettle, in her memoir, *The Ways of War*, p.3.
13. Ibid., p.10.
14. Ibid., p.11.
15. Terence Denman's *Ireland's Unknown Soldiers*, p.145. It was also published in *Blue Cap*, the journal of the Royal Dublin Fusiliers Association.
16. Mary Sheehy Kettle, p.40.
17. Richards Holmes, *Tommy*, p.361, reprinted by permission of HarperCollins Publishers Limited, 2005. It was also published in *Blue Cap Journal of the Royal Dublin Fusiliers Association*, (vol.9,

p.2007), by Tom Burke, 'In Memory of Tom Kettle'.

18. Terence Denman, *Ireland's Unknown Soldiers*, p.85.

19. By kind permission of the Francis Ledwidge Museum, Janeville, Slane, Co Meath.

20. In a letter to the mayor of Derry (R. N. Johnston) on Irish achievements in the war, on the 21 September 1918, many months after the attack on Wijtschate, the *Galway Observer* published this account of a conversation between, Captain Stephen Gwynn of The 16th (Irish) Division and Colonel F. J. M. McRory of the 36th (Ulster) Division.

21. Tom Burke, in the 2010 edition of *Blue Cap*, the Journal of the Royal Dublin Fusiliers Association.

22. John Weafer's article about his great-uncle, published in the *Dun Laoghaire Borough Historical Society's Journal*, No. 9, 2000.

23. Declan and Hugh Sweeney in their unpublished work, *A Tale of Two Brothers*.

24. Liam Dodd in conversation with the author.

25. Published in Dublin by the *Irish Times* on 1 May 1915.

26. Patrick Sarsfield O'Hegarty, *The Victory of Sinn Féin* (Dublin, 1998), p.3.

27. Ibid.

28. Terence Denman, *Ireland's Unknown Soldiers*, pp.114, 451.

29. Published by the *Evening Herald* on 30 October 1915.

30. Published by the *Irish Times*, on Wednesday, 20 September 1916, previously published in *The Times*, by its military correspondent.

31. Adam Hochschild, *To End All Wars*, p.188.

32. Wilfred Owen, soldier and Great War poet, with kind permission of the Wilfred Owen Association, *The War Poems* (Chatto & Windus, 1994), editor, Jon Stallworthy.

33. Published by the *Evening Herald* on 11 November 1918.

34. Published by the *Irish Times* on Armistice Day, 11 November 1918.

35. Captain Terence B. Poulter, Wikipedia, the free encyclopaedia. http://en.wikipedia.org/wiki/File:Irish-peace-tower-terence-poulter-belgium.redvers.jpg (accessed 1 December 2013).

36. Geraldine Plunkett, *All in the Blood*, a memoir of the Plunkett Family in the 1916 Easter Rising and the War of Independence, edited by Honor O Brolchain, p.269.

37. The Sisters of the Dominican Convent, Dun Laoghaire, Co Dublin.

38. Bridget Haggarty, *The Irish Soldiers in World War I*, from her website, Irish Customs and Culture.

39. The Royal Dublin Fusiliers Association archive and website.

40. Terence Denman, *Ireland's Unknown Soldiers*, p.181.

41. Marshal Foch's Tribute to the Irish Soldiers who died in the First World War, delivered in Paris on 9 November 1928.

42. Dr T.K. Whitaker, architect of the Modern Irish Economy, in an article written for *Out of the Dark, 1914–1918*.

43. A Committee was formed in November 1924 to consider proposals for a site to build a Great War Memorial. The statement was made by W.T. Cosgrave, as President of The Irish Free State Executive Council, following the acceptance of his proposal on 16 December 1931.

44. A statement made on 10 September 1988 by the trustees responsible for the restoration of the Great War Memorial at Islandbridge, Dublin.

45. This account of the north–south project to construct a round tower at the Island of Ireland Peace Park, Messines Ridge, in Flanders, Belgium, was included in a letter to the author in 2006 from Paddy Harte, former Fine Gael TD for Donegal, who was the driving force behind the initiative.

46. Ibid.

47. Published by the *Irish Times* on 25 March 1914, following the visit of President Mary McAleese to Green Hill Cemetery in Turkey to unveil a plaque commemorating nearly 4,000 Irishmen, who fought and died in the Gallipoli campaign.

CHAPTER TWO

1. Rob Goodbody, *On the Borders of the Pale*, a history of the Kilgobbin, Stepaside and Sandyford area, p.86.

2. Ibid.

3. Ibid.

4. Padraig Laffan, *Forge Farriers and Smiths*, Foxrock Local History Club, Publication 54 in February 1991.

5. First World War original documents for officers in the WO339/ series, with the kind permission of the National Archives, Kew, London.

6. Anne Pedley in her recently unpublished work, *The Gunners Hell*, at Zillebeke Lake, Near Ypres in Belgium, July 1917.

7. Rudyard Kipling wrote this following a request from the people of the Canadian town, Saulte St Marie, who requested him to write a verse for the face of their War Memorial.

8. Tom Johnstone, *Orange Green & Khaki*, the story of the Irish Regiments in the Great War, 1914–1918, p.209.

9. World War One army of occupation war diaries in the WO95/ series, with the kind permission of the National Archives, Kew, London. For the Royal Dublin Fusiliers, 8th Battalion.

10. Wilfred Owen, recognised as the greatest English poet of the Great War, from a stanza of his haunting poem, 'Dulce et decorum est'.

11. First World War service records in the WO363/ series with the kind permission of the National Archives, Kew, London.

12. Philip Lecane, World War One researcher and author of *Torpedoed!*

13. War Time Memories Project – The Great War. http://www.wartimememoriesproject.com/ greatwar/allied/royalengineers5fldcoy-gw.php (accessed 1 December 2013).

14. Published by the *Evening Herald* on 14 August 1915.

15. John Byrne, great-uncle of Private Laurence Mooney.

16. Ibid.

17. World War One army of occupation war diaries.

18. Jane Morgan (deceased), Barnacullia, Co. Dublin.

19. Patrick Ryder, great-nephew of Private James Robinson and Private John Robinson of Kilgobbin, Co Dublin.

20. Ibid.

21. Beatrice Elvery (later Lady Glenavy), *Today We Will Only Gossip*, p.19.

22. World War One army of occupation war diaries, in the WO95/ series at the National Archives, Kew, London for the Irish Guards, 1st Battalion.

23. Published in the *Evening Herald* on 29 September 1915.

24. World War One army of occupation war diaries.

25. Patrick Ryder.

CHAPTER THREE

1. *Thoms Directory* 1914 – Kilternan.

2. South Dublin Libraries' Headquarters, Unit 1 Square Industrial Complex, Tallaght, D. 24

3. Geraldine Plunkett Dillon, *All in the Blood*, edited by Honor O Brolchain, p.22.

4. With the kind permission of Honor O Brolchain, granddaughter of Geraldine Plunkett Dillion.

5. Geraldine Plunkett Dillon, p.65.

6. Ibid.

7. Eilís Dillon, *A Victorian Household in Victorian Dublin*, p.69, edited by Tom Kennedy (Dublin: Albertine Kennedy Publishing with the Dublin Arts Festival, 1980), courtesy of the estate of Eilís Dillon as copyright holder.

8. World War One army of occupation war diaries for the Leinster Regiment at Birr County Library, Birr, Co Offaly.

9. The Army List at the National Archives, Kew, London.

10. *Thoms Directory.*

11. Ibid.

12. G. O. Simms, Archbishop of Dublin (1956–1969) in his book, *Tullow's Story*, p. 14

13. *Thoms Directory* 1853.

14. South Dublin Libraries.

15. Ibid.

16. Tom and Patricia Farrell are the owners of Knockrose, which was used as a home and hospital for wounded soldiers in the period 1914–1918.

17. First World War original documents for officers.

18. All information in the book on the formation of regiments serving in the Great War is by kind permission of Chris Baker, from his website, The Long, Long Trail.

19. Last Will and Testament at the National Archives, Dublin.

20. Rudyard Kipling, *The Irish Guards in the Great War*, The First Battalion, p.60. Rudyard Kipling wrote the Regimental History of the Irish Guards in two volumes. His son, John, was an officer in the first battalion, and when he was reported missing, his father spent many years after the war searching for his son's body, without success. Lieutenant John Kipling's body was identified in 1991, and his remains are today buried in St Mary's Advanced Station Cemetery in Haisnes, France.

21. Irish Guards attestation papers from Regimental Headquarters, London.

22. Published in the *Evening Herald*, December 1915.

23. From an interview with Ambrose Connolly, a great-nephew of Private Edward Byrne, in 2012.

24. Ibid.

25. From interviews with Elizabeth Geraghty (deceased) and Kate Sinnott (deceased) in 2003.
26. Rudyard Kipling, p.59.
27. Ibid., pp.61, 62.
28. From interview with Kate Sinnott (deceased) in 2003.
29. First World War army of occupation war diaries.
30. General Sir Ian Hamilton GCB, *Gallipoli Diary*, Vol.1, p.131.
31. Refers to the text on a poster printed in Dublin by Alex Thom in May 1915.
32. First World War service records for other ranks.
33. Chris Baker's website, The Long, Long Trail.
34. 1st Battalion, Royal Dublin Fusiliers, in Gallipoli. See: http://www.dublin-fusiliers.com/battalions/1-batt/campaigns/1915-gallipoli.html (accessed 1 December 2013).

CHAPTER FOUR

1. Wilfred Owen, a poem comprising of four stanzas, written in November 1917 while he was in Craiglockhart as 'Killed Asleep' and edited in May 1918.
2. *Thoms Directory* 1914.
3. Ibid.
4. Ibid.
5. *De Ruvigny's Roll of Honour, 1914–1918,* (1916), Part One, p.204.
6. First World War army of occupation war diaries.
7. First World War original documents for officers in the WO339/ series at the National Archives, Kew, London.
8. Chris Baker.
9. By kind permission of the archivist at Monkton Combe School, Bath, England.
10. First World War original documents for officers.
11. Last will and testament from the National Archives, Dublin.
12. *The Cruel Clouds of War*, a book about the sixty-four former pupils, three Jesuit priests and one lay teacher from Belvedere College SJ, who fell in the military conflicts of the 20th century, compiled by Oliver Murphy, p.60.
13. Ibid., p.61.
14. Ibid.
15. Ibid., p.60.
16. Dr Brian Beveridge, nephew of Captain James Beveridge.
17. *The Cruel Clouds of War*, p.61.
18. Reported in a supplement of the *London Gazette* in 1918.
19. Dr Brian Beveridge.
20. Ibid.
21. Dr Joe Duignan, surgeon, from an RTÉ Radio interview with Pat Kenny on 23 May 1913.
22. Dr Brian Beveridge.
23. Ibid.
24. Ibid.

25. Ibid.
26. Ibid.
27. With the the kind permission of his grandson, Ian Ainslie and Ian's wife Ann.
28. First World War original documents for officers.
29. *London Gazette*, p.8817.
30. Ann and Ian Ainslie.
31. First World War original documents for officers.
32. Ann and Ian Ainslie.
33. Ibid.
34. Ibid.
35. Ibid.
36. RTÉ Radio broadcast on the 10 October 1974. The programme, Voices of Men who had survived the Great War, was produced by Kieran Sheedy and presented by Tom McGuirk.
37. Ibid., broadcast on the 10 November 1974.
38. Ibid., broadcast on the 8 December 1984.
39. First World War original documents for officers.
40. Ibid.
41. Lieutenant Harry Laird, *Personal Experiences of the Great War*, pp.122, 134, 135, 174.
42. First World War original documents for officers.
43. Ibid.
44. Virginia, Mason, *Gens Van Scuylen, 600 Years of Verschoyle History,* pp.283, 284. With grateful thanks to Joan McPartland (née Verschoyle).
45. Ibid., p.284.
46. World War One army of occupation war diaries.
47. Virginia Mason, p.285.
48. With the kind permission of the archivist at Marlborough College, Wilshire, England.
49. Virginia Mason, p.285.
50. Ibid.
51. Chris Baker.
52. First World War original documents for officers.
53. Ibid.
54. By kind permission of the archivist at Leys School in Cambridge, England.
55. James Henderson, *From Tee to Green – Irish Life,* 27 August 1915, courtesy of Eamon Beale, golf historian.
56. First World War original documents for officers.
57. Ibid.
58. Ibid.
59. Last Will and Testament at the National Archives.
60. *The Clongownian*, by the kind permission of Margaret Doyle, archivist at Clongowes Wood College, Co Kildare.
61. Anthony Quinn, *Wigs and Wars*, Irish Barristers in the Great War, p.32.
62. *The Clongownian*.
63. First World War original documents for officers.

64. Ibid.
65. With the kind permission of John Lennon, Dundrum District Historical Society.
66. First World War army of occupation war diaries, for the 42nd Canadian Battalion Canadian Infantry (Quebec Regiment).
67. Will R. Bird, *Ghosts Have Warm Hands*, p.46.
68. With the kind permission of Scott Rossiter, researcher of the Rossiter family and military history. Original sources also include the National Archives in Canada.
69. Ibid.
70. From his service record at the National Archives in Canada.
71. Scott Rossiter.
72. Ibid.
73. Ibid.
74. Ibid.
75. Ibid.
76. Ibid.
77. *The Cruel Clouds of War*, pp.69, 70.
78. Geoffrey Sparrow MC and J N Macbean MC, surgeon in the Royal Navy, *On Four Fronts*, pp. 80, 81.
79. Anthony P. Quinn, p.44.
80. www.britisharmedforces.org/li_pages/regiments/rmli/marine_ww1.htm.
81. Geraldine Plunkett Dillon, *All in the Blood*, pp.4, 6, 8.
82. Ibid., p. 20.
83. Ibid., p.268.
84. Anthony P. Quinn, *Wigs and Guns*, p.109.
85. Shivaun Gannon is a daughter of Germaine Plunkett, Geraldine Plunkett's sister.
86. Honor O Brolchain.
87. Shivaun Gannon is a daughter of Germaine Plunkett, Geraldine Plunkett's sister.
88. First World War original documents for officers.
89. Ibid.
90. Nonie Robinson (deceased), of Dun Laoghaire, Co Dublin.
91. World War One army of occupation war diaries.
92. By kind permission of Father Philip Tierney OSB, Glenstall Abbey, Co Limerick, nephew of the officer. The letter was also published in *The Cruel Clouds of War*, p.34.
93. First World War original documents for officers.
94. Ibid.
95. Ibid.
96. Ibid.
97. The Belvederian is the Journal of Belvedere College, Dublin. The extract was published in *The Cruel Clouds of War*, p.34.
98. The extracts of five letters to parents are by kind permission of Father Philip Tierney OSB, Glenstall Abbey, Co Limerick. A larger selection of his letters were also published in Anthony Quinn's, *Wigs and Wars*, pp.136, 137, 138, 140.
99. *De Ruvigny's Roll of Honour*, 1914–1918, Part Two, p.231.

100. Henry Hanna, *The Pals at Suvla Bay*, p.110.

101. Ian Lowe, 2nd Leinsters at Prémesques, 18 to 20 October 1914, in the 40/10 published by The Prince of Wales Leinster Regiment Association, HYPERLINK "http://www.leinster-regiment-"www.leinster-regiment-association.org.uk

102. In correspondence with the author from Mrs Maureen Martin, a great-niece of Private Fleming.

103. First World War army of occupation war diaries. This was researched by his great-nephew, David King.

104. World War One army of occupation war diaries

105. E. P. F. Lynch, *Somme Mud, The War Experiences of an Infantryman in France*, p.210, 211.

106. From his service record at the Australian National Archives for the Australian Infantry, 25th Battalion at National Archives, Australia.

107. Gerarda Mullane, a great-granddaughter of Private Langan.

108. Ibid.

109. First World War army of occupation war diaries.

110. Ibid.

111. Fintan Byrne, Sandyford Village, Co Dublin, great-grandson of Corporal George Mason.

112. RTÉ's Hidden History series, directed by Geraldine Creed and presented by the late Cathal O'Shannon, journalist and ex RAF pilot, in November 2005.

113. World War One army of occupation war diaries.

114. Ronan Lee, relative of Private Michael Richardson.

115. Family information came from his relatives, Ronan Lee, Mary White and Michael Richardson.

116. First World War army of occupation war diaries for the New Zealand Expeditionary Force.

117. Last will and testament from his service record at the New Zealand National Archives.

118. World War One army of occupation war diaries.

119. Declan and Hugh Sweeney, *The Tale of Two Brothers*, an unpublished work, about their great-uncles, Private George Sweeney and Lieutenant Michael Sweeney.

120. Ibid.

CHAPTER FIVE

1. With the kind permission of the Francis Ledwidge Museum, Janeville, Slane, Co Meath.

2. Beatrice Elvery (later Lady Glenavy), *Today We Will Only Gossip*, p.16.

3. Anecdotal information about Glenamuck Road being a 'famine road'. Confirmation that the road was already in existence in 1845 was confirmed by historian, Liam Clare of Foxrock.

4. Rob Goodbody, *On the Borders of the Pale*, a history of the Kilgobbin, Stepaside and Sandyford area, p.29.

5. The late Brendan Reynolds in his article, *Foxrock Estate*, published in the Foxrock Local History Club, Journal No 32, on 11 September 1991. Other information on the Foxrock Estate was courtesy of Brendan in interviews before he died.

6. Dr G.O. Simms, *Tullow's Story*, p. 60.

7. Published in *Nebraska State Journal* on 31 January 1923, with thanks to Liam Clare, historian of Foxrock, Co Dublin.

8. Liam Clare, *Arson at Kilteragh*, Foxrock Historical Club Journal, No 1, in January 1981, p.10.

9. Brendan Reynolds.

10. Ibid.

11. Ibid.

12. World War One army of occupation war diaries.

13. The website of the *Royal Army Medical Corps in the Great War*, a profile of Lieutenant-Colonel Hugh Stewart DSO MC.

14. Alan Grevenson's World War One Forum, Circle City Communities. http://www.circlecity. co.uk (accessed 1 December 2013).

15. Details of Hugh Stewart's Distinguished Service Order were published in the London Gazette on 4 June 1917. Mentioned in Despatches was recorded in the officer's service Record on p.123, Return No 6533 from the AMS Museum at Keogh Barracks, Mytchett in Surrey.

16. Niall Brannigan & John Kirwan, *Kilkenny families in the Great War*, p.488.

17. Alan Grevenson.

18. The Carrickmines Golf Club Centenary Book in 2000, with the kind permission of Cedric R. Bayley, Honorary Secretary.

19. British Government Information Services, Order No Order No 112805/2 on 29 October 1917.

20. Alan Grevenson.

21. London Gazette 2 September 1918, p.1025.

22. Alan Grevenson.

23. Cedric R. Bayley.

24. First World War original documents for officers.

25. Paul Leichar, present owner of Gwalia Farm, which is located 400 meters from the cemetery. The information was given to the author during a visit to the Leichar Farm.

26. London Gazette on 11 October 1917, p.10488.

27. Alan Grevenson.

28. First World War original documents for officers.

29. Ibid.

30. World War One army of occupation war diaries.

31. First World War original documents for officers.

32. Ibid.

33. World War One army of occupation war diaries.

34. Published in a supplement to the London Gazette on 18 June 1917 p.6001.

35. Long, Long Trail.

36. World War One army of occupation war diaries.

37. Ibid.

38. With the kind permission of Graeme Donald, a relative of the Halpin and Corrigan families.

39. Bill Webster, a relative and family historian of the Halpin family.

40. Ibid.

41. Graeme Donald.

42. Bill Webster.

43. With the kind permission of Turtle Bunbury, *Dublin Docklands – An Urban Voyage*.

44. Ibid.

45. Ibid.
46. Ibid.
47. Bill Webster.
48. Ibid.
49. World War One army of occupation war diaries.
50. Captain David Campbell, *Forward the Rifles*, p.52.
51. First World War original documents for officers.
52. Captain David Campbell, p.14, 15.
53. 'First World War original documents for officers
54. Long, Long Trail.
55. Philip Lecane, *Torpedoed! The RMS Leinster Disaster*, p.52.'
56. Ibid., p.223, 224.
57. Information on the cause of death was not available in the officer's First World War original documents, but grateful thanks to the military experts, members of Chris Baker's Great War Forum.
58. First World War original documents for officers.
59. www.geneaology.com (accessed 1 December 2013).
60. In a letter to the author, Dr Claude Cronhelm of Canada, a cousin of Lt A. G. Cronhelm, kindly offered this additional information on the Cronhelm family in the Great War.
61. First World War original documents for officers.
62. Published in the *Evening Herald* during September 1916.
63. By kind permission of Aravon School, Bray, Co Wicklow.
64. The Carrickmines Golf Club Centenary Book in 2000, courtesy of Cedric R. Bayley, Carrickmines Golf Club.
65. First World War original documents for officers.
66. World War One army of occupation war diaries.
67. First World War original documents for officers.
68. Ibid.
69. By kind permission of the archivist at Winchester College, Winchester, England.
70. First World War original documents for officers.
71. The Royal Dublin Fusiliers, 8th Battalion, war diaries available at the National Archives at Kew in London, for the period including the 7 September 1916 are missing and this version of the action on the day that 2nd Lieutenant Geoffrey C. M. Hamilton was killed comes from unofficial sources, but may be taken as a fair account of the action on this day.
72. Brendan Reynolds.
73. World War One army of occupation war diaries.
74. James W. Taylor, *The 2nd Royal Irish Rifles in the Great War, relating to a letter from Corporal Robert Platt* (4/7413) of the 'Rifles', p.67.
75. First World War original documents for officers.
76. Courtesy of the Bob Speel website. Please see http://www.speel.me.uk/sculpt/brucejoy.htm (accessed 1 December 2013).
77. Philip Lecane, *Torpedoed!*, p.230
78. Ibid.

79. World War One army of occupation war diaries for soldiers of the Canadian Mounted Rifles, 1st Battalion (Saskatchewan Regiment).

80. Australian Service Records from World War I on the National Archives of Australia website.

81. Service Records from the Australian National Archives.

82. Rootsweb, finding our roots together. In the IRL-Cavan-L Archives.

83. Cracroft's peerage – Guillamore, Viscount (1, 1831 – 1955).

84. World War One army of occupation war diaries.

85. By kind permission of Mrs Nancy Corcoran, Foxrock. A postcard was sent to her grandparents by a friend, Private Dick Byrne of the Foxrock Hotel.

86. Nancy Corcoran.

87. World War One army of occupation war diaries.

88. History of the South Irish Horse at, www.southirishhorse.com Dough Vaugh and his brother Hugh are working on a biographical history of the men who had a connection with the South of Ireland Imperial Yeomanry or the South Irish Horse. (accessed10/01/2014).

89. World War One army of occupation war diaries.

90. The Long, Long Trail.

91. Enda Cullen, great-nephew of Private S.T. Hayden. The story, 'A Forgotten Soldier' first appeared in *Three Rock Panorama*, Volume 33, No. 10 in November 2007.

92. World War One army of occupation war diaries.

93. Tom Burke MBE, *The 16th (Irish) and the 36th (Ulster) Divisions at the 'Battle of Wytschaete – Messines Ridge', 7 June 1917*. The match took place on 29 April 1917 at Loker, between the 6th Connaugh Rangers and the 9th Royal Irish Fusiliers pp.205, 206.

94. Commonwealth War Graves Commission's information service for war cemeteries.

95. 'British Service Records for other ranks.

96. By kind permission of Patsy Mooney, grandson of Private Joseph Mooney, and owner of the Mooney farm at Carrickmines.

97. Rudyard Kipling, p.97, 98.

98. Published in the *Evening Herald*, 22nd November 1915.

99. Rudyard Kipling, p.70.

100. British service records for other ranks.

101. The Long, Long Trail.

102. British service records for other ranks.

103. World War One army of occupation war diaries.

104. 'The Long, Long Trail.

105. Published in the *Evening Herald* on Tuesday 30 November 1915.'

106. 'World War One army of occupation war diaries.

107. Tom Johnstone, *Orange Green & Khaki, The Story of the Irish Regiments in the Great War 1914–1918*, p.211.

108. British Army First World War Service Records for other ranks.

109. Brendan Reynolds.

110. Ibid.

111. Ibid.

112. Rudyard Kipling, p.84.

CHAPTER SIX

1. *Thoms Directory* 1911 & 1914.
2. Ibid.
3. Alan Grevenson.
4. Ibid.
5. Ibid.
6. First World War original documents for officers.
7. Ibid.
8. Commonwealth War Graves Commission Website.
9. Published in the *London Times* on 11 May 1918, under the heading 'Fallen Officers'.
10. Benoit Douville, Irish Military Records at www.findmypast.ie (accessed 1 December 2013).
11. First World War original documents for officers.
12. *London Gazette* on 26 July 1918.
13. Published in the *London Times* on 11 May 1918.
14. Ibid.
15. Chris Baker's Great War Forum website.
16. Courtesy of Peter Mitchell from his website, 'Submerged' on 4 July 2007.
17. Ibid.
18. Published in the *London Times* on 13 March 1914.
19. House of Commons report in the sitting of 26 February 1914, with grateful thanks to www.hansard.millbanksystems.com (accessed 1 December 2013).
20. The author is most grateful to his grandson, Dr Patrick Henley of New Zealand, who offered family information.
21. World War One army of occupation war diaries.
22. By kind permission of Rodney Mason, Kilburn Grammar School, Old Boys Association.
23. First World War original documents for officers.
24. World War One army of occupation war diaries.
25. First World War original documents for officers.
26. Ibid.
27. World War One army of occupation war diaries.
28. First World War original documents for officers.
29. Ibid.
30. World War One army of occupation war diaries.
31. First World War original documents for officers.
32. The *Worcesterian,* with kind permission of the archivist at Royal Grammar School Worcester.
33. Rudyard Kipling, *The First Battalion*, p.268.
34. First World War original documents for officers.
35. Last Will and Testament at the National Archives, Dublin.
36. Published in the *Irish Times* on 19 August 1915.
37. Henry Hanna KC, *The Pals at Suvla Bay*, p.15.
38. Ibid., p.20.

39.   Mary Sheppard and husband John Sheppard, relations of Harold Trevor Marrable, through www.ancestry.com (accessed 1 December 2013).

40.   With the kind permission of Carmel Forrestal, a relative of Acting Sergeant Higgins.

41.   Long, Long Trail.

42.   Carmel Forrestal.

43.   Rudyard Kipling, p.268.

44.   Irish Guards attestation papers from Regimental Headquarters, London.

45.   Service Records for other ranks at the National Archives, Kew, London.

46.   World War One army of occupation war diaries.

47.   Service Records for other ranks at the National Archives, Kew, London.

48.   Rudyard Kipling, p.234.

49.   Irish Guards attestation papers.

50.   Brendan Reynolds.

51.   Tom Johnstone, *Orange Green & Khaki*, p.415.

52.   Dermot Kennedy, *Local Heroes of the 1914–1918 War*, Publication No 41 on 11 November 1998 of the Foxrock History Club Journal, p.24.

53.   Long, Long Trail.

54.   In conversation with Father Jack Slater, nephew of Private Patrick Slater.

CHAPTER SEVEN

1.   *Thoms Directory* 1914.

2.   Published in the *Evening Herald* on 22 April 1916.

3.   *Thoms Directory* 1911.

4.   Sir William N. Orpen KBE, RA, RHA, *An Onlooker in France*, p.28.

5.   Ibid.

6.   Published in the *Daily Mirror* of Tuesday 2nd August 1918.

7.   First World War original documents for officers. An account of his death was also published in the book, *Consuelo Remembers,* by Consuelo O'Connor, a niece of the Cruess Callaghan brothers killed in the war, pp.44, 47, 48.

8.   Ibid.

9.   Ibid.

10.   *London Gazette* on 13 February 1917.

11.   Peter Hart, *Somme Success: The Royal Flying Corps and the Battle of the Somme 1916*, p.124.

12.   First World War original documents for officers.

13.   The Aerodrome website at http://www.theaerodrome.com (accessed 1 December 2013).

14.   First World War original documents for officers.

15.   The Aerodrome website at http://www.theaerodrome.com (accessed 1 December 2013).

16.   Louise C. Callaghan, 'Brothers', from her book of poetry, *Remember the Birds*, p.22.

17.   Consuelo O'Connor, p.41.

18.   Ibid.

19.   Consuelo O'Connor, p.42. Another account of the incident was published in *Cruel Clouds of War,* p.51.

20. Consuelo O'Connor, p.41.
21. By kind permission of the archivist at Stoneyhurst College, Clitheroe, Lancashire, England.
22. First World War original documents for officers.
23. Stoneyhurst College.
24. British Army WW1 Service Records for other ranks.
25. The Long, Long Trail.
26. First World War original documents for officers.
27. World War One army of occupation war diaries.
28. The Long, Long Trail.
29. World War One army of occupation war diaries.
30. First World War original documents for officers.
31. *London Gazette*, 22 September 1916.
32. First World War original documents for officers.
33. Published by the *Uttoxeter Advertiser* in October 1916, having previously been published by the *The Motor News*.
34. First World War original documents for officers.
35. Ibid.
36. Ibid.
37. With the kind permission of Michael Lee, a great-grandson of Edward Lee.
38. Ibid.
39. First World War original documents for officers.
40. Courtesy of Michael Lee, a great-nephew of Captain Robert Ernest Lee.
41. Ibid.
42. Ibid.
43. Ibid.
44. Ibid.
45. World War One army of occupation war diaries.
46. A report published in the *Irish Times* on Monday 6 September 1915 from a Methodist Minister, Reverend Robert Spence, who discovered his body. Courtesy of Michael Lee.
47. First World War original documents for officers.
48. The Long, Long Trail.
49. First World War original documents for officers.
50. World War One army of occupation war diaries.
51. Courtesy of his nephew, District Justice Michael Coghlan, of Dublin.
52. Courtesy of his nephew, Lieutenant Noel Coghlan (rtd.), 39th Regiment, Royal Artillery of Dublin.
53. Published in the London Gazette on 9 January 1918.
54. First World War original documents for officers.
55. Lieutenant Noel Coghlan (rtd.).
56. Published in the London Gazette in 1917.
57. Lieutenant Noel Coghlan (rtd).
58. Baccame, R, *Poelcapelle 1917; A Trail of Wrecked Tanks,* (Ypres: P1917TA, 2007), courtesy of his nephew, Lieutenant Noel Coghlan (rtd).

59. Lieutenant Noel Coghlan.

60. District Justice Michael Coghlan.

61. World War One army of occupation war diaries.

62. First World War original documents for officers.

63. From the Dorothea Healy scrap book relating to her son Jack. At the exhibition 'Soldiers and Chiefs' at the National Museum, Collins Barracks, Dublin in 1912 and courtesy of his great-niece, Jean Kelly (deceased) of Dun Laoghaire, Dublin.

64. Ibid.

65. Ibid.

66. By kind permission of the archivist at Elstow School, Bradford, England.

67. From the Dorothea Healy scrap book relating to her son John.

68. James Morton, *The Journal of the Irish Medal Society*, 'Ref. JAR McCormick' Volume 21, p.331.

69. Geoffrey Sparrow MC and J M MacBean-Ross, *On Four Fronts with the Royal Naval Division*, p.81.

70. World War One army of occupation war diaries.

71. Rudyard Kipling, *The Second Battalion*, p.176, 177.

72. First World War One original documents for officers.

73. With kind permission of the late John Maher and his wife Margaret, Ballinkeele Country House, Enniscorthy, Co Wexford.

74. With kind permission of the archivist at St Michael's University School, Victoria BC, Canada.

75. The late John Maher and his wife Margaret, Ballinkeele Country House, Co Wexford. This family information was also published in the book, *The Wexford Gentry*, Volume 2, by Art Kavanagh and Rory Murphy.

76. Ibid.

77. World War One army of occupation war diaries.

78. The Long, Long Trail.

79. This information comes from different sources gathered over the years, including anecdotal notes by forum contributors who had relatives serving on the *Clan McNaughton*.

80. From the Obituary Notices published in the Monthly Journal of the Royal Astronomical Society, Vol. 79, p.234, 235.

81. George Francis Weldrick and Rosa Mulholland Gilbert were associated with the publication of the *Calendar of Ancient Records of Dublin*.

82. First World War original documents for officers.

83. World War One army of occupation war diaries.

84. Published in the *Irish Times* on the 2 August 1917.

85. Published in a supplement to the London Gazette on 16 August 1917.

86. First World War original documents for officers.

87. Ibid.

88. Ibid.

89. *Irish Times*, 15 June 1917.

90. World War One army of occupation war diaries.

91. First World War original documents for officers.

92. The William Purser Geoghegan family information was taken from, David Hughes, *A Pint of Guinness Please: The Colourful History of Guinness*, with the kind permission of Gregory Geoghegan, a relative of Second Lieutenant William George Geoghegan.

93. With the kind permission of the archivist at Uppingham School, Rutland. England.

94. Gregory Geoghegan.

95. World War army of occupation war diaries. With grateful thanks to Anne Pedley of the Royal Welsh Fusiliers Association.

96. With the kind permission of the archivist at Rugby School, Warwickshire, England, 2012.

97. First World War original documents for officers.

98. Nevile Shute, *Slide Rule*, p.17.

99. First World War original documents for officers.

100. Nevile Shute, p.14.

101. Ibid., p.22.

102. Ibid., p.25.

103. Professor Keith Jeffery, *The Sinn Fein Rebellion as They Saw It*, incorporating Arthur Hamilton Norway's *Irish Experience in War* and Mary Louisa Hamilton Norway's, *The Sinn Fein Rebellion as I Saw It*, p.93.

104. Mary Louisa Norway, in *The Sinn Fein Rebellion as I Saw It*, p.62.

105. Ibid., p.58.

106. Nevile Shute, *Slide Rule*, pp.14, 15.

107. Ibid., pp.27, 28, 30.

108. Nevile Shute, the information on his private life was taken at different intervals from his book, *Slide Rule*.

109. World War One army of occupation war diaries.

110. Ibid.

111. Niall Brannigan and John Kirwan, p.482.

112. First World War original documents for officers.

113. Ibid.

114. Ibid.

115. Long, Long Trail.

116. Last Will and Testament at the National Archives, Dublin.

117. First World War original documents for officers.

118. Ibid.

119. With the kind permission of John Stein Joyce, who lives in Germany, and is a nephew of 2nd Lt John Francis Stein.

120. First World War original documents for officers.

121. John Stein Joyce.

122. First World War original documents for officers.

123. John Stein Joyce.

124. *Our War*, edited by John Horne, p.140.

125. John Stein Joyce.

126. With the kind permission of Rita Lett, Co Wexford.

127. World War One army of occupation war diaries.

128. Connolly, Sean, *A Forlorn Hope* (published by The Royal Dublin Fusiliers Association in 2008).

129. World War One army of occupation war diaries.

130. Long, Long Trail.

131. In conversation with Liam Dodd, great-nephew of Sergeant William Dodd.

132. The Ernie O'Malley Papers courtesy of the archivist at University College Dublin and with the kind permission of Liam Dodd.

133. In conversation with Liam Dodd.

134. World War One army of occupation war diaries.

135. Published in the *Evening Herald* at the end of 1916.

136. Long, Long Trail.

137. World War One army of occupation war diaries.

138. Published in the *London Gazette* in November 1916.

139. Recorded on his Medal Index Card.

140. Long, Long Trail.

141. World War One army of occupation war diaries.

142. Rudyard Kipling, The First Battalion, p.240.

143. British Army WW1 Service Records for other ranks.

144. First World War army of occupation war diaries.

145. Ibid.

146. Tom Johnstone, *Orange, Green & Khaki*, p.248.

147. British Army WW1 Service Records for other ranks.

148. Ibid.

149. Ibid.

150. Courtesy of the Francis Ledwidge Museum, Slane, Co. Meath.

151. World War One army of occupation war diaries.

152. Long, Long Trail.

153. World War One army of occupation war diaries.

154. Canadian Army World War One Service Records 1914–1920 for other ranks, courtesy of the National Archives, Canada.

155. Ibid.

156. In conversation with the late Drew Kinsella, grandson of Private James Joseph Dwyer.

157. Ibid.

158. Rudyard Kipling, The Second Battalion, p.132, 133, 136.

159. With the kind permission of Colette Mannion, a relative of John and Philip Kearney.

160. Ibid.

161. World War One army of occupation war diaries.

162. With the kind permission of Patrick and Catherine Kelly, grandchildren of Private Myles McNally.

163. Rudyard Kipling, *The Irish Guards in the Great War*, The First Battalion, p.283.

164. In correspondence with Dolores Gobbett, (née Mahon) a great-niece of Private John Mahon and Private Michael Mahon.

165. Published by the *Evening Herald* on 18 November 1914.

166. Royal Dublin Fusiliers Association website, Major Battles – Salonika.

167. Ibid.

168. The Commonwealth War Graves Commission website – Struma Military Cemetery, Greece.

169. Liam Dodd. It is believed this document is in the Royal Dublin Fusiliers archives at the Gilbert Library, Pearse Street, Dublin.

170. Remembering Father William Doyle SJ, from the website, frwilliedoyle@gmail.com.

171. World War One army of occupation war diaries.

172. Stonyhurst College.

CHAPTER EIGHT

1. *Thoms Directory* 1914.

2. Ibid.

3. Ibid.

4. Ibid.

5. First World War One army of occupation war diaries.

6. First World War original documents for officers.

7. Published in the London Gazette on 16 September 1918.

8. Published in the London Gazette on 11 December 1917.

9. First World War original documents for officers.

10. Alan Grevenson's World War One Forum, Circle City Communities.

11. Ibid.

12. First World War original documents for officers.

13. World War One army of occupation war diaries.

14. First World War original documents for officers.

15. Ibid.

16. Ibid.

17. Ibid.

18. Long, Long Trail.

19. By kind permission of Morgan Dockrell, great-nephew of Major George Dockrell.

20. L.A.G. Strong, *The Forty-Foot: Retrospect*, a poem in remembrance of friends, including George Dockrell, who frequented the 'Forty Foot' bathing area in Sandycove, Co Dublin. With the kind permission of Sharon Rubin, Drury House, 34-43 Russell Street, London.

21. With the kind permission of Morgan Dockrell.

22. First World War original documents for officers.

23. Ibid.

24. Peter Hart, *Somme Success*, The Royal Flying Corps and the Battle of the Somme 1916, in an article by Second Lieutenant Harold Balfour, p.124.

25. Published in the London Gazette on 4 January 1917. First mentioned in the London Gazette on 8 December 1914.

26. First World War original documents for officers.

27. Karl E. Hayes, *A History of the Royal Air Force and United States Naval Air Service in Ireland 1913–1923*, pp.3, 4.

28. The contention by Dr Vincent Orange, Oxford University Press Directory, that Major F.F. Waldron was an old Etonian, was confirmed to be incorrect on 18 June 2013 by Mark Curthoys, Research Editor, Oxford University Press Directory.

29. In a letter from Lieutenant General Sir Arthur Singleton Wynne, Secretary of the Selection Board, War Office, Liddell Hart Centre for Military Archives at King's College, London.

30. Last Will and Testament.

31. First World War original documents for officers.

32. Jerry Murland, *Departed Warriors: The Story of a Family in War*, pp.2, 287, 288.

33. With the kind permission of Andrea Tingleff and family, relatives of the former Bateman family of Kingstown, Co Dublin.

34. Ibid.

35. Ibid.

36. First World War original documents for officers.

37. Ibid.

38. Ibid.

39. Ibid.

40. Ibid.

41. Ibid.

42. Published in the London Gazette on 26 September 1917.

43. Extracted from the archives of the Irish Cricket Union.

44. World War One army of occupation war diaries.

45. An extract from the website of the Saskatchewan Dragoons, a unit of the Canadian Forces.

46. First World War original documents for officers.

47. Professor Donald Cameron Kerr BA, MA, University of Saskatchewan, Canada. By kind permission of Cheryl Avery, History Department, University of Saskatchewan, Canada.

48. First World War original documents for officers.

49. Information from the Royal Engineers Museum, Chatham, England.

50. First World War original documents for officers.

51. Extracted from Wikipedia, the free encyclopedia.

52. Published by the *Bray and South Dublin Herald* in January 1916.

53. With the kind permission of Ishbel Lee, wife of the late John Lee, nephew of Captain Valentine Arthur Cranwill MC.

54. By Tony Allen of the 'Wrecksite' website.

55. By kind permission of Lesley Whiteside MA (Mod), DPAA (Liverpool), HDipEd (NUI), Archivist at Kings Hospital School, Dublin 20. This piece was also published in the *Blue Coat*, Midsummer and Christmas 1932 and written by the late Paddy Hogarty of the Royal Dublin Fusiliers Association.

56. Ishbel Lee.

57. World War One army of occupation war diaries.

58. Ishbel Lee.

59. First World War original documents for officers.

60. World War One army of occupation war diaries.

61. First World War original documents for officers.

62. Ibid.

63. Ibid.

64. Published in the London Gazette on 2 October 1915.

65. First World War original documents for officers.

66. Courtesy of the Irish Rugby Football Union archives.

67. Arnold E.A. Bousfield, *Corrig School, Kingstown*, pp.5, 6, 7, 8. The author failed to get a response from the publisher, The Dargle Press.

68. Father Doyle's original documents at the National Archives in London, contained a review titled 'Hero and Mystic – Father William Doyle, S J', for the book *Father William Doyle, SJ*, by Professor Alfred O'Rahilly.

69. Father William Doyle, SJ, by Professor Alfred O'Rahilly, p. 237- 245. With thanks to Pearson Publishing, London and proprietor of title, St Francis Xavier's Church, Upper Gardiner Street, Dublin.

70. Ibid., p.273.

71. Ibid., p.251.

72. Written by Percival Phillips and published in the *Daily Express* and *Morning Post* in August 1917.

73. First World War original documents for officers and with kind permission of his great-nephew, Hugh Cumiskey, from the family archives.

74. First published in the *Glasgow Weekly News* on 1 September 1917. It was also published in Professor Alfred O'Rahilly's book, *Father William Doyle, SJ*, pp.32, 331.

75. Lieutenant Frank Laird, *Personal Experiences of the Great War*, p.109–110.

76. Paddy Harte, former Fine Gael TD, in a letter to the author in 2007.

77. Professor Alfred O'Rahilly, *Father William Doyle, SJ*, pp.315, 316.

78. With the kind permission from the family archives of his great-nephew, Hugh Cumisky.

79. A report that appeared in the *Guardian* on Friday 12 November 1999.

80. A reply received following a letter sent by the author to the Commonwealth War Graves Commission in 2006 concerning a report in the *Guardian* on Friday 12 November 1999. This concerned a request made by an 85-year-old retired Belgian teacher, Denise Dael, to the Commonwealth War Graves Commission for the exhumation of an anonymous grave in a British war cemetery outside a Flemish town to establish whether it contained the remains of Father Willie Doyle, one of the British army's most celebrated heroes.

81. Published in the London Gazette on 1 January 1917.

82. This information was obtained following an email to the author in 2006 from Brother Nigel Cave of Ratcliffe, the Roman Catholic College, in Leicestershire, England.

83. First World War original documents for officers.

84. Ibid.

85. With the kind permission of Hugh Cumiskey, great-nephew of Father William Doyle SJ MC.

86. Ibid.

87. Professor Alfred O'Rahilly, *Father William Doyle, SJ*, pp.12–21.

88. Hugh Cumiskey.

89. The officers' Medal Index Card at the National Archives, London.

90. The Long, Long Trail.

91. In correspondence with his cousin, Alex Findlater, (Edinburgh) and also in Alex Findlater's book *The Story of a Dublin Merchant Family, 1774–2001*, p.57.

92. First World War original documents for officers.

93. Ibid.

94. The officers' Medal Index Card at the National Archives, London.

95. First World War original documents for officers.

96. Last Will and Testament.

97. World War One army of occupation war diaries.

98. The Long, Long Trail relating to the Battle of Loos on 25 September to 18 October 1915.

99. World War One army of occupation war diaries.

100. First World War original documents for officers.

101. Ibid.

102. Ibid.

103. This page is taken from the battalion's regimental history courtesy of Conor Dodd.

104. The Long, Long Trail.

105. Turtle Bunbury, *Dublin Docklands – An Urban Voyage*.

106. Courtesy of his nephew, Professor John H. C. McCormick.

107. Ibid.

108. World War One army of occupation war diaries.

109. First World War original documents for officers.

110. Ibid.

111. Ibid.

112. First World War original documents for officers.

113. Ibid.

114. Ibid.

115. Ibid.

116. Ibid.

117. Published in the London Gazette in 1917.

118. With the kind permission of Joan McKeever of Sandycove, niece of Captain McKeever.

119. Ibid.

120. Caroline Mullan, archivist at Blackrock College.

121. Joan McKeever.

122. First World War One army of occupation war diaries.

123. First World War original documents for officers.

124. Ibid.

125. Ibid.

126. Ibid.

127. Ibid.

128. The Long, Long Trail.

129. First World War original documents for officers.

130. Sister Isabelle Smyth, Medical Missionaries of Mary, (MMM) Booterstown, Co Dublin.

131. Sister Isabelle Smyth, *A Dream to Follow*, Booterstown, Co Dublin. The story of Mother Mary Martin, founder of the Medical Missionaries of Mary, based on letters to her mother, Mrs Mary Martin, p.6.
132. With the kind permission of Clive C. Martin, a relative of the Martin family, from Mrs Martin's diary written for her son, Captain Charles A. Martin, during the period that he was missing in action.
133. Ibid.
134. Ibid.
135. Sister Isabelle Smyth, p.9.
136. Ibid., pp.10, 11, 12, 13.
137. Ibid., pp.15, 17.
138. Ibid., pp.12, 19.
139. Ibid., the story of Maire Martin founder of the Medical Missionary of Mary MMM, pp.21, 37.
140. Clive C. Martin.
141. The Peerage, a genealogical survey of the peerage of Great Britain as well as the royal families of Europe, p.41142.
142. *The Cruel Clouds of War*, compiled by Oliver Murphy, by kind permission of Belvedere College SJ, p.12.
143. Belvedere College, *Tragic Loss, First World War*, a profile of the O'Brien Butler brothers, who perished in the Boer and First World Wars.
144. First World War original documents for officers.
145. *The Cruel Clouds of War*.
146. The Peerage, a genealogical survey of the peerage of Great Britain as well as the royal families of Europe, p.41143.
147. *The Cruel Clouds of War*, p.50.
148. Published in the London Gazette in 1917.
149. First World War original documents for officers.
150. Ibid.
151. Ibid.
152. Ibid.
153. Ibid.
154. Ibid.
155. Ibid.
156. With the kind permission of Noel Kidney, grandson of Lt Francis Burke Close.The work is titled, *The Picture on the Mantelpiece*.
157. Elizabeth Dowse, *A Jackdaw's Gleanings* (published by author in Victoria, Australia 2003), p.85, 170.
158. Ibid., pp.84, 88.
159. Ibid., p.91.
160. First World War original documents for officers.
161. Elizabeth Dowse.
162. Étain Murphy, *A Glorious Extravaganza*, a history of Monkstown Parish Church, Co Dublin, p.345.

163. Ibid., p.345.
164. Étain Murphy was informed by Edith, Charles Dowse's sister, that her brother, Richard, made the point that Charles's height made him more vulnerable, p.345.
165. Ibid.
166. Ibid., p.342.
167. First World War original documents for officers.
168. Ibid.
169. With the kind permission of Rob Goodbody, great-nephew of Lieutenant Owen Goodbody. The passage was quoted from his relative's book, Michael Goodbody, *The Goodbodys: Millers, Merchants and Manufacturers*, p.395.
170. Rob Goodbody.
171. Courtesy of Sue Light, a member of the Great War Forum.
172. First World War original documents for officers.
173. World War One army of occupation war diaries.
174. First World War original documents for officers.
175. Anthony P Quinn, *Wigs and Guns*, pp.94, 95.
176. First World War original documents for officers.
177. Courtesy of the archivist at Charterhouse School, Godalming, Surrey, England.
178. Anthony P Quinn, *Wigs and Guns*, p.94.
179. First World War original documents for officers.
180. www. AngloBoerWar.com.
181. First World War original documents for officers.
182. Ibid.
183. Ibid.
184. Ibid.
185. According to 'Flight' of 23 October 1976, in a review of the book *Pioneer Pilot: The Great Smith-Barry, who taught the world how to fly* by F. D. Tredey. At the 1939 dinner of the Central Flying School, Lord Trenchard described Smith-Barry as the man who taught the air forces of the world how to fly. This piece was the subject of a programme based on David McKenna's article; Robert Smith-Barry: 'The man who taught the world to fly', broadcast on the BBC in February 2013. With Thanks to Andy Jordan of the BBC and Graeme of The Great War Forum.
186. With kind permission of Robert M. Morley relating to his thesis, 'Earning Their Wings: British Pilot Training, 1912–1918', submitted to the College of Graduate Studies and Research at University of Saskatchewan, Saskatoon, Saskatchewan, Canada, in December, 2006.
187. With kind permission of Charles Lillis, great-nephew of Lieutenant Martin Lillis.
188. Ibid.
189. Ibid.
190. Ibid.
191. James W. Taylor, *The Second Royal Irish Rifles in the Great War*, p.319.
192. Ibid., p.59.
193. First World War original documents for officers.
194. Published in the London Gazette on 22 June 1951.

195. With the kind permission of the Francis Ledwidge Museum, Slane, Co Meath.
196. With the kind permission of Rob Ruggenberg, professional journalist, author and editor of his website, The Heritage of the Great War.
197. With the kind permission of Jasper Brett, nephew of Second Lieutenant Jasper Brett.
198. First World War original documents for officers.
199. Henry Hanna, *The Pals at Suvla Bay*, pp.39, 40.
200. First World War original documents for officers.
201. World War One army of occupation war diaries.
202. First World War original documents for officers.
203. Ibid.
204. Published in the *Bray & South Dublin Herald* in September 1915 following report that a comrade wrote to his mother.
205. Bryan Cooper, *The Tenth (Irish) Division in Gallipoli*, wrote about the preparation for the attack on 21 August 1915 at Kabak Kuyu, pp.106, 107, 108.
206. Ibid., p.110.
207. The Long, Long Trail.
208. The correspondence between Lieutenant-Colonel H.F.N. Jourdain, Commanding Officer of the 5th Battalion, Connaught Rangers and Brigadier-General C.F. Aspinall-Oglander CB, CMG, DSO, dated 11 February 1931 was filed with the World War One army of occupation war diaries for soldiers at the National Archives, London.
209. Bryan Cooper, *The Tenth (Irish) Division in Gallipoli*, p.89.
210. Jim Herlihy, *Royal Irish Constabulary officers – A Biographical Dictionary & Genealogical Guide*, p.77.
211. Ibid.
212. Ibid.
213. Ibid.
214. First World War original documents for officers.
215. Jim Herlihy, p.77.
216. First World War original documents for officers.
217. Ibid.
218. World War One army of occupation war diaries.
219. First World War original documents for officers.
220. With the kind permission of Owen Lemass.
221. Ibid.
222. This statement was made by Taoiseach, Seán Lemass, in February 1966, on the occasion of the 50th anniversary of the 1916 Easter Rising.
223. With the kind permission of Owen Lemass.
224. John Horne, editor of *Our War: Ireland and the Great War*, p.140.
225. First World War original documents for officers.
226. Ibid.
227. Ibid.
228. Ibid.
229. With the kind permission of Patrick Vaughan, nephew of 2nd Lieutenant McFarland.

230. Published by the London Gazette in 1918.

231. First World War original documents for officers.

232. Ibid.

233. Patrick Vaughan.

234. Ibid.

235. Ibid.

236. Ibid.

237. First World War original documents for officers.

238. Ibid.

239. Ibid.

240. Ibid.

241. With the kind permission of Ruth Kinsella, great-niece of Lt James Stanley McFerran.

242. Ibid.

243. World War One army of occupation war diaries.

244. Bryan Cooper, *The Tenth (Irish) Division in Gallipoli*, p.102.

245. Philip Orr, *Field of Bones, an Irish Division at Gallipoli*, p.26.

246. With the kind permission of Caroline Mullan, archivist at Blackrock College, Co Dublin.

247. First World War original documents for officers.

248. The Long, Long Trail.

249. First World War original documents for officers.

250. Ibid.

251. World War One army of occupation war diaries.

252. Ibid.

253. With the kind permission of David Leslie Orr, great-nephew of Second Lieutenant, Walter Leslie Orr.

254. Ibid.

255. First World War original documents for officers.

256. World War One army of occupation war diaries.

257. First World War original documents for officers.

258. The Long, Long Trail.

259. With the kind permission of Michael Lee, a cousin of Second Lieutenant Richard Shackleton.

260. First World War original documents for officers.

261. With the kind permission of David Millar, nephew of Sergeant Edward Millar.

262. Ibid.

263. Ibid.

264. Ibid.

265. Ibid..

266. Henry Hanna K.C., *The Pals at Suvla Bay*, p.87.

267. John A. Mizzi, The Malta Connection, 1925 (Tecnografica Publications, 1991) 'Remembering Gallipoli'. HYPERLINK 'http://www.timesofmalta.com' www.timesofmalta.com (accessed 1 December 2013).

268. First World War original documents for officers.

269. David Millar.

270. Published by the London Gazette in 1915, p.1204.
271. David Millar.
272. The Long, Long Trail.
273. David Millar.
274. Étain Murphy, pp.130, 341.
275. Alex Findlater, p.264.
276. Ibid., pp. 262–263.
277. Published by the Evening Mail, on 12 December 1916.
278. Ibid., p.259.
279. Henry Hanna KC, p.20.
280. Alex Findlater. p.260, 261.
281. Ibid., 260.
282. Ibid.
283. Ibid.
284. Ibid.
285. Ibid.
286. Ibid.
287. Bank of Ireland, The Great War 1914–1918, Bank of Ireland Staff Service Record.
288. From the website of the Commonwealth War Graves Commission, The Battles of the Somme: The Battle of Ginchy, 9 September 1916.
289. Tom Kettle's widow, Mary Sheehy Kettle, p.12, 13.
290. With the kind permission of Lieutenant Matt Comiskey (rtd.), nephew of Private Keegan-Comiskey.
291. Ibid.
292. With the kind permission of Peter Kelly, great-nephew of Privates Thomas and James Kelly.
293. World War One army of occupation war diaries.
294. Peter Kelly.
295. Rudyard Kipling, pp.61, 62.
296. Étain Murphy, p.348.
297. From his Service Record at the National Archives, London.
298. With the kind permission of Leslie Shaw, relative of Able Seaman Richard McClatchie.
299. From his Service Record at the National Archives, London. No change.
300. With the kind permission of Gerard Mahony, great-nephew of Stoker Bernard Mahony, Royal Navy.
301. Courtesy of the Ministry of Defence, Naval Historical Library, London and Gerard Mahony.
302. From 'Harley' member, of the Worlds Naval Ships Forums, on 25 February 2008.
303. This Day in History – 20 January 1914: http://www.history.com/this-day-in-history/goeben-and-breslau-battle-the-allies-in-the-aegean (accessed 1 December 2013).
304. Ian Buxton, Big Gun Monitors (World Shipping Society and Trident Books, 1978), pp.34, 35, 36, 37. Courtesy of Gerard Mahony.
305. From his Service Record at the National Archives, London.
306. With the kind permission of Roseleen Whelan, a grand-niece of Stoker Bernard Mahony.
307. World War One army of occupation war diaries.

308. With the kind permission of John Weafer, great-nephew of Private Jack Weafer. All information given to the author by John, was also published in his article in the Dun Laoghaire Borough Historical Society's journal No 9 in November 2000.

309. The Long, Long Trail.

310. John Weafer.

311. Ibid.

312. World War One army of occupation war diaries.

313. John Weafer.

314. World War One army of occupation war diaries, together with information from John Weafer.

315. Elizabeth Petcu, Art and Ceramics: http://elizabethpetcu.com/art-ceramics.htm (accessed 1 December 2013), together with information from John Weafer.

Bibliography

INTERVIEWS

Brian Beveridge	Elizabeth Geraghty	Bernadette O'Brien	Owen Lemass
Jasper Brett	Patrick Glynn	Consuelo O'Connor	Joan McKeever
Fintan Byrne	Paul Glynn	Brendan Reynolds	Joan McPartland
Michael Coghlan	Nuala Howell	Nonie Robinson	Gerard Mahony
Hugh Comiskey	John Kelly	Kate Sinnott	Margaret Maher
Ambrose Connolly	Peter Kelly	Father Jack Slater	J.A. Manly
Nancy Corcoran	Tommy Kenny	John Weafer	Patsy Mooney
Morgan Dockrell	Noel Kidney	Drew Kinsella	
Brendan Doyle	Jane Morgan	Michael Lee	
Matthew Fitzgibbon	Joseph Murphy	Ronan Lee	

PRIMARY SOURCES

The National Archives (London)
Sources for First World War service information: Original documents for army officers are in the series, WO339/, WO338/ and WO374/. Service records for other ranks are in the WO363/ and WO364/ series. Royal Naval Reserve, officers are found in the ADM 240 and 340 series and information for officers in the Royal Naval Division are in the WO339/ series. Royal Air Force officers are in Air 76 and Royal Flying Corps officers in WO339/ series. World War One army of occupation war diaries are in WO95/ series. Details of World War One campaign medals are in WO329/ series.

The Irish Guards Regiment
Attestation papers for other ranks were courtesy of D.P. Cleary MBE, Irish Guards Regimental Headquarters, London.

SECONDARY SOURCES
Bird, W.R., *Ghosts Have Warm Hands* (Ontario: Cef Books, 1997; Toronto: Clarke, Irwin, 1968).
Bousfield, A.E.A., *Corrig School, Kingstown* (Bray: The Dargle Press, 1958).
Bowman, T., *Irish Regiments in the Great War* (Manchester: Manchester University Press, 2004).
Brannigan, N. and J. Kirwan, *Kilkenny Families in the Great War* (Kilkenny: OLL Editions, 2012).
Bunbury, T., *From Dublin Docklands: An Urban Voyage* (Dublin: Montague Publications Group, 2009).
Burke, T.S., *The 16th (Irish) and 36th (Ulster) Divisions at the 'Battle of Wijtschate–Messines Ridge'*
   (Dublin: The Royal Dublin Fusiliers Association, 2007).

Burke, T.S., *The Second Battalion Royal Dublin Fusiliers and Tragedy of Mouse Trap Farm: April and May 1915* (Dublin: The Royal Dublin Fusiliers Association, 2005).

Buxton, I., *Big Gun Monitors* (Windsor: World Ship Society, 1978).

Callaghan, L.C., 'Brother', in *Remember the Birds* (Co Clare: Salmon Publishing, 2005).

Campbell, Captain David MC, *Forward the Rifles: The War Diary of an Irish soldier, 1914–1918* (Dublin: The History Press Ireland, 2009).

Carrickmines Croquet and Tennis Club, *Centenary Book 1903–2003* (Dublin, 2003).

Connolly, S., *A Forlorn Hope* (Dublin: Royal Dublin Fusiliers Association, 2008).

Cooper, B., *The Tenth (Irish) Division in Gallipoli* (Dublin: Irish Academic Press, 1993).

Denman T., *Ireland's Unknown Soldiers* (Dublin: Irish Academic Press, 1992).

De Ruvigny's Roll of Honour, 1914–1918 (London, 1916)

Dillon, E. and T. Kennedy (ed.), *A Victorian Household in Victorian Dublin* (Dublin: Albertine Kennedy Publishing with the Dublin Arts Festival, 1980).

Dowse, E., *A Jackdaw's Gleanings* (Australia, 2003).

Dodd, C. and L. Dodd, *Lieutenant-Colonel R.G.B. Jeffreys: A Collection of Letters 1916–1918*, The World War One letters of an RDF officer (Dublin: Old Tough Publications, 2007).

Dungan, M., *They Shall Grow Not Old* (Dublin: Four Courts Press, 1997).

Dungan, M., *Irish Voices from the Great War* (Dublin: Irish Academic Press, 1995).

Elvery, B. (later Lady Glenavy), *Today We Will Only Gossip* (London: Constable & Company, 1964).

Findlater, A., *The Story of a Dublin Merchant Family, 1774–2001* (Dublin: A. & A. Farmar, 2001).

Fitzpatrick, G., *St. Andrew's College, 1894–1994* (Dublin, 1994).

Goodbody, M., *The Goodbodys: Millers, Merchants and Manufacturers* (Dublin: Ashfield Press, 2011).

Goodbody, R., *On the Borders of the Pale* (Dublin: Pale Publishing, 1993).

Hamilton, General Sir Ian, *Gallipoli Diary* (London, 1920).

Hanna, H., *The Pals at Suvla Bay* (Dublin: Ponsonby, 1916).

Hart, P.M., *Somme Success* (Barnsley: Pen and Sword Military, 2012).

Harte, P., *Dublin City & County Book of Honour: The Great War 1914–1918* (Dublin: The National Book of Honour Committee, 2004).

Hayes, K.E., *A History of the Royal Air Force and United States Naval Air Service in Ireland, 1913–1923* (Dublin, 1988).

Henderson, J., *From Tee to Green* (Dublin, 1915). Courtesy of Eamon Beale, golf historian.

Hennessy, T.F., *The Great War, 1914–1918: Service Record of Bank of Ireland Staff* (Dublin, 1920). Courtesy Gordon Henderson.

Herlihy, J., *Royal Irish Constabulary Officers: A Biographical Dictionary & Genealogical Guide, 1816–1922.* This book lists the 1700 officers of the Royal Irish Constabulary officers, including birth, marriage and death dates; service in the British army, yeomanry and militia; dates of appointment and retirement, resignation, discharge or dismissal and a list of officers who later served as lawmen elsewhere (Dublin: Four Courts Press, 2005).

Hitchcock, Captain F.C., MC, *Stand To: A Diary of the Trenches 1915–1918* (Sussex: The Naval & Military Press, 2001).

Hochschild, A., *To End All Wars: A Story of Loyalty and Rebellion, 1914–1918* (New York: Mariner Books, 2011).

Hogarty, P., *Remembrance: A Brief History of 'The Blue Caps': The First Battalion, Royal Dublin Fusiliers, 1914–1922* (Dublin, 2005).

Holmes, R., *Tommy, The British Soldier on the Western Front 1914–1918* (London: Harper Perennial, 2005).

Horne, J., *Our War* (Dublin: Royal Irish Academy, 2008).

Hughes, D., *A Pint of Guinness Please: The Colourful History of Guinness* (Berkshire: Phimboy, 2006).

Jeffery, K., *The Sinn Fein Rebellion as They Saw It*, incorporating *The Sinn Fein Rebellion as I Saw It*, by Mary Louisa Hamilton Norway and *Irish Experiences In War* by Arthur Hamilton Norway (Dublin: Irish Academic Press, 1999).

Johnstone, T., *Orange, Green and Kahki* (Dublin: Gill and Macmillan, 1992).

Kavanagh, A. and R. Murphy, *The Wexford Gentry, Volume 2* (Irish Family Names, 1996).

Kettle, T. and M. Kettle Sheehy, in her memoir, *The Ways of War*, about the writings of her late husband, Lieutenant Tom Kettle (New York: Charles Scribner's, 1917).

Kipling, R., *The Irish Guards in the Great War*, Vol. 1 and 2, (London, 1923).

Laird, F., *Personal Experiences of the Great War* (Dublin, 1925).

Lecane, P., *Torpedoed! The RMS Leinster Disaster* (Cornwall:Periscope Publishing, 2005).

Lynch, E. P. F., *Somme Mud, The War Experiences of an Infantryman in France 1916–1919* (London, 2008).

Mason, V., *Gens Van Scuylen, 600 Years of Verschoyle History* (London, 2001).

Murland, J., *Departed Warriors, The Story of a Family in War* (Leicester: Metador).

Murphy, É., *A Glorious Extravaganza*, A history of Monkstown parish church (Dublin: Wordwell, 2003).

Murphy, O., compiled by, *The Cruel Clouds of War*, a book about sixty-four former pupils, three Jesuit priests and one lay teacher from Belvedere College SJ, who died in the military conflicts of the twentieth century.

O'Connor, C., *Consuelo Remembers* (Dublin, 2000).

O'Hegarty, P.S., *The Victory of Sinn Fein* (Dublin: University College Press, 1998).

O'Rahilly, A., *Father William Doyle, SJ* (London: Longmans, Green & Co., 1922) Proprietor of title, St Francis Xavier's Church, Upper Gardiner Street, Dublin.

Orpen, Sir W.N., *An Onlooker in France* (London: Williams and Norgate, 1921).

Orr, P., *Field of Bones*, an Irish Division at Gallipoli (Dublin: Lilliput Press, 2006).

Pearson, P., *Between the Mountains and the Sea* (Dublin: O'Brien Press, 1999).

Plunkett Dillon, G., and Honor O Brolchain (ed.), *All in the Blood* (Dublin: A.&A. Farmar Book Publishers, 2006).

Quinn, A.P., *Wigs and Guns* (Dublin: Four Courts Press, 2006).

Majors C.F. Romer & A.E. Mainwaring, *The Second Battalion Royal Dublin Fusiliers in the South African War* (London: A.L. Humphreys, 1908).

Ryan, N., *Sparkling Granite* (Dublin, 1992).

Shute, N., *Slide Rule: An Autobiography* (London: House of Stratus, 1954).

Sparrow, G. MC and J.M. MacBean-Ross (surgeon with the Royal Navy), *On Four Fronts with the Royal Naval Division* (London: Hodder & Stoughton, 1918).

Taylor, J.W. *The 2nd Royal Irish Rifles in the Great War* (Dublin: Four Courts Press, 2005).

Tredey F. D., *Pioneer Pilot: The Great Smith-Barry, Who Taught The World How To Fly* (Published by P. L. Davies London 1976).

Westlake, R., *British Regiments at Gallipoli* (London: Pen & Sword, 1996).

Index